Modern
Federalism

Modern Federalism

An Analytic Approach

Peter W. House
Office of Environmental
Analyses, U.S. Department
of Energy

Wilbur A. Steger
CONSAD Research Corporation

LexingtonBooks
D.C. Heath and Company
Lexington, Massachusetts
Toronto

Library of Congress Cataloging in Publication Data

House, Peter William, 1937–
  Modern federalism.

  Includes bibliographical references and index.
  1. United States—Economic policy—1971-   2. Regional planning—United States. 3. Federal government—United States. I. Steger, Wilbur A. II. Title.
  HC106.7.H695   338.973   81–47972
  ISBN 0-669-05208-6   AACR2

Copyright © 1982 by D.C. Heath and Company

All rights reserved. No part of this publication may be reproduced or transmitted in any form or by any means, electronic or mechanical, including photocopy, recording, or any information storage or retrieval system, without permission in writing from the publisher.

Published simultaneously in Canada

Printed in the United States of America

International Standard Book Number: 0-669-05208-6

Library of Congress Catalog Card Number: 81-47972

To Friendship

Contents

	Figures	xi
	Tables	xii
	Preface and Acknowledgments	xv
Part I	*Context and Objectives*	1
Chapter 1	**Problem Context**	3
	Considering Frostbelt and Sunbelt Issues at the National Level	6
	Federal Policy and Subnational Consequences and Trends	11
Chapter 2	**Some Definitions and Concepts**	19
	A Hierarchical Typology of Policies and Programs	19
	Key Analytic Research Issues	24
	Is This a New Problem?	26
Chapter 3	**The Current State of the Art: Theory**	31
	Some Regional Economic Evidence	33
	Does It Have to Be a Zero-Sum Game?	34
Chapter 4	**Policy Research: Contributions by the Disciplines to the National/Subnational Discussion**	39
	Contributions of Economics and Planning	39
	Contributions of Public Administration, Management, and Political Science	52
	Some Cautionary Observations about Analytic Approaches to Policymaking	54
	Concluding Remarks	56
Part II	*Top-Down/Bottom-Up Approaches to National-Subnational Analysis*	61

Chapter 5	**How Can Analytic Methods Assist in Federal/Subfederal Processes?**	63
	Special Features of National-Subnational Modeling	63
	Other Desirable Conceptual Properties of Modeling Approaches	66
Chapter 6	**Top-Down Analysis Methods**	75
	Evolution of a Top-Down Policy from a Specific Local Instance	76
	Some Representative Available Analytic Top-Down Models	78
	BLS Economic Growth Model	81
	Department of Energy Midrange Energy Forecasting System (MEFS)	87
	The Strategic Environmental Assessment System (SEAS) Model	100
	Top-Down Approaches to Developing Energy and Environmental Policy: Illustrative Applications	111
	Summary and Conclusions	129
Chapter 7	**Some Bottom-Up Techniques**	135
	The Advantages of Bottom-Up Methodology	136
	Jurisdictional Levels Suitable for Analytic Purposes	139
	Traditional Methods for National-Subnational Analysis	143
	The National-Regional Impact Evaluation System (NRIES)	155
	Concluding Remarks	161
	Appendix 7A: References to State Economic Models	167
Part III	*Discovering Some Two-Way Methods*	171
Chapter 8	**Some Two-Way Applications for Modeling National-Regional Analysis**	173
	Regional Environmental Assessments—DOE Style	176
	Regional Characterization: The Use of Factor- and Cluster-Analysis Techniques	209
	Urban- and Community-Impact Statements	228

Contents

	Subnational Programming of Public-Works Investment within the Federal System	259
Chapter 9	**Summary and Conclusions**	275
	Politics	280
	Budget	282
	Institutional-Organizational Issues	284
	Methodology	287
	Index	293
	About the Authors	303

Figures

6-1	Flow Chart of the BLS Model	82
6-2	Schematic of PIES/MEFS	89
6-3	PIES Satellite Models	91
6-4	DOE Regions	92
6-5	PIES Coal Regions	94
6-6	PIES Oil Regions	96
6-7	PIES Natural-Gas Regions	97
6-8	PIES Refinery Regions (PADD Regions)	99
6-9	SEAS Block Diagram	102
6-10	Regionalization of Coal Mining	116
6-11	Major Regional Trends Associated with Energy Development	121
6-12	Trends in Point-Source Discharges of Major Water Pollutants, 1975-1990	123
6-13	Trends in Water Consumption, by Energy and Manufacturing Sectors, 1975-1990	124
6-14	Trends in Solid-Waste Generation, 1975-1990	125
6-15	Major Regional Environmental Trends Associated with Two World-Oil-Price Scenarios	130
7-1	Projected National Framework of Production Requirements: Agricultural Sector	147
7-2	Modeling of State Economies: Generalized Framework	151
7-3	Endogenous Sectors	152
7-4	NRIES Flow Diagram for a National Coal Scenario	158
8-1	Conceptualization of the RIIA Process	177
8-2	Federal Regions Assigned to Each National Laboratory	179

8-3	RIIA Development Program	181
8-4	ORNL Siting-Analysis Approach	186
8-5	Projected Electrical-Generating Capacity, by Technology: Region 5	195
8-6	Relative Contribution of Major Energy Activities to Energy-Related Occupational Deaths under the Mid-Mid Scenario: Region 5	200
8-7	Range of Potential Accidental Deaths in Coal Mines under the Mid-Mid Scenario: Region 5	200
8-8	Range of Potential Deaths and Cases of Chronic Respiratory Disease Due to Coal-Mining Occupational Exposure under the Mid-Mid Scenario: Region 5	201
8-9	Range of Potential Deaths from Sulfate Exposure Due to Utility and Industrial Use of Fossil Fuels under the Mid-Mid Scenario: Region 5	202
8-10	Potential Air-Quality Impact Areas: Illinois	205
8-11	River Basins: Illinois	206
8-12	Projected Increases in TDS Loadings in the Northern Illinois and Sangamon Rivers, 1975–1990	207
8-13	Regional-Issue Identification and Assessment: Lead-Lab Process	210
8-14	Factor-Analysis Data Base	216
8-15	BEA Economic Areas	224
8-16	Schematic of Community Growth Induced by Industrial Development	243
8-17	Projected X Low Annual Population Impact of Fischer-Tropsch Synthetic-Fuels Development: Torrance, New Mexico	245
8-18	Illustration of a Time Impact: Maximum-Growth Effect of Commuting Distance on Available Construction Workforce	246
8-19	Summary of Maximum-Growth Construction Potential, by Technology	247
8-20	Type C Analysis Impact Quadrants	252

Tables

1-1	Regional Economic-Analysis Units in the Federal Government	13
2-1	Proposed Coverage of Consequences, Trends, and Affected Parties	22
4-1	Economic-Impact Analysis: Scope and Methods	42
5-1	Our Current Data World (Illustrative)	68
5-2	The Complete Data World	70
6-1	Projection Series C Energy-Supply Projections	113
6-2	Trends in Macroeconomic and Energy Consumption, 1975–1990	115
6-3	1985 Coal Production and Consumption under Various Cases	117
6-4	Projected Consumption of Electricity, by Region and Sector	119
6-5	Energy Supply, by Source, Present and Projected	126
6-6	Present and Projected Annual Particulate Emissions, by Federal Region	128
7-1	Partial List of Comprehensive Regional Models of the United States	149
7-2	Partial List of Regional Modeling Efforts	150
7-3	Regional Impacts on State Gross Product Originating in a National Coal-Development Scenario, Present and Projected	159
8-1	Definition of Criteria for Rating of Impacts	188
8-2	Electrical-Generating Capacity, Coal Extraction, and Industrial Fuel Use: Region 5	196
8-3	Disaggregation of National Impacts to the Regional Level: Region 5	196
8-4	Projected Increases in Electrical-Generating Capacity under the Mid-Mid Scenario: Illinois	203

8-5	Environmental Impacts of the EIA Trendlong Mid-Mid Scenario at the State Level: Illinois	204
8-6	Cluster-Analysis Results	238
8-7	Characteristics of Analyses of Varying Complexity	240
8-8	Synthetic-Fuel Technologies Incorporated in Analysis	244
8-9	Variables Used to Characterize a High-Btu Coal-Gasification Plant	248
8-10	Workforce Requirements for Characteristic Synfuel Plants	249
8-11	Characterization of Illustrative BEA Areas by Two UCIA Major Impact Categories: Springfield, Illinois	250
8-12	Employment Impacts for UCIA Variables	251
8-13	PWI Programs: Factors in Top-Down/Bottom-Up Needs Assessment	262

Preface and Acknowledgments

There are times when a review of specific federal policies or regulations as they affect individual states must remind the reviewer of the anecdote of the six-feet-tall man who drowned in the river that was only a foot deep—on the average. Examples abound of federal mandates that are either too closely tailored to unique situations found in only one or a few states and inapplicable or inappropriate for the rest or, more characteristically, of situations in which a general goal is lost when each state tries to implement it. Grand designs and grand schemes are fun to dream about; making them happen is harder. Our country is not a conglomeration of homogeneous areas that just happen to be states. In many ways, these locales are each unique, so that it is necessary to craft carefully any national action to ensure that the differences are taken into consideration. Given the way the federal lawmakers currently make policy, this is a formidable undertaking.

On the other hand, allowing each state to go its own way also has serious drawbacks. Not only does this conjure up an image of independent fiefdoms and principalities feuding and fussing, but also we quickly see an undeniable need for expertise to address the avalanche of issues that appear time and time again. Naturally, we balk at the resource duplication (and drain) attendant to such reported analysis. Clearly, there are many issues that have to be addressed, at least initially, including safety, inflation, sound economic growth, and matters of national security.

Both perspectives have merit. We want to ensure that federal policies take local initiatives, conditions, and wishes into consideration. But the desired actions of scores of states, regions, or localities cannot be carried out independently of their effects on one another. The question, and challenge, is how these seemingly mutually exclusive, yet equally valid, goals can be accomplished.

This book addresses that question. Over the past several years federal, regional, and state bodies have designed and implemented several approaches, both organizational and technical, that have made it possible to address the issue of top-down versus bottom-up government. Some have been experimental; others were intended for real applications. We discuss several such techniques and applications and propose a strategy for resolving this seeming dilemma.

The subject area has been among our professional interests for more than a decade. Each of us has written extensively and been a part of or led several research efforts in related areas. But technology, techniques, and information have progressed so rapidly that what seemed like wishful thinking a few years ago has potential today for implementation. This book explores how far and how fast such planning can take effect. Each of us, working for the federal government in different capacities, has developed a keen awareness of the need for better analytic tools to improve the flow of communication and information among levels of government. In no case, however, do the findings presented here necessarily represent those of the agencies we are working or have worked for.

We want this work to help stimulate a process of discussion and feedback: we hope the stimulus will be efficient and the process effective.

Acknowledgments

This book evolved slowly over a period of two years. Some portions were speeches or papers by one of the authors and a colleague; others were part of technical reports. In all cases, these reports were rewritten, but many of the original concepts remained. Because of this we wish to thank the staff of the Office of Environment for thoughts and comments over this protracted period. Of special note were Ted Williams, Dario Monti, Roger Shull, Joan Hock, and Ted Harris. Nazir Dossani of CONSAD provided many insights and other contributions as did Sheila Steger with bibliographic and editorial assistance. Although many typed and edited, the contributions of Carol Bochert, Monica Brodine, and Tina Shaw deserve special recognition.

The authors take full responsibility for the book as it now stands. It does not represent the views of the U.S. Department of Energy, CONSAD Research Corporation, or any of our colleagues.

Part I
Context and Objectives

1 Problem Context

The orientation of this book is analytical: it examines the replicable objective methods for developing and using information to help public decision makers make difficult public-sector choices and to allow responsive public comment on the results of such analysis. Analytic information is designed to help the decision maker select among alternative means for reaching a solution by assessing their relative worth. The decision makers of most interest to us here are those who help make federal-level policy, policy that affects both the entire nation and every geographic area in it—the Congress, the executive branch, the states, and other political jurisdictions operating below the national level.

We intend this book to be useful at all levels of government, wherever public decision makers are seeking ways to make better decisions. The title, *Modern Federalism: An Analytic Approach,* reflects our deep interest in reaching all those who are bringing about—or who will be affected by—the emerging, rapidly changing nature of federal, state, and local relations. The "new federalism," as we see it, will evolve out of several philosophical and operational strands: the Reagan administration's interest in returning many, if not most, federal operational programs and some policy choices to the states through block grants and other mechanisms; politically moderate governors (such as Babbitt of Arizona, Alexander of Tennessee, Lamm of Colorado, Rockefeller of West Virginia) seeking to help taxpayers determine which level of government should be responsible for which functions;[1] the view, held by the Advisory Commission on Intergovernmental Relations, of an "evolving consensus" of partners in a federal system;[2] and an emerging, rich body of literature reexamining the federalist traditions within a modern society.[3]

There are many diverse approaches here, to be sure, and very little experience with any but the current system as it has evolved in recent years. We will therefore focus on where policy decision making has taken place—primarily at and within the federal level. In the 1980s, as and if decision-making responsibilities devolve more to states and localities, what is said here about the federal level will apply equally (or perhaps even more) at subnational levels.

Notwithstanding its ultimate applicability to all decision-making levels, our major concern in most of this study is that federal policymakers frequently neglect to take into account, analytically or otherwise, the consequences of government programs on subfederal regions and localities, where implementation of these policies achieve their ultimate impact. This represents a major deficiency in the process of policy analysis and in the formulation of federal policy. It also represents a major problem for a system of federalism that relies heavily on top-down policymaking.

A second, related concern is that some programs also fail to take into consideration major trends that can be expected to change the character of one or more of the nation's regions. These changes, though purportedly outside the immediate purview of a specific policy, may dramatically affect its successful implementation. These two shortcomings are exacerbated if the regional impacts of policies are not accurately forecast into the future, when longer-term and more-widespread geographic ripple effects will have had time to take effect.

The first of these concerns helps account for the failure to feed back to federal policymakers either the actual or anticipated effects of national programs on subnational areas. This failure often results in unrealistic, misguided, and possibly pernicious national policymaking. Furthermore, unrealistic and incomplete assessments may lead to policies that engender state and local resistance, seriously diminishing the effectiveness of federal legislation and regulations, or even perverting their intentions and objectives. This is an increasingly important issue as the new federalism assumes an increasingly state and local orientation.

The second deficiency, failure to take account of subnational differences and trends, often exacerbated the shortsighted practice of extrapolating impacts, implicitly or explicitly, along narrow programmatic lines whose effectiveness is measured in terms of total or average national impacts. This practice can be very misleading, particularly if the effects of regional economic and demographic trends on the particular federal program under investigation are important enough seriously to deflect that program's purpose.

Although it is our premise that all federal policies should be reviewed for their subfederal (frequently termed *subnational* or *regional*) impact, such reviews may be especially necessary for federally sponsored energy, environmental, and economic-development policies, taken either separately (as they often are in federal agencies) or interdependently. Some economists advise that, in most cases, the federal government's best policy for resolving, say, the nation's energy problems, would be to create a climate in which the private sector invests in techniques or creates output in a socially productive fashion that would not have resulted without government stimulus. Similarly, state or local governments may be encouraged to engage in, or permit, the mining of ores or siting of some stage of the fuel cycle in a fashion or at a rate different from what they otherwise would plan to do. In the same way, environmental policies generated at the federal level usually have their most meaningful consequences when the emissions from the various productive processes are related to the ambient conditions of a specific locale or region; moreover, administration of the majority of these regulations is largely a state function. Both energy and environmental policies affect local or regional jobs, investment, output, unemployment, and economic development generally. As such, these changes are of local concern and will cause local reactions that may significantly modify the anticipated results of a national policy.

Traditional federal policymaking, in almost every substantive policy area, does not usually take subfederal issues into account in a sufficiently detailed and meaningful way. Various reasons are assigned, including lack of staff, inadequate time, and absence of an agreed-upon methodology. There are also some in the national government who believe that the job of the federal establishment is to do little more than set policy at the strategic level, letting subnational government institutions attend to details as they wish, within the bounds set by the general policy. Equally important is the growing concern that the federal government—perhaps the executive branch in particular—is becoming more and more remote from the people. The increased currency of the term *citizen participation* is an illustration— nonanalytic but representative of an important trend—of the powerful support for the principle that the populace has a right to participate in the policymaking process. At the very least, a wider range of desires and biases must be considered as policies evolve; at the other extreme, localities, states, and citizens are claiming veto power over federal policy.

Merging subfederal interests is a clear requirement from the perspective of the myriad locales, but it also makes sense from the perspective of federal decision makers and their attainment objectives. The majority of federal programs implicitly assume that the targets will be developed by integrating various performances locally. But time and time again, local desires and capabilities turn out not to be those anticipated at the federal level and thus place federally constructed policy in jeopardy.

Examples of national policies with sizable subnational impacts abound: U.S. pollution standards may limit the development of new energy facilities, and attendant job growth and economic development, to relatively few areas in the country;[4] incentives are proposed for areas many hundreds of miles from a nuclear power-plant facility to provide waste-storage facilities for spent nuclear fuel; strip-mining control standards increase demand for eastern coal and result in rail-transportation "squeak-points" and eastern versions of boom-town conditions.

The Frostbelt-Sunbelt conflict illustrates many facets of the general set of national and regional issues, the sort of subnational trends federal policymakers should consider. If the shift in growth from the Frostbelt to Sunbelt is real, such movement in population and economic activity should be taken into account in the development of national-policy analyses. Greater sensitivity to and understanding of the unique regional features and characteristics of Frostbelt and Sunbelt states would allow federal policymakers—such as those involved with energy, environmental, and economic-development policies and programs—better to anticipate barriers and to plan more effectively national growth and change, with far more local, state, and regional support and understanding.[5]

Considering Frostbelt and Sunbelt Issues at the National Level

It is easy to embrace the belief that the nation's key economic and demographic movements are irreversibly toward the sun. Yet it is not at all obvious how long and to what extent this trend will actually persist. A simple-minded, somewhat exaggerated extrapolation would forecast total abandonment of the frozen North for the sunshine. The issue, however, is not whether the country's population is moving toward the warmer areas, but the extent and timing of the movement, what changes it may bring, and whether federal policies exacerbate, condition, or otherwise affect these shifts, both intentionally and unintentionally. A study for the Department of Housing and Urban Development (DHUD) has examined these issues.[6] In this book we review perspectives developed from that study, addressing both the environmental parameters and energy issues that may moderate continued regional development in the Sunbelt, as well as the economic attributes of existing northeastern areas that may ward off terminal decay.

Sunbelt Issues

A few regional Sunbelt issues are indicative of the subnational differences of concern to people living in these areas:

Air Quality. A quick review of the existing regional characteristics of parts of the U.S. South and West reveals that many of the environmental amenities perceived by Americans as necessary to a suburban life-style are already present there. Some amenities, however, such as clean air and abundant water, are in short supply, both in the Sunbelt and elsewhere. If present air-pollution standards remain in effect, and if the nondegradation and visibility regulations of the Environmental Protection Agency survive, the population and economic-activity absorption rate of the South and West may become a serious issue.⁷ Atmospheric monitoring suggests that western regions may have a low capacity for handling atmospheric pollutants, particularly during certain times of the year.

One of the largest sources of air pollution in the West is the automobile, according to recent studies of automobile-oriented urban areas (such as Los Angeles, San Francisco, and Atlanta), and little potential exists for further switching from the private car to mass transit, at least in the short-to-medium run. Large-scale growth of western cities may not, therefore, be inevitable: the life-style of the West suggests sprawl, wide-open spaces, and access by automobile, practically regardless of the increasing cost of this mode of transportation. Thus, the very technical device that has allowed the characteristic growth pattern of these cities may now be a primary cause of change in the urban form and a substantial contributor to limiting its growth.

Water—Quantity and Quality. Although the cost of water-pollution control will be a significant burden for some cities, the principal difference between the new cities in the Sunbelt and the established ones in the Frostbelt (after industrial sources are required to clean up their own pollution) is the upgrading required by new regulations versus the cost of providing resources for new growth. If the federal government equalizes the economic burden, control costs may not be much of a factor influencing regional-growth trends.

The difficulties of an inadequate water supply are more serious in the Sunbelt states: most of the western and southwestern states have historically been short of readily available water, and recent droughts have revived attention to the problem. In times of scarcity, questions of water rights for existing and proposed uses and arguments about the construction of new dams or the economic rationality of desalinization assume new importance. Most important, water availability in the West is a matter that necessarily cuts across state lines, frequently requiring intervention at regional and federal levels or compacts at local levels.

Energy. Although the definitive future effects of present-day energy policies on various regions can be debated, some statements concerning energy development in the South and West are likely to meet with general agreement. For example, increased need to supply energy before the year 2000 from domestic energy sources will almost inevitably mean an increase in the development of western coal reserves. The processes of extraction and energy conversion or the desire to be near the source of the energy resource will probably mean building new western energy towns. It is not clear how viable these towns are likely to be. The West is dotted with ghost towns left from gold, silver, and other mining efforts. These communities were dependent on a single industry, and when the resource was gone the towns died. If such communities spring up in the coal belt, they will have little long-term effect on regional migration figures even though the short-run impact on specific areas may be considerable. On the other hand, the coupling of coal extraction with a form of on-site power generation or synthetic-fuel development could result in a significant influx of people and in the birth of communities akin to those of early New England or of the post–Civil War South. The long-run staying power of such areas is difficult to predict, but their future is likely to be substantially different from that of the early western mining towns.

The recent creation of the Synthetic Fuels Corporation suggests enormous potential for growth in the West. If direct federal investment in synthetic fuels over the next decade or so is, say, in the neighborhood of $90 billion, and investment by the private sector about $60 billion, and if much of this activity is expected to be in the West, then there is substantial reason to suppose that an energy-prompted boom will result. One recent study by the Western Governors' Policy Office (WESTPO) suggested that there may be as many as 400,000 new dwelling units in the mountain states by the end of the century. These represent only the *direct* impacts of energy development.

The implications of current federal energy policy for energy consumption in the Sunbelt are even more difficult to project. Transportation, particularly by means of private auto, accounts for almost a quarter of the total energy used in both the Frostbelt and Sunbelt states. One popular idea is that higher fuel prices will lead to a shift from the automobile to mass transit. Not unexpectedly, however, recent studies measuring mass switching from automobiles to public transit on the Washington, D.C., Atlanta, and San Francisco mass-transit systems do not augur well for immediate, or even longer-term, success for fixed-guideway modes, even in densely settled areas. Other urgent questions of efficacy arise in the sprawling cities of the West. Energy-use patterns for residences vary greatly depending on the specific location in the region. In the West, housing styles are apt to be larger and more rambling than the traditional ones of the Frostbelt, making insulation and other energy-saving devices even more necessary. Economic, political, and social uncertainties make forecasts of consumption patterns chancy at best.

The western phenomenon of urban-suburban sprawl chews up land resources. Albuquerque, New Mexico had a population of about 300,000 in 1978, spreading through a valley for about 200–250 square miles. There is still a lot of unused land in the West, but substantial tracts are unsuitable for development because of such factors as slopes, water scarcity, and individual or federal ownership. As a result, in the West of the wide-open spaces, land suitable for residential development could become a very scarce commodity.

Scarcer, costlier energy generally suggests the future evolution of more-densely-settled cities, regardless of region. Because multifamily homes are less expensive to heat and cool, because sprawling cities require more cross-hauling trips that use greater quantities of energy (and generate more pollution), and because the cost of land is potentially high, patterns of greater concentration may develop in the Sunbelt states than have done so up to now. The increased use of coal for power generation in the West and development of synthetic fuels for eastern markets are also bound to have significant environmental, energy, and economic impacts on the fragile western ecology.

Frostbelt Issues

Coincident with the environmental impacts on the Sunbelt states, certain economic attributes of northern urbanized areas argue against continued relocation of northeastern and midwestern populations to Sunbelt states. Long-term balancing forces appear to be at work.

Agriculture and Resources. Because the United States will probably continue to import energy and other raw materials in massive amounts for some time, there will be a strong demand for continued production of food and fiber in sufficient quantities to export. To achieve a balance in international payments, the federal government probably will provide more-favorable conditions for agricultural and extractive industries and for the states producing these goods. Recently, there has been additional demand for agricultural produce as a raw material in the production of gasohol, biomass, and other crops-for-energy resources. With changes such as these, there would be less reason for the rural populace to migrate to southern and western cities for higher wages and better living conditions.

Agglomeration Benefits. Because of their size and in-place infrastructure, large metropolitan areas of the Northeast and Midwest may have certain advantages that will eventually reverse their downward cycle. These areas have large consumer markets and labor pools that can attract new industries; such areas with diverse manufacturing offer a corresponding benefit to skilled laborers, who have greater choices there among potential employers.[8] The growth of the minicomputer industry in New England is representative of a variety of new, light-manufacturing industrial sectors helping this region reestablish an export base to the rest of the United States and the world.

Transportation and Communication. Barring the overnight development of an exotic new form of transportation, we must assume that our major transportation networks are now in place. Although a program to maintain the existing highway system and to upgrade and then maintain the railroad beds and inland-waterway facilities is only partially complete (for example, the Northeast Corridor project), individuals' ability to move about by means of the automobile and the airlines has never been better. Coupled with vastly improved communications facilities, this system has allowed corporations to carry out their headquarters functions almost anywhere. Despite the fact that this improved technology allows a wide distribution of physical locations, it has not eliminated the need for personal contact in business relationships. Industries will still require the face-to-face communications characteristically associated with the headquarters function, and many of these financial and administrative offices are already located in the Northeast Corridor, serving as a magnet for other firms.

Briefly stated, there has been a definable movement from the northeastern part of the nation to the South and West, and long-term structural counterforces are at work. Such trends have been operating for decades and continued to be reflected in the recent results of the 1980 census.[9] The current Sunbelt phenomenon is, in one sense, little more than an extension of the past. In any case, national-level policymakers face some difficult decisions. One is whether to accept the trend and express little need, power, or ability to intervene. National issues cut across all regions, with different effects, and these effects must play a role in federal policymaking. At the other extreme, policymakers interested in federal intervention must consider how either to take advantage of or to combat these trends.

The population shifts in the Sunbelt and Frostbelt regions and their potential impact on other related factors raise a host of interesting policy questions and issues, including:

Will the current rate of emigration from the Frostbelt continue?

What type of people and industry will remain in the Frostbelt? Which will move to the Sunbelt?

How long can a region sustain emigration before it undergoes fundamental change of a terminal nature?

What kind of region will the Sunbelt become if all the growth projected actually occurs?

What should the federal government do, if anything, given these developments?

What is the quality-of-life likely to become for the various regions of the country?

There are dozens of such questions. Our main concern about them is this: Should such issues be included as fundamental components of current analyses of federal policy? Under the new and evolving federalism, with a great deal more state and local involvement in decision making, how should subnational interests best be represented in federal policymaking?

Regions from a National Viewpoint

As complex as regional and local growth patterns are when viewed dynamically, they become even more complex as seen by the federal decision maker, who frequently receives only forecasts with the abstractness of a top-down or macro perspective. Such examples as the Sunbelt-Frostbelt shift could be described at even greater length here, but the message they all convey could not be clearer. Taking subnational consequences, requirements, and objectives into account when creating federal policy should not only be a necessary condition for the assurance of a viable, implementable policy, but also can provide a broader, possibly even national-level perspective that shares and supports the views of locally affected parties. Such a two-way perspective can be extremely useful in addressing and resolving regional issues such as Frostbelt versus Sunbelt, and many other, similar subnational controversies over emerging structural trends.

Federal Policy and Subnational Consequences and Trends

Given these initial observations, we can turn to the fundamental questions addressed in this book: What influences should subnational concerns have on those making federal policy, and to what degree can federal and subfederal levels of sophisticated analysis assist in the policymaking process?

It is still an open question whether analysis per se can affect regional outcomes. There is no evidence, for example, that such analysis would do more than generate the enormous flurry of activity, charges, countercharges, denials, and political name-calling that followed a 1977 *National Journal* analysis entitled "Where the Funds Flow: A *National Journal* Survey Shows That There Is a Massive Flow of Wealth from the Northeast and Midwest to the Faster-Growing West and South."[10] The journal updated its analysis a year later with 1976 data and reached the same general conclusions. Newspapers, politicians, regional interest groups, and government agencies have since flooded the media with similar stories.[11]

This battle over the regional policies of the federal government has been referred to as *the new sectionalism,* differentiating the new battle from regionalism, the more time-honored and less narrowly parochial of the various forms of federalism.

> If a broad agreement could be reached on the desirable regional consequences of federal policy, the "regional warfare" would be over. . . .

> If the battle over distribution continues to rage on a "where's mine?" level, it will simply result in more money going to *all* regions through programs with obvious regional biases—a gain in appearance only. . . .[12]

The sentiment reflected in these paragraphs, particularly in the first, is perhaps too pat, too optimistic a solution. But it does, appropriately, raise the issue of national goals and national welfare, as opposed to more narrowly regional and/or sectional goals and welfare. And it raises another question: Does federal policy and programming that impacts at the subnational level invariably imply national betterment? Does it also include betterment, for regions most affected, for the regional or for the national good?

The Overriding National Criterion

For such policies and programs to benefit the national welfare would require first defining and then actively seeking something similar to the economist's concept of Pareto optimality. A policy or program activity is considered to be Pareto optimal if it is impossible to improve the position of any one affected party without making someone else worse off.[13] (The problem of assessing whether a policy is desirable, however, is more complex if a redistribution of income is also involved.) Subnational geographic areas are not individuals, the entity with which economic Pareto optimality deals, and are therefore theoretically not subject to the same rules. There is certainly common sense, however, in rephrasing Pareto optimality in terms of areas rather than individuals: if a national policy can make some subnational units better off with no unit worse off,[14] then it is a desirable policy in that national welfare is also increased.[15]

This is the most basic challenge for analytic approaches to federal policymaking either within or outside a context of new federalism. In assessing all the costs and benefits, both public and private—and, to the extent feasible, those that are measurable in dollars and those that are not—do federal policies benefit some subnational areas at the undue expense of others?[16] And could residents of those geographic areas that might suffer negative net benefits be compensated (at least in theory)? If, in other words, residents of gaining areas can compensate residents in losing areas and still have something positive left over—including all transfer and other real costs—the policy can be considered as contributing to national welfare; that is, a Pareto optimality of a sort would have been reached. (Granted, this is only a crude approximation to increasing people's economic welfare.)

Analytically, these estimates of projected costs and benefits at national and subnational levels are considerably more difficult to make than they are

Table 1-1
Regional Economic-Analysis Units in the Federal Government

Units	Collects Information	Forecasts Models	Receptions for Officials	Legislative Support	Public Information	Staff Support	Coordinates Interagency	Prepares Options
Department of Agriculture								
Agriculture Stabilization and Conservation Service	✓							
Economic Statistics and Cooperative Service	✓	✓	✓	✓	✓	✓	✓	✓
Forest Service	✓	✓	✓	✓	✓	✓	✓	✓
Department of Commerce								
Office of Chief Economist		✓	✓	✓	✓			
Bureau of Economic Analysis			✓	✓	✓		✓	✓
Office of Assistant Secretary for Policy	✓	✓	✓	✓		✓	✓	✓
Industry and Trade Administration	✓		✓	✓				
Department of Defense								
Office of Economic Adjustment		✓	✓	✓	✓	✓	✓	✓
Federal Communications Commission								
Common Carrier Bureau		✓						
General Services Administration								
Emergency Economic Stabilization Division	✓		✓	✓	✓	✓		
Resources Management Division	✓		✓	✓	✓	✓	✓	✓
Economic Preparedness Division						✓		
Applied Economic Division		✓	✓		✓			✓

Table 1-1 continued

Units	Collects Information	Forecasts Models	Receptions for Officials	Legislative Support	Public Information	Staff Support	Coordinates Interagency	Prepares Options
Housing and Urban Development								
Office of Policy Development and Research	✓	✓						
Interstate Commerce Commission								
Bureau of Economics	✓					✓	✓	
Department of the Interior								
Bureau of Mines	✓	✓	✓	✓	✓	✓	✓	
Bureau of Reclamation		✓	✓	✓		✓	✓	
Office of Minerals Policy and Research Analysis	✓	✓	✓	✓		✓	✓	✓
Bureau of Land Management	✓	✓	✓	✓		✓	✓	
Department of Labor								
Office of Trade Adjustment Assistance	✓	✓	✓	✓	✓	✓	✓	✓
Bureau of Labor Statistics (Office of Wages and Industrial Relations)			✓	✓	✓	✓		
Bureau of Labor Statistics (Office of Price and Living Conditions)	✓		✓	✓	✓	✓		✓
Bureau of Labor Statistics (Office of Product and Technology)	✓		✓	✓	✓	✓	✓	✓

Agency							
Bureau of Labor Statistics (Office of Employment Structure and Trends)	✓				✓		
Employment and Training Administration (Unemployment Insurance Services)	✓	✓			✓		
Department of Transporation							
Office of Systems and Economic Development	✓	✓		✓	✓	✓	
Research and Special Programs Direction (Materials Transportation Bureau)	✓	✓		✓	✓	✓	
Federal Highway Administration	✓						
Office of Environmental Quality	✓		✓				
Assistant Secretary for Policy and International Affairs	✓	✓		✓	✓		
Department of the Treasury							
Office of State and Local Finance	✓	✓		✓	✓		✓
International Trade Commission	✓	✓		✓			

Source: President Carter's Reorganization Project, *Economic Analysis and Policymaking Project*, Survey I (Washington, D.C.: U.S. Office of Management and Budget, 1978).

Note: Based on incomplete information as of February 1978. The Department of Energy was only a few months old, although regional energy analysis was being conducted in the predecessor Federal Energy Administration and Energy Research and Development Administration at the time. Other agencies such as EPA or DHEW have increased their interest and activity in regional analyses in recent years. The omission of these and other agencies does not mean that no such activity was taking place.

to conceptualize. We believe that each federal/subnational program—and there are literally hundreds of such programs—has a responsibility to make such estimates, both on an *ex ante* (before-the-fact) basis and then as an *ex post* (after-the-fact) assessment of what actually occurred as a result of the program. Indeed, were it done as it should be, such estimation would entail the analysis of combined programs, not of each program individually, one at a time. Clearly, this is a formidable task.

Doesn't Everybody Consider Regional Impacts?

Given the importance of subfederal consequences, it is justifiable to ask whether or not policymakers habitually and adequately take into account the regional impacts of federal programs. For some departments and programs, the question would be superfluous, for their legislatively mandated *raison d'etre* is to serve a regional clientele. Consequently, a considerable amount of regional analysis already occurs at the federal level (see table 1-1). But although much is done in some departments, much is not done in others. In any case, close examination of the activities of federal agencies dealing with subnational programs and/or consequences leads to the conclusion that there are several ways to look at the federal-regional impact question.

At this point, some discussion of definitions and concepts is in order: what is meant by the terms *federal, regional* (or *subnational*) *policy, program, impact?* Can regionalism and sectionalism be defined in these terms? What are some implications for the evolving new federalism? Chapter 2 addresses these questions.

Notes

1. National Governors' Association Annual Meeting, Washington, D.C., February 1981. Also, Jay Rockefeller and Richard D. Lamm, "Balanced U.S. Growth," *Washington Post,* 28 February 1981.

2. Carl W. Steinberg, "Beyond the Days of Wine and Roses: Intergovernmental Management in a Cutback Environment," *Public Administration Review* 41, no. 1 (January/February 1981):10–20; U.S. Advisory Commission on Intergovernmental Relations, *A Crisis of Confidence and Competence: The Federal Role in the Federal System—The Dynamics of Growth* (Washington, D.C.: Government Printing Office, 1980).

3. For example, Garry Wills, *Explaining America: The Federalist* (Garden City, N.Y.: Doubleday, 1981).

4. Office of Technology Impacts, *Environmental Analysis of Syn-*

thetic Liquid Fuels (Washington, D.C.: U.S. Department of Energy, Office of the Assistant Secretary for Environment, 1980).

5. Peter W. House and Robert G. Ryan, *The Future Indefinite* (Lexington, Mass.: Lexington Books, D.C. Heath and Company, 1979). Some of the observations of this section are adapted from this book.

6. Irving Hock, "The Relationship between Natural Resources and Patterns of Urban and Regional Development," mimeographed, Report to the Department of Housing and Urban Development, (Washington, D.C.: Resources for the Future, 1974).

7. Symptomatic of the fragile ecosystem is the Four Corners area in the western Rockies: the particulate emissions at Four Corners are higher than in Los Angeles and about the same as in Chicago, Detroit, and Cincinnati.

8. CONSAD Research Corporation, *Impact of Regulation on Industrial Location Decisions* (Washington, D.C.: U.S. Department of Commerce Regulatory Reform Seminar, 25 August 1978); John R. Meyer and Robert A. Leone, "The New England States and Their Economic Future: Some Implications of a Changing Industrial Environment," *American Economic Review* 68, no. 2 (1978), pp. 110-115.

9. Movement to the Sunbelt during the 1970s appears to have even exceeded the expectations of demographers and social scientists: see C.M. Slater and Martha Davis, "Population Shift to Sunbelt States in Seventies Greater than Expected," *Business America* 4, no. 4 (23 February 1981):19-21.

10. *National Journal,* July 1977, pp. 1028-1034. An earlier comprehensive study by CONSAD Research Corporation in a report to the President's Independent Study Board titled *Regional Effects of Government Procurement and Related Policies* (Washington, D.C.: U.S. Department of Commerce, 1967), and later studies, such as idem, *Public Works Investment in the United States* (Washington, D.C.: U.S. Department of Commerce, 1980), covered similar topics, but without corresponding journalistic coverage.

11. See, for example, the following articles in the *National Journal:* N.R. Pierce and Jerry Hagstrom, "Regional Groups Talk about Cooperation, but They Continue to Feud," May 1978, pp. 844-846; Dick Kirschten, "There's More Rhetoric than Reality in the West's 'Sagebrush Rebellion,' " November 1979, pp. 1928-1932; and Richard Corrigan and R.L. Stanfield, "Rising Energy Prices—What's Good for Some States Is Bad for Others," March 1980, pp. 468-474.

12. A.R. Markusen and Jerry Fastrup, "The Regional War for Federal Aid," *Public Interest* 53 (1978):98-99. This generalization could well apply to policy-oriented approaches to the Sunbelt-Frostbelt issues discussed above.

13. See J.E. Meade, *Trade and Welfare* (London: Oxford University Press, 1955); I.M.D. Little, *Welfare Economics* (London: Oxford University Press, 1950); R.J. Arnott and J.E. Stiglitz, "Aggregate Land Rents, Expenditure on Public Goods, and Optimal City Size," *Quarterly Journal of Economics* 93, no. 4 (1979), pp. 472-500; and William J. Baumol, "Theory of Equity in Pricing for Resource Conservation," *Journal of Environmental Economics and Management* 7 (1980):308-320.

14. Here, we refer to all measures of well-being as reflected in the richest quality-of-life measure.

15. Again, this is so only if the redistributive effects are ignored. In reality, such consequences cannot be ignored—so that subnational redistributive consequences should be estimated and considered in any overall subnational policy assessment of a federal policy or program. See J.S. Chipman and J.C. Moore, "Real National Income with Homothetic Preferences and a Fixed Distribution of Income," *Econometrica* 43 (1980): 401-429; P. Samuelson, "Evaluation and Real National Income," *Oxford Economic Papers,* n.s. (1950):1-29; and A.C. Pigou, *The Economics of Welfare,* 4th ed. (New York: Macmillan, 1932).

16. I.E. Raskin, "A Conceptual Framework for Research on the Cost-Effective Allocation of Federal Resources," *Socioeconomic Planning Sciences* 9 (1975):1-10.

2 Some Definitions and Concepts

A Hierarchical Typology of Policies and Programs

This book is concerned with all federal policies and programs for which improved national planning necessarily entails taking into account subnational perspectives, impacts, trends, interests, and concerns. Such federal programs are (and have been) of three types: (1) *expressly national programs* that refer to subnational consequences only obliquely or not at all (many federal energy and environmental policies and programs are of this type); (2) *expressly regional programs* that have national funding and overtones, such as the Appalachian Regional Commission, the Title V Commissions (Ozarks, Old West, New England, and so on); or (3) *nationally funded programs targeted to local regions* (such as the planning and other programs of the Economic Development Administration's (EDA) economic-development districts, DHUD's community-action grants, the joint Corps of Engineers (Corps)/Department of Interior (DOI) waterway/dam infrastructure projects, and the Department of Transportation's (DOT) Northeast Corridor project).

A convenient grouping of such programs, primarily of types 2 and 3, was developed about 1978 for President Carter's Reorganization Project, to facilitate dealing with so-called major federal local development programs. This grouping is listed below.[1]

> *Community-Facilities Programs,* including the community-development block-grant program of the Department of Housing and Urban Development (DHUD); the water and sewer programs and related community-facility programs of the Departments of Agriculture (USDA) and Commerce (DOC), and the Environmental Protection Agency (EPA); and the Title V and Appalachian Regional Commission programs.
>
> *Housing Programs,* including those in USDA, DHUD, the Veterans Administration, and the Bureau of Indian Affairs (BIA), as well as related activities of the Government National Mortgage Association, the Federal National Mortgage Association, and the Federal Home Loan Mortgage Corporation.

Business-Assistance Programs, including programs of the Small Business Administration, the Economic Development Administration, the Community Services Administration, the Office of Minority Business Enterprise, the Farmers Home Administration, and BIA.

Transportation Assistance Programs, including the urban-mass-transit program and the airport-construction-program aspects of the federal-aid highway programs.

Employment and Training Programs, including the Comprehensive Employment and Training Act programs, the local public-works employment program, the job-opportunities program, and the work-incentive program.

Planning-Assistance Programs, including those of the Departments of Housing and Urban Development, Commerce, Agriculture, Transportation, and the Environmental Protection Agency.

Energy and Resources Programs, such as the state and local conservation and solar DOE programs, regional land-management and recreation programs of the Department of the Interior, and regional forestry programs of the Department of Agriculture.

There is admittedly only a fine line between the Department of Energy's National Energy Act or the EPA's Clean Air Act (type 1) policy, programming, and planning process, which affects regions differentially, and the national/regional/local programs (types 2 and 3—including the Economic Development Administration (EDA), DHUD, Corps, DOI, and DOT—which are explicitly and intentionally regional). In the latter programs, there is an explicit presumption that the nation as a whole somehow benefits from each of these regionally and locally (that is, subnationally) targeted programs. Emphasis is on an *entire* type 2 or 3 program (such as all Corps of Engineers projects) benefiting the nation—not necessarily that individual projects (funded as an element of any of these programs) separately benefit the entire nation.

What is common to all three program types, notwithstanding their other differences, is the presence of public-sector decision making—decisions that consider each federal action and that either unintentionally (as in type 1 cases most typically) or intentionally (as in the case of EDA, DHUD, Corps, type 2 and 3 cases) have differential subnational impacts. The informed and well-meaning decision maker, when subnational considerations can and should be made explicit, might ask: "What does my decision do (that is, impact upon), both at the national level (in some aggregate sense) and also at whichever subnational levels are affected?" Then, knowing this, and granting the uncertainty of estimates, the decision maker asks:

Some Definitions and Concepts

"Is my decision good both for the subnational jurisdictions directly and indirectly affected and for the nation as a whole? Do any subnational units benefit solely at the expense of other units, and by how much?"

Table 2-1 is intended to make these distinctions, similarities, and overlapping a bit clearer. The subdivisions in the table cover and include:

Major consequences and trends (such as Sunbelt/Frostbelt and center city/suburban migration)[2]

Affected parties, places, factors, and elements, such as land uses (agriculture, natural resources), middle- and poverty-income socioeconomic classes, transportation and communication, housing costs, private and public infrastructure costs (housing, factors of production), energy resources, and environmental quality

Most of the entries we want to discuss—the ones that are generally ignored in current agency policy—are those called *settlement patterns:* land-use and socioeconomic impacts at any subnational level affected. Unlike the national-program half of the table, where the argument is "What's good for the nation is good for each region (unless it can be proved otherwise)," the argument for the subnational programs, in the bottom half of the table, is "What's good for each subnational area (assisted by federal policy, program, and the like) is good for the nation."

Subnational programs, of course, are more closely tied to federalist concepts of regionalism and sectionalism. Some political scientists hold that federalist concepts are opposed to centralist notions, and, in theory, that is correct. We are arguing here that *allegedly*-federalist policymaking becomes more like arbitrary and ill-considered centralism to the degree that subfederal (subnational) considerations are ignored in federal decision making. Indeed, in either the extreme or moderate versions of the new federalism, such seeming arbitrariness not only will be rejected but also may lead to a reduction of the federal policymaking role, even when significant national-interest rationale exists.

Illustrative Situations

We use the term *subnational* or *subfederal* to describe activities, effects, and consequences at the regional, multistate, state, or substate local levels. All of these have increasing relevance in our emerging system of federalism. Below are four situations in which subnational policy/program activities are generated.

Table 2-1
Proposed Coverage of Consequences, Trends, and Affected Parties

	Impacts at the Federal/National Level: Direct, Indirect, Induced		Impacts at the Subnational Levels: Direct, Indirect, Induced	
	Intended Impacts Short Term–Long Term	Unintended Impacts Short Term–Long Term	Intended Impacts Short Term–Long Term	Unintended Impacts Short Term–Long Term
Federal programs, policies, budgets, regulations (such as NEA and CAA)	Increased prices for imported fuels	Costlier U.S. production processes: lower comparative advantage	Increased use of Western coal	Uncontrolled growth, Western boom towns
	Increased expenditures on air-quality anti-pollution equipment		More rigorous treatment of air quality in steel-producing regions	Loss of jobs in steel-producing regions
Subnational programs, policies, budgets, regulations, managed by the federal government (such as ARC, Title V's, EDA Corps of Engineers, DHUD, DOI, and DOT)	Improved highway programs, Appalachian region	Increased truck competition for rail service	Increased support for Northeast and Appalachian region(s) (with more depressed local areas)	Nondepressed Sunbelt areas receive proportionately less public-investment funding
	Increased works in economically depressed areas	Increased competition for nondepressed areas		

Note: Subnational includes regional metropolitan, county groupings, urban, center city, neighborhood, rural areas, etc. Both categories 2 and 3 are included. NEA = National Energy Act; CAA = Clean Air Act.

Some Definitions and Concepts

Situation 1. The nation uses public and private infrastructure, generated by or through subnational development, to accelerate the pace of economic, social, and cultural growth on a national scale. The characteristic features of this situation might be summarized as follows:

1. Interareal-development schemes are promoted by the central government via a central policy or programming agency.
2. The interareal-development plan or program is designed for the whole country, in most cases within the framework of a general development plan or program. In this case, the development program is composed of four interrelated sets:
   a. the general program
   b. the sectoral program
   c. the subnational area program
   d. the interareal program.
3. *Interareal development* in this case means the subnational and sectoral disaggregation of national economic and social policies.

Situation 2. The subnational development or policy activity is generated by integrating local activities to solve problems on a subnational scale that cannot be solved at a local scale. An example of this would be a program designed to overcome obstacles created by traditional administrative divisions for urban development by promoting metropolitan planning and metropolitan government. There are also programs promoting the modernization of agriculture on a subnational scale, not only to resolve problems of technical and managerial innovations in agricultural production and services, but also to bring about changes in the quality of life for the population in rural areas and small towns. The concept of growth centers, focusing on new productive and infrastructural investment, is applicable here.

Situation 3. A special action for subnational development is designed and implemented in order to accelerate the economic, social, and cultural change in an underdeveloped or depressed area. Such an action can be performed within the framework of general planning or programming machinery (such as the EDA) or through establishing a set of institutions that have no counterparts in the more developed regions of the country (such as the Appalachian Regional Commission or the Title V Commissions).

Situation 4. The subnational-development activity is started and implemented as a consequence of a sectoral-investment decision. In this case, the primary motivation for subnational development is not that of geographic areas but of sectoral forces. An example is the TVA, organized around the energy-production sector. In most such cases, the sectoral decision-making unit also recognizes the necessity of designing and implementing at its own level a development plan that establishes relationships between the sectoral and nonsectoral activities of that area. Such a plan also seeks to foster a set of social and cultural institutions and investments for its area.

These four situations are all characterized by combinations of conflict, dialogue, and compromise among national, local, subnational, and sectoral forces, but all are national-level policies implemented through and affecting differentially the nation's subnational areas. Until now, these policies have been too frequently national, not national-subnational. The new federalism—with or without analytic support—will considerably alter this situation. The question to be answered in the remainder of this book is whether or not analytics can be helpful in this new context.

Key Analytic-Research Issues

For the most part, managers of public programs that are predominantly subnational (or regional) in orientation (situations 2, 3, and possibly 4 in the preceding section) have not sought to estimate, or even to define, the larger consequences of their activities. For one, the federal unit might look exclusively at the direct effects of agency programs on the single activity within its purview—the Federal Highway Administration might evaluate road networks in a specific local area or region, for example. Investigation into a specific functional-area federal program, whether it be highways or airports or industrial parks, frequently reveals a lack of perspective: more often than not, regional impacts of these federal programs are ignored. In addition, the analysis performed by many of these specific substantive functional programs is often retrospective: it seeks to estimate the impacts of programs and policies already imposed. Typically, the analysis—if performed at all—does not attempt to differentiate the impact of a particular agency policy from those of other policies that also impact on the activity under scrutiny. Moreover, to the extent that policy-directed studies are made of the anticipated regional impacts of a particular policy, they tend to be special-purpose, one-time efforts rather than matters of routine.

As recently as a decade ago, experts studying this array of situational contexts would characterize only situation 1 types genuinely interregional activities and consequences.[3] Today, however, there is little disagreement worldwide that there are very few federal policies and programs whose consequences are so geographically isolated that they can be segmented, studied, and treated separately from all the rest. Admittedly, not every federal policy or program requires a comprehensive, integrated, intersectoral, interareal review—across economic, social, and physical dimensions. In fact, the very essence of policy formulation requires that scarce analysis resources be

Some Definitions and Concepts

devoted to situations where the potentially most-significant interareal and intersectoral unintended consequences must be discovered and assessed. In most federal policy-analysis situations, the most skillful and successful managers know when to apply quick-and-dirty analysis methods and what, at the margin, the addition of more resources might yield in terms of additional knowledge, insight, and creative surprises about unintended consequences.

The notion that federally designed and supported subnational policies and programs are important at a national level is certainly not new. Almost fifty years ago, the National Resource Committee's Task Force on Regional Factors in National Planning and Development stated:

> Major problem areas frequently overlap state boundaries and yet cover only a part of the whole nation. Production areas, manufacturing areas, lines of transportation, corn, cotton, citrus, coal, watersheds, timber, are no respecters of political boundaries, yet many create problems that require public attention. Some of these areas, such as the Northeast, the Northwest, the Southeast, are marked by so many fundamental natural, population, and cultural factors that they create a regional consciousness in the minds of their inhabitants. The fact that state boundaries are firmly embedded in the Constitution has led to a search for means of setting these regional or subnational interests into the framework of the American nation. . . .
>
> If regions with serious problems were to be given geographic boundaries, the tendency to defend their regional interest at the boundary, so characteristic of Europe, might be encouraged in America. On the other hand, a series of interrelated regions, closely cooperating with the federal establishment, would tend to cement the Union and to promote the solution of intersectional adjustments.[4]

This statement of the problem is equally valid today. And there are dozens of subsequent investigations of what different visions of federalism—regionalism, sectionalism, and other intergovernmentalisms—engender for the nation as a whole.[5]

Although national attention on subnational issues was centered, during the first years of the Carter administration, on so-called urban policies, increased attention turned increasingly to multistate subnational levels in the last years of the 1970s, promising to continue into the 1980s with strength.

The most widely discussed federal/subfederal issue of the late 1970s was surely the so-called Sunbelt-Frostbelt conflict, over public-sector policies and programs that allegedly exacerbated the resource and income migration from the more densely populated northeastern states. The recent White House Conference on Balanced Growth and Economic Development, for example, focused much attention on the meaning of regionally disparate growth rates and on ways to deal with resulting economic-welfare distortions. Furthermore, a number of active legislative proposals in 1977, 1978, and 1979 addressed the future of the several Title V Regional Commissions (such as adding to their current number)—covering the nation with such commissions in a wall-to-wall fashion, revising and/or enlarging the Appalachian Regional Commission program, concepts, and other multistate/regional proposals—all dealing with this relatively new governmental tier between (and alongside) states and the federal government. And, as it has done since its inception, the Economic Development Administration (EDA) continues to define and refine its role in the economic development of the nation's less developed and/or high-unemployment areas.[6]

Despite this outpouring of studies of subnational matters, consequences, and trends, there has also been little (if any) observable surge of research into operational methodologies potentially useful to interested and involved federal policymakers. Some research into subnational questions has, of course, taken place in previous years, supported primarily by the federal government, with the variable results to be anticipated from such a difficult research arena.[7] Nevertheless, several research issues urgently require further attention, because their resolution can make an important contributions in this important policy debate.

Rephrasing the analytic challenges posed in an earlier section, we believe this is the key analytic-research issue: Does explicit consideration of (a) subnational trends and subnational consequences of federal actions or (b) federal policy and program actions that explicitly affect specific subnational activities contribute not only to subnational but also to the national welfare? If so, to what extent and under what conditions?

Related analytic issues, pending an affirmative answer, include:

What methods are most viable, effective, and efficient for use in conducting such national/subnational analyses of consequences and socioeconomic welfare?

How can analysis play a more effective role in the design and development of federal policies and programs that either implicitly or explicitly impact differentially on subnational areas?

Is This a New Problem?

Inevitably the question arises, Why hasn't this set of issues been addressed more seriously in the past? Possibly one reason no serious effort has been made to measure the local/regional impacts of a national policy or more seriously to estimate the federal consequences of local feedback is the belief

Some Definitions and Concepts

that a process doing just that was already at work. After all, the founding fathers, when they designed the federal system of a Congress, foresaw the utility of a structure in which subfederal interests were to be well represented. In general, the system as designed postulated that at least one chamber of the national legislature (the House of Representatives) should have a membership representing the citizenry in direct proportion to its size. The other chamber (the Senate) was also to be representatively constructed, but with a more geographic orientation. In either case, both houses of the legislature were to represent clearly defined subfederal interests. With such a design, it might be expected that enlightened self-interest would take over and each subnational entity could be expected to favor (or oppose) policies or programs that related to their area.

In the main, most would agree that this expectation has proved fairly valid. Several developments over the years, however, have made this arrangement inadequate as the only guardian of subfederal interests. In the first place, the historical relationships between the legislative branch and the executive branch have meant that the formulation of laws designed to set the policy for the nation as a whole may or may not have taken subnational interests into account; the operation of these general guidelines may not prove to do so. For by precedent, the laws enacted by the Congress normally leave much discretion to the president and the executive branch in the execution stage, and there are few formal institutional arrangements available to the executive branch for the explicit recognition of subnational interests, concerns, and consequences.

Second, because of improvements in transporation and communication networks, change occurs considerably faster in today's world than it did two centuries ago. The decennial census, used to apportion political power in the nation as a whole among the various states and regions, tends to lag considerably behind the actual movement of people and, more important, seems to lag behind the institutional, organizational, economic, and political shifts that both accompany and lead these population movements. The Sunbelt-Frostbelt phenomenon discussed here and the so-called sagebrush rebellion prompted by energy and economic developments illustrate where a great deal of national and regional policy has been and will continue to be focused, say between 1971 and 1989; but only one national census to reapportion the House of Representatives will have taken place during that eighteen-year period: the 1980 census.

Third, the role of the public sector in our lives has increased considerably since the early days of the nation. Not only has the fraction of total national income that is touched by the public sector risen dramatically in the last fifty years, but also each facet of our everyday lives is affected by public- was well as private-sector decisions. Further, the whole society has become more complex, with improved transportation and communication blurring geographic distinctions and at the same time accelerating the impacts of policy decisions. Equally obvious is the fact that not only our technology, but indeed our whole culture, has evolved so that the difference, speed, number, and variety of primary and secondary impacts of the myriad of public policies can no longer be expected to be attended to by the informal, unknowing, and often insensitive model of enlightened self-interest. Many of these impacts are spillovers, affecting others outside the purview (and often interest) of the parties responsible for the original action. Long-range transport of air pollutants is one example, mandatory school busing is another, and deregulation of the price of natural gas still another.

One can imagine the debates possible—in today's terms—over the creation of a national postal system. For example:

> Why should it cost the same to mail a letter from New York to California as from New York to New Jersey? Doesn't this subsidize the western states at the expense of the eastern states? What are the national as opposed to the regional and/or the sectional interests?
>
> Which industries are hurt? Which are helped? Are private postal firms helped or injured? What supplier firms and labor organizations are helped, which hurt, and where are they located?
>
> What states and regions are likely to develop faster as a result? Which are likely to be relatively injured?

No technological, environmental, economic, or subnational impact analysis was conducted prior to establishment of a national postal system. Today we can identify many lasting consequences, both intended and unintended; moreover, a much larger public is aware of such effects, both national and subnational: today we would most likely subject such a proposal to intensive and searching analytical investigation, some of it perhaps along subnational lines.

Not only does no formal institutional mechanism exist in the executive branch for heeding and mitigating the unintended and undesirable subnational impacts of policy applications, but also the representative structure of the legislative branch is probably inadequate to the task of equitably overseeing the consequences of present-day national policy. The reactive political, adversarial process of lawmaking, as it has evolved through the decades, is found wanting when Congress attempts to address itself simultaneously to setting major energy, economic, transportation, and health objectives that accord with some agreed-upon *national* objective, and to avoiding setting off some undesirable or unanticipated reaction in one of the other functional areas (such as environment). As difficult as this is in the abstract, it is made even more complex by congressional committee struc-

Some Definitions and Concepts 29

tures, which, except for the Congressional Budget Office, the Joint Economic Committee, and the Office of Technology Impacts, tend to be overly specialized and institutionally incapable of analyzing, either before or after the fact, the total impacts of the dozens of laws investigated, formulated, updated, and enacted each year. How much more difficult it is when the task is complicated by a set of subnational units with their own desires, needs, histories, problems, people, and resource bases!

Without adequate national and subnational analysis, properly institutionalized in both the legislative and executive branches, this federal shortcoming will be exacerbated and may become even more damaging to the public interest. This will be even more true under extreme versions of the new federalism, if subnational decisions are made with no consideration of the national public interest.

Is this a new problem? In the sense that substantial subnational interests have always existed, the answer must be no. But it is only recently that we have been able to use modern public-sector analytic problem-solving techniques—extensive data bases, complex and reliable analytic models, and efficient field-survey capabilities. In this sense, the problem emerges in a new form: Can analytic methods help assess subnational impacts and take subnational trends into account so as to restore a valid, sensitive, and meaningful subnational presence at the federal level? Can such methods not only help those who wish to take currently unintended and undesirable subnational consequences into account, but also promote subnational activities for which there is a substantial nationwide benefit? In this sense, we do have a new problem—and a new opportunity for analysis, properly set within a context of institutional policy analysis.

These important questions deserve response first on a conceptual level, before we attempt to fit a helter-skelter of existing models and data bases to problems for which they might not be well suited. We will discuss some of these concepts in the next chapter; in chapter 4 we will assess the disciplinary contributions to the implementation of those concepts.

Notes

1. These have been modified here to add certain energy, natural-resources, and environmental programs. Similar groups have been developed and analyzed in Harold F. Wise, *Conflicts in Federal Subnational Development Programs* (Washington, D.C.: Economic Development Research Report, U.S. Department of Commerce, 1976).

2. Both phenomena are actual trends that most likely would happen without any federal programs; however, they may be stimulated, exacerbated, mitigated, or stifled in unanticipated and unintended ways by such federal policies and programs.

3. A.R. Kuklinski, "Trends in Research on Comprehensive Regional Development" (paper prepared for the United Nations Research Institute for Social Development, [UNRISD], 1968).

4. U.S. Natural Resources Committee, *Regional Factors in National Planning and Development* (Washington, D.C.: Government Printing Office, 1935).

5. Advisory Commission on Intergovernmental Relations, *Regional Decision-Making: New Strategies for Sub-State Districts* (Washington, D.C.: Government Printing Office, 1973); idem, *Multistate Regionalism* (Washington, D.C.: Government Printing Office, 1972); idem, *An Agenda for American Federalism: Restoring Confidence and Competence* (Washington, D.C.: Government Printing Office, 1981); Albert Breton and Anthony Scott, *The Economic Constitution of Federal States* (Toronto: University of Toronto Press, 1978); Donald J. Bogue and Calvin J. Beale, *Economic Areas of the United States* (Glencoe, N.Y.: The Free Press, 1961); State University of New York-Binghamton, Center for Social Analysis, "Title V Regional Commissions: An Evaluation" (Binghamton, N.Y. 1977); Martha Derthick and Gary Bombardier, *Between State and Nation: Regional Organizations of the United States* (Washington, D.C.: Brookings Institution, 1974); David K. Hartley, James G. Coke, and Ralph R. Widner, "Interstate and Substate Approaches to Growth Policy" (Paper prepared for the Committee on Public Works, U.S. House of Representatives, 1974); National Governors' Association, *Report to the White House Conference on Balanced National Growth and Economic Development* (Washington, D.C.: Government Printing Office, 1980); Monroe Newman, *The Political Economy of Appalachia* (Lexington, Mass.: Lexington Books, D.C. Heath and Company, 1972); Robert Rafuse, "New Regional Debate: A National Overview" (paper presented to National Governors' Association, Washington, D.C., 1977; Donald N. Rothblatt, *Regional Planning: The Appalachian Experience* (Lexington, Mass.: Lexington Books, D.C. Heath and Company, 1971); James L. Sundquist, *Making Federalism Work* (Washington, D.C.: Brookings Institution, 1969); and Andrew M. Isserman, "The Allocation of Funds to Small Cities under the Community Development Block Grant Program: An Evaluation," *American Planning Journal* 47 (1981):3-24.

6. EDA's regions are typically not multistate but are, instead, multicounty districts that sometimes involve more than one state.

7. Sponsored, for example, by the EDA's Office of Economic Research, the Corps of Engineers, and the Appalachian Regional Commission.

3
The Current State of the Art: Theory

Can federal policy actions seek to achieve a national objective with little or no negative impact on any subnational area? Alternatively, can it initiate actions to increase the economic and social welfare of specific subnational regions and still promote the general national welfare? What is the current state of the art in the capability for making this determination?

The potential conflict between the welfare function of a subnational area and that of the parent nation has been a recurrent theme throughout the literature of subnational economic planning and decision making. Boudeville's assessment was written more than ten years ago:

> If the objective were to maximize, in a given period, the income of each region, national growth might be slowed down to a considerable extent. National resources are always limited, regional productivities are unequal, and regional interconnections different. Investment in the less productive, less well-endowed regions would put a brake on the development of more productive ones. Investment in regions less closely linked with the economic core of the nation than others would make a lower impact on total growth. Conversely, it is socially unacceptable to invest in the expanding and richest regions only. Thus, every time choice has to be made of a set of final goods, problems of social and political welfare are bound to arise.[1]

The size, variety, and relative importance of these regions—frequently multistate in nature—make any question about their net contribution to the total social and economic fabric of the nation far from academic. Unlike individual metropolitan areas, where no more than 0.5 to 2 percent of the gross national product (GNP) may be produced, a large fraction of the nation's production, population, and political support are found in each of the nation's major subnational regions: Appalachia, the ten standard federal administrative regions, the Title V regions, and others. Each of these regions contains several, perhaps dozens, of these metropolitan areas. Economists and economic-development specialists have devoted considerable attention to this matter, although until recently few have wrestled with the difficult problems of attribution and aggregation. For many years, regional economists were alone in the criticism of traditional regional-accounts systems, whose underlying concept is that the national economy is solely the sum of its parts—that is, that the national growth rate is merely the (weighted) average of the growth rate of its parts. Macroeconomists generally believe, in fact, in this primary top-down approach to national-income measurement.

Edgar Hoover and Benjamin Chinitz are regional economists who have stated on a number of occasions that even a full and current set of separately developed regional accounts would not be adequate to ensure the availability of the data inputs required for either a valid regional study or a study of the nation and its component regions. Comprehensive and interactive demographic, economic, and land-use impacts, they maintain, could not be accurately calculated from such a picture of separate, individual regions. Chinitz said, even before the current emergence of the intense subnational concerns, that the national trend cannot be independent of its parts; in other words, *it is not only—and should not be only—a top-down process*

> in reconciling metropolitan goals with national goals if we define an objective not in terms of grabbing a bigger piece of the nation for ourselves but rather in terms of raising the productivity of this piece of the nation. If we succeed, it is not at the expense of the world around us.[2]

Here, and in many places since, Chinitz contends that, for a variety of reasons, we cannot study hierarchical systems only from the top down.[3] The total at the "top," though certainly and ultimately the algebraic sum of all that is below it, is affected by what goes on below it—within geographic areas, between sectors, over time, and among productive factors—and by how these activities are located relative to, and how they deal with, one another.

In coping with these regional-level issues recently, macroeconomists have tended to lump the many factors that contribute to this synergistic regional feedback under the term *regional underemployment* or *structural unemployment,* sometimes even *spatial disequilibrium.* And more recently, in the mid-1970s, there was increasing recognition that the measure of net national product (NNP) as conceptualized by welfare economists is a flawed measure, or proxy, of economic welfare occurring at regional levels where:[4]

> Substantial unemployment, underemployment, and/or otherwise inefficient employment of factors exist at regional levels;

> Substantial income-distribution differences exist that should not be ignored; and

> Possibilities for perverse interregional repercussions (externalities) exist, arising from the impact of uneven development policies in each region upon other regions.

Some Regional Economic Evidence

Despite the importance of this subject, there has been little conceptual and empirical work on the questions that opened the chapter.[5] Some economists have surrendered to the overwhelming complexity of interregional policy-making and programming. Instead of attempting to coordinate interareal activities, they have proposed that individual areas should attempt to become as independent from outside influences as possible. Doctors Gar Alperwitz and Norton Long, for example, have recently called for individual urbanized areas to develop increasing degrees of economic self-sufficiency in exploring ways to achieve full employment.[6]

In some respects, these advocates of self-sufficiency—whatever the geographic dimensions—are recommending a policy designed to offset the advantages gained over the years from both specialization and the application of comparative-advantage principles to geographic areas. There is, of course, a fine line between each local area's seeking economic self-sufficiency and each area's maximizing what it can do and does do best. Generally, an objective of areal economic self-sufficiency alone cannot achieve the latter.

Specialists in regional economics and policy analysis such as Dr. Robert Rauner have begun to identify the assumptions of public policy that are the basis for promoting subnational activities with positive national consequences. Dr. Rauner's conclusions and recommendations can be summarized as follows:[7]

1. Public activities should have sufficient strength, as either incentives or the removal of deterrents, to effect national distribution of resources in favor of the designated regions.
2. There is sufficient resilience in the national economy to permit without major objection these public-policy-promoted deviations from purely market-located economic activities.
3. These deviations must be politically acceptable to both the electorate and the economic power-structure of business and labor.

Although some of the legislative responses to the problems of subnational diversity may have been premised on these beliefs, there has been comparatively little research on the validity of these assumptions. However, although additional research is urgently needed, both conceptual and empirical work exists that can be built upon.[8]

There is substantial evidence that jurisdictions need not pursue a "beggar-thy-neighbor" policy in achieving national and subnational objectives. Indeed, the few empirical analyses that do exist indicate that jurisdictions throughout the nation can and do provide considerable (and often indispensable) economic and social invisible support for other jurisdictions,[9] thus creating a net benefit for geographic areas larger than themselves. For example, the infrastructure provided by each subnational jurisdiction for the others (such as transportation and communication investments)—presently unmeasured, for the most part, as public capital stock yielding a rate of return—needs increasingly to be recognized as explicitly affecting total national welfare.

There is also ample evidence that underemployed and underutilized subnational units can increase their activities, in a local and regional macro sense, so that other localities and regions are not necessarily affected adversely; indeed, evidence exists that overall national-income (macro) objectives can be enhanced if subnational underutilization is properly reduced without beggar-thy-neighbor consequences.[10] In recent years, major metropolitan areas and city centers such as Boston, St. Paul-Minneapolis, and Pittsburgh have made major recoveries—with significant but not overwhelming public-investment assistance—with substantial beneficial effects upon their adjacent suburban and urban communities, as well as their larger regions and the nation in general.

Clearly, these processes cannot go on indefinitely: when resources are fully employed in each subarea, one area's gain will then occur at the expense of another. The evidence for an apparent "beggar-thy-neighbor" consequences, in any case, is not overwhelming; furthermore, results of piecemeal research yielding contrary conclusions can be found.

Research supporting this and analogous speculations has, for the most part, proceeded at an all too leisurely pace. No current research, for example, can demonstrate that subnational/jurisdictional assistance grants—be they adaptive or developmental—have positive external (spillover) economies for other jurisdictions (Rauner's point 1, above), and/or expansive (positive) impacts upon national income (Rauner's point 2). Clearly, this is a serious shortcoming of current regional-economics research and policy analysis.

Does It Have to Be a Zero-Sum Game?

Elements of competition and complementarity exist in the dealings between subnational regions—so much so that one might ask if one area's gain always has to be at the expense of another. In mathematics, when one player's loss is another player's gain it is called a *zero-sum game*. These game-theory notions of strategy and payoff (or von Neumann-Morgenstern utility) were created as part of decision theory and the formal representation of a decision-making organization called *team-theory*.[11] If the game played among a nation's subnational areas were truly zero-sum, a situation of pure conflict would obtain. (Here, the main body of game-theory results would apply, providing a rationale for the minimax criterion of strategy choice.) If the payoffs are not zero-sum, however, the selection of the criterion for a good decision is unresolved except in certain special game-theory cases. Compounding the difficulty is the fact that there are numerous decision makers involved at all levels—national, regional, and subregional—with differing objectives as to the distributional consequences of varying growth rates and differing sectoral and demographic composition. Another difficulty exists in the uncertainties inherent in the situation. Not only does each region have less-than-perfect information concerning the impacts of its public-sector actions on its own regional net product, but also there are the uncertainties caused by each region's economic actions being taken somewhat independently of one another, reinforcing the complexities of this already-difficult decision problem. (Major regional and interregional decisions on transportation and communication infrastructure are illustrative of this planning problem.)

In summary, the situation is so complex that federal policies are often made that benefit one region at the expense of another. There is no reason, conceptually, to believe that this has to be so, but the real-world situation is so complex that it would be hard to make a case either way.

Different approaches and disciplines have attempted to address this matter of the benefits and costs of national and subnational actions in situations that some economists believe to be zero-summed, and many—in our opinion, more correctly—recognize the out-of-equilibrium, dynamic, uncertain situations that are not zero-summed in nature. Economists, political scientists, public administrators, systems experts, and geographers have made contributions to the discussion of national-subnational issues and their resolution, some of which we shall summarize in the next chapter.

The focus in chapter 4, the last in part I, concentrates more on conceptual approaches than on empirically analytical or modeling approaches. We shall discuss the latter two approaches in parts II and III. Chapter 4 helps lay the groundwork for these later discussions.

Notes

1. J.R. Boudeville, *Problems of Regional Economic Planning* (Chicago: Aldine Publishing Co., 1966), p. 19.

2. Benjamin Chinitz, "Economic Goals for the Metropolitan Community" (Address at a conference held in Cobo Hall, Detroit, May 1963).

3. Benjamin Chinitz, ed., *Central City Economic Development* (Cambridge, Mass.: Abt Books, 1979).

4. Fuller elaboration is contained in J.T. Romans, "Welfare Economics and the Measurement of NNP" (Paper presented at the Fourteenth

Conference of the International Association for Research in Income and Wealth, Auranko, Finland, 1975); and Richard Cooper, "Macroeconomic Policy Adjustment in Interdependent Economies," *Quarterly Journal of Economics* 83 (1969):1-24.

5. Walter Isard, the founder of regional economics, summarizes his views of the still-very-elementary nature of the state of the art in "Discussion," *American Economic Association Proceedings* 68, no. 2 (1978), pp. 116-117.

6. In addresses to the annual convention of the National League of Cities, Washington, D.C., March 1978. Secretary of Commerce Dr. Juanita M. Kreps also appeared to support aspects of this concept at this meeting.

7. Robert Rauner, "Multistate Regional Development: Some Economic and Legislative Perspectives" (Paper presented at the Special Conference on Economic Development, San Juan, Puerto Rico, April 1976).

8. W.A. Steger, "Competition for Public Resources Based upon Jurisdictional Contributions to National Growth and Development" (Report prepared for the White House Conference on Balanced National Growth and Economic Development, February 1978).

9. There are many studies bearing upon this finding: CONSAD Research Corporation, *A Study of the Effects of Public Investment* (Report prepared for the Economic Development Administration, Washington, D.C.: U.S. Department of Commerce, 1969); George S. Tolley, "The Welfare Economics of City Bigness," *Journal of Urban Economics* 1, no. 3 (1974), pp. 324-325; Frederick N. Cleaveland, *Congress and Urban Problems* (Washington, D.C.: Brookings Institution, 1969); W. Baumol, "Macroeconomics of Unbalanced Growth," *American Economic Review* 57, no. 3 (1967), pp. 415-536; Richard L. Meier, "The Organization of Technological Innovation in Urban Environments," in *The Historian and the City*, ed. Oscar Handlin and John Burchard (Cambridge, Mass.: MIT Press, 1966), pp. 74-83; Herbert A. Simon, "Effects of Increased Productivity upon the Ratio of Urban to Rural Population," *Econometrica* 15 (1947):31-42; and George Vernez and Roger Vaughan, *Assessment of Countercyclical Public Works and Public Service Employment Programs* (Santa Monica, Calif.: RAND Corporation, 1978).

10. Benjamin Chinitz, "Economic Goods for the Metropolitan Community"; W.A. Steger, "Inventing Economic Institutions for Urban Survival" (Report prepared for the Carnegie-Mellon Conference on Advanced Urban Transportation Systems, Carnegie Mellon University, Pittsburgh, 1970); Charles M. Tiebout, "A Pure Theory of Local Expenditure," *Journal of Political Economy* 64 (1956):416-424; Benjamin Chinitz and T.G. Cowing, "The Impact of Local Public Service Consolidation on Urban Spatial Structure," in *Local Service Pricing Policies and Their Effect on Urban Spatial Structure,* ed. Paul Downing (Vancouver: University of

British Columbia Press, 1977); and Edgar M. Hoover, "Some Old and New Issues in Regional Development" (Center for Regional Economic Studies, University of Pittsburgh, Occasional Paper no. 5, 1967).

11. Jacob Marschak, "Elements for a Theory of Teams," *Management Science* 2 (1955):127-137; idem, "Toward an Economic Theory of Organization and Information" in *Decision Processes,* ed. Robert Thrall, C.H. Coombs, and R.L. David (New York: Wiley, 1954), pp. 197-219.

4 Policy Research: Contributions by the Disciplines to the National/Subnational Discussion

Contributions of Economics and Planning

Several analytical contributions have been made to the study of national-subnational interactions: (1) investigations of what factors contribute to efficient and effective subnational arrangements; (2) economic-impact-analysis methods, at varying geographic levels; (3) methods for delineating subnational areas; and (4) economic-planning concepts.

Factors Contributing to Efficient and Effective Subnational Arrangements

Most studies have focused, as one would expect, on matters of scale economies. Economists have wrestled primarily with matters relating to the economies of scale involved at differing hierarchical levels. Dr. Robert Rauner, with the Title V Regional Commissions in mind, has stated:

> Regional and subregional problems come in many different sizes and scales. For the most part, governmental organizations generally align with those problem scales. . . . The concept of scale of economic problem and its broad correspondence with scale of institution carries with it a sense that some kind of organization efficiency is being served: that programs and responsibilities will be carried out at the level best fitted for them, that unnecessary or deleterious duplication will be avoided, and that no organization will be required to deal with problems that exceed its capacity or legitimacy. Federalism, itself, is but a version of this notion of organizational scale efficiency.[1]

Rauner notes that there is a rough correspondence, in certain functional activities, between governmental organizational level and the scale of the economic problem. Areal costs and benefits are appropriately matched with relatively few spillovers to other geographic areas, as in the case of subnational (large-scale regional) institutions:

The textbook examples of such scale are the river system encompassing several states, or a natural resource lying within several states and necessary for industrial or commercial development, or a transportation system spanning several state borders. Within the last decade a number of multistate organizations have been authorized for purposes of facilitating multistate planning and development. The objectives here are to institutionalize joint efforts among neighboring states. . . . The idea, in short, is simply to recognize the benefits of addressing another class of problems with an institution keyed to their unique scale.[2]

Multiple-jurisdiction regionalization—whether at multicounty, state, or multistate level—has been alleged to benefit from the following types of scale economies:

Improved staff utilization and increased quality for areal planning, programming, consensus development, promotion, and political show of strength and unification

Larger selection of potential growth centers on which to focus scarce development resources

Aggregation of the public/private markets for specific developmental and/or adaptive services (transportation, specialized health sources, vocational education, environmental protection)

Internalization of benefit spillovers (such as trained workers) and resulting recapture of investment costs to appropriate area

Better planning of large-scale, indivisible projects requiring integrated, multiarea coordination

The theory is simple and readily comprehended; however, with the relatively small budgets available to the Title V commissions or to the Department of Commerce, which monitors their activities, no rigorous evaluation of these concepts has in fact been performed. Small budgets have prevented effective implementation of multistate regional-scale projects and programs for these Title V agencies, so that few, if any, of the five types of scale economies listed above have actually been used, particularly at the multistate regional levels.[3] Attempts at further conceptualization of the scale-economies argument have not gone uncriticized, however. Geof Brennan recently wrote of the Breton-Scott report,[4] the latest study of this approach:

There are three major problems with this [economic] approach. First, the analysis implies a different level of government for each public service: the number of such levels would hence be extremely large. This arrangement is not congruent with any federal system we know, nor does it seem intuitively likely that such an arrangement would in fact be optimal. Second, the theory does not explain why genuine political decentralization is necessary to achieve the desired results: an appropriately benevolent (or electorally constrained) central government could achieve precisely the same results purely by administrative delegation. Thirdly, the theory is institutionally void. The "optimal" allocation of function is derived on the assumption that governments operate "perfectly" in accord with the demands of those who consume the various goods. It seems unlikely that the same allocation of functions would emerge as desirable when plausible assumptions about the operation of the political mechanism are inserted.[5]

Clearly, a meshing of the narrowly economic point of view about scale economies and those of the public administrator (see below) is called for, in terms of practical application to a realistic national/subnational context.

Economic-Impact Analysis

Dozens of economic-impact analyses have been completed at different subnational levels and across economic sectors. Table 4-1 summarizes some of the methods used to perform these studies at different sectoral and areal levels.[6] Notwithstanding the diversity of methods indicated, none yet treats interregional, intersectoral relationships in a sufficiently rich, believable manner.[7]

The leading edge of assessments in the field, as supported and encouraged at the federal level, are urban- and community-impact analyses. Unlike environmental-impact analyses (EISs), urban- and community-impact analyses (UCIAs) are intended to be policy oriented:[8]

> For example, a UCIA might look at the effect of EPA clean air standards on cities across the country; a typical EIS, however, would try to measure the effects of a specific project (e.g., a new highway) on a single city or small cluster of jurisdictions. . . .
>
> The current UCIA procedures are concerned primarily with gross, or macroeconomic views of impacts of policies. Distributional issues and noneconomic variables are given considerably less importance. Thus, UCIA generally attempts to estimate the absolute levels of the direct and indirect effects of policies on the employment and income of a city type.[9]

The analytic-modeling activity supporting the UCIA effort is still distinctly experimental (see chapter 7). A multiregion econometric model, the National-Regional Impact Evaluation System (NRIES), is being developed in the U.S. Department of Commerce[10] (see chapter 7). There are many conceptual and empirical difficulties with subnational, multisectoral modeling:[11] to date, the efforts are almost exclusively experimental, with many conceptual and empirical problems remaining to be addressed and solved. More will be said about such modeling efforts in chapters 6 and 7.

Table 4-1
Economic-Impact Analysis: Scope and Methods

Effects	(1) Individual Firm	(2) Industrial Segment	(3) Industrial Sector	(4) Community
Wage Effects	Combine employment, productivity, and cost impacts; bargaining and information models	Combine employment, productivity, and cost impacts; bargaining and information models	Combine employment, productivity, and cost impacts; bargaining and information models	Combine employment, productivity, and cost impacts; bargaining and information models
Financial Impacts (such as, profits/migration/closure)	Cost-price/rate-of-return analysis, simulation; cash-flow analysis; behavioral analysis	Cost-price/rate-of-return analysis, simulation; cash-flow analysis; behavioral analysis	Cost-price/rate-of-return analysis, simulation; cash-flow analysis; behavioral analysis	Cost-price/rate-of-return analysis, simulation; cash-flow analysis; behavioral analysis
Distribution of Impacts	Incidence (shifting) analysis for factors of production, including degree of market imperfection	Incidence (shifting) analysis for factors of production, including degree of market	Incidence (shifting) analysis for factors of production, including degree of market imperfection	Incidence (shifting) analysis for factors of production, including degree of market imperfection
Technological Constraints and Opportunities	Analysis of supply functions, providing industries, by factors of production	Analysis of supply functions, providing industries, by factors of production	Analysis of supply functions, providing industries, by factors of production	Analysis of supply functions, providing industries, by factors of production
Estimates of Health and Safety Benefits	Analysis of firm's medical records; apply discounting and damage functions to unit/days	Analysis of firm's medical records; apply discounting and damage functions to unit/days	Analysis of firm's medical records; apply discounting and damage functions to unit/days	Analysis of firm's medical records; apply discounting and damage functions to unit/days
Computation of Direct and Indirect Macroeconomic, Energy, and Environmental Consequences	Not relevant unless dominant firm	Utilize adapted Wharton, DRI, and INFORUM	Utilize adapted Wharton, DRI and INFORUM	Utilize adapted Wharton, DRI and INFORUM; regionalize
Overall Evaluation	Compute difference between social and private rate of return	Compute difference between social and private rate of return	Compute difference between social and private rate of return	Perform C-E and B/C analysis

Cost-of-Production Changes	Technology option/marginal cost/investment and annualized operating-cost analysis	Cost-abatement model -segment analysis	Cost-abatement model -sectoral analysis	Induced price changes; firm locational shifts
Price Impacts	Supply/demand analysis for firm's product; microindustry analysis (including forward and backward shifting)	Supply/demand analysis for firm's product; microindustry analysis (including forward and backward shifting)	Supply/demand analysis for firm's product; microindustry analysis (including forward and backward shifting)	Induced price changes; firm locational shifts; community cost-abatement and cost/price model
Productivity Impacts	Engineering economics/process-control study, including production-function impacts (such as reduced illness)	Engineering economics/process-control study, including production-function impacts (such as reduced illness)	Engineering economics/process-control study, including production-function impacts (such as reduced illness)	Engineering economics/process-control study, including production-function impacts (such as reduced illness)
Market-Structure Impacts	Study of firm's competitive position	Study of firm's competitive position	Study of firm's competitive position	Study of interindustry competitive effects
Employment/Output Effects	Determine output effect: supply/demand industry study; convert output to employment	Determine output effect: supply/demand industry study; convert output to employment	Determine output effect: supply/demand industry study; convert output to employment	Determine output effect: supply/demand industry study; convert output to employment

Table 4-1 continued

Effects	(5) Regional	(6) National	(7) International
Wage Effects	Combine employment, productivity, and cost impacts; bargaining and information models	Combine employment, productivity, and cost impacts; bargaining and information models	Combine employment, productivity, and cost impacts; bargaining and information models
Financial Impacts (such as, profits/migration/closure)	Cost-price/rate-of-return analysis, simulation; cash-flow analysis; behavioral analysis	Cost-price/rate-of-return analysis, simulation; cash-flow analysis; behavioral analysis	Cost-price/rate-of-return analysis, simulation; cash-flow analysis; behavioral analysis
Distribution of Impacts	Incidence (shifting) analysis for factors of production, including degree of market imperfection	Incidence (shifting) analysis for factors of production, including degree of market imperfection	Incidence (shifting) analysis for factors of production, including degree of market imperfection
Technological Constraints and Opportunities	Analysis of supply functions, providing industries, by factors of production	Analysis of supply functions, providing industries, by factors of production	Impact on exports and imports
Estimates of Health and Safety Benefits	Analysis of firm's medical records; apply discounting and damage functions to unit/days	Analysis of firm's medical records; apply discounting and damage functions to unit/days	Analysis of firm's medical records; apply discounting and damage functions to unit/days
Computation of Direct and Indirect Macroeconomic, Energy, and Environmental Consequences	Utilize adapted Wharton, DRI, and INFORUM; regionalize	Utilize adapted Wharton, DRI, and INFORUM; regionalize	Utilize adapted Wharton, DRI and INFORUM; regionalize
Overall Evaluation	Perform C-E and B/C analysis	Perform C-E and B/C analysis	Not relevant

Cost-of-Production Changes	Induced price changes; firm locational shifts	Induced price changes; firm locational shifts	Induced price changes; firm locational shifts	Induced price changes; firm locational shifts; comparative-advantage analysis
Price Impacts	Induced price changes; firm locational shifts; community cost-abatement and cost/price model	Induced price changes; firm locational shifts; community cost-abatement and cost/price model	Induced price changes; firm locational shifts; community cost-abatement and cost/price model	Induced price changes; firm locational shifts; comparative-advantage analysis; community cost-abatement and cost/price model
Productivity Impacts	Engineering economics/process-control study, including production-function impacts (such as reduced illness)	Engineering economics/process-control study, including production-function impacts (such as reduced illness)	Engineering economics/process-control study, including production-function impacts (such as reduced illness)	Engineering economics/process-control study, including production-function impacts (such as reduced illness)
Market-Structure Impacts	Study of interindustry competitive effects	Study of interindustry competitive effects	Study of interindustry competitive effects	Study of interindustry competitive effects
Employment/Output Effects	Determine output effect: supply/demand industry study; convert output to employment	Determine output effect: supply/demand industry study; convert output to employment	Determine output effect: supply/demand industry study; convert output to employment	Determine output effect: supply/demand industry study; convert output to employment

Source: W.A. Steger, "Economic Impact Analysis: Scope and Methods" (Pittsburgh: CONSAD Research Association, 1976)

The primary effects of the UCIAs have been those of heightened urban sensitivity and some impact on national-level policy:

> Not every review, of course, has led to policy changes. . . .
> But that's fine, say Administration officials. The most important thing, they say, is that more and more policy makers are becoming aware of the problems and are taking them into consideration when making their decisions.[12]

Urban- and community-impact analysis, as an embryonic policy-analysis tool to examine one facet (the urban) of subnational consequences of federal policies, is off to a good institutional beginning. Evaluation of its utility, validity, and impacts, however, will possibly require several years.

How to Delineate Subnational Geographic Areas

Economists and representatives or practitioners of other disciplines have begun to address the difficult question: What physical boundaries for the nation's subnational areas would contribute most to analysis of the nation's economic welfare as it is affected by national policies and programs? Putting aside the far-from-unimportant political and sociocultural realities that have already led to such decisions as establishment of the Northeast Corridor, and the Title V Commission regions, the Appalachian Regional Commission, as well as the several river-basin and other specific, functionally oriented multistate organizations: were this matter of boundaries to be determined more by economic criteria, would some standardization of geographic boundaries be desirable?

Many disciplines besides economics have studied aspects of this question. Political science, geography, planning, sociology, and history have all made significant contributions to the theory and practice of both subnational and multinational regionalism. Geography, for example, has devoted considerable attention to classifying regions—most typically discovering that "a region is essentially what we want it to be"—with the proviso that regional delineation can and does serve a number of descriptive as well as evaluative purposes.[13]

This is far from an academic question. National task forces and commissions have frequently studied it (as in the recent U.S. Department of Commerce Regional Round Table, July 1978). If the United States is to embark actively and knowledgeably, formally and comprehensively, in the next few years on a multistate regional reorganization, policymakers and system planners need to know more than the relative political clout of each alternative regional delineation. Furthermore, even if no such formal and total national subnationalization occurs, it would be most useful to know the benefits and disadvantages, such as the economies of scale, potentially available to alternative subnational patterns.

Economic research has dealt with the problem on both a conceptual and an empirical level. At the theoretical level, economists have discussed the concept of partitioning systems when development of a rational hierarchy depends upon minimizing direct interactions between ostensibly separate elements of a system. Practitioners responsible for shaping very complex systems—for analytic as well as for organizational and administrative purposes—have distinguished between two types of interaction; for example:

> Systems may be said to exhibit interactions of the *first kind* if their respective aggregate levels of effectiveness influence the performance of other systems independently of *how* they achieve their effectiveness. Systems exhibit interactions of the *second kind* if their performance depends not only on the performance of other systems, but also on the *kind* of systems they are. . . . The distinction is important because it is related to the possibility of decomposing a larger problem of choice into smaller subproblems.[14]

Whether dealt with in mathematically formal terms or not, the business of subdividing complex problems, often referred to by economists as suboptimization, is the very essence, the object of regionalization organization and boundary-setting analysis. In practice, it is necessary first to guess roughly at alternative gross regional partitions, and then to study the effects of partitioning on the whole (and, to an extent, vice versa).[15] We would not expect to find totally interaction-free regions, for in reality national subareas are typically very interdependent economically, politically, physically, socially, and culturally. What analysts try to do is to search for regional grouping the interaction is—in some relevant sense—weak. There are many degrees of meaning in the notion of relevant interaction; however, although the economic theory dates back to Adam Smith's concepts of specialization and weak interactions between atomistic economic entities, the recent formalization and mathematization have not yet led to a flurry of empirically based studies of interaction. Rather, economists have, for the most part, been hopeful that it is sufficient to study the interactive nature of entities as though they were black boxes, and that it need not be necessary to delve into the internal components of these entities. This lack of empirical content renders much of the analysis to date esoteric and ethereal, and therefore generally irrelevant for policy purposes.

These various disciplines are useful to draw upon for regional-partitioning studies. A thorough review, however, is likely to reveal a number of shortcomings relative to U.S. needs in regionalization-policy analysis. To remedy this situation, it would be desirable to:

Categorize regional public undertakings into functional and scale classes—examples include vocational-education systems, regional (third-tier) air-carrier networks, river-basin projects, environmental and energy-development projects and programs, housing programs—and determine the presence or absence of economic, as well as political, scale economies.[16]

Determine the true system costs of regional organizations, including the opportunity costs of personnel, as well as the conventional administrative costs.

Investigate the extent to which spillovers/externalities—both benefits and costs—of a resources-flow (manpower and capital), environmental, and interregional trade nature accompany regional projects of differing scales.

Admittedly, much of the regionalization we see today is as likely to be based on political realities as on the economist's considerations of scale economies, spillover/externalities, and/or optimal partitioning. Nevertheless, we can learn, from carefully selected projects and programs at a regional scale, whether or not they are currently part of a multistate regional organization. Ideally, it would be useful to differentiate between the scale economies and externalities planned for by multistate regional agencies and those that are not. However, if the sample of such projects and programs is too small, carefully selected multistate regional programs of any kind will likely provide useful insights into this recommended partitioning analysis. How useful operations and systems research into preferred boundaries can be is a big question mark—but research into these topics needs to begin.

Below, in chapter 8, we shall review contributions by statistical experts to regional characterization. These methods utilize factor-analysis techniques to select geographic boundaries or to create separations between heterogenous areas and thus maximize intraregional similarities and inter-areal variation. In such cases, factor analysis becomes a partitioning technique with operational significance.

National/Subnational Economic-Planning Concepts

Economic planning—first at the macro (national) level and increasingly at subnational levels—often plays an important role in the formulation of national policy.[17] Long-term economic planning has been conceived largely in global and sectoral terms. Typically, an economic plan outlines a schedule of public-sector investments, targets for growth, and a variety of monetary, fiscal, and manpower-training programs. These analyses and guidelines are generally macro level in character, dealing with national aggregates such as investments, consumption, exports, imports, and desired rates of growth.

The problem of sectorally balanced versus unbalanced development has been addressed for some time;[18] however, spatial balance or imbalance received little attention until the 1960s.[19] Until recently, spatial or locational analysis of the economic plan was limited. Economic planning in the 1950s focused on capital use and did not explicitly address land use, locational analysis, or subnational economies more generally.[20] The implicit but untenable assumption during these years was that if an appropriate allocation of capital were obtained, appropriate allocations of labor, management, and land would naturally follow.

National economic growth has a very definite spatial manifestation; however, the settlement pattern—the manner in which population and economic activities are organized in settlements of various sizes and attributes—is dynamically affected by economic growth. Further, there are consequences for national economic development that derive from the attributes of a settlement pattern. At any point in time, the settlement pattern signifies certain opportunities and constraints on subsequent stages of economic development: it determines the market size for goods and services, the degree of labor specification feasible, and the effectiveness of capital utilization. Consequently, economic development in practice must incorporate an explicit treatment of a settlement pattern for the nation or region that is conducive to rapid development. This issue, as well as the related issue of regional disaggregation of national plans (intersectoral, interregional reconciliation and consistency), began to attract attention during the late 1960s.[21]

Another traditional area of economic planning that has serious consequences for the outcome of efforts at the subnational level is the matter of making the choice between investment in infrastructure- or amenity-investment choices. The stock of social-overhead capital available to a region is regarded as one of the most important determinants of growth potentials in a region. The triggering event produced by social-overhead investment in the industrial infrastructure of a region is a reduction in the price of resources supplied by public-investment projects at a given level of output. This confers on the region a competitive advantage for industrial location. Not only do social-overhead investments lead to directly productive activities; they also increase the amenity level of the region through facilities for education, health, recreation, and the like. Amenity-oriented investments contribute to economic growth by improving public health and the skills of the labor force, and thus, productivity.[22] Yet, until very recently, these amenity-oriented investments were often made by physical planners without any serious participation by economic planners and with only a dim awareness of consequences in economic growth or income distribution.[23]

"Balanced" Planning

Dr. Robert Rauner, in addition to his excellent conceptual work on the rationale for subnational units (see page 39) has also written about planning and the planning process as an essential ingredient in a hierarchically, federally structured system for the achievement of an improved balance in national/subnational policy:

> All these factors together generally point toward one critical element: that virtually none of these objectives can be achieved unless and until explicit plans are called for at the operational regional levels and until such plans in the aggregate are harmonized with priorities at the national level. The basic purposes of such plans are to ensure unity in understanding and commitment within and among governmental agencies and jurisdictions.[24]

Rauner goes on to urge, for a variety of reasons, that a successful subnational planning process must be a two-way process, from the top down and the bottom up: appropriateness of the match of planning and economic scale, the command over subnational resources, scale economies in plan preparation, and comparative advantage in the partitioning of complex problems are convincingly offered as rationales. Given the lack of subnational programmatic resource commitments to date, it is not surprising that no effective top-down or bottom-up, let alone combined top-down/bottom-up, regional plans have yet been developed. By effective, we mean a plan that genuinely commits all concerned parties, at all affected levels in the hierarchy, to a specific course of action to achieve a prespecified objective.

Many action plans have been prepared but, as might be anticipated because of the difference between available Title V Regional Commission budgets and the scale of regional problems posed by these regional plans, these plans have had little or no influence on specific Title V commission projects and resource allocations. Furthermore, Chinitz found in a recent evaluation that, up to now, political rather than economic-development strategy appears to have been the dominant factor in the planning process. Chinitz proposes that, with expanded funding and a clearer articulation of purpose, activities of these regional agencies

> should serve to improve governmental processes so that in combination with private organizations, the economic and social development of these regions is encouraged. . . . Within a Commission, these efforts can be harmonized with regional perspectives and the national interest to produce wiser applications of public resources. Regional Commissions are supportive of a federal system of government by providing a mechanism for intergovernmental, cooperative activities.[25]

Chinitz further advocates more bottom-up planning in each region and an equitable distribution of costs regionwide, with more emphasis on developmental than on piecemeal ("adaptive") mitigation of economic distress wherever it is found.

Is improved economic planning in a predominantly private-enterprise, market-oriented democracy—or, as Charles Edgar Lindblom in *Politics and Markets* calls it, a "polyarchy"—doomed to failure, or at least ineffectuality? Lindblom, in his provocative new book, believes so:

> Why, then, has no polyarchy tried to plan production centrally in peacetime? . . . A superficial explanation is that historical and contemporary problems call for solutions more specific than central production planning. Inflation and unemployment, for example, call for the management of money and credit. . . . And specific production shortages—medical care or housing, for example—call for subsidies or other specifics.[26]

Lindblom later advances the notion that the costliness and difficulty of "synoptic"—complete, broad, and competent—planning and analysis increases the attractiveness of the type of incremental and piecemeal planning and analysis that currently predominates and that is characterized by "limited intellectual aspiration . . . and inevitably incomplete analysis":[27]

> Strategic planning people also depend, we saw, on social interactions to reach outcomes that they are not competent to reach analytically. Market interactions, voting, and negotiation are among them. One such possibility among many others is drastic decentralization: to fragment the problem and its analysis. . . . Much of mutual adjustment among authorities, we have already noted, is problem-solving interaction of this kind.[28]

We do not have to agree totally with Lindblom to grant the seriousness of the challenges that he and Chinitz have presented to the national/subnational planner. Lindblom in particular and Chinitz to a lesser degree have presented the multistate regional planner/analyst with a number of researchable hypotheses:

> Comprehensive, synoptic planning—even when scale economies, regional levels, and budgets come appropriately together—cannot be developed and implemented in a polyarchy such as the United States.
>
> Significantly more attention to bottom-up planning will improve the planning process—synoptic or strategic—significantly.

Effective and useful plans can be—indeed, need to be—developed for the activities of subnational agencies and for each subnational area itself.

These are sensible and, to some extent, testable and research-worthy hypotheses. Others less so, but equally important with respect to planning and the planning process, include:

Until there is a national plan for subnational development, no adequate and effective regional plan can be developed.

To be effective, planning needs to be able to command and allocate resources.

It is difficult to say, at this juncture, how each of these hypotheses about planning effectiveness can best be subjected to an empirical, research-worthy design, test, and analysis; however, it is not overly dramatic to say that unless we can discover which methods can be made effective within the socioenvironmental context of current U.S. private/public-sector relationships, we will not have effective national/subnational programs operating through a viable and operable planning process.

Contributions of Public Administration, Management, and Political Science

Clearly, any hierarchical structure such as federalism and its attendant subnational, multinucleated political units, is a complex organization. Studies of federalism by public administrators and political scientists have typically focused less on the policy aspects of federalism than on questions of implementation such as coordination, decision making, and preferred degree of centralization and decentralization. Martha Derthick, perhaps the leading authority on the development and effectiveness of subnational political forms in the United States, has stated:

> There has never been a sustained movement for regional organization that left its impress across the United States. Regionalism (it is not quite accurate to use so concrete a term as "regional organization") is one of those ideas that grips a few minds or much of an academic discipline, as it gripped sociologists and planners in the 1930s and economists and planners in the 1960s, but then disappears for a while.
>
> The principal thing that experience suggests is that pragmatism is the *best* policy: it leads to the most effective regional organizations. It is no accident that the leading cases of regional organization are accidents. Any one of the

executive organizations of government needs to be sustained by some constituency or underlying set of interest as well as by the force of the formal instrument that created it. Or it needs to be autonomous: it must have the means to sustain itself. For a regional organization, which runs counter to the deep institutional grain of American government, these needs are especially exigent.[29]

There is here no theoretical statement about the "goodness" of federal/subnational policies as exercised through an effective federalist management structure—only a statement about what makes the complex whole work better.

James Sundquist also sees federalism in its current form as a means of getting national policy implemented; at one time, however, such was not the case:

Before 1960 the typical federal assistance program did not involve an expressly stated *national* purpose. It was instituted, rather, as a means of helping state or local governments accomplish *their* objectives. It was the states that set the goal of "getting the farmers out of the mud" through improved state highway networks; federal highway aid was made available simply to help them reach that goal sooner. Communities needed hospitals and sewage treatment plants and airports; the leading lobbyists for expansion of federal assistance for community activities were the national organizations of municipal officials, and they sought it for specific and accepted functions of local government.

Policy making for the established functions, in the older model, remained where it resided before the functions were assisted—in the state and local governments. Federal review and control, accordingly, sought primarily the objectives of efficiency and economy to safeguard the federal treasury, and did not extend effectively to the substance of the programs.[30]

But after 1960:

As a major internal problem develops—or comes to public attention—public attitudes appear to pass through three phases. As the problem begins to be recognized, it is seen as local in character, outside the national concern. Then, as it persists and as it becomes clear that the states and communities are unable to solve it unaided (partly because the same political groups that oppose federal action are wont to oppose state and local action too), the activists propose federal aid, but on the basis of helping the states and communities cope with what is still seen as *their* problem. Finally, the locus of basic responsibility shifts: the problem is recognized as in fact not local at all but as a *national* problem requiring a national solution that states and communities are mandated, by one means or another, to carry out—usually by inducements strong enough to produce a voluntary response but sometimes by more direct, coercive means. By now, the first phase has become a matter of history in virtually every field of governmental action save a few remnants like fire protection and sidewalk construction—and even in those fields, federal public works funds are from time to time available.[31]

Leaving the major question:

> But the questions of how to design and operate a structure of creative federalism were not resolved. The basic dilemma of the Great Society—or, for that matter, one with humbler aspirations—is how to achieve goals and objectives that are established by the national government, through the action of other governments, state and local, that are legally independent and politically may even be hostile.[32]

Later commentators have continued to study the multiplicity of arrangements, attempting to divine which levels could perform which functions best and whether cooperation and coordination were effective.[33] Occasionally, specialists find new signs of effective bottom-up policymaking, as in the case of states and energy policy:

> My findings, based on state activities within the past decade, seem to point toward an affirmation of a strong state role in energy policy formation. As a result of the states' efforts, the tardy formulation of national policy objectives is being reshaped in several important respects in order to encompass an expanded view of collective state interests.[34]

Clearly, opinions differ about the efficacy and desirability of policymaking from the bottom up; but that it takes place, and perhaps does so increasingly where tremendous subnational diversity and interests exist (as in energy policy), is indisputable. This two-way policy-development process if anything exacerbates the growing need for federal/subfederal impact-analysis procedures that are credible at all hierarchically impacted levels. In other words, appropriately designed analytic methods will not only reflect the top-down allocation of national policy, which disregards subnational impacts and interests; instead, subnational impact-analysis feedback to national (macro) analyses will have to play a useful, perhaps a key, role in such analyses.

Some Cautionary Observations about Analytic Approaches to Policymaking

Despite our bias in favor of analytic approaches to recognizing and including subnational consequences and trends, we are aware of several serious shortcomings in such methods and techniques, particularly as these may be used in the policymaking process. We must also recognize and understand the dynamics of this process. Planning theories advocating management-science principles of rational objectivity, functional comprehensiveness, and hierarchical integration assume that rational policies cannot be made through complex, multinucleated, noncentrally coordinated decision-making structures. Yet decisions *are* made. Policy is formulated and implemented through processes of interaction and calculation evincing a high degree of subjective rationality. Decisions are coordinated through political interaction and mutual adjustment. Analysis and forethought enter policy formulation and implementation—albeit incrementally and disjointedly. Policies evolve from organizationally complex environments under the very conditions that make traditional planning prescriptions inoperable: with imperfect information, uncertainty, risk, and cognitive limits on comprehensive analysis.

If well-executed policy analysis is to support public decisions effectively, policy analysts must have—and know how to work with—a realistic understanding of the pluralistic, multinucleated, dynamic, decentralized, and open-to-external-influence political interaction and organizational complexities. Easier said than done: but two decades of experience make it more comprehensible, manageable, and, possibly, doable.

Equally clearly, we cannot fail to recognize that policy analysts are, after all, influenced by the complex bureaucracies in which they function. Halperin and Schlesinger[35] have analyzed analytic biases and shortcomings extensively:

> In understanding [study] results we must bear in mind that analytical work is performed and decisions are reached, not by disinterested machines, but by individuals with specific views, commitments, and ambitions. The normal bureaucratic tendencies may be weakened, but will not disappear.[36]

Halperin and Schlesinger's observations are no more or less correct today, one or two decades later. Policymakers, however—those who use what policy analysts do—appear to be taking results of analyses more seriously. Internal reviews of such analyses, and processes to ensure these assessments, are much more common, and interagency conflict over the merits and shortcomings of different analytic approaches and findings will often force the better—or at least the more persuasive—analysis to the surface. Nor do we necessarily believe in the counter to Gresham's law, that is, that good policy research always drives out bad. Our experience has been that good analysis often receives an increased hearing and, with even the federal level becoming more nucleated, is not permanently banished upon losing but tends to resurface later, in the same or similar form.

Concluding Remarks

The state of the art reviewed in chapters 3 and 4 consists primarily of contributions to the theory of how a nation and its subnational parts coexist and potentially contribute to one another's well-being. The remainder of this book examines the more empirical, modeling-base contributions. Many are made by members of the same disciplines—economists, systems analysts, regional scientists, and public-administration specialists. The objectives for these analytic approaches, and the criteria employed to differentiate good from bad national-subnational policy, can be based substantially upon the contributions already described above in part I.

Notes

1. Robert Rauner, "Regional Development in a Federal System" (Draft of a report for the U.S. Department of Commerce, 1977), p. 7.

2. Ibid., p. 12.

3. The sole exception being, perhaps, that of the Appalachian Regional Commission, where several of the types of scale economies have been exercised to some degree, such as interstate highways and Appalachia-wide health, vocational education, and environmental-protection investments and systems.

4. A. Breton and A. Scott, *The Economic Constitution of Federal States* (Toronto: University of Toronto Press, 1978).

5. Ibid., p. 145.

6. W.A. Steger, "Economic Impact Analysis: Scope and Methods" (Pittsburgh: CONSAD Research Corporation, 1976).

7. R.J. Vaughan, *The Urban Impacts of Federal Policies,* vol. 2. *Economic Development* (Santa Barbara, Calif.: RAND Corporation, 1977; and S. Barro, *The Urban Impacts of Federal Policies,* vol. 3. *Fiscal Conditions* (Santa Barbara, Calif.: RAND Corporation, 1978).

8. Norman J. Glickman, "Urban Impact Analysis: Its Role in Federal Decision-making" (Paper presented to the Regional Science Association, November 1979); Sheldon Danziger, Robert Haveman, Eugene Smolensky, and Karl Taeuber, "The Urban Impacts of the Program for Better Jobs and Income," in *The Urban Impacts of Federal Policies,* ed. Norman J. Glickman (Baltimore: Johns Hopkins University Press, 1980), pp. 219–242; and Lester Salamon and John Helmer, "Urban and Community Impact Analysis: From Promise to Implementation," in *Urban Impacts of Federal Policies,* pp. 33–66.

9. Norman G. Glickman, "Urban Impact Analysis."

10. F. Gerard Adams and Norman J. Glickman, eds., *Modeling the Multiregion Economic System: Theory, Data and Policy* (Lexington,

Mass.: Lexington Books, D.C. Heath and Company, 1980); and Kenneth Ballard, Richard Gustely, and Robert Wendling, *The National-Regional Impact Evaluation System: Structure, Performance, and Application of a Bottom-up Interregional Econometric Model* (Washington, D.C.: U.S. Bureau of Economic Analysis, 1980).

11. For an excellent review of the problems, see Nazir Dossani, "An Evaluation of Current Regionalization Procedures" (Report prepared by CONSAD Research Corporation for the U.S. Environmental Protection Agency, 1979).

12. R.L. Stanfield, "Federal Policy Makers Now Must Ask: Will It Hurt the Cities?" *National Journal,* July 1979, pp. 1203-1206.

13. Albert Z. Guttenberg, "Classifying Regions: A Conceptual Approach," *International Regional Science Review* 2, no. 1 (1977), pp. 1-13, also B.S. Cohn, "Regions Subjective and Objective: Their Relation to the Study of Modern Indian History and Society," in *Regions and Regionalism in South Asian Studies,* ed. Robert I. Crane Program in Comparative Studies on Southern Asia (Durham, N.C.: Duke University, 1966), pp. 5-37. D. Grigg, "The Logic of Regional Systems," *Annals of the Association of American Geographers* (1955); D. Whittlesey, "The Regional Concept and the Regional Method," in *American Geography, Inventory and Prospect,* ed. Preston James and C.F. Jones (Syracuse: University of Syracuse Press, 1954).

14. A.C. Enthoven and H.S. Rowen, *An Analysis of Defense Organization,* (Santa Monica, Calif.: RAND Corporation, 1959).

15. See Robert H. Strotz, "The Empirical Implications of a Utility Tree," *Econometrica* 25 (1957):269-280; Thomas Marschak, "Centralization and Decentralization in Economic Organizations," *Econometrica* 27 (1959):399-430; and, for an optimization approach, S.M. Montias, "Planning with Material Balances in Soviet-Type Economies," *American Economic Review* 49, no. 5 (December 1959), pp. 963-985. These early writings have led to a substantial literature on partitioning, decentralization, and optimization.

16. For the most part, Title V Regional Commissions and Appalachian Regional Commission programs remain largely unevaluated. See Robert W. Haisten, "Evaluating Regional Programs: A Beginning," *Appalachia,* December 1977-January 1978, pp. 9-17.

17. The discussion below is adapted from T.R. Lakshmanan, *Integration of Physical and Economic Planning* (Pittsburgh: CONSAD Research Corporation, prepared for the United Nations Development Program, 1973).

18. P.N. Rosenstein-Rodan, *Notes on the Theory of the Big Push* (Cambridge, Mass.: MIT Press, 1957); Albert O. Hirschman, *Strategy of Economic Development* (New Haven, Conn.: Yale University Press, 1958).

19. Harvey S. Perloff and John Friedman, "Education and Research

in Planning: A Review of the University of Chicago Experiment," in H.S. Perloff, *Education for Planning: City, State and Regional* (Baltimore: Johns Hopkins University Press, 1957); J.R. Boudeville, *Problems of Regional Economic Planning* (Chicago: Aldine Publishing Co., 1966); and John Friedmann, "Planning as Innovation," *Journal of the American Institute of Planners* 32 (1966):194-204.

20. Charles Haar, Benjamin Higgins, and Lloyd Rodwin, "Economic and Physical Planning: Coordination in Developing Areas," *Journal of the American Institute of Planners* 24 (1958):167-173.

21. T. Hermansen, "Development Poles and Development Centers in National and Regional Development," in *Growth Poles and Growth Centers in Regional Planning,* ed. A.R. Kuklinski (The Hague: Mouton, 1972); L.B.M. Mennes, Jan Tinbergen, and J.G. Waardenburg, *The Elements of Space in Development Planning* (Amsterdam: North-Holland Publishing Co., 1969); and Ricardo Carrillo-Arronte, *An Empirical Test of Interregional Planning: A Linear Programming Model for Mexico* (Rotterdam: Rotterdam University Press, 1970).

22. Leo H. Klassen, *Social Amenities in Area Economic Growth* (Paris: Organization for Economic Co-operation and Development, 1968); CONSAD Research Corporation, *Study of the Effects of Public Investment* (Pittsburgh: 1968); and T.R. Lakshmanan and Arthur Silvers, "Adaptive and Developmental Planning in Developing Economies," in *Regional Planning: Concepts, Techniques, Policies and Case Studies,* ed. R.P. Misra (Prasarange, India: University of Mysore, 1969).

23. T.R. Lakshmanan, *Design of Analytical Studies for Planning in Puerto Rico* (Pittsburgh: CONSAD Research Corporation, 1968).

24. Robert Rauner, "Multistate Regional Development: Some Economic and Legislative Perspectives" (Paper presented at the Special Conference on Economic Development, San Juan, Puerto Rico, April 1976).

25. Benjamin Chinitz, "Evaluating Title V Commission Plans" (Report prepared for the U.S. Department of Commerce, 1978). Thus, Chinitz discusses the need for two levels of planning: one for the region and one for commission programs.

26. Charles E. Lindblom, *Politics and Markets* (New York: Basic Books, 1978), p. 311.

27. Ibid., p. 314; Lindblom calls the latter "strategic" planning.

28. Ibid., pp. 314-315.

29. Martha Derthick, *Between States and Nation: Regional Organizations of the United States* (Washington, D.C.: Brookings Institution, 1974), pp. 3, 226.

30. James L. Sundquist, *Making Federalism Work* (Washington, D.C.: Brookings Institution, 1969), p. 3.

31. Ibid., p. 11.

32. Ibid., p. 12.

33. Including Brevard Crihfield and H.C. Reeves, "Intergovernmental Relations: A View from the States," *Annals of the American Academy of Political and Social Science (AAAS)* 416 (November 1974):99-107; J.B. Aron, "Intergovernmental Politics of Energy," *Policy Analysis* 5, no. 4 (1979), pp. 451-471; and D.S. Wright, "Intergovernmental Relations: An Analytic Overview," *Annals of the AAAS* 416 (November 1974):1-16.

34. Aron, "Intergovernmental Politics of Energy," p. 452.

35. See Martin H. Halperin, "Why Bureaucrats Play Games," Brookings Reprint no. 199 (Washington, D.C.: Brookings Institution, 1971); James Schlesinger, *Systems Analysis and the Political Process* (Santa Monica, Calif.: RAND Corporation, 1964); see also idem, *Organizational Structures and Planning* (Santa Monica, Calif.: RAND Corporation, 1966).

36. Schlesinger, *Systems Analysis and the Political Process,* pp. 1-2.

Part II
Top-Down/Bottom-Up Approaches to National-Subnational Analysis

5 How Can Analytic Methods Assist in Federal/Subfederal Processes?

Part I of this book has identified a number of substantive criteria to apply to analytic modeling efforts to determine validity and effectiveness in national/subnational policy-analysis contexts. The ideal set of features for a hierarchically useful, decision-oriented, multilevel, multiobjective system is one that represents the national level in two ways: first, as a system within a larger (such as an international economic) setting, to capture such factors as the essential balance of trade (and payments) and changes in sectoral advantage relative to other nations elsewhere; and second, as a system spanning a tier of subnational geographic settings, to capture and reflect the essential ties of the nation to regional, state, and more-local economies, and vice versa. Theoretically, the structure of such a system would include spatial, sectoral, functional, and intertemporal components. The hierarchical organization would be composed of vertical arrangements of subsystems whereby higher-level units have some priority of control and action—but not veto power—over the lower-level ones. These higher and lower subsystems would be interdependent and require information flow between them.

In this context, the feedback loops between levels and among geographic units at the same level become very important. The manner in which this feedback is communicated (by machine or by human) also helps decide the accuracy, bias, and speed with which policy questions can be analyzed. There is also consensus, again at the contextual level, that a multilevel modeling system built around a unified national-regional accounting framework is the correct way to analyze energy-economic-environmental interactions.

Special Features of National-Subnational Modeling

Although much has been written in general about how complex modeling can and should be done, little has been said specifically about establishing specific criteria for analytic efforts designed to:

> Identify and estimate, in detail, the direct, indirect, and induced effects of specific federal policies (taken individually or together) at different subnational geographical levels and for differently impacted groups

Identify and estimate in detail the direct, indirect, and induced effects of specific subnational federal policies (that is, types 2 and 3 in chapter 2, above), which impact on both the national and subnational levels

We have discussed the following desiderata relative to modeling efforts, the objective of which is to permit the use of one or both of these types of analyses:

Intra-areal Detail and Structural Validity

Most analysts would agree that the only legitimate reason for making a model more complex is to increase its accuracy. A number of assessments have reviewed models in terms of the tradeoff between degrees of error (error of specification and error of measurement) versus model complexity.[1] Geisler and Steger, arguing for modeling-technique complexity for problems requiring detail to achieve accuracy, maintain that

> high [levels of] abstraction (e.g., simple, non-simulation models) . . . delimit the kinds of questions that can be examined. . . . The degree of abstraction required for analytic techniques is not obtainable for studying even the broad trade-offs, so that computer simulation is the [frequently] used alternative in this role as well.[2]

The question we are addressing here is not one of using simulation per se. Real-world problems are characteristically so complex that some simplification of models is necessary. However, there are questions concerning the *degree* of simplification for which models should be designed. How much abstraction can be tolerated and still yield results meaningful to the policy-making process? Quite often, the virtues of greater realism and accuracy—accompanied by increased costs of complexity and the possibility of greater measurement error of details—lead to the selection of increasing regional (or subnational) in-depth scope and knowledge. Aggregation problems can lead to the obscuring of crucial structural interstices within each area and can generate significant specification errors that are difficult to detect and correct. Basically, this argument for subnational input is tantamount to that time-honored phrase, "You've got to know the territory."

Interarea Flows

Any detailed subnational impact analysis should consider the interactive effect on all affected subnational areas. A federal policy affecting subnational areas A and B directly needs to consider the resulting interactive efforts: between A and B; between A and B and any other indirectly affected area C; and any economic (or other) feedback of effects on A, B, and C, back up to the national level. These interactions might be demand/consumption oriented; for example, areas may change their buying habits vis-a-vis other areas, leading to different interarea trade and travel patterns. Previous interarea migration and commuting patterns for resources/manpower, capital, natural resources, and entrepreneurial skills might be altered. And flows (people, pollutants, resources, capital) between the nation and other nations might be directly and/or indirectly affected and altered. Clearly, the complexity of the interareal flow depends on the level of detail represented within each subnational area. If there is a highly detailed sectoral, demographic, environmental, and energy-technology representation within each geographic area, there is need for—and benefit from—a detailed intersectoral-flow representation.

Scale Economies

In chapter 4 we suggested that one of the most pressing arguments for federally sponsored and encouraged subnational relationships and arrangements is the effectiveness gained from the achievement of scale-economy advantages. These scale economies can take a number of different forms: projects that cut across jurisdictional boundaries to permit interareal network connectivity (such as transportation and communication); projects requiring a certain minimum size designed to reduce the unit costs of providing a certain service and/or producing a specific product (such as a dam providing flood control, power, recreation, and other services to a region with many jurisdictions, or a courthouse serving many small cities and a rural area); projects producing research and information results of use to many jurisdictions; and so on. Economies of scale are not restricted to physical structures but can apply at least equally to decision-making and planning activities, where the inclusion of larger geographic areas or populations helps produce better decisions.

We can advance three basic rationales for greater input from, and consideration of, detailed knowledge of subnational areas, their interrelationships, and cost functions (as the last might be shaped by scale economies). We do not claim that policy analysts have these three dimensions—interareal flows, areal detail, and scale economies—in mind as they construct their models, either of the nation or of the nation and its subareas. Indeed, we might not expect to find all these ingredients represented in any given analysis, because typically the subnational argument has not been made in as focused and demanding a fashion as we have presented it in the preceding chapters. Nevertheless, we consider them a crucial set of criteria, the absence of any of which would indicate a fundamental conceptual deficiency in an analytical approach to the real-world situation it is attempting to capture.

Other Desirable Conceptual Properties of Modeling Approaches

Several other properties in addition to the three above are desirable for a properly structured analytic system if it is to be of help to federal decision makers and policy analysts whose choices affect subnational areas. Ten of the most important are listed below.[3]

1. *Prevention of the "chamber-of-commerce" effect.* Previous attempts to build and link regional models from a bottom-up point of view have led to a phenomenon we call the chamber-of-commerce effect (that is, information that is perceived as desirable at the subnational level is overreported relative to what is objectively supportable), whereby the sum of all regional projections in any area exceeds the national total for that area—for example, the sum of projected population increases to the year 2000 for all counties is greater than the total population expected in the nation as a whole.

2. *Modularity.* In general, we recommend that a core set of relatively simple analytic and informational systems be established, in contrast to a single, complex model. A system should be such that modules for analyzing different impacts could be detached or attached with relative ease. The system could be modular in its choice of sectors, geographic regions, and impact areas.

3. *Consistency.* Consistency among different models (and accounting frameworks) is an essential characteristic in providing reliable comparisons of different projections in areas such as energy, environment, and economics. One way to ensure such consistency is to base the core set of models on an interindustry accounting framework with built-in mechanisms for aggregating or disaggregating the sectoral and geographic breakdown. Furthermore, the core set of models needs to be planned and reviewed carefully to provide consistent and comprehensive linkages at the sectoral and geographic level of detail. This may be a difficult task, for the core models would undoubtedly include elements using different analytic techniques representing various approaches.

4. *Valuation.* Conceptually, there is often resistance to quantification of many classes of consequences, particularly those arising from disruption of environmental and social processes, as well as lack of agreed-upon procedures for monetary valuation of even those consequences that might be

quantified; furthermore, there is generally uncertainty concerning monetary abatement and avoidance costs until specified abatement and avoidance schemes under consideration have actually been implemented. These valuation problems are likely to be even more troublesome at subnational levels, where local variations in damage, avoidance, abatement, transaction, and other costs are both poorly documented and not well understood.

5. *Dynamic.* The planning and review of the core model system ought to be a continual process so that both the modeling techniques and data bases can be updated. This may require changes in technical and location coefficients as well as in geographic and sectoral detail.

6. *Statistical properties.* In complex systems, it is generally desirable that statistical estimates of the uncertainties in projecting energy, environmental, and economic effects be included in the data used in calculating the parameters of the assessment models and in presenting model-based results. Without knowing how accurate these numerical values are, the analyst cannot tell whether the differences obtained are statistically significant. This difficulty arises because the accuracy of the data used in the model is not often known, or if it is, the models are so complex that the uncertainties in data are not easily translated into uncertainties in results. As difficult as it is to give proper statistical treatment of national-level aggregates, the difficulty is compounded when a large number of subnational units are represented.

7. *Data.* The models that are currently used for subnational policy analysis are quite complex, with a high degree of regional and sectoral disaggregation. The quality of the data currently available and of the data that might be available in the foreseeable future is not generally adequate for such detailed models. Similarly, the ultracomprehensiveness of large national models (and national/subnational models) is not justified by the data inaccuracies inherent in substantive fields as uncertain as energy, environmental, and economic-development planning. Tables 5-1 and 5-2 depict the difference between the real world of data availability and what might be required for a complete intra/interareal-sectoral study although data worlds located in between those portrayed in the exhibits are constantly evolving and improving.

8. *Validation.* Validation and verification of data and of independent models must be emphasized if energy-environmental-economics policy modeling is to be credible to peers, policy analysts, and those affected by model-based policy decisions. Validation and verification are even more important for credibility and psychological acceptability when subnational forecasts are present. At lower-than-national levels, more observable, discernible activities exist against which estimated forecasts can be compared and validated "on the ground," that is, ground-truth.

9. *Subnational involvement.* There are a number of ways in which the

Table 5-1
Our Current Data World (Illustrative)

	Outflow									
	Region 1					Region 2				
Inflow	Sector 1	Sector 2	Sector 3	Sector 4	Rest of World	Sector 1	Sector 2	Sector 3	Sector 4	Rest of World
Region 1										
Sector 1										
Sector 2										
Sector 3										
Sector 4										
Rest of world										
Region 2										
Sector 1						X	X		X	
Sector 2							X			
Sector 3								X		
Sector 4							X			
Rest of world										
Region 3										
Sector 1										
Sector 2										
Sector 3										
Sector 4										
Rest of world										
Region 4										
Sector 1										
Sector 2										
Sector 3										
Sector 4										
Rest of world										
Total Inputs										

Analytic Methods

	Outflow										
	Region 3					Region 4					Total Output
	Sector 1	Sector 2	Sector 3	Sector 4	Rest of World	Sector 1	Sector 2	Sector 3	Sector 4	Rest of World	
Region 1											
Sector 1											
Sector 2											
Sector 3											
Sector 4											
Rest of world											
Region 2											
Sector 1											
Sector 2											
Sector 3											
Sector 4											
Rest of world											
Region 3											
Sector 1	X	X	X	X	X	X	X	X			
Sector 2		X	X	X		X	X	X			
Sector 3		X	X		X			X			
Sector 4	X	X	X	X							
Rest of world	X	X		X							
Region 4											
Sector 1	X	X		X				X			
Sector 2	X		X				X	X			
Sector 3	X		X			X	X				
Sector 4									X		
Rest of world											
Total Inputs											

Table 5-2
The Complete Data World

	Outflow									
	Region 1					Region 2				
Inflow	Sector 1	Sector 2	Sector 3	Sector 4	Rest of World	Sector 1	Sector 2	Sector 3	Sector 4	Rest of World
Region 1										
Sector 1	X	X	X	X	X	X	X	X	X	X
Sector 2	X	X	X	X	X	X	X	X	X	X
Sector 3	X	X	X	X	X	X	X	X	X	X
Sector 4	X	X	X	X	X	X	X	X	X	X
Rest of world	X	X	X	X	X	X	X	X	X	X
Region 2										
Sector 1	X	X	X	X	X	X	X	X	X	X
Sector 2	X	X	X	X	X	X	X	X	X	X
Sector 3	X	X	X	X	X	X	X	X	X	X
Sector 4	X	X	X	X	X	X	X	X	X	X
Rest of world	X	X	X	X	X	X	X	X	X	X
Region 3										
Sector 1	X	X	X	X	X	X	X	X	X	X
Sector 2	X	X	X	X	X	X	X	X	X	X
Sector 3	X	X	X	X	X	X	X	X	X	X
Sector 4	X	X	X	X	X	X	X	X	X	X
Rest of world	X	X	X	X	X	X	X	X	X	X
Region 4										
Sector 1	X	X	X	X	X	X	X	X	X	X
Sector 2	X	X	X	X	X	X	X	X	X	X
Sector 3	X	X	X	X	X	X	X	X	X	X
Sector 4	X	X	X	X	X	X	X	X	X	X
Rest of world	X	X	X	X	X	X	X	X	X	X
Total Inputs										

	Outflow										
	Region 3					Region 4					Total Output
	Sector 1	Sector 2	Sector 3	Sector 4	Rest of World	Sector 1	Sector 2	Sector 3	Sector 4	Rest of World	
Region 1											
Sector 1	X	X	X	X	X	X	X	X	X	X	X
Sector 2	X	X	X	X	X	X	X	X	X	X	X
Sector 3	X	X	X	X	X	X	X	X	X	X	X
Sector 4	X	X	X	X	X	X	X	X	X	X	X
Rest of world	X	X	X	X	X	X	X	X	X	X	X
Region 2											
Sector 1	X	X	X	X	X	X	X	X	X	X	X
Sector 2	X	X	X	X	X	X	X	X	X	X	X
Sector 3	X	X	X	X	X	X	X	X	X	X	X
Sector 4	X	X	X	X	X	X	X	X	X	X	X
Rest of world	X	X	X	X	X	X	X	X	X	X	X
Region 3											
Sector 1	X	X	X	X	X	X	X	X	X	X	X
Sector 2	X	X	X	X	X	X	X	X	X	X	X
Sector 3	X	X	X	X	X	X	X	X	X	X	X
Sector 4	X	X	X	X	X	X	X	X	X	X	X
Rest of world	X	X	X	X	X	X	X	X	X	X	X
Region 4											
Sector 1	X	X	X	X	X	X	X	X	X	X	X
Sector 2	X	X	X	X	X	X	X	X	X	X	X
Sector 3	X	X	X	X	X	X	X	X	X	X	X
Sector 4	X	X	X	X	X	X	X	X	X	X	X
Rest of world	X	X	X	X	X	X	X	X	X	X	X
Total Inputs	X	X	X	X	X	X	X	X	X	X	X

core set of models could provide an effective means of communication among modelers in different subnational areas as well as among modelers specializing in different sectors of the economy and the environment, thus permitting subnational entities to communicate (through computerized models or through other organizational structures) with each other as well as with modelers and policymakers at the national level. One of the goals such interaction would achieve is separation of costs and benefits geographically, over time, and/or across socioeconomic classes.

10. *Policy-analysis sensitivity.* It must be possible—with relative user ease and face validity—to introduce changes in a model's inputs or structure to simulate conditions that occur in conjunction with a given exogenously engendered policy change. Although all policy-analysis models permit changes in policy-relevant variables, they differ in the completeness and degree to which the policy changes can be realistically and validly represented.

These ten properties do not exhaust the list of desirable characteristics of national/subnational analytic systems. As specific modeling systems are described in the next chapters, still others may become obvious. In addition, all good policy-analysis modeling systems should have the following characteristics:

The modeling technique should be capable of dealing with both short-term, specific (tactical) and longer-term, structural (strategic) assessments; the latter capability is particularly important in cases where the duration of impacts is likely to be lengthy.

Output displays need to be understandable to both lay people and policy analysts.

The possibility for model misinterpretation and misuse should be minimized through high-quality documentation.

These criteria are not precisely measurable; however, they provide some useful benchmarks whereby differing analytic systems can be compared, at least in rough terms. As more experience with modeling accumulates, more precision and quantification of these system dimensions will surely emerge.

In the remainder of part II we discuss two primary methods for modeling national-subnational effects and interrelationships: the first, the so-called top-down approach; the second, those known as bottom-up approaches. In general, neither approach by itself captures within any given system all the dozen or so criteria that a total national-subnational one should possess. Some, however, are more complete than others.

These goals for constructing a good modeling system remain only goals. No system exists that embodies all the criteria discussed above, and none is likely to. But they indicate the direction toward which we must strive. Further, there are enormous implementation and maintenance problems attendant with such a sophisticated system: Where is it best located? how is it kept current? who pays for its upkeep? and who sets and evaluates the standards through which its data and technique are fashioned? These and similar questions are discussed in chapter 9.

Notes

1. R.M. Rauner and W.A. Steger, "Simulation and Long-Range Planning for Resource Allocation," *Quarterly Journal of Economics* 76 (1962): 219-245; M.A. Geisler and W.A. Steger, "The Combination of Alternative Research Techniques in Logistics Systems Analysis," *Management Technology* 3 (May 1963):68-77; D. Leinweber, "Essay on Data Quality, Model Complexity, and Uncertainty" (Paper presented for the RAND Corporation at Proceedings of the Workshop on National/Regional Energy-Environmental Modeling Concepts, Reston, Virginia, May 1979).

2. Geisler and Steger, "Combination of Alternative Research Techniques," p. 75.

3. R.L. Ritschard, ed., "Proceedings of the Workshop on National/Regional Energy-Environmental Modeling Concepts" (Berkeley, Calif.: Energy Analysis Program, Lawrence Berkeley Laboratory, 1979); Geisler and Steger, "Combination of Alternative Research Techniques;" Lawrence Berkeley Laboratory, "Report on a Workshop: Integrated Assessment—Can We Do It?" (Berkeley, Calif.: Lawrence Berkeley Laboratory, 1978).

6 Top-Down Analysis Methods

Although the general meaning of the term *top-down analysis* might be intuitively obvious when used to describe an analytic technique, it is relatively difficult to describe with precision. Generally, it means that the projective analysis is performed at the highest level of aggregation consistent with the spatial unit being analyzed. This carries with it the expectation that the data used will also be consistent with this level of analysis and that other levels below the one being analyzed will be derived from the level of this data by one or another means of apportionment after the level is simulated. Where the top is depends on where the analysis is starting from—the world, the nation, the region, a state, county, or city. Consequently, data needs and confidence in forecasts of impacts on a specific region or locale depend, among other things, on how far the study information is from the specific data used to study the region in question to the more aggregate data used to perform analyses at the top from which the study data were devised. In the context of this study, the top is the national level.

Each legislative session produces several federal laws intended to benefit a particular region or locale.[1] Our primary focus, however, is on legislative actions and the executive implementation thereof that are intended to be more broadly national in scope. In developing and implementing such policies, federal policymakers allegedly adopt a strategic perspective and consequently view the impacts of the intended policy in a particular way. By *strategic,* we mean that the policy grows out of a perceived national-level problem that the policy is designed to solve. The solution could take several forms—a regulation, financial inducement, or direct intervention by the public sector. These strategic solutions tend to be stated in very specific terms: if the problem is scarce energy, the solution is generally stated in terms of means to more energy; if the problem is deemed to be too much pollution, the solution tends to be aimed at actions that directly lessen pollution; if it is underdevelopment of a region, the objective is typically worded in terms of increasing that region's employment; and so forth.

Until very recently, all such analyses of potential strategic policies could be anticipated to be almost entirely of primary impacts, devoid of indirect and induced secondary consequences. In the last few years, with the advent of the environmental movement and the legitimization of the ecological concept of system holism, there has been at least lip service paid to the effect that everything is related to everything else. Trying to put the holistic approach into practice has proved to be extremely difficult. A number of attempts at holistic analyses and implementation of strategic policies will be described in the following chapters in conjunction with various comprehensive national-level analysis techniques.

Reference to the various bureaucratic attempts to consider the secondary impacts of national policies directed at a specific goal can be found in the growing number of impact statements now required: environmental, inflationary, energy, community, and urban, to name a few. These statements are formally required by legislation or by executive order to accompany any major policy initiative and thus are necessarily a formal part of the budgetary and decision-making process. Few of these documents and reports are truly comprehensive, or even-handed in the treatment of indirect effects.

From a top-down perspective, the most characteristic form of attention paid to the expected subnational impacts of federal policy is anecdotal. This approach provides impressions of the magnitude of a particular problem across the country. Public and private lobbying and interest groups representing areal or subject-matter interests provide a perspective on each issue. Attention is frequently focused on worst-case situations or potentials. These cases are used to illustrate the nature and extent of the problem and often become the focal point of a policy solution. A specific instance is found in the development of one aspect of the 1970 Clean Air Act.

Evolution of a Top-Down Policy from a Specific Local Instance

Krier and Ursin recount the socioeconomic evolution of one aspect of the Clean Air Act, that pertaining to mobile sources.[2] This history begins in the 1940s in southern California, which even then had chronic air inversions and smog. In 1943 a serious smog attack focused political attention on the clean-air issue. Scientific evidence about how bad the smog was for health and what was causing it was generally lacking. Krier and Ursin trace this historical pattern: before early 1950, the automobile was not considered to be a serious source of the pollution, and attention was on stationary sources; in 1953 the auto industry claimed that automobile emissions were not a problem; in 1954 the industry admitted that there "could be" a problem; in 1955 it admitted that automobiles were a source of air pollution but not of smog; in 1956 the industry admitted that autos were a key source of smog.

The public reaction in California, because of the lack of definitive evidence, was threefold: preoccupation with obvious stationary-source emissions; dependence on a technological fix and a search for a reasonable solution; and use of regulation as opposed to other solutions.

With this view of policy history as a series of unfolding perceptions, one can better understand the development of the 1970 Clean Air Act with regard to mobile-source emissions. Given that there was a great deal of work to be done in setting the mobile-source emissions as demanded by Congress, the Department of Health, Education, and Welfare (the predecessor of EPA) had little choice but to make use of whatever information and experience were available. Clearly, there was a strong carry-over of California's three strategies for pollution control. Many of the bases for the mobile-emissions standards also come from the California experience (although California tended to be tougher). Even after passage of the basic act and promulgation of the standards, California was used as a test area for developing implementation strategies.

In December 1973 the RAND Corporation performed an analysis for the Office of Environmental Management of San Diego County.[3] San Diego was chosen as a test case for analysis for a number of reasons, including the existence there of an active planning department and of extensive data for planning purposes. Air pollution also was an obvious problem in San Diego County. The RAND report stated that in 1970, the primary-oxidant standard (not formally established until 1971) would have been exceeded by 400 percent for the worst day and, in general, for a total of 226 days that year. Given the plans available in the early 1970s, by 1975 the county was still expected to exceed the standard on about 40 days and to exceed it by 200 percent on the worst day. The study was undertaken to analyze alternative air-pollution strategies in terms of their environmental, economic, transportational, and spatial impacts in San Diego and to identify the most promising. The report presented a mixed strategy of fixed-source controls, retrofit devices for light-duty vehicles, and transportation management.

Since the early days of mobile-source emissions strategy there have been some questions raised as to whether there really was a need for such stringent pollution control of automobiles as was developed in the early 1970s—largely on the basis on information gathered from the early California experience. Despite the fact that cars sold in California have to meet even stricter air-pollution-control standards than those sold elsewhere in the nation, there is still some reason to believe that the costs incurred (by the control-strategies requirement based on the California experience) in automotive performance, purchase, and gasoline mileage are likely to be overly severe when implemented in areas in the mountain and plains states. Here, longer distances separate population centers, and sustained, high-speed driving in relatively clear airsheds is the rule rather than the exception. Questions such as these are presently being investigated by the National Commission on Air Quality.[4] Furthermore, there is a question as to whether this additional analysis would have been necessary if techniques had been available earlier to analyze in depth various regional issues such as the mobile-standard impacts while the national clean-air standards were being promulgated. Instead, a considerable portion of the 1970 Clean Air Act was forged from experience in one state, and within that state, in one county, Los Angeles. Other case studies could be presented to make the point, but the principle is clear: regional differences in resources and institutions make such analyses imperative before national policies are promulgated. Even granting this general statement, however, there are some very real technical difficulties in analytical implementation.

To provide a better perspective on how models perform their top-down functions—and some of the difficulties occasioned at the subnational levels—the remainder of this chapter describes several modeling systems, focusing on the aspects important to an understanding of these hierarchical features.

Some Representative Available Analytic Top-Down Models

Much of the analysis performed at the national level is done with the aid of computer models. These models are used to stimulate the impact of proposed policies on selected variables incorporated in the model and to forecast the change in the national system if no changes were made in existing policies. Some of the better-known of these models are those used to forecast national economic growth, the macro models of the U.S. economy. Although several such models exist and there are many different methods used to build them, a brief description of several, in the context of energy-policy analysis, will help make it clear that although the nation, on the whole, is being represented in these models; variation and diversity across regions is necessarily restrained, averaged, and to an extent disguised. This is less conspiracy against individuality and uniqueness than it is necessity of the statistics involved—to find and use what is common across regions, not to dwell on, extol, or highlight spatial differences. National-level (macro) modeling must search for similarities, not differences, among the nation's regions. This and other reasons tend to make national macro models not very relevant for regional analytic concerns.

For example, selected DOE policies, programs, and regulations may generate a wide range of economic and employment effects. These could include microeconomic impacts on affected industries and macroeconomic impacts on national and regional economies. Most of the national models deal exclusively with macroeconomic impacts, but even these receive and use more micro-level impacts as basic inputs. For example, initially, any energy-related cost increases at the micro level (such as costs to comply with federal regulations and conversion to an alternative fuel type) can be estimated for each affected industry. Typically, these costs are then consolidated into four categories: total capital investment, annualized capital costs, annualized operating costs, and total annualized costs. Given these cost estimates, direct impacts at the industry level can be developed and include: *price effects,* the extent to which incremental costs associated with energy-related activities increase industry prices; *changes in market structure,* whereby increased capital requirements and reduced demand caused by higher prices could change the size and number of firms in affected industries; and *employment changes,* as when the closing of marginal firms could reduce employment in affected industries or employment could increase due to accelerated government incentives (such as solar-energy tax credits).

The macroeconomic impact analysis most typically involves estimating the magnitude of compliance costs for both industry and the government. The effects of these costs on selected macroeconomic variables would include:

Aggregate price (or inflationary) effects. These trace the effects of price changes in the affected industries on the national economy. Through the use of input-output techniques, for example, price changes can be calculated in terms of the relative or percentage changes in final prices for select industrial products, and aggregated price deflators can then be estimated.

National effects on employment. Given the direct employment effects, which are estimated as macroeconomic impacts, the indirect and induced employment effects associated with a given energy incentive can be estimated.

Effects on domestic energy production. Compliance with environmental legislation may lead to increased consumption or decreased production of energy by the affected industries, possibly increasing energy imports. Energy legislation in the area of conservation, for example, could directly reduce energy demand in some sectors while increasing it in others.

Balance-of-trade effects. The most important impact may involve importation of crude oil, but price changes indirectly caused by federal regulations could also increase the demand for increased imports.

A number of econometric models are available to estimate these types of economic and employment impacts. At the national level, the most frequently used models are: the Data Resources, Inc. (DRI) macroeconomic model of the U.S. economy; the Chase Econometric Model; the Wharton EFA Annual and Industry Forecasting Model (commonly known as the Wharton model); the INFORUM Input-Output model; the Economic Growth Model of the Bureau of Labor Statistics (BLS, Department of Labor); the Department of Energy's Midrange Energy Forecasting System (MEFS); the Department of Energy and Environmental Protection Agency's Strategic Environmental Assessment System (SEAS); and others. These are representative of a somewhat larger set of models.

The DRI macroeconomic-impact model of the U.S. economy, for example, currently has the capability to forecast some 800 endogenous variables on a quarterly basis through 1990. It also can forecast industrial output for seventy-six economic sectors. Through various respecifications of forecasting equations, the DRI model can be applied to a variety of energy-policy/economic-impact analyses.

The Wharton model is designed to prepare medium-to-long-term projections of the major components of the U.S. economy and to simulate the potential effects of proposed changes in public policies. It contains forty-two final-demand components of GNP and converts these components to industrial output for fifty-six economic sectors. This detailed sectoring scheme permits the user to examine comparative impacts—including employment requirements—across a number of industries.

The INFORUM model provides still another alternative for estimating national economic impacts. It is a 200-sector input-output model designed to produce annual projections over a ten-to-fifteen-year period. A run of the INFORUM model yields a number of key direct, indirect, and induced consequences of various energy-policy alternatives.

The BLS Economic Growth Model combines a macroeconomic model with an input-output system to make medium- and long-term projections of output and employment by industry. The BLS model has the capability to forecast through 1990. As part of an ongoing project, an analytical procedure has been devised that enables the BLS model to compute construction and operational-employment multipliers for emerging energy technologies and to estimate the direct and indirect employment impacts of alternative-energy scenarios.[5] For purposes of this study, the BLS model is an excellent illustration of the current state of the art of the best of the macro-structural models, and of its potential strengths and weaknesses for use as a regional, as well as national, analysis tool. The BLS modeling system has been developed primarily by the federal government for use at the federal level, to study national—not subnational—impacts; nevertheless, regional impacts can be determined, albeit with some difficulty. Following that are descriptions and reviews of the PIES and SEAS systems. Each of these models was supported and developed by federal funding for specific agency purposes. The DRI, Chase, and Wharton models are all privately developed and, though very widely used, have no specific federal-agency designation.

BLS Economic Growth Model

Description

Conceptually, the BLS Economic Growth Model combines a macroeconomic model with an input-output system to make medium- and long-term projections of output and employment by industry:[6] in this sense, the BLS is more an economic model than it is an environmental or energy model. This macro model of the U.S. economy is relatively aggregated (containing about fifty equations), whereas the more micro-level analysis of industry-output and employment projects covers about 160 sectors of the economy. The model is comprised of a set of well-defined procedures or steps that are operated primarily in a recursive manner, with some feedback and consistency checks. Typically, a run of the model consists of five separate steps:

1. Projection of the macroeconomic aggregates for the U.S. economy
2. Disaggregation of the GNP forecast to individual-demand components
3. Translation, through appropriate bridge matrices and equations of these final-demand components, to purchases from individual industries
4. Solution for the total output of each industry needed to support this level of final demand through an input-output system
5. Projection of productivity and employment, also by individual industry

Figure 6-1 diagrammatic representation of these steps; a brief description of each follows.

Step 1—The Macro Model. The macro model is structured through a general-equilibrium framework, equilibrating output produced with output demanded via income flows. As a result, the model can be segmented into three blocks: supply, demand, and income. Though distinct, these blocks interact with each other.

The supply block is divided into private and public GNP. Private GNP is estimated through an aggregate-production function that uses labor and capital as inputs. The labor input consists of average annual hours times the number of employees, which is estimated through equations. Exogenous estimates of federal military and civilian employment and an endogenous

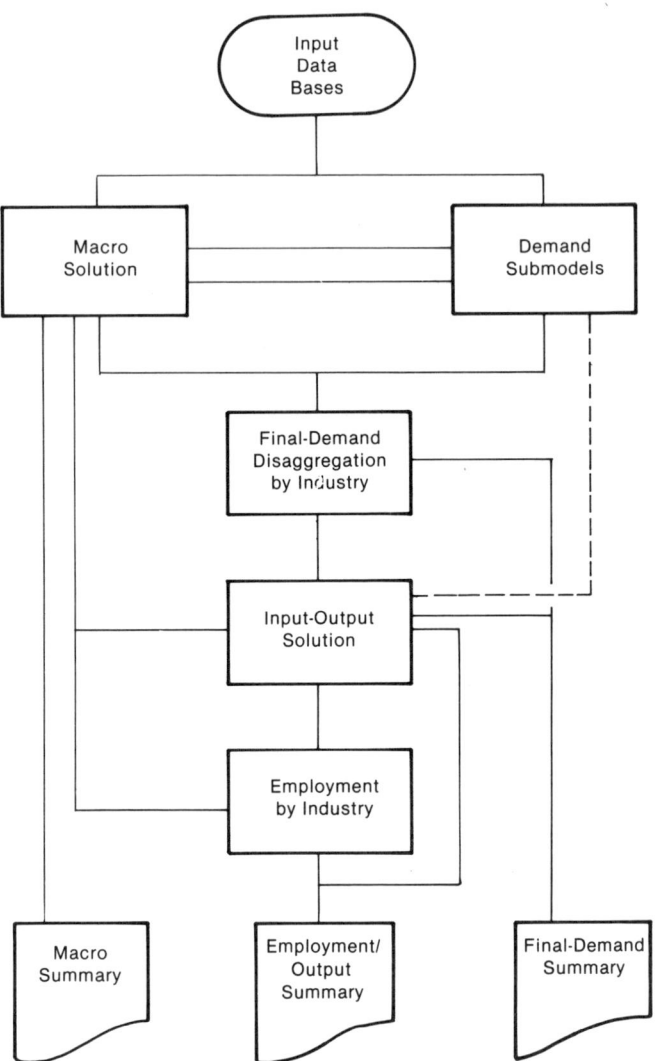

Figure 6-1. Flow Chart of the BLS Model

estimate of state and local government employment are subtracted from total employment to obtain private employment. The capital input is obtained from the capital stock and net real investment. Net investment is related to private-sector output and corporate cash flow, among other variables. Capital and labor, after entering the production function, determine the supply side of private GNP. In the government sector, GNP is defined as employment compensation (after adjusting from changes in grade structure of the personnel) plus purchases of goods and services.

The income block in the model is comprised of a set of relationships that determine personal and disposable income and can be divided into corporate and personal income. Corporate profits, dividends, internal funds, and other related variables are estimated through a series of equations. Median family income is a function of the employment rate, GNP per worker, and the share of GNP going to personal income. Disposable income is then derived by subtracting personal taxes; personal consumption is determined as an identity after deducting personal saving from income.

The demand block in the model contains three equations for personal-consumption expenditures (durable, nondurable, and services). Investment, which is estimated as a factor demand, is determined through four equations (nonfarm equipment, nonfarm structure, farm equipment and structures, and residential investment). One equation estimates imports, while government demand and net exports are exogenously determined.

In the macro model, the supply and demand blocs are determined in constant prices, while the income block is expressed in current prices. Given this discrepancy, the model contains a price/wage block to provide internal consistency between wage and price determination and to endogenize the rate of inflation. Necessary adjustments are accomplished through private GNP, personal-consumption expenditures, and other deflators. A final adjustment eliminates any gaps between supply and demand blocks of the model or balances them through adjustments in various federal-policy variables—such as changes in expenditures or in' taxes. These adjustments create balanced projections to achieve internal consistency among outputs, income, government policy, and demand.

Step 2—Final-Demand Disaggregation of GNP. In this step, the level of GNP and its composition, which were determined by the macro model (step 1), are disaggregated into final-demand components. For example, individual equations determine personal-consumption expenditures for a set of eighty-two commodities. Similar disaggregations are determined for gross private domestic investment; federal, state, and local government expenditures; and net foreign demand. Overall, GNP is divided into 207 categories or variables.

Step 3—Application of Bridge Matrices. After final-demand components are disaggregated in the categories above, they are transformed into a set of final demands consistent with the input-output framework. This is accomplished through bridge matrices, which relate final-demand components to purchases from individual industries. Essentially, each demand component is converted into a bill of goods or product. These matrices bridge or distribute product forecasts into 160 producing industries. A product, as defined in national-income accounts, may be the aggregate of many different types of goods. In these cases product value includes the value received by the producing industry. Trade, transportation, and distribution margins that occur between the time a product is produced and the time it is actually consumed are, in turn, reallocated to the margin-producing industries. Thus, the bridge matrix has a dual purpose: it allocates each product-class expenditure among the various producing industries involved; and it removes the cost margins from the producing industries and reallocates them to the insurance, trade, and transportation industries.

Step 4—Input-Output Solution. After final demand in each industry is determined, the output required to meet this projected final demand is derived. This solution for total output of each industry is computed through an input-output system. In the BLS model, this system follows a conventional input-output format:

$$AX + Y = X$$

where Y = the final-demand bill of goods determined the previous step;

X = total output vector;

A = direct-requirements matrix.

Initially, the BLS model was comprised of 134 industries; currently it contains 160. The basic input-output table in the model was originally constructed for the year 1967 by the Bureau of Economic Analysis but has been modified and updated within the BLS model. Input-output realtionships are expressed in producer's value, or the price received by the producer. As previously indicated, trade margins and transportation costs related to these inputs are contained under direct purchases by the consuming industry from the trade and transportation industries. The input-output system assigns all output of a product or service to a particular primary industry. Under this framework an industry that produces a product as a secondary good sells or transfers this product to the primary industry. With this approach, the final-demand bill of goods is classified only by primary product.

A set of projections is necessary to transform input-output relationships in the base year to an updated year and the forecasted years (say, 1980 and 1985). These projections require not only that all parts of the system be estimated but also that the parts be incorporated into a balanced system. Projection techniques are available to determine both input-output coefficients and interindustry relationships. The former examines specific data changes for individual coefficients that include possible changes in price, product mix, and/or technology. Interindustry-relationship projections examine such factors as changes in the sales of an industry to other sectors over time.

Several steps are required to update input-output relationships. First, industry output and final demand by industry are estimated. Second, the differences between actual intermediate demand and derived intermediate demand for each industry are calculated and then compared to identify significant deviations in derived output. Third, a final balancing is performed to develop a consistency among final demands, value added by detailed sector, and also the independently estimated cells. Similarly, input-output relationships are projected for future years (say, 1982–1985). Next, estimates of final demands by industry are determined for the projected years. Total output is then estimated as a function of the independently projected coefficient matrix and the final-demand projections.

Step 5—Productivity and Employment Projections. Employment projections are derived from the projections of output by sector. Before industry employment is projected, however, it is necessary to determine industry productivity (or the change in industry output per hour). Either a regression or least-square approach can be utilized to project productivity. The primary approach, however, uses a historical least-square time trend and adjusts this trend by some percentage difference between projected and historical output trends. After industry-productivity projections are derived, estimates are made for changes in the average work week for each industry. Then, employment projections for each industry are determined from the projected levels of output, output per hour, and average annual hours. Employment estimates are comprised of wage and salary workers, unpaid family workers, and the self-employed.

Finally, a series of checks and balances is available within the BLS model to monitor the various stages of projections. This feedback and balancing procedure is designed to establish consistency between micro and macro projections of imports, investments, and employment.

Critique of the BLS Model from a National and Subnational Standpoint

Recent critiques prepared for the Department of Labor have characterized the BLS model as one in which many key economic variables are introduced exogenously. The behavioral model is straightforward and thus very dependent on initial values chosen for exogenous variables: though difficult to estimate and forecast such exogenous variables at a national level, they are even more difficult and suspect if required at each of several interrelated regional (subnational) levels. A second cited shortcoming of the BLS model is the lack of consistency in the price-determination processes between micro (such as sectoral or subnational) and macro behavior. Most relationships in the model are between real quantities (real output, employment). On the other hand, prices are entered into the model as nominal terms in the model's income block. Thus, a significant number of price and technological adjustments are necessary to achieve comparability. These adjustments make it difficult to judge the economic reasonableness of the real-resource allocations implied for the growth of output and employment at the industry and the national level. Substantially greater difficulty would accompany attempts to develop similar, regional price-determination processes.[7]

One of the major weaknesses of the BLS modeling scheme is its lack of adequate specification of the behavioral relationship underlying price determination in the industry equations. Price equations are available to determine aggregate deflators (for GNP, Personal Consumption Expenditures (PCE), and the like) based on a simple Phillips-curve concept, but no attempt is currently made to assure sector-by-sector consistency between real flows and money flows. (This is generally true of most input-output work, although some noticeable progress in this regard appears to have been made in the recent development of the Wharton energy model.[8]) To achieve sector-by-sector consistency at subnational levels, including interareal trade and flows, would tremendously complicate the BLS model.

Another difficulty in this context relates to employment estimation at a sectoral level. Typically, these estimates are made by multiplying the output vector from the input-output solution by productivity equations, defined as output per employee. This is true of most input-output models, including INFORUM, the Wharton model, and the BLS model. For consistency, however, the equilibrium conditions should be derived simultaneously for employment and investment from a given production function. Here, further research appears to be needed to develop viable and reliable methods for estimating productions functions (capital, labor, energy, and materials are the major inputs) for each major industry. A two-step approach could be used, for example, as in the Wharton model, where substitutions among the four major inputs are modeled at a first level, with a detailed specification of substituton within each input category (say, interfuel substitution) at a second level. The two levels are solved simultaneously, however.

The technical issues of input substitution and relative price changes—important for both further sector and regional (subnational) delineation and analysis—are summarized by Eckstein and Heien as follows:

> In addition to finding a method for adjusting I-O coefficients for relative price changes, the BLS macro model could also be modified to incorporate

Top-Down Analysis Methods   87

energy into the projections in a simple way, as has been attempted in other macro models. This could be done by introducing an energy variable into the aggregate production function—i.e., in the price equation. If employment demand is then made endogenous, solution of the macro model would then be given some indication of feasible sets of price, output, employment, productivity and demand configurations compatible with a given set of energy price assumptions. A second, somewhat more ambitious project would involve estimation of production functions for the key industries which produce intermediate outputs in the economy. In this way, real wage rate changes in various inputs would cause factor demands to adjust in response to price variation.[9]

Clearly, the BLS model is a top-down formulation, making little or no provision for extensions to subnational areal levels; the model was not designed to address regional issues, and substantial difficulties would be encountered if regionalization analyses were attempted with this system. Later we shall compare the features of the BLS model and the other top-down formulations with the criteria specified in chapter 5.

Department of Energy Midrange Energy Forecasting System (MEFS)

Description

The MEFS model was originally called PIES, the Project Independence Evaluation System.[10] Project Independence was the generic title used to describe activities organized by the Federal Energy Administration in the development and implementation of a national-energy policy for the United States in the early and mid-1970s. The MEFS model is constantly evolving and its data bases are updated regularly. In general, though, its form and structure remain as described here. The MEFS generates estimates of possible energy-system variables, taking into consideration the effect of relative prices, the potential for fuel substitution, and technological constraints inhibiting increased energy supplies. Among the objectives considered by the MEFS model in analyzing alternative strategies are:

1. Price sensitivity—the impact of relative prices
2. Fuel competition—the substitution of one energy source for another
3. Technology—the variation of production and conversion technologies within the energy system
4. Resource limitations—physical capacities and other resource limitations
5. Externalities—by-products or side-effects of energy production and consumption

6. Economic impact—interaction with the total energy production and consumption
7. Regional variations—the geographic distribution of energy production and consumption
8. Dynamics—lead times, capacity in previous periods, and other time-dependent conditions

Thus, the energy system is depicted as a kind of network wherein production, processing, conversion, distribution, transportation, and consumption activities take place. The prices and capacities for these activities are presented so as to be consistent with the dual objectives of preserving price sensitivity and recognizing potential constraints on the system. This framework is structured by separating the supply and demand sectors. Figure 6-2 shows a process-schematic diagram of MEFS; detailed description of MEFS follows.

The supply system is conceptualized as nodes of activity that produce, process, and convert raw materials within an energy network. These nodes are connected by links depicting the transportation and distribution system. Potential energy-production system activities are described by a set of supply curves, identifying prices to be paid and nonenergy resources to be consumed at each possible level of operation. Important physical or technological limitations affecting the production of energy are also described within the transportation and distribution network. The refining and conversion sectors are included as the intermediate nodes of the network, each with a description of its capacities. Conversion activities are then joined with the demand or consumption sectors through an additional set of transportation and distribution links. These links are subject to capacity restrictions that can be modified. The supply curves, conversion technologies, transportation possibilities, costs, and resource requirements are produced by supply submodels of the evaluation system and linked within this framework.

Estimates of the demand for energy are produced by a demand model. Demand for energy products originates in different geographic regions and varies with energy prices. A selection of activities is described as demand and can be thought of as the final demands for energy. Fuel substitution is simulated by the demand model through the empirical development of relationships between demands and relative prices.

Given the prices, resource requirements, and capacity constraints, an integration model is utilized to construct a feasible set of energy flows that satisfies the final demands for energy. Energy-supply activities and demand prices are adjusted during this market simulation to obtain a balanced solution that is in equilibrium.

The supply, demand, and equilibrium-balancing components describing the energy system are combined with models of the economy and assessments of nonenergy-resource availability to evaluate energy solutions

Top-Down Analysis Methods

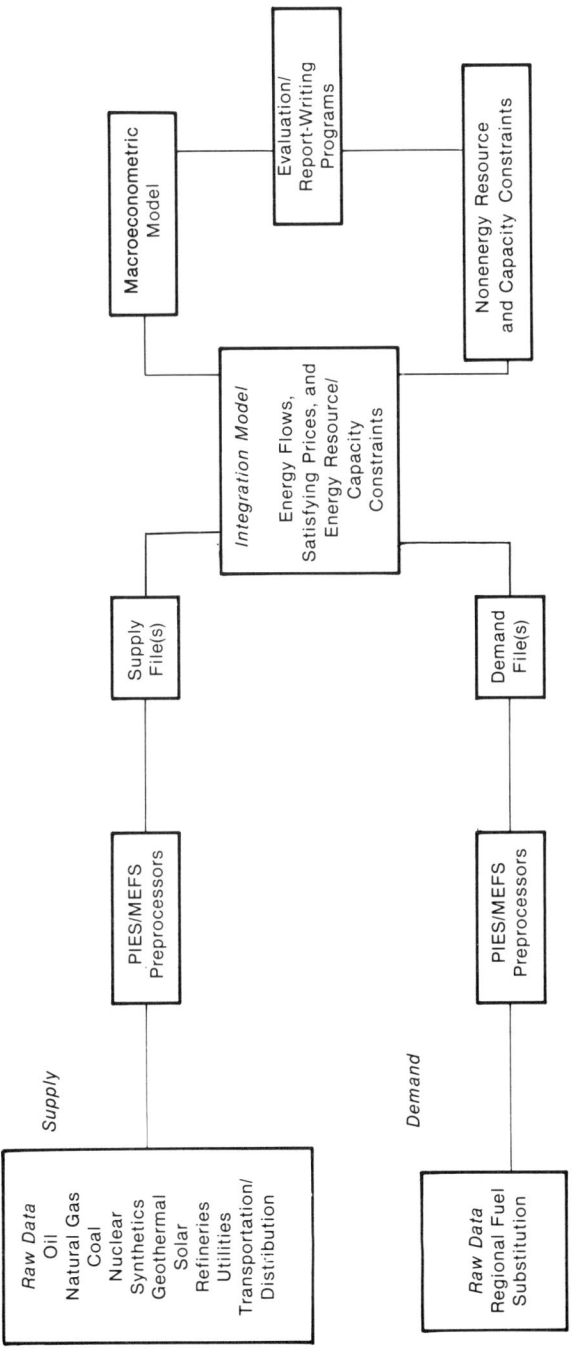

Figure 6-2. Schematic of PIES/MEFS

in terms of environmental, economic, or resource impacts. Econometric, simulation, accounting, and optimization models are included, each exploiting special capabilities for the relevant components of the problem. The model of macroeconomic activity is the system developed by Data Resources, Inc.

The resource-constraint elements are contained in a large data base that records the coefficients of demand for nonenergy resources for the alternative-energy activities included in the system. These coefficients are employed to construct constraints for the equilibrium solution of supply capacities or to prepare *ex post* summaries for off-line evaluation of potential bottlenecks. The supply components consists of a variety of procedures used to construct stepwise approximations to the energy supply curves. These range from case-specific engineering analyses in the instance of coal to the complex software developed by the National Petroleum Council for estimation of the supply of petroleum and gas.

The demand model is a behavioral econometric model. The demand for energy is not represented in terms of its final use as energy but as the demand for the variety of energy products in the end-use sectors. The structure of demand and any potential substitutions are postulated in terms of relative prices, and the parameters of these relationships are further estimated using econometric techniques. The resulting system consists of over 800 behavioral relationships governing the demand for energy in forty product and sectoral combinations.

The demand, supply, and resource-assessments models are combined through the series of programs constituting the integrating model. A partial equilibrium is obtained by balancing prices and quantities for all energy products. Through this model, the quantity flows and prices of the equilibrium energy-sector solution provide the input to a series of evaluation or report-writing programs that relate the solution to particular problems under consideration. These reports, over twenty in all, range from an executive summary of the energy balance to detailed classification and compilation of associated environmental residuals, water requirements, or implied nonenergy-resource usage for inputs that have not been considered directly in the energy-system network.

Unlike the BLS model, MEFS provides for regional breakouts, since *interareal* flows of energy, for example, are an important feature of the system. Production, distribution, conversion, and consumption of energy material each have a regional structure in MEFS. The primary purpose of the regional detail is not to provide results for regional analyses, but to develop more-representative national figures. In this sense, the regionalization capability of MEFS exists for the convenience of the MEFS top-down approach. The choice of regional structure is governed largely by the availability of data for that segment of the energy system. Specific regional details are included in the following descriptions of each primary MEFS submodel.

Top-Down Analysis Methods

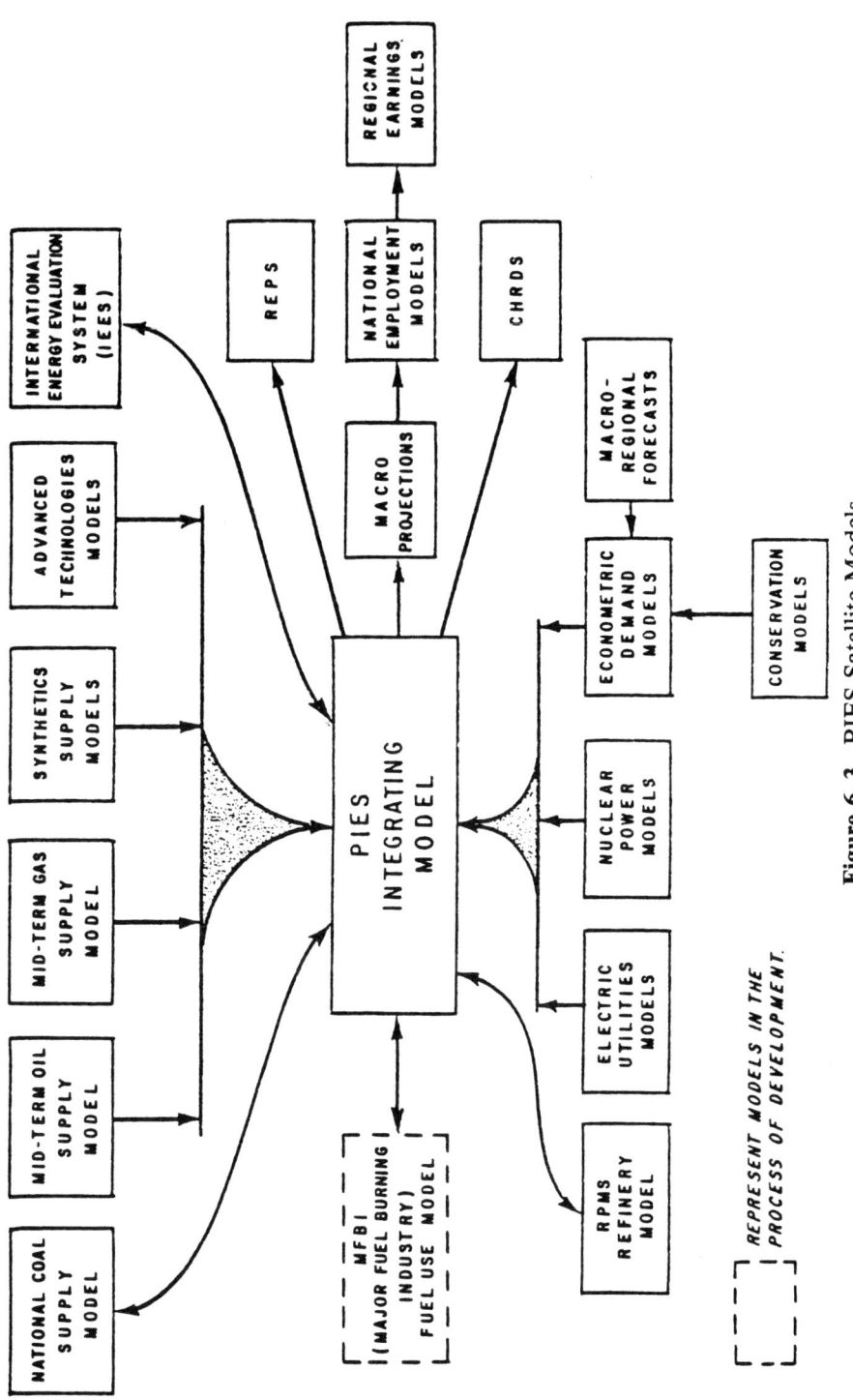

Figure 6-3. PIES Satellite Models

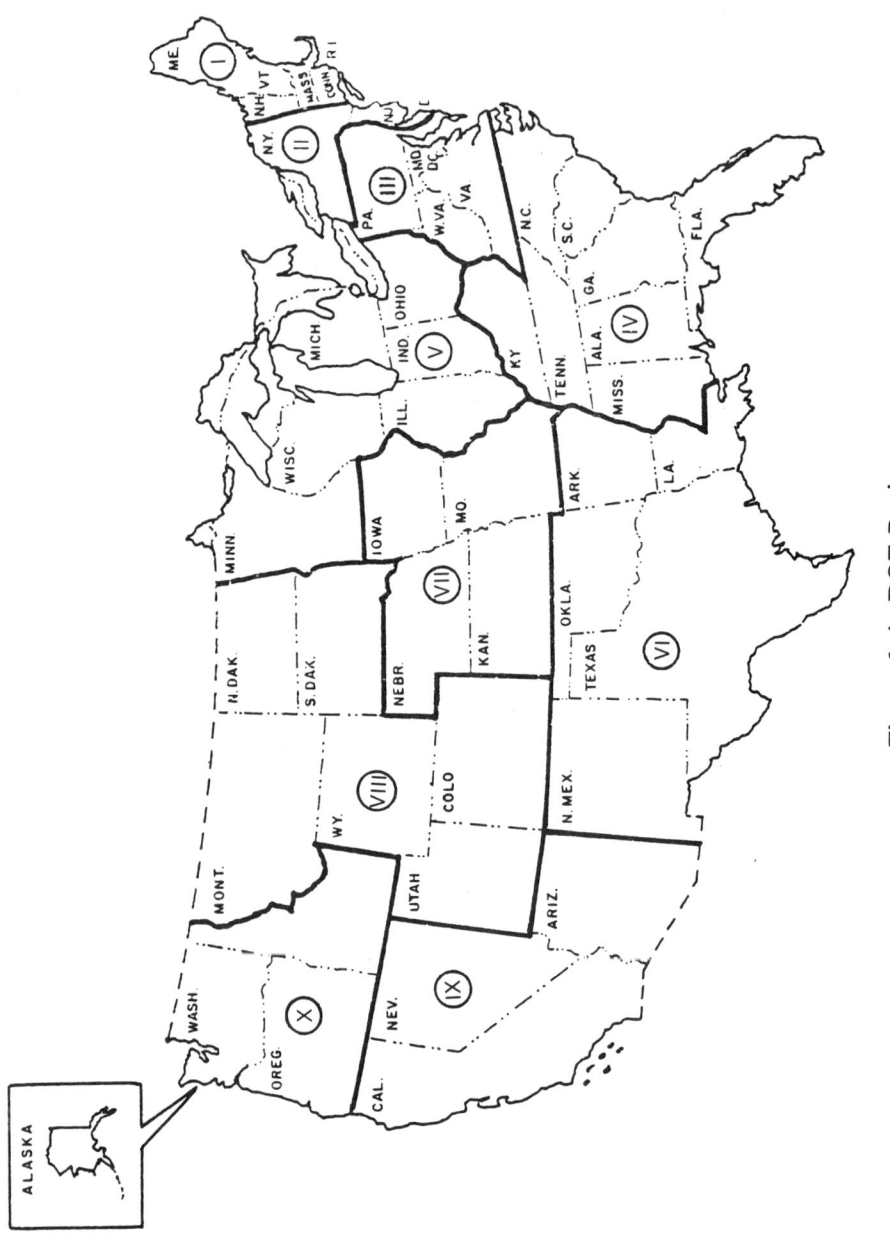

Figure 6-4. DOE Regions

Demand Models. The demand models are satellites of the MEFS integrating model and are depicted as such in figure 6-3.[11] Outputs from the demand models, which include price elasticities (including cross-elasticities for thirty sector-specific products in each of ten regions for the target year), are used as inputs to the integration model. Demand regions are the ten DOE federal regions shown in figure 6-4.

The Supply and Conversion Submodels. In the past, many economists have estimated output as a function of capital and labor, without giving adequate attention to the resource base. This is particularly inappropriate in energy-supply modeling, for the resource base is the most important factor affecting the level of output. Although the 1970s witnessed a remarkable growth in interest in the economics of natural resources, the technical methods are still in an embryonic stage.

Rather than using the more typical extrapolation of historical time-series data to predict future raw-material and product availability, production models within MEFS are constructed so as to simulate the actual production capabilities, given the resource base of the energy sector considered and the economic presumption that each producer seeks to maximize its profits.

Possibly the most important feature of the regionalization subroutines of MEFS is that they are designed, not to illuminate the energy impacts of national policies on localities, but more to enrich the macro forecasts presented at the national level. This rationale is in contrast with the regionalization aims of the SEAS model, discussed next, where the more detailed impacts are a function of the desire to learn potential impacts of national policy on local regions—where the true environmental impacts are to be measured.

Coal. The PIES/MEFS national coal model is used to develop supply functions for eleven different categories of coal in the thirteen MEFS coal-supply regions. These regions, shown in figure 6-5, were chosen to correspond to the traditional mining regions defined by the Bureau of Mines. Within MEFS, coal is differentiated by its sulfur and Btu content and by type.

As for all supply functions in MEFS, step functions are used to approximate individual coal-supply curves. For each type of coal, the steps of the coal-supply curve represent the development of a specific mine type. The lowest-cost steps on these curves generally correspond to existing mines or to mines that are about to be opened. In such instances, capital costs are sunk or mostly sunk, and the mines will be operated as long as the marginal revenue is at least equal to the operating cost. The higher-cost steps reflect the capital recovery necessary for opening new mines.

The production capacity for new mines is estimated as the maximum annual production that the former Bureau of Mines estimated-reserve base

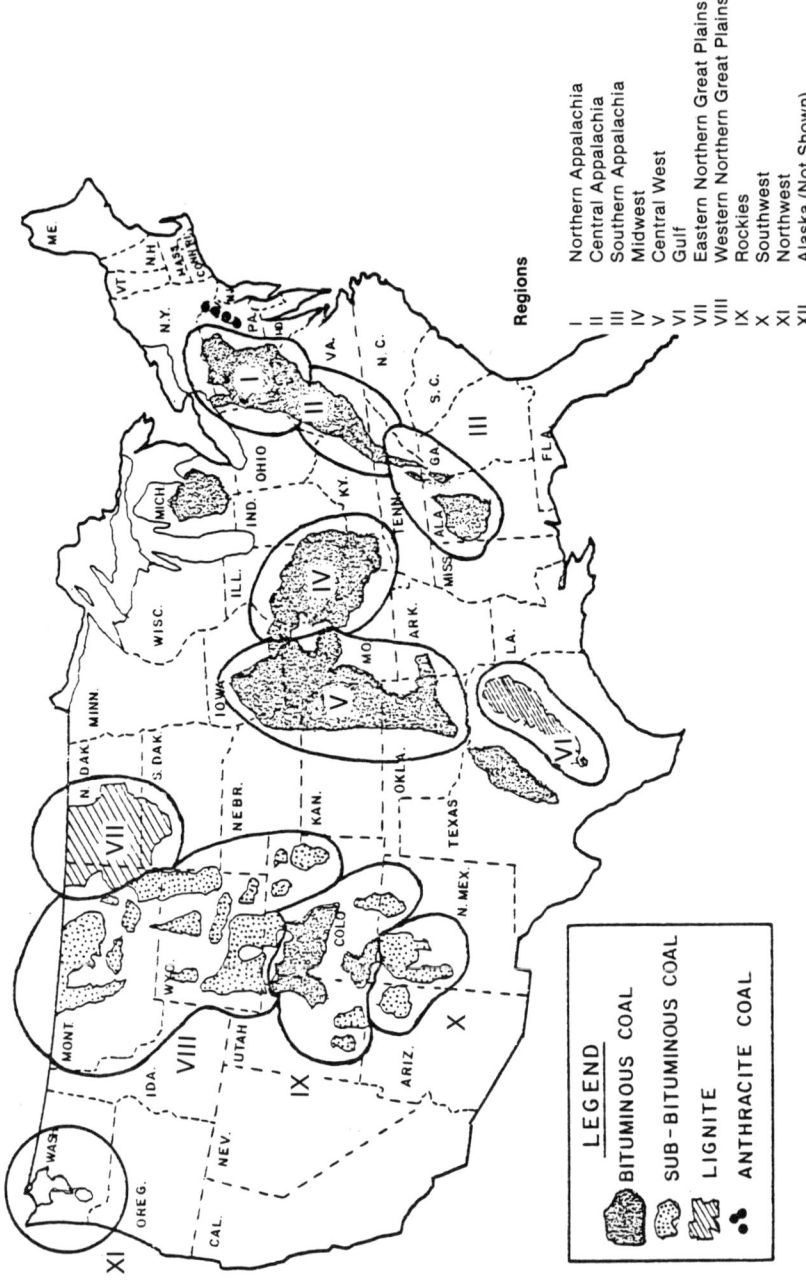

Figure 6-5. PIES Coal Regions

could sustain for twenty years or so. The amount of coal in each cost category is estimated by means of statistical distributions appropriate for the region and coal type. The cost of coal is determined through an income-statement simulation in which there are four major determinants of cost: capital, labor cost and productivity, power and supplies, and rate of return. Transportation, which represents a substantial portion of the delivered cost of coal, is also estimated, utilizing transportation-cost functions that include considerations of rail, barge, and multimodal rates by distance and type of shipment.

Oil and Gas. Oil production is modeled in thirteen regions, consisting of eight regions on-shore in the lower forty-eight states, three regions on the outer continental shelf, the Alaskan North Slope, and south Alaska. These regions are based on the National Petroleum Council (NPC) classification, with Alaska being split into two regions and NPC regions 8, 9, and 10 being aggregated (see figure 6-6).

An oil-supply model provides supply functions for approximately twenty different domestic crude oils in the appropriate oil-production regions, plus associated gas and coproducts. The crude oils are differentiated by sulfur content and American Petroleum Institute (API) gravity (see figure 6-7). A gas-supply model provides supply functions for natural gas and coproducts in each of the gas regions.

Fourteen natural-gas regions are modeled. They are identical to the oil regions, except that the NPC regions 8, 9, and 10 form two natural-gas regions—one composed of NPC regions 8 and 9, the other of NPC region 10.

Oil discovered in-place in a region is partitioned into primary, secondary, and tertiary reserves by barrel, based on historical regional recovery factors. An exponentially declining curve is used to represent production over time. Secondary production starts several years after the oil is added to reserves, tertiary even later. The recent history of barrels of oil (and/or thousand cubic feet of gas) is used to establish an initial finding rate per foot. Once the value of a unit of reserves is added and the cost of discovering the reserves is known, the cumulative feet worth drilling for each price level is determined.

Electric Utilities. The electric-utilities submodel of MEFS simulates the capacity and mix of generating-plant types required to meet load demands that vary daily and seasonally. It models the consumption of fuels (coal, residual oil, distillate oil, natural gas, and uranium), including transportation to utilities from domestic producing and importing regions. Fuels are converted to electricity taking account of energy losses, and then sent through the transmission and distribution network to satisfy sectoral demands for electricity in the individual demand regions.

MEFS utility regions correspond to the ten DOE federal regions

96   Modern Federalism

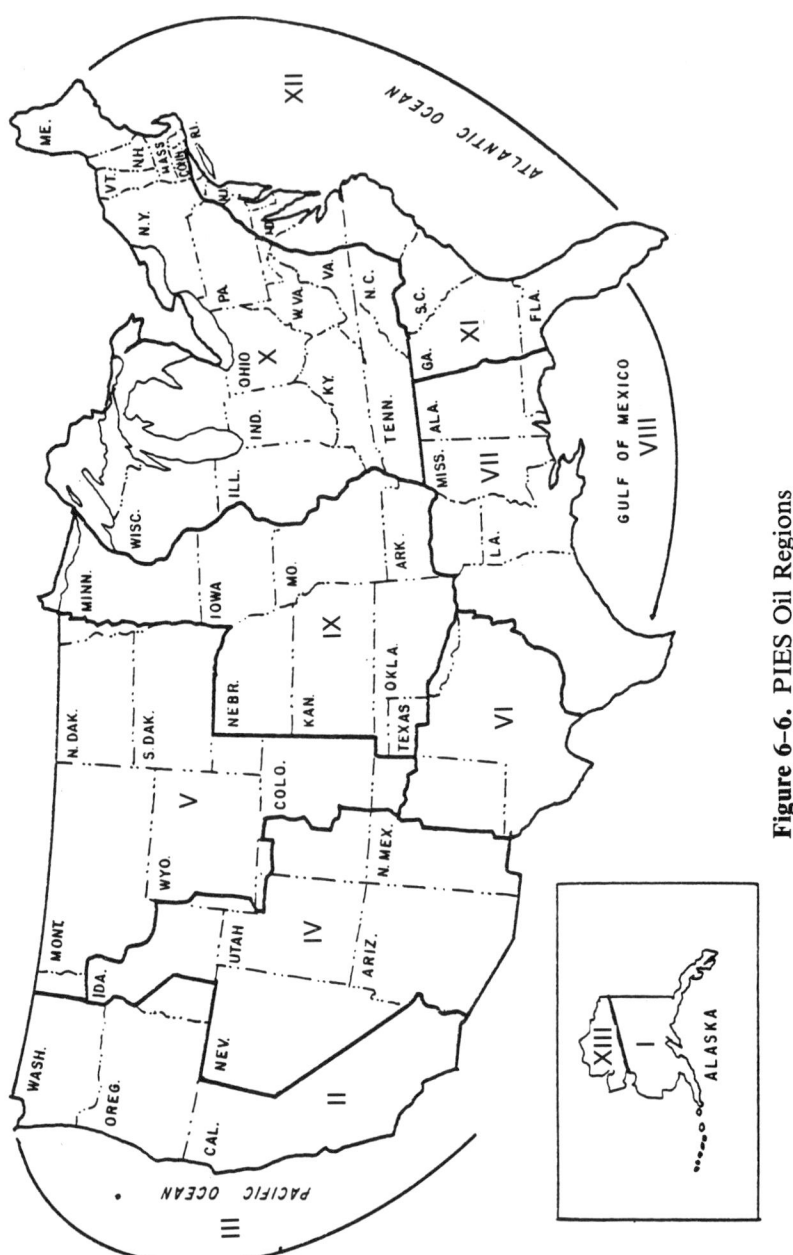

Figure 6-6. PIES Oil Regions

Top-Down Analysis Methods

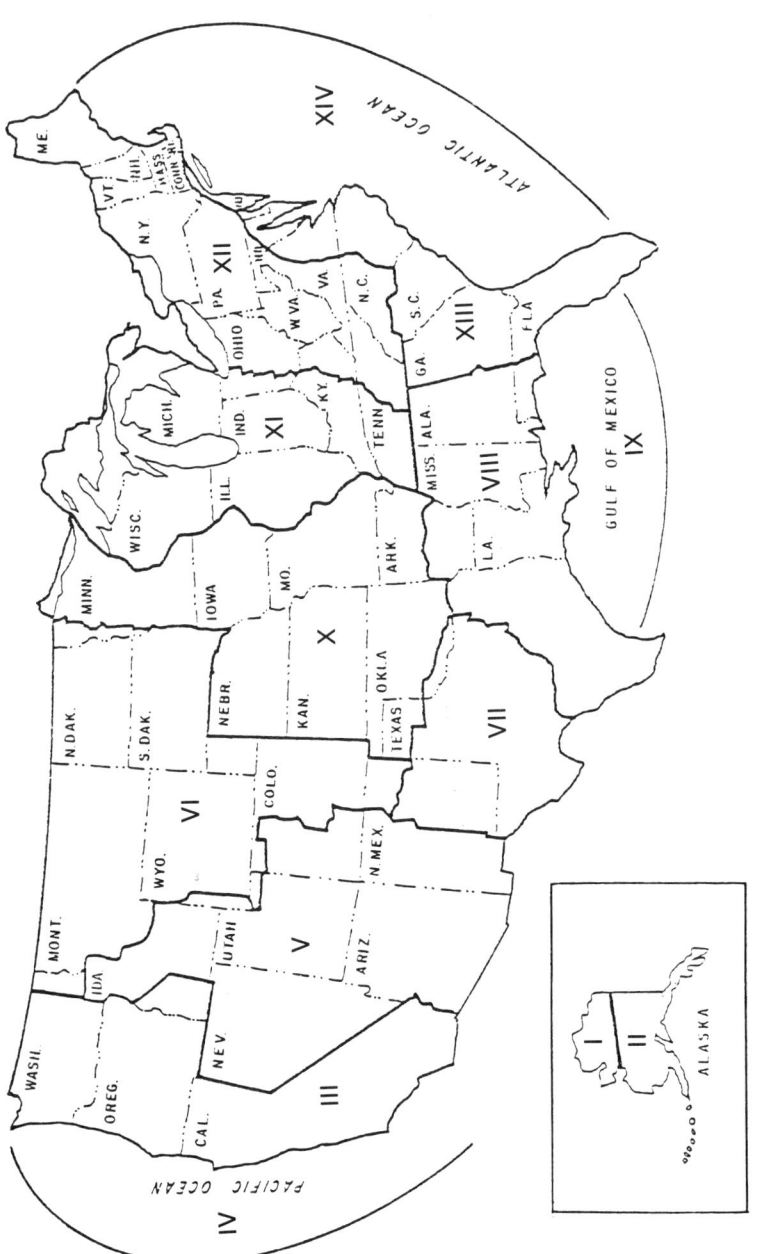

Figure 6–7. PIES Natural-Gas Regions

depicted in figure 6-4. The model allows electricity demand to be satisfied by generation only in the same utility region. MEFS models base, cycling, daily-peak, and seasonal-peak modes of operation. The types of generation equipment that can be represented include nuclear power, coal-fired steam (with or without scrubbers), residual-fired steam, gas-fired steam, simple-cycle turbines, combined-cycle distillate turbines, and hydroelectric power. Each type of generation plant has its own cost and load-factor characteristics.

Refineries. The refineries submodel represents the conversion of crude oils (both domestic and imported) to seven major refined products (naptha, gasoline, jet fuel, distillate, residual, liquefied petroleum gases, and other). Crude oils processed by refineries differ in physical and chemical characteristics, meaning that each crude type must be processed slightly differently, with processing costs varying slightly from crude to crude, and each operating mode producing a different mix of products. The MEFS refineries submodel has the capability to differentiate crude oils by characteristics such as specific gravity and sulfur content and distinguish approximately forty-five different domestic and imported crude types. Expansion of the refinery industry is accomplished by providing a spectrum of choices for construction of new capacity.

Consistent with the general MEFS modeling approach, the refineries submodel selects and transports specific crude types to refinery regions, chooses specific operating models, specifies necessary types of capacity for expansion, and produces and transports refined products to the consumers, all in a way that minimizes the refiner's costs.

The refinery regions are the five Petroleum Administration for Defense Districts (PADDs), with PADDs 1 and 2 being divided into two regions as shown in figure 6-8. These regions were originally defined for the administration of refiners by the navy during a national emergency. Within MEFS, crude oil is transported into refinery regions from the oil-production or import regions, and refined products are transported from the refinery regions to either the utility or demand regions by pipeline, barge, or tanker.

Transportation. All production, conversion, and consumption activities MEFS are linked by a transportation network. The transportation submodel provides interregional links to model coal transportation by barge and rail, gas by pipeline, and oil and refined products by tanker, barge, and pipeline. It also calculates the cost for shipping each material by the potential transportation models for each link.

Critique of MEFS from a National and Subnational Standpoint

Clearly, MEFS has a substantial regional orientation. All the important models and submodels have regional breakouts, required for the interareal-

Top-Down Analysis Methods

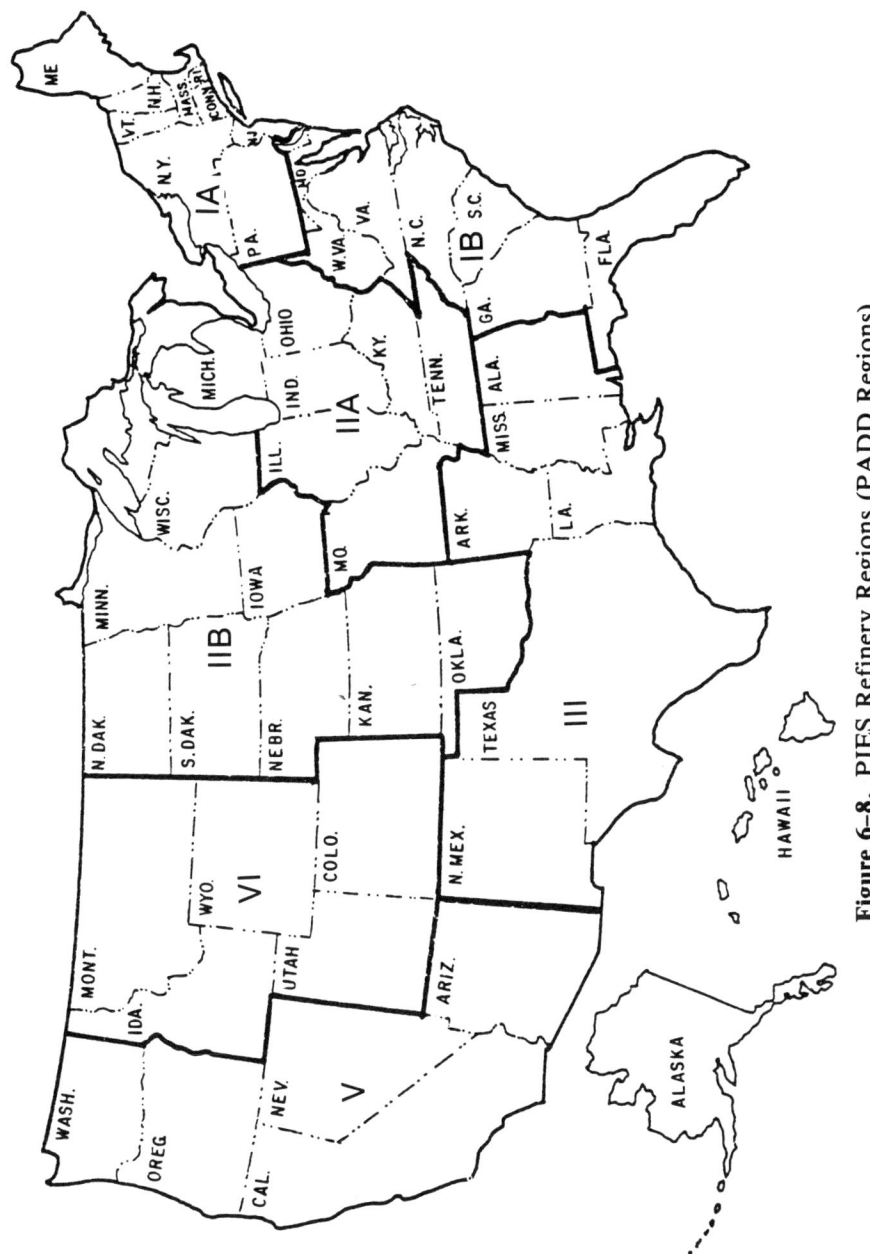

Figure 6-8. PIES Refinery Regions (PADD Regions)

network flows developed within MEFS. However, the MEFS regions are not to be taken as realistic depictions of each included geographic area: different geographic delineations are used primarily for modeling and data convenience. Because MEFS operates with a number of other artificial conversions, such as not permitting the interregional transfer of energy supplies, the regionalization projections may not be an accurate reflection of reality. No comprehensive, integrated analytic description of any one region is developed. Rather, as stated above, MEFS regionalization is almost entirely for the benefit of the comprehensive, top-down MEFS model: PIES/MEFS recognizes that regional differences and similarities can and do affect national energy and economic totals and includes regional activities only insofar as they are needed to reflect this very limited bottom-up recognition. There is no attempt to model all sectors within each geographic area comprehensively, either by the area itself (intra-areal equilibrium), or by interaction with others (interareal equilibrium). This does not necessarily mean that nothing significant can be learned about subnational structures and processes from MEFS; however, it does call for judicious use that recognizes the obvious shortcomings of MEFS as a regional-analysis tool, or even as a regional-analysis technique housed within a national framework. For the most part, the many uses and users of the PIES/MEFS modeling systems do not utilize the areal disaggregation of PIES per se as accurate forecasts of regional energy and economic activities.

The Strategic Environmental Assessment System (SEAS) Model

Description

SEAS has been described as "a system of special-purpose models linked to a macroeconomic model and an interindustry input-output of the United States economy."[12] Economic forecasts to estimate pollutant levels and associated abatement costs such as pollution-abatement benefits, energy demands, solid-waste generation and associated recycling, land-use requirements, mineral-use and virgin-stock status, processed-ore inventories, transportation demand, and relative commodity price changes, are used by other models in this system. At present, this model is used to build on economic and energy policies and forecasts made primarily by government agencies in order to forecast pollution loadings, costs of cleanup, and associated direct and indirect economic impacts that are likely to flow from these policies and forecasts.

In the Department of Energy, SEAS has a very particular use. In DOE's Office of Environment, SEAS is used to predict the environmental impacts of energy policies and scenarios produced by other parts of the agency. To accomplish this, it is necessary for analysts to map the energy and economic forecasts onto the SEAS system of modeling and then to use the system to calculate the environmental residuals and impacts from these forecasts.

The model, as currently used, forecasts up to a twenty-five year period; produces forecasts at national and regional levels; provides for regional variation of industrial pollutants; allows for variation in assumptions regarding pollution-control regulations; has a detailed disaggretation of the economy for environmental analyses; emphasizes pollution from energy industry in conjunction with major polluting nonenergy industries; permits users to trace effects throughout the system; has a rich data base containing a comprehensive set of environmental, energy, and economic variables and parameters; and, finally, allows for extensive user options, particularly in the selection of output reports.

SEAS is designed to operate as a set of integrated submodules that can be run either alone or as part of the overall system. These submodels can be divided into four general areas: energy, economics, regional disaggregation, and environment. Within each major category there is a further breakdown. The economics section has four models: energy investment, interindustry input-output, sector disaggregation, and pollution abatement costs. Energy consists of three submodels: electric utilities, industrial combustion, and an energy-supply-network simulator. Regional disaggregation is carried out using a single submodel. The environmental portion, clearly the single most important feature of SEAS, uses five models: transportation, residuals generation, land use, solid waste, and environmental-quality indicators.

Figure 6-9 shows a schematic diagram of the SEAS model; details of the components submodels of SEAS follows.

The Economic Models. The SEAS economic forecasts are developed at several levels of detail. The first, the macroeconomic forecast, provides the general parameter projection on an annual basis through 1985. These general values include employment, general production-sector output volumes, personal consumption, disposable income, and capital investment and allow projections of the general subaccounts of the GNP. Basic structural relationships between these economic variables are developed from BLS and Department of Commerce models and data bases.

The second level of forecast is the calculation of interactions among industries in order to meet the levels of output in the demand forecast of the macro model. This economic input-output model provides the yearly economic projections for 185 sectors of the economy and statistics for each sector such as employment, output sold for final demand, total output, durable goods and construction expenditures, exports, imports, and inven-

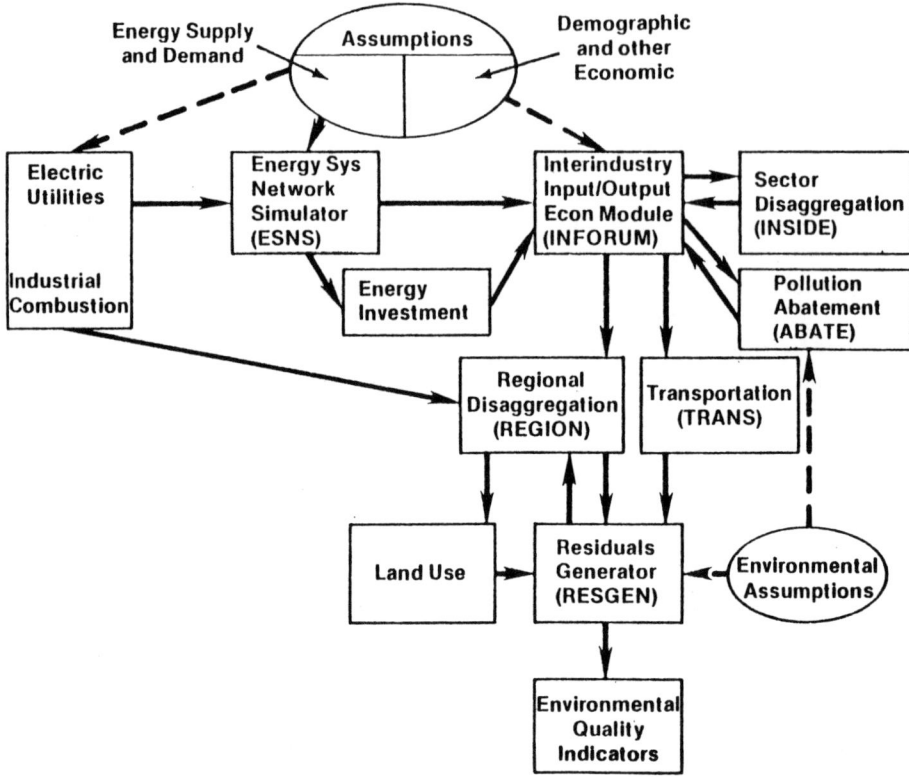

Figure 6-9. SEAS Block Diagram

tories. The model, called INFORUM, is a rigorous input-output system that provides great detail and balanced accounting of values that can act as physical goods flow among sectors and to the final consumers. The INFORUM model is maintained by a staff at the University of Maryland.

A third level of forecast detail of economic activity is produced by the SEAS design and systems teams and deals with procedures that break the specific (185) industry forecasts into richer information (where required) for specific analysis questions, using official estimates from the Department of Commerce, Agriculture, and Interior for more-detailed economic-activity levels. This last level of detail in SEAS is readily expanded and now represents three times the detail available from the original INFORUM sectors.

A fourth level is found in the pollution-abatement cost model, ABATE.

ABATE estimates the investment, operating, and maintenance costs associated with abating the emissions of air and water pollutants by each economic sector. It also feeds back to INFORUM the increased monetary and goods demands created by pollution-control investment and operating purchases on the industrial sectors that supply construction materials and labor, abatement equipment, chemicals for abatement, energy sources, and operating-manpower requirements. INFORUM uses this information to rebalance its forecasts of sector economic activity. Nonindustrial consumption and disposal processes such as utilities, sewage-treatment plants, and commercial and residential spaceheating consumption are handled by INFORUM, RESGEN (see discussion of the environmental models, below), and ABATE in concert, in the same manner as the industrial sectors.

The fifth and final level of detail of the SEAS economic models is in the treatment of energy investment. Demands on the energy supply, unit capital costs, the forecasted construction period, and materials requirements are loaded into the model as inputs. These are then fed into an energy-investment model, which calculates the impact on the composition of GNP, output of selected sectors, indirect energy use for capital resources, and sectoral employment. These calculations are then fed back into INFORUM and are used to update the economic forecasts.

The Energy Models. There are three energy models in SEAS: electric utilities, industrial combustion, and an energy-supply-network simulator (ESNS).

The electric-utility model forecasts air-emissions and fuel-consumption levels for electric utilities operating after 1976 by fuel type, and regionalizes state electric-utility fuel mixes to the county level. It considers various fuel types and takes as inputs items such as total demand for electric power, fuel mix, capacity factors, retirement factors, and environmental considerations.

The industrial-combustion model has as its purpose the regionalization of industrial-fuel combustion and the calculation of regional air-pollution emissions. It takes as inputs future coal distribution, boiler size, various assumptions about the status of coal technology, and relevant environmental factors. Forecasts are made at the county level and normally aggregated to a higher level, such as air-quality-control region (AQCR).

Finally, the energy-system-network simulator (ESNS) is designed to determine the environmental/economic consequences of a specific energy policy. The candidate energy policy is translated into changes in the demand for energy and adjustments in various stages of the fuel cycle. It is divided into subprocesses relating to energy demands, intermediate activities, and energy-supply sectors. The network detail is determined by environmental issues, investment implications, and the calibration requirements fostered by mapping it onto other models (such as MEFS). The changes forecast by this model lead to adjustments in other models in SEAS: for example, in energy activities (both nationally and regionally), economic forecasts and pollution forecasts.

The Environmental Models. There are five environmental modules in SEAS: transportation, residuals generation (RESGEN), solid waste, land use, and environmental-quality indicators.

The transportation module forecasts demand for automobiles, buses, trucks, railroads, and aircraft in terms of miles traveled for both passenger and freight transportation purposes, using the DOT forecasted total of miles traveled. It estimates the annual volume of controlled emissions produced by mobile sources. It has the ability to vary emission standards by model year, average age of the auto fleet, modal splits for Standard Metropolitan Statistical Areas (SMSA), occupancy ratios, and the miles per gallon of various model years. It can also take into consideration the transportation-control plans of regions.

The residuals module estimates annual emissions of air and water pollutants and of solid wastes for the most significant polluting industries. It estimates first the potential environmental emissions before abatement, then the emissions actually reaching the environment; the latter depends on the degree of pollution abatement in each sector and its subprocesses. The released emissions include not only untreated primary pollutants, but also significant secondary pollutants produced by the pollution-treatment processes themselves (such as sludges).

The solid-waste-recycling module estimates the amounts of solid wastes from nonindustrial sources, the expected method of disposal, and the costs associated with each method. For incineration and open-burning disposal methods, it also estimates the annual levels of air-pollution emissions. Recycling levels are applied to the product classes that constitute significant elements of the solid-waste stream to calculate total amounts of materials available for recycling and the levels actually recycled.

The land-use module estimates amounts of land used in broad categories as a function of forecasts of economic activity. It also calculates nonpoint sources of water pollution. For nonpoint rural pollution sources such as agriculture, construction, forestry, mining, and drilling, it calculates soil loss, sedimentation, and pesticides/fertilizer loading. For urban runoff as well as naturally occurring pollution sources, it forecasts levels of air, water, and solid-waste-pollution emissions.

The final module, environmental-quality indicators, is designed to translate air emissions and water effluents into indicators of environmental quality to allow regional and temporal comparisons of air- and water-pollutant levels. For air pollution, for example, the indicators used are concentration ranges and ratios, emissions per square mile, emissons per cubic meter of ventilated flow, and population at risk for both total suspended particulates (TSP) and Sulfur-Oxide (SO_x).

The Regional-Disaggregation Model. To enrich the forecast of economic and environmental impacts, this model provides a forecast of distributions of industry outputs and the associated environmental emissions to a number of geographical subdivisions. The subdivisions include states, SMSA, river basins, air-quality-control areas, and basic economic areas (BEA). The OBERS projections developed by the Departments of Commerce and Agriculture are employed in this model (for a description of OBERS, see chapter 7).

The analyses performed outside the computer system are most important and are made up of two elements: (1) the analysis used to develop the experimental design of alternate scenarios to modify the specific input data for each scenario, and (2) the analysis of the computer outputs to show impacts of scenario changes, and, hence, insight into probable effects of specific national policies and regulations, including public and insitutional consequences.

The purpose of the regionalization model is to allocate the present and future industrial, commercial, and consumer activity to lower levels of aggregation. The model has four separate regionalization modules: (1) a permanent share file based on OBERS projections (OBERS is a forecast of county-level employment and economic activity issued jointly by the Departments of Agriculture and Commerce); (2) an ability to manually override these coefficients; (3) a dynamic forecasting capability; and (4) special regionalization programs for utilities, boilers, and coal mining.

The model has several special features that make it unique as a regionalization system. It reflects changing pollution-control technologies or standards over time. It also incorporates changing process technologies within sectors over time. In addition to allowing for differences in pollution per unit of output for the same sectors in different regional locations, it allows user override of all the above. Finally, it automatically identifies secondary residuals produced by the treatment of process streams.

Critique of SEAS from a National and Subnational Standpoint

SEAS is one of the most ambitious analytic modeling efforts ever undertaken.[13] As such, its design is constantly under review, and redesign efforts are continually under way. Given our emphasis on subnational levels of analysis, it is appropriate to describe in some detail the relatively naive state of the art in the current regionalization procedures used in SEAS, difficulties encountered in remedying the technical problems involved, and some approaches to improved regionalization concepts and procedures.

The term *regionalization* in SEAS has typically been used very broadly. It is used to denote forecasts of regional economic activity, including industrial output, energy supply and demand, regional population, and other variables. It is also used in reference to regional environmental forecasts of such widely differing variables as air-pollution emissions, land use, occupational safety, and water use. In the latter context, it is recognized that the same level of economic activity in two regions can lead to different environmental impacts because of differences in local pollution-control standards, climate, population density, equipment vintage, and other factors. Of the two broad contexts, however, it is the regional economic forecasts that are the principal focus of discussion in the sections immediately following.

The SEAS regional forecasts are based, we have seen, on a top-down approach. National forecasts of GNP, its composition, sectoral output, and other variables are made first; sectoral output (but not GNP) is then allocated to regions such as states, AQCRs, and Standard Metropolitan Statistical areas, using a mix of analytic techniques. Because the level of disaggregation in INFORUM is not detailed enough to distinguish among products and processes with significantly different residual coefficients (tons of pollutant per unit output), the forecasts from INFORUM are disaggregated into approximately 300 additional subsectors using functions of the following form:

$$\bar{X}_i = \sum_{J=1}^{185} \bar{A}_{ij} X_j + \sum_{k=1}^{m} \bar{C}_{ik} F_k$$

where $\bar{X}_i$ = the production of a given good (say, titanium dioxide) measured in quantities such as tons or Btus;

F_k = the kth component of final demand (such as consumption or imports); $k = 1, \ldots m$;

X_j = the constant dollar output of sector j $j = 1, \ldots 195$;

$\bar{A}_{ij}$ and $\bar{C}_{ik}$ = estimated parameters.[14]

$\bar{X}_i$ is, in several cases, further disaggregated into the amounts that are produced by alternative processes:

$$_l \bar{X}_i = {_l^\alpha} \bar{X}_i$$

Top-Down Analysis Methods

where
$_\ell \bar{X}_i$ = the amount of the good produced by process ℓ;

$_\ell^\alpha$ = a parameter estimated for the base year and user specified for forecast years.

The regional allocation of the values X_j, $\bar{X}_i$ and $_\ell \bar{X}_i$ in earlier phases of SEAS emphasized the development of a valid set of regional shares for the base year. In the process, the accuracy of forecast values was given less consideration than the base-year data. The procedures subsequently used to remedy the weaknesses have significantly improved the forecasts in some sectors (primarily energy sectors) but not in others. Several weaknesses remain in the overall forecasts, however, and design remedies are continually under reivew to reduce the consequences of these remaining weaknesses.

In the original regionalization procedure used in SEAS, the national value of X_j, X_i, and $_\ell \bar{X}_i$ for the base year were disaggregated using available data sources on county production of the good or proxies for these measures. In general, $\bar{X}_i$ and $_\ell \bar{X}_i$ were allocated to counties using information from trade directories, DOC, DOE, and other sources on base-year production. The principal errors, here, in the current running version of the model and by DOE, arise from the use of data from variable years (1971-1976) to apply to 1971 national values, the use of capacity measures where production data were unavailable, and the occasional use of proxy measures such as population to allocate national production of a good where no reliable regional series was available. These difficulties are currently being remedied.

A significant problem has been present in allocating the X_j's or constant-dollar outputs to regions. Census data on the value of shipments at a four-digit Standard Industrial Classification (SIC) level contains major disclosure problems at a detailed regional level. Consequently, a four-digit employment data was used to allocate national X_j's, thereby assuming that regional shares of output are roughly equal to regional shares of employment.[15]

Another weakness relates to the forecasting procedures. No general interregional econometric or multiregional model was available in the initial development stages of SEAS. Conventional wisdom regarding future regional activity was best exemplified by the Office of Business and Economic Research Services (OBERS) forecasts of the Department of Commerce, and this still is used extensively in SEAS.

The regional forecasts of X_j, $\bar{X}_i$, and $_\ell \bar{X}_i$ were obtained by deriving growth indexes from the relevant OBERS sectors and multiplying the base-year values by these indexes. All INFORUM sectors and INSIDE subsectors (that is, those which are more refined sectoral breakouts than exist in INFORUM) that were a subset of a given OBERS sector (there are thirty-seven

OBERS sectors) used the same growth rate or index in a given region. The resulting forecasts were scaled to meet national control totals. One feature of this scheme was that regional shares of national totals were, in this procedure, invariant across scenarios. The OBERS forecasts were, as the name implies, a forecast for a given scenario and not an analytic tool for making alternative forecasts.[16]

This feature (the so-called permanent-share file) was particularly unacceptable when SEAS entered a new development phase beginning with its use as the principal analytic tool for the Department of Energy's *Annual Environmental Analysis Report* (two of which have been released by the Department, first in 1979, then in 1980). The focus here was on analyzing the impact of various energy policies on environmental trends. To avoid the weaknesses inherent in the use of fixed shares, two new procedures were developed.

The first was simply an override option. Here, the user specifies the regional shares exogenously, based on analysis of specific technologies or processes. These shares are used to allocate the national production to various regions, particularly states. This method (called the manual-share file) has been used for several energy sectors and a few nonenergy sectors, thus providing a framework to avoid sole reliance on the OBERS forecasts. The three primary weaknesses of this approach are that: first, it is difficult, in practice, to generate a new set of shares for each scenario (many of these shares files have also been scenario-independent); second, although it is feasible to specify a share file for regions such as states, it would clearly have been a major effort to specify shares for all regions such as AQRCs and Aggregated Statistical Areas (ASAs), so that some flexibility was lost; and, third, shares are specified on a sector-by-sector basis (interindustry linkages at a regional level are not considered).

The second regionalization extension was the development of special modules for important sectors such as electric utilities, industrial boilers, and coal mining. The principle feature of these modules is the specification at a county level of the location of facilities likely to begin operation in the near-to-mid term (one to ten years), based on criteria such as environmental constraints, industry plans, and other factors. Because these facility sites are rank ordered along a time dimension, the shares can be scenario sensitive and because they were county based, they can be aggregated to any desired regional level.

Another feature of the new modules is a linkage of the modules' forecasts to those of other regional energy supply-and-demand modules, particularly the Department of Energy's MEFS (formerly PIES).[17] These other energy models are used to forecast energy supply/demand at the federal regional level, with SEAS providing the framework for the more detailed forecasts of energy activity at AQCR states and other regions. These activity forecasts, combined with residual coefficient data, yield residual trends.

Critique of SEAS from a Regional Standpoint

Several criticisms can be directed against the current system. These relate to the analytical approaches and the data bases.

One problem is related to sectoral aggregation: the regionalization of sectors at various levels in the hierarchy—INFORUM, INSIDE product levels, INSIDE process level, and energy sectors—is essentially done independently. The user specifying an override on the regional shares for a given INFORUM sector should be aware that the override does not affect the regional product-level forecasts (which are measured in tons). Or, an override imposed at the product level will not carry over automatically to the INSIDE process or INFORUM sector level. Likewise, making different assumptions about regional production regarding one part of the cycle—such as coal mining—does not affect any other part of the cycle, such as coal preparation. Consistency across sectors is essentially handled at the national level, not at a regional level.[18]

There are also, in the current regionalization procedure, a number of consistency problems related to the use of proxy variables. As explained above, different variables are used in the estimation of regional production. First, regional employment is used to allocate product for all INFORUM sectors in the base year. Because regional productivity can differ significantly, such a procedure would result in overestimates of residuals (for the base year) for regions with lower productivities than the national average. This is true for those residuals calculated at the INFORUM sector level. Second, the OBERS earnings forecasts are used to shift the base-year production, implying that changes in regional two-digit earnings are identical across all INFORUM sectors within a given two-digit sector. It also implies that shifts in output are proportional to shifts in earnings. The reasonableness of this assumption should be tested in historical data.

Still another problem, related to the one above and present also in the MEFS regionalization procedure, is the lack of a comprehensive picture of regional economic activity. Different measures of sectoral activity are not consistently related to one another. For example, regional-population shares are derived from the OBERS forecasts and, although they change over time, they remain constant across scenarios. Variations in regular energy production, for example, have not been related to population nor have the factors affecting migration been evaluated in the model. Similar comments apply with regard to regional employment. Interest in regional employment forecasts has been increasing, partly due to national trends in productivity growth, energy policies that result in excessively rapid growth in some regions, and known or suspected relations among environmental policies, industrial location, and jobs created or lost. Clearly, a methodology to analyze these tradeoffs is needed.

Another weakness lies in the linkage of energy demand, supply, and regional activity: as currently structured, the system cannot adequately estimate the regional economic impacts of changes in energy-supply activities. Consider, for example, a major synfuels program with locations of plants concentrated in the western regions. Such a program would result in direct, indirect, and induced economic effects with accompanying environmental consequences. The direct environmental effects are captured in a straightforward manner through multiplying the measure of energy output (such as Btus of coal mined or Btus of synfuels produced) by residual coefficients to derive direct environmental effects.

The only direct measure of economic activity here is Btus or energy output. Direct regional employment, in either the construction or operational phase, is not estimated. More important from the viewpoint of environmental effects, the regional system does not endogenously capture indirect economic effects such as additional employment in the industries materials supplying or any of the induced effects resulting from income generated, such as higher levels of consumption and accompanying employment. Supply-industry effects are captured in the national model, but because regional shares of INFORUM sectoral output are static across scenarios, the western regions would, in most representative runs of SEAS, not gain a reasonable share of the incremental production. This would lead to underestimates of residuals for the region in supply sectors as well as transportation emissions and others affected by aggregate regional economic activity.

On the demand side, both the electric-utilities and industrial-boilers modules have made a significant contribution to understanding the role of these sectors in aggregate emissions, as well as in helping assess the impacts of various policies such as variations in New Source Performance Standards (NSPS) standards on trends in regional emissions. One of the remaining weaknesses is the somewhat rigid relationship between regional forecasts of fuel use in utilities and boilers and regional industrial output. Shifts in aggregate manufacturing activity from the OBERS forecasts have been used as one independent variable affecting growth in electricity supply and boiler activity. There are two problems here. First, rates of growth or decline within manufacturing sectors have not been considered. Second, with regard to utilities, such a procedure fails to recognize possible trends toward mine-mouth generation that would result in a divergence over time between the location of electricity supply and demand. Moreover, there is the continuing problem that OBERS shift factors are invariant across scenarios. And, if the user chooses to impose manually a different scenario regarding location of key industries, under the current system this element would not be input to the utilities and boiler modules, producing inconsistent process residuals and energy-related residuals estimates from the same sector.

One final weakness regarding the way OBERS is used in the SEAS regionalization needs noting. The state level growth rates are derived from a special OBERS run completed in 1978 for EPA. However, growth rates for other regions are derived from the earlier OBERS study published jointly by the Bureau of Economic Analyzer (BEA) and the Water Resources Council. The two sets of forecasts differ at both the national and regional levels, resulting in forecasts at the SEAS sector level that are not consistent across various regional groupings. For example, the forecast for the pulp-mills sector in the Northeast would differ if derived by summing across states from results of summing across BEA areas. Finally, OBERS forecasts were not made for AQCRs. Here, a crude procedure was used to derive growth indexes for an AQRC based on OBERS forecasts for SMSAs and on SMSA parts of BEA areas. The error here is significantly less than one would expect, because AQRCs are primarily used for air-pollution analysis and the most important sectors here are utilities, boilers, and transportation, for all of which special modules exist with regional controls given from sources other than SEAS.

In the current use of SEAS, none of these regionalization weaknesses is fatal primarily becuase there are a number of existing remedies involving a series of validation tests, simple improvements, and system overrides used as needed. Furthermore, the regionalization estimates are never made independently (that is, outside the system), but, instead, are always estimated together with other means of obtaining the subnational estimates. Research and development of SEAS regionalization procedures is promising; however, much remains to be done before completely satisfactory, valid, and policy-useful estimates are obtainable using SEAS regionalization as the primary subnational-impact estimating technique. Unlike BLS, where no regionalization attempt is made, or MEFS, where regionalization is estimated only to serve a top-down purpose, there is great need for such valid procedures in SEAS. Users of SEAS are interested in the subnational environmental (and related energy and economic) effects of national policies and scenarios (see chapter 8). For valid regional results using SEAS, much research remains to be done. Both SEAS and MEFS, though presenting reasonably accurate pictures of some parts of the regional energy/environment picture, cannot be used alone as tools for regional analysis; they are highly mechanistic, rely partially on outdated data, and are dependent on several artificial conventions for showing the regionalization. The ability to gauge the subjective factors that impinge on regional circumstances is, of course, critical, and cannot be supplied by a model.

**Top-Down Approaches to Developing Energy and
Environmental Policy: Illustrative Applications**

Having described SEAS and MEFS, which could be and have been used to forecast regional impacts of energy policy and environmental impacts, it remains to demonstrate how these are employed in realistic policy-analysis situations.[19] We shall provide examples from two sources, focusing on the environmental consequences and, when available, subnational estimates.

The first is the development of the National Energy Plan, required by Congress of the Department of Energy every two years, and the second is the annual report to Congress of DOE's Energy Information Administration (EIA). From a technical perspective, environmental assessment is carried out similarly for both analyses. In general, the energy and economic forecasts used in these two analyses are accepted as givens and are used to calibrate the economic- and energy-forecasting portions of the SEAS model. Once the SEAS submodels are constrained so that the forecasts they produce duplicate those of the official DOE forecasts of energy and economic futures, the model is considered calibrated and thus ready to be used to forecast conditionally the environmental impact of these futures. In fact the feedback to DOE from the national labs concerning the reality of the control totals for energy supply and demand is used to update the next year's forecast.

Energy Information Administration (EIA) Forecasts

Let us first turn to the EIA forecasts of energy supply and demand for its annual report to Congress.[20] In April of 1978, the EIA sent to the Congress a set of six scenarios, which varied based on the assumptions made as to the amount of oil and gas recoverable, the expected economic growth rate, and the world price of oil. Energy policies anticipated at that time were assumed constant. The six cases were a combination of three levels of economic growth taken from econometric forecasts made using the DRI model (see page 80, above). Forecasts were estimated to the year 1990 and were based on assumptions of low, medium, and high growth rates in GNP (ranging from 4.3 to 2.5 percent annually). The energy-supply scenario was similarly designed to range from low to high, differing also by special fuel type. The five base scenarios were derived by taking the corners of the 3 × 3 matrix produced by the economic and energy assumptions of low to high (four cases) and taking the single medium economic and medium energy scenario to represent the rest of the potential six medium related cases. A final excursion was made using this medium-medium case by changing the world oil price to give the reader a feel for the sensitivity of MEFS to the variable of price (table 6-1). The environmental impacts of the energy scenarios were primarily based on the so-called business-as-usual or mid-mid scenario (Projection Series C), described in more detail in the next section.

Mid-Mid Scenario Description. The basic assumptions of the business-as-usual scenario (Projection Series C) are medium economic growth, medium

Table 6-1
Projection Series C Energy-Supply Projections

	1975		1985		1990	
	Quads	Percentage of Total Supply	Quads	Percentage of Total Supply	Quads	Percentage of Total Supply
Domestic production						
Crude oil	17.9	24	19.0	20	18.0	16
Natural-gas liquids and butane	2.6	4	2.0	2	1.8	2
Shale oil	0	0	0.1	*	0.3	*
Natural gas	19.0	26	17.2	18	16.7	15
Coal	14.6	20	23.1	24	27.5	25
Nuclear	1.8	3	6.2	6	10.3	9
Hydro and Geothermal	3.2	4	4.2	4	5.0	4
Total domestic production	59.1	81	71.8	74	79.6	71
Imports						
Crude oil	8.7	12	16.5	18	20.9	19
Petroleum products	3.8	5	6.7	7	7.8	7
Natural gas	1.0	2	1.9	1	2.6	3
Total imports	13.5	19	25.1	26	31.3	29
Total supply	72.6	100	96.9	100	110.9	100

Source: Energy Information Administration, *Administrator's Annual Report to Congress* (Washington, D.C., 1977).
Note: One quad equals one quadrillion (10^{15}) Btus.
*$p < 0.01$.

energy demand, medium energy-supply expansion, and constant world oil prices.[21] In several, energy-demand assumptions are related to the general level of economic activity and other factors. Energy-supply assumptions relate to the availability of basic resources and to the costs of finding, producing, converting, and delivering energy to its end use.

Future domestic oil and gas prices are the forcing variables in the EIA Project Series scenarios. The costs of production and distribution for all energy sources except oil and gas were held constant and are based on the medium estimate from the U.S. Geological Survey (USGS) of oil and gas resource availability used in Project Series C.[22]

Changes in oil and gas costs, however, are induced through assumptions regarding their physical availability. The Projection Series C case assumes a real price of imported oil of $15.32 per barrel in 1978 dollars and no change in the qualitative nature of energy-producing and -consuming technologies between 1985 and 1990. However, considerable variability is assumed in the quantitative mix of technologies used to satisfy forecasts of energy supply and demand, including such factors as the degree of energy conservation in general and of oil and gas in particular.

For the mid-term, the Projection Series C scenario includes several other important assumptions, such as:

Domestic oil production will increase slightly over current levels due to the development of Alaskan oil fields and Outer Continental Shelf.

Lower-48 production of natural gas will continue to decline, although less rapidly, after Alaskan North Slope gas-distribution systems are completed. This suggests that fuel shares in the industrial economic sector will shift from gas to oil and, to a lesser extent, to electricity, reflecting these declining gas supplies.

Coal production, particularly in the West, will increase dramatically, reflecting increased demand brought about by higher prices of oil and gas, particularly for electricity generation.

Electricity sales will grow at 4.8 percent per year, rather than the historic 7 percent, reflecting saturation of electric-home-appliances market.

Based on these assumptions, the Projection Series C scenario projects the following trends in macroeconomic and energy consumption.

Regional Analysis. As we discussed earlier several submodels of the MEFS are used to forecast energy supply and demand by region. We shall focus here on the cases of coal and electricity, to illustrate how regions are taken into account in the EIA analysis.

Table 6-2
Trends in Macroeconomic and Energy Consumption, 1975-1990

	1975	*1985*	*1990*
GNP (billions of 1972 dollars)	$1,202	$1,803	$2,107
Energy consumption (quadrillion Btus)	70.6	94.6	108.5

Source: Energy Information Administration, *Administrator's Annual Report to Congress, 1977* (Washington, D.C.: U.S. Department of Energy, 1978).

In this system, coal is projected for twelve regions of the country: Northern Appalachia, Central Appalachia, Southern Appalachia, Midwest, Central West, Gulf, Eastern Northern Great Plains, Western Northern Great Plains, Rockies, Southwest, Northwest, and Alaska. (See figure 6-10). Using the various scenarios of the EIA, table 6-3 shows the growth forecasted in millions of tons per year from 1976 to 1990. Areas such as the Gulf and Great Plains show four-to-fivefold increases, whereas Southern Appalachia shows a decrease, and Alaska and the Central West are depicted as relatively stable in coal output.

Table 6-4 lists the regional estimates of the pattern of electricity consumption and the associated growth rates for each of the ten federal regions. The national trend away from residential consumption is apparent in all but three regions: the South Atlantic (IV), North Central (V), and Northwest (X). Increased consumption in the industrial sector is evident in every region. Another result: except for New England (I) and the West (XI), the growth rates in electricity consumption are forecast to decline over time.

Major Environmental Trends. Following production of the official energy and economic forecasts, the SEAS model is calibrated as described above and is used to produce estimates of associated environmental impacts. The picture of the future (as of 1980) that emerges from this analysis is, as anticipated, mixed. Significant national reductions are forecast by 1990 in the emissions of particulates, hydrocarbons, carbon monoxide, and major point-source water pollutants such as biochemical-oxygen demand, suspended solids, total phosphorus, and numerous metals. However, little or no improvement is shown for sulfur-oxide emissions and point-source nitrogen releases to water. Large increases are anticipated for nitrogen-oxide releases to air, dissolved solids released to water, ash and sludge generation, and water consumption.

Largely because of the stricter standards for new sources, increased coal combustion is not anticipated to cause significant changes in total national sulfur-oxide emissions by 1990. In fact, the heavily industrialized

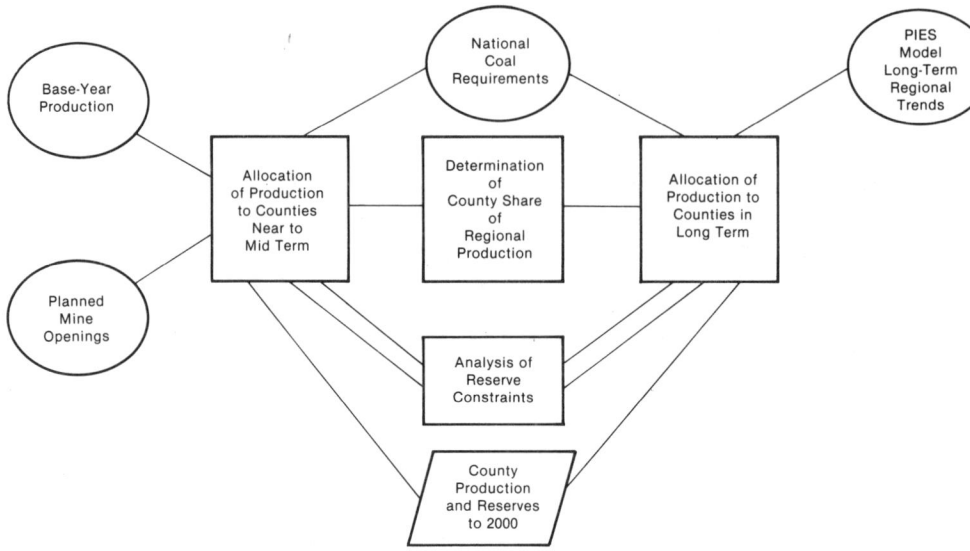

Figure 6–10. Regionalization of Coal Mining

areas in the northeastern quadrant of the country[23] which produced the largest sulfur-oxide emissions in 1975, are expected to show significant reductions in emissions by 1990; however, much of the rest of the nation is anticipated to experience some increase in sulfur-oxide emissions, for the base there is presently low.

Increased coal combustion is expected to contribute to increased release of nitrogen oxides, because no control technology is really effective at present, and to be responsible for significant increases in sludge and ash generation, much of which is a by-product of other control technologies. The remainder of the coal fuel cycle is not expected to produce significant national environmental effects; however, regional impacts may result where particular activities are concentrated.

Continually increasing generation of electricity is expected to contribute significantly to increased releases to water of total dissolved solids and several specific metals. Further, nuclear- and coal-powered electricity generation and other manufacturing industries will contribute substantially to increased water consumption by 1990. Development of both energy and manufacturing activity may be seriously limited by existing or anticipated

Table 6–3
1985 Coal Production and Consumption under Various Cases
(millions of tons per year)

		1986 Projection Series					
	1976[a]	C Medium Demand, Medium Supply	A High Demand High Supply	B High Demand Low Supply	D Low Demand High Supply	E Low Demand Low Supply	F Medium Demand, Medium Supply High Oil Price
Coal Production							
Northern Appalachia	176.8	164.9	164.9	169.5	161.7	163.9	164.9
Central Appalachia	207.7	271.4	269.7	277.3	260.9	270.0	277.3
Southern Appalachia	21.7	21.1	21.1	21.1	21.1	21.1	21.1
Midwest	136.4	221.1	218.0	228.3	211.7	222.1	221.8
Central West	11.4	11.0	11.1	11.2	10.9	11.0	11.1
Gulf	14.1	51.9	51.9	51.9	48.0	48.0	51.9
Eastern Northern Great Plains	11.4	31.8	36.9	31.8	33.7	30.3	31.8
Western Northern Great Plains	57.1	184.4	183.9	196.6	169.4	175.0	201.7
Rockies	17.1	24.2	23.9	24.2	22.9	23.8	24.2
Southwest	20.2	45.7	47.6	47.1	47.1	46.1	45.7
Northwest	4.1	5.7	5.7	5.7	5.7	5.7	5.7
Alaska	0.7	0.8	0.8	0.8	0.8	0.8	0.8
Total[b]	678.7	1,034.0	1,035.4	1,065.4	993.9	1,017.9	1,057.8

Table 6-3 continued

	1976[a]	1986 Projection Series					
		C Medium Demand, Medium Supply	A High Demand High Supply	B High Demand Low Supply	D Low Demand High Supply	E Low Demand Low Supply	F Medium Demand, Medium Supply High Oil Price
Coal Consumption							
Electrical Generation	448.5	745.5	750.2	755.7	720.9	724.9	771.0
Metallurgical	84.7	96.8	98.9	98.9	95.9	95.9	95.8
Industrial[c]	56.5	106.0	89.9	124.1	80.7	110.4	104.4
Synthetics	—	13.7	23.5	13.7	23.5	13.7	13.7
Exports	59.4	74.0	74.0	74.0	74.0	74.0	74.0
Domestic Consumption	589.7	961.0	962.4	992.4	920.9	944.9	984.8
Total[b]	649.1	1,034.7	1,036.9	1,066.4	995.9	1,018.9	1,058.9

[a] 1976 data are derived from the Federal Power Commission, *Form 4, Monthly Powerplant Report for Utilities* (Washington: v.d.) and the Bureau of Mines *Coal Distribution Report 1419* (Washington: n.d.), for other domestic sectors. They differ from historical data presented with the mid-term forecasts for this chapter and in the Energy Information Administration *Annual Report*. vol. 3 (Washington, D.C.: Government Printing Office, 1980) which use the BOM Fuel Consumption Report for the industrial sector. The Consumption Report is under revision.
[b] Totals may not equal columnar totals due to rounding.
[c] Includes general industry, residential and commercial.

Table 6-4
Projected Consumption of Electricity by Region and Sector

Region	Sector	Billion kWh			Growth Rates	
		1976	1985	1990	1976-1985	1985-1990
I	Residential	28	27	29	-0.40	1.44
	Commercial	23	30	35	3.00	3.13
	Industrial	20	31	36	4.99	3.04
II	Residential	46	60	63	3.00	0.98
	Commercial	52	72	82	3.68	2.64
	Industrial	45	72	88	5.36	4.10
III	Residential	63	76	84	2.11	2.02
	Commercial	50	69	82	3.64	3.51
	Industrial	79	134	168	6.05	4.63
IV	Residential	143	245	343	6.16	6.96
	Commercial	84	130	160	4.97	4.24
	Industrial	167	302	390	6.80	5.25
V	Residential	116	137	149	1.87	1.69
	Commercial	91	121	142	3.22	3.25
	Industrial	173	284	358	5.66	4.74
VI	Residential	73	99	110	3.44	2.43
	Commercial	63	88	101	3.78	2.79
	Industrial	93	164	204	6.51	4.46
VII	Residential	34	44	49	2.91	2.18
	Commercial	26	34	39	3.03	2.25
	Industrial	28	55	71	7.79	5.24
VIII	Residential	15	32	38	8.78	3.50
	Commercial	17	35	41	8.35	3.22
	Industrial	15	32	37	8.78	2.95
IX	Residential	57	56	63	0.20	2.38
	Commercial	71	78	86	1.05	1.97
	Industrial	57	70	81	2.31	2.96
X	Residential	40	64	84	5.36	5.59
	Commercial	25	38	47	4.76	4.34
	Industrial	48	81	89	5.99	1.90

water shortages in several regions of the country, especially the West and the mountain states.

This brief summary of some of the overall findings of the national environmental analysis emphasizes the energy-related environmental effects resulting from the mid-mid scenario assumptions concerning the forecasted national-energy supply and demand from EIA. The following sections identify and analyze projected trends in environmental releases of specific pollutants from 1975 to 1990. Trends in overall releases, specific industrial and energy contributions, and significant regional and local impacts are selectively examined for each pollutant. These trends are analyzed in the context of existing regulations, scenario assumptions, and identified environmental issues.

Air Pollution. Assuming compliance with applicable emission regulations, total national emissions of particulates are forecast to decline from 1975 to 1990, while emissions of sulfur oxides (SOx) remain unchanged. These trends are shown in figure 6-11. Highlights are discussed below.

Sulfur oxides. The national level of sulfur-oxide emissions is projected to remain relatively constant between 1975 and 1990. This national picture is a composite of varying trends among different federal regions. Emissions are forecast to decline from 1975 to 1990 in region 8 (West) and in those regions where emissions were highest in 1975, region 3 (Middle Atlantic) and region 5 (Great Lakes). This includes significant decreases in parts of the Ohio River basin. All other regions are expected to show increased sulfur-oxide emissions over the study period with the greatest relative (but not absolute) increase (fourfold) projected to occur in states within federal region 6 (South Central).

The projected regional increases in sulfur-oxide emissions are generally due to increased coal combustion, primarily as already noted, in existing rather than new facilities, except in region 6 (South Central), where coal combustion replaces extensive use of natural gas. The decline in emissions in the major polluting regions resulting primarily from an assumption of enforcement of relatively strict standards for existing sources together with even more stringent control for new sources.

Particulates. National particulate emissions are projected to decrease by one-third between 1975 and 1990. This trend is found in all federal regions except the New England and South Central regions, where very small increases occur due to stringent controls mandated for facilities existing prior to 1975.

Water Pollution—Point-Source. Assuming full industrial compliance with Best Practicable Control Technology (BPCT) standards in 1979 and Best Available Technology (BAT) standards in 1985, point-source discharges of several major water pollutants—biochemical-oxygen demand (BOD) and total suspended solids (TSS)—are expected to decline from 1975 to 1990, whereas discharges of total dissolved solids (TDS) are expected to increase (figure 6-12). Except for some dissolved solids, energy technologies are not responsible for significant releases of water pollutants over the forecast period. Discharges of total dissolved solids from point-sources are expected

Top-Down Analysis Methods

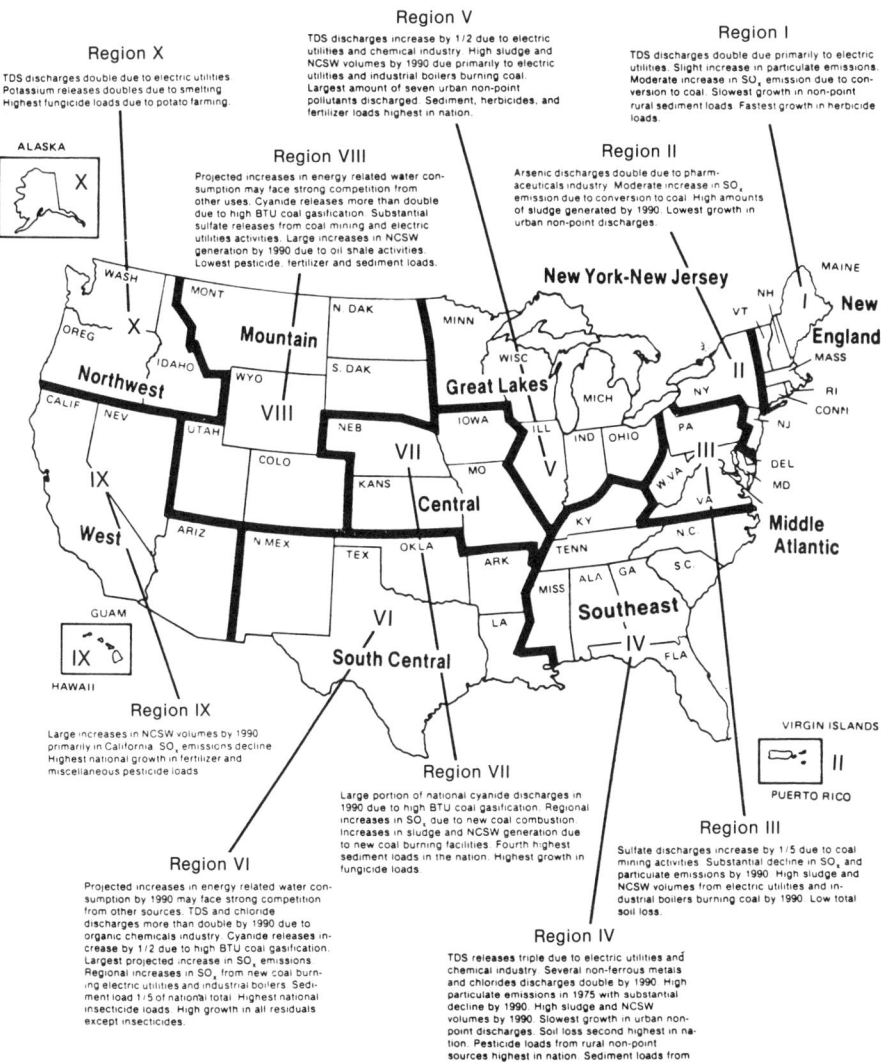

Figure 6-11. Major Regional Trends Associated with Energy Development

to double between 1975 and 1990. The major source of TDS is the organic-chemicals industry, which accounts for more than half of these discharged by 1990. Energy technologies (primarily boiler blowdown from electric utilities) are another significant source of total dissolved solids, accounting for approximately one-third of total releases throughout the forecast period. Three-fourths of the nation's discharges of TDS in 1990 are projected to be released in the Southeast, Great Lakes, and South Central regions.

Water Consumption. Total water consumption by energy and manufacturing industries is expected to more than double the 1975 levels by 1990 (figure 6-13). Energy and manufacturing, however, will account for only 5 percent of total annual water consumption. Throughout the forecast period electric utilities are expected to consume as much water as all other energy and manufacturing sectors combined. However, the utility mix is projected to change between 1975 and 1990, with a large increase expected in the nuclear-utility sector and a significant decrease in the oil and gas electric sectors. By 1990, other energy-related activity is expected to be responsible for 5 percent of total water consumption, most of which will be for coal gasification. Among the manufacturing industries, the largest water consumers are the iron and steel, pulp and paper, and food-processing industries.

Throughout the forecast period, water consumption for energy and manufacturing sectors is concentrated in the major industrial regions—Middle Atlantic, Southeast, and Great Lakes—and in the South Central region. Parts of this region are currently susceptible to drought and water shortages. Because the already-large consumption levels by the energy and manufacturing sectors in this region are projected to triple by 1990, this anticipated new consumption is likely to face competition from alternative water uses.

Solid Waste. Increased coal use in electric utilities and industrial boilers, coupled with more-intensive use of scrubbing systems to meet Clean Air Act requirements, is expected to lead to substantial increases in both scrubber-sludge and ash volumes generated by the utility and industrial sectors between 1975 and 1990 (figure 6-14). Sludge generated is expected to increase sixfold during this period, while ash production is expected to triple. By 1990, electric utilities and industrial boilers together may account for two-thirds of scrubber sludge and two-fifths of noncombustible solid-waste production. The Middle Atlantic, Southeast, and Great Lakes regions are projected to generate significant amounts of both sludge and ash in 1990.

The National Energy Plan—National Perspective

In contrast with the EIA scenario, which represents forecasts that are purportedly unaffected by the DOE energy policy plan, produced every other year, is meant to encompass all relevant energy and associated environmental policies of the agency for the upcoming budget periods.[24]

Top-Down Analysis Methods

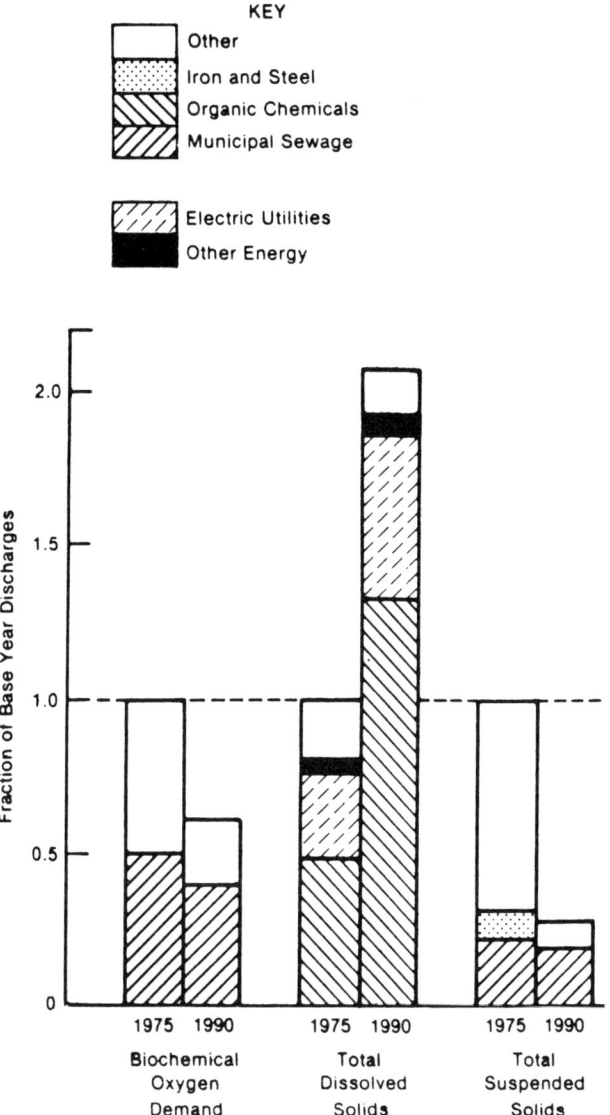

Figure 6-12. Trends in Point-Source Discharges of Major Water Pollutants, 1975-1990

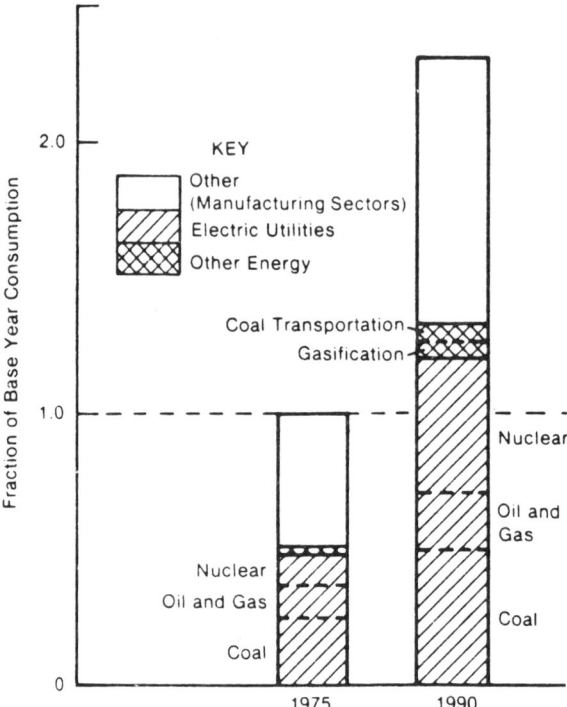

Figure 6-13. Trends in Water Consumption, by Energy and Manufacturing Sectors, 1975-1990

The *Second National Energy Plan* (NEP II) presented a set of actions designed both to reduce demand for energy in the United States through conservation and to increase domestic energy production, thereby reducing the nation's dependence on foreign oil supplies. The plan was meant to alter the mix of fuels used in the United States over the next twenty years or so away from oil and gas toward coal and nuclear power. Table 6-15 presents the projected mix of energy sources in 2000 under two sets of assumptions concerning worldwide energy supply/demand relationships and a likely range of prices of imported oil.

Domestic production of energy is expected to increase from 60 quads in 1975 to about 97 quads under the low-oil-price scenario, an increase of about 60 percent, and to about 113 quads under the high-oil-price scenario, or about 90 percent of the 1975 production level.

The largest energy-supply increases are generally expected in coal and nuclear energy. The production from coal would more than double under

Top-Down Analysis Methods 125

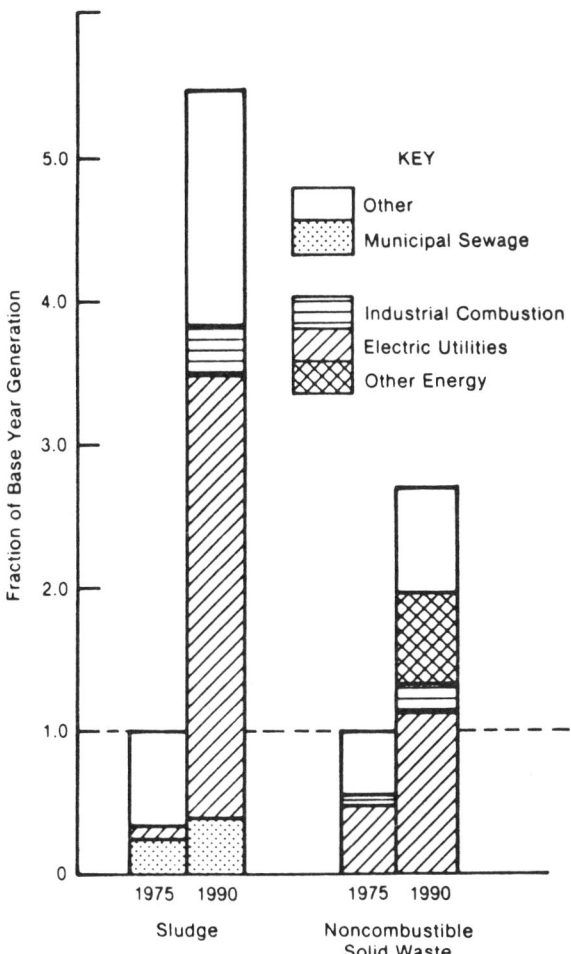

Figure 6-14. Trends in Solid-Waste Generation, 1975-1990

the low-price scenario and almost triple under the high-price scenario. Nuclear energy was expected to increase roughly eight to nine times by 2000.

Under the low-price scenario, energy imports would nearly triple from 1975-2000. At higher oil prices, however, imports would decline by about 30 percent. Because of price-induced conservation, total U.S. demands for energy in 2000 are anticipated to be lower by about 5 percent in the high-oil-price scenario than under the low-price scenario.

Table 6-5
Energy Supply, by Source, Present and Projected
(quads)

	1975 World Oil Price ($11.60/bbl)	2000 Low World Oil Price ($21.00/bbl)[a]	2000 High World Oil Price ($30.00/bbl)[a]
Domestic			
Synthetics,[b]	(0)	(2.3)	(5.6)
Fossil Fuels			
Coal	14.9	35.4	43.9
Oil	17.7	19.0	23.4
Conventional[b]	(17.7)	(17.2)	(20.8)
Shale[b]	(0)	(1.8)	(2.6)
Gas	22.2	18.1	18.6
Total Fossil Fuels	54.9	72.5	85.9
Nuclear	1.8	14.9	16.5
Hydro, Solar, and Geothermal	3.1	9.8	10.1
Total Domestic	59.7	97.2	112.5
Imported			
Crude Oil	8.7	20.8	5.4
Refined Oil Products	3.8	7.7	2.3
Natural Gas	0.7	0.8	0.1
LNG	0.1	0.8	1.6
Total Imported	13.2	30.1	9.4
Coal Exported	−1.8	−2.4	−2.4
Grand Total	71.1	124.9	119.5

Note: One quad equals one quadrillion (10^{15}) Btus.
  These values differ slightly from those in the plan due to rounding and slight changes made in the final version of the plan. These differences do not change the overall finding of this report.
[a] 1979 dollars.
[b] Not included in total.

Given the energy future projection, the environmental analysis was carried out, as in the earlier NEPI, on the basis of initial exogenous inputs, estimates of the forecast economic and regional impacts of the plan, although many of the latter were not part of the published results. Following are selected summary environmental impacts that were estimated given the forecasts mentioned above.[25]

Air-Emission Trends. The emissions of air pollutants related to energy processes, because of improved controls and stricter emission standards for all sources, for hydrocarbons, carbon monoxide, and particulates are generally projected to remain at 1975 levels or to decrease between 1975 and 2000 under both scenarios. Sulfur-oxide levels in 2000 are anticipated to remain at the 1975 level under the low-world-oil-price scenario and decrease slightly under high world-oil-prices. Nitrogen-oxide emissions are expected to increase by one-third in both the low- and high-price cases over the twenty-five-year period.

Each pollutant and each region was subjected to more-detailed analyses. Rather than summarize all pollution forecasts, we attempt to provide a capsule summary of air emissions and focus on total suspended particulates (TSP) as an example of the information available.

Projections of particulate emissions at the federal-region level (table 6-6) show a decrease between 1975 and 2000 in the Middle Atlantic, Southeast, and Great Lakes regions, where emissions were highest in 1975. This decline is due to the assumed compliance of existing energy facilities and industrial sources with emissions standards. Decreases are also seen in the New York-New Jersey and Central regions for similar reasons. The regions that exhibit increases in particulate emissions by 2000 are those with fairly low emissions in 1975 that experience relative increases as a consequence of increased industrial activity or coal use.

The regional trends indicate that air-quality improvement would occur in areas such as the Great Lakes region that are highly industrialized and, as of 1975, emitted large quantities of particulates. The projected emissions in terms of total tonnage (whether increasing or decreasing by the year 2000) do not appear alarming at the federal-region level but may present localized problems in some areas of the regions.

Similar assessments were carried out by pollutant for water, solid-waste, and nuclear-emissions streams. We shall briefly summarize some of the other environmental impacts found by the analyses, highlighting those due to energy activities.

Water-Consumption and -Pollution Trends. Water consumption by the nation's energy industry is expected to increase almost fourfold from 1975 to 2000. This increase is caused primarily by both growth in steam-electric generation by coal and nuclear-fuels facilities and by more-stringent water-pollution-control regulations, which encourage the use of cooling towers that consume larger quantities of water than currently popular once-through cooling systems.

National efforts to improve water quality during the last decade promise some continued success. In general, pollutant loadings are being reduced, but of those that remain, energy use would be responsible for the major share of point-source releases of total dissolved solids, sulfates, and other pollutants. Releases from coal-mining and -processing operations and

Table 6-6
Present and Projected Annual Particulate Emissions, by Federal Region
(millions of tons)

Region	Base Year (1975)	2000 Low World Oil Price	2000 High World Oil Price
New England			
Energy	0.05	0.31	0.36
Nonenergy	.15	.18	.17
Total	.21	.50	.53
New York, New Jersey			
Energy	.15	.24	.25
Nonenergy	.40	.29	.29
Total	.55	.52	.53
Mid Atlantic			
Energy	1.26	.55	.63
Nonenergy	1.22	.69	.64
Total	2.48	1.23	1.28
Southeastern			
Energy	1.39	.54	.62
Nonenergy	1.60	1.91	1.86
Total	2.99	2.45	2.48
Great Lakes			
Energy	1.87	1.18	1.31
Nonenergy	1.82	1.23	1.20
Total	3.70	2.41	2.52
South Central			
Energy	.22	.41	.40
Nonenergy	.94	1.37	1.37
Total	1.16	1.78	1.77
Central			
Energy	.20	.17	.18
Nonenergy	.56	.45	.44
Total	.76	.62	.62
Mountain			
Energy	.27	.50	.61
Nonenergy	.18	.21	.20
Total	.45	.71	.81
West			
Energy	.08	.14	.18
Nonenergy	.51	.57	.53
Total	.60	.71	.71
Northwest			
Energy	.07	.23	.26
Nonenergy	.28	.34	.33
Total	.35	.56	.58

Top-Down Analysis Methods

electric utilities would be the main source of TDS (which alone is expected to increase) and are projected to contribute about three-fourths of the nation's sulfate effluents by 2000.

On the other hand, energy industries would be responsible for a minor share of the other water pollutants analyzed (biochemical-oxygen demand, total suspended solids, nutrients, and chlorides). Total suspended solids from energy sources are projected to decrease slightly over the period, while nutrients and BOD from energy sources are projected to remain at their 1975 levels.

Solid-Waste Trends. Solid wastes, currently produced at a level of 487 million tons per year, include industrial solid wastes and sludges, municipal refuse, and municipal wastewater-treatment sludges. Noncombustible solids remaining after conversion of solid fuels, and sludges from pollution-control devices and from wastewater treatment currently represent about 17 percent of all these wastes. That portion resulting from fuel use is expected almost to triple during this time as a result of electric-utility and industrial use of coal, combined with new pollution regulations that require greater scrubbing. Another area of projected solid waste of interest to the Department of Energy is that remaining after oil-shale retorting. This emerging fuel source is expected to result in 372 to 537 million tons of noncombustible wastes annually by 2000 for the low and high world prices, respectively.

This discussion of environmental trends emphasizes expected changes at the national level. Regional variations will occur depending on local energy supply-and-demand patterns. Figure 6-15 summarizes the major regional environmental trends anticipated under both world-oil-price cases. These environmental issues are similar to those found in the EIA mid-mid scenario, discussed earlier.

Summary and Conclusions

It is unfeasible to assess—positively or otherwise—the validity, reliability, and overall utility of the national and subnational environmental-quality (and associated other variables) conditional forecasts resulting from the top-down modeling efforts described in this chapter. It will be several years before real events catch up with the projected years, permitting at least minimal verification. Real-world ground-truths are never adequate checks for conditional forecasts, because many of the basic assumptions underlying forecasts may not have materialized, thereby denying the basic requirements for any total verification. Thus, validation of forecasts outside the national and physical sciences is a chancy, if not quixotic, enterprise. Nevertheless, several observations can be made about top-down modeling, based on the discussion in this chapter and the preceding ones.

Figure 6-15. Major Regional Environmental Trends Associated with Two World-Oil-Price Scenarios

First, for some purposes, convincing, realistic, detailed, and sensible conditional forecasts of important policy-relevant variables *can* be produced, using top-down models, to the levels of major subnational regions. Although there may be disputes over individual pollution media and geographic areas, much about the forecasts appears to be valid.

Second, and counter to the first, is the fact (as just stated) that adequate ground-truth testing and validation of these regional forecasts have not yet been made, although a first step in this direction was taken using the research-and-development exercises discussed above. These exercises took the energy forecasts of the EIA as given and presented them to regional analysts for environmental-impact assessments. During this procedure several problems surfaced with the regional energy forecasts. For example, the assumption that each region's energy demand is met by supplies from that same region caused artificial capacities (and generated more pollution) in some regions and less in others than actual. Further, existing and reported data sets were found wanting. These and several other details were fed back to the EIA and used to update subsequent forecasts. But a concerted follow-up effort still waits to be done.

Third, top-down models are not designed to produce detailed, verifiable media-area results. In fact, in several of the top-down models—the BLS model being one of the more extreme illustrations—there is little or no subnational-level design present in the model system. Nearest to the BLS in terms of regional-analysis capability is the MEFS: here, we have seen, the subnational areas are used more to develop realistic interareal flows and improve national forecasts than to generate realistic and valid depiction of the regional area. Even the regionally-sensitive SEAS modeling process develops its regional estimates solely from the top down, thereby negating any influences at local levels that might alter these strictly macro-oriented estimates.

Fourth, and possibly most important, is the obvious fact that none of these top-down models comes very close to meeting the criteria set out in chapter 5, above; none fulfills the three key desiderata posed there. Proper treatment of intra-areal detail and structure, interareal flows and trade, and subnational-scale economies are the absolutely *minimum* technical characteristics for modeling systems whose objectives are to treat adequately the subnational consequences of national-policy choices. The presence of these three fundamental criteria and their correct technical use are minimum conditions for the proper incorporation and representation of subnational trends and structure in national-policy analysis. As for the additional characteristics described in chapter 5, none can be considered vital in the same way. The top-down models discussed in this chapter do have a number of these characteristics, however (such as modularity and prevention of chamber-of-commerce effects).

We do not know, and cannot say with any certainty, what such shortcomings mean in terms of model validity and utility. Certainly none of the top-down models can be used to study detailed subnational consequences (such as counties, county groupings, and development districts crossing state lines) with any degree of confidence. Nor do any of these systems properly treat subnational trends such as the Sunbelt-Frostbelt phenomenon discussed earlier. Most of the systems ensure that subnational forecasts cannot exceed the national totals in top-down models. However, if interarea scale economies, or subnationally underemployed resources, or some set of system dynamics not observable at the national levels are present—as we feel they are in significant degree—the top-down modeling will completely miss these. Finally, as we have already discussed, the seeming reasonableness of forecasts at the national level may be less so if they are disaggregated to regional areas. Energy supplies that are highly region-specific as to source would tend to be most susceptible to perception errors of this type (including oil shale, hydro power, and geothermal power). Other features of data that look reasonable at the macro scale but prove specious when detailed can be found in such activities as institutional constraints (legal or economic—utilities do not plan to build forecasted plant capacity) or indirect consequences of environmental regulations (pollution levels or regulations do not permit growth to forecast).

The bottom-up modeling approaches described in the next chapter are much more likely to begin to treat these phenomena more accurately and with greater validity—but with some obvious concomitant disadvantages.

Notes

1. These are the extreme types 2 and 3 or situations 3 and 4 as discussed in chapter 2.

2. James E. Krier and Edward Ursin, *Pollution and Policy—A Case Essay on California and Federal Experience with Motor Vehicle Air Pollution: 1940-1975* (Berkeley: University of California Press, 1977).

3. Bruce Geoller et al., *San Diego Clean Air Project: Executive Summary* (Santa Monica, Calif.: RAND Corporation, 1973).

4. National Commission on Air Quality, "Draft Plan of Study," *Federal Register,* 9 May 1979, p. 27271. In general, the commission's approach could be deemed more bottom up than top down: several regions (including the Four Corners and the Ohio River basin), more or less independently of one another and of the nation, are being separately analyzed from the standpoint of Clean Air Act impacts and alternatives.

5. CONSAD Research Corporation, *Joint DOE/DOL Project to Improve Employment/Energy Economic Analysis* (Pittsburgh: CONSAD 1979).

6. Documentation of the BLS model was obtained from information supplied by BLS staff, in particular from the Bureau of Labor Statistics, "Methods and Data Sources: BLS Revised 1980 and 1985 Projections" (Washington, D.C.: Office of Economic Growth, 1977). A brief description and evaluation of the model is contained in A.J. Eckstein and D.M. Heien,

"A Review of Energy Models with Particular Reference to Employment and Manpower Analysis" (Report prepared for the Employment and Training Administration, U.S. Department of Labor, 1978).

7. Eckstein and Heien, "Review of Energy Models."

8. Y. Sheinin, *Alternative Technologies for Energy in the Production Process* (Philadelphia: Wharton EFA, Inc., 1977).

9. Eckstein and Heien, "Review of Energy Models," pp. 78-79.

10. The section on the MEFS leans heavily on the exposition developed in Peter W. House and John McLeod, *Large Scale Models for Policy Evaluation* (New York: John Wiley & Sons, 1977).

11. The following description of PIES/MEFS is based heavily on FEA and DOE material used to document and describe these modeling systems.

12. Peter House, *Trading Off Environment, Economics, and Energy: A Case Study of EPA's Strategic Environmental Assessment System (SEAS)* (Lexington, Mass.: Lexington Books, D.C. Heath and Company, 1977).

13. This section has been adapted from Nazir Dossani, "An Evaluation of Current Regionalization Procedures" (Report prepared by CONSAD Research Corporation for the U.S. Environmental Protection Agency, 1979).

14. Note that each subsector is not a function of all sectoral outputs and final demands. The number of nonzero elements in A_{ij} and C_{ik} varies from one equation to another.

15. There are likely to be significant errors here, for labor productivities in a given sector vary significantly across regions. There was also undercoverage of small firms in the employment file. The data base known as the Economic Information System file is best on its coverage for the larger firms. Very small firms (with less than twenty employees) are not covered, and no attempt was made to control for these.

16. Thus, for example, the growth rate of iron-ore mining is the same as that of nonferrous-ore mining.

17. A simpler version of the analytical methods incorporated in some of these special modules is the so-called dynamic regionalization process, in which counties are rank ordered with an estimated production assigned to each county. A fixed-share file is used to allocate any national production that is not met from this rank-ordered list. In this process, no internal constraints or regional balancing are imposed.

18. In terms of the technical discussion of SEAS, this problem is, in essence, a questioning of the use of a constant-share file and associated internal table lookups, which fail to represent simulated reality with changes in input assumptions.

19. We have not used a BLS model illustration, because we wished to focus here on energy and environmental applications. Only recently has

BLS been adapted to more detailed energy technology–employment applications. See CONSAD Research Corporation, *Joint DOE/DOL Project*. This application, as might be expected, is developed only at the national, not the subnational, level.

20. Energy Information Administration, *Annual Report to Congress, Volumes I and II, 1977: Projections of Energy Supply and Demand and Their Impacts* (Washington, D.C.: U.S. Department of Energy, 1978).

21. Based heavily on U.S. Department of Energy, *The First National Energy Plan* (NEPI) (Washington, D.C., 1978).

22. U.S. Geological Survey, *Geological Estimates of Undiscovered Oil and Gas Resources in the United States,* Circular 725 (Reston, Va., 1975).

23. The northeastern quadrant includes the Great Lakes, New England, New York, New Jersey, and Middle Atlantic regions.

24. This discussion is based heavily on the environmental appendix to the U.S. Department of Energy (NEPII) *Second National Energy Plan* (Washington, D.C., 1979).

25. These environmental implications are addressed in this analysis in the form of projected environmental-pollution levels, water requirements, and solid-waste production. They were derived from the Strategic Environmental Assessment System (SEAS). The national energy-production and -consumption levels used as input to the SEAS model were projected by DOE's FOSSIL 2 model: regional distributions are based on data from the Midrange Energy Market Model (MEMM) operated by the Energy Information Administration. The discussion is based heavily on the environmental appendix of the *Second National Energy Plan*.

7 Some Bottom-Up Techniques

We have seen in chapters 5 and 6 not only that top-down analysis entails difficulty with the data used but also that the models themselves have deficiencies in their representation of, and feedback from, subnational geographic areas—their sectors, people, and institutions. Regional impacts are without qualification *spatial* in nature. They happen to particular people in specific areas. They are not homogeneous over an entire forecast area. Such impacts are stressed in the models developed for urban growth and transportation but are characteristically utilized to study individual urban areas. There is a need to develop coefficients for use in such models that are more than averages of more-geographically-specific data. The obscuring of regional differences in national modeling markedly increases the potential for producing forecasts that ignore or miss subnational impacts of policies that are analyzed only through the use of such averages. Although it would be mechanically possible to use these spatial-modeling techniques in an attempt to study the local impacts of national policies by treating either the whole nation or large regions as if they were the urban, metropolitan and nonmetropolitan areas that the models were designed to simulate, it is doubtful whether such "mechanization" would prove valid or useful results. On the one hand, if these techniques were used to study broad general areas of the nation, say federal regions, the resultant information could be said to be of questionable value because the theory underlying these spatial models was never intended to deal with the forces that result in interregional transfers and impacts. It is also unlikely that the data would be adequate.

On the other hand, if the multiplicity of regions were somehow all individually modeled using a consistent and calibrated data base, and then the model runs integrated, it might well be possible to obtain information to estimate the total change in selected variables through time.

In addressing these issues, we have already discussed why subnational consequences and trends are important to consider at the federal level (chapters 1-4), and what characteristics of analytic efforts help (chapter 5) and often do not help (chapter 6). There are repeated calls in the literature for a two-way communication to assist in reflecting subnational interests at the national level (see, for example, criterion 9, page 67, above); some of the discussions cite one or another subnational jurisdictional level where this type of activity should be focused. In the first section of this chapter, we shall briefly explore some of the available alternatives. Following that, we shall examine analytic approaches for achieving bottom-up representation: both the traditional techniques and others more recently arrived at and still somewhat experimental.

This discussion is not merely an academic exercise, or a wasteful excursion by bureaucrats seeking to enlarge their responsibilities and turf. An extensive literature expresses the concerns of private-sector market forecasters who are faced with determining conditions under which: the sum of forecasts of sales in market segments (aggregation) is preferred to a forecast of the whole market; and forecasts of individual market segments are preferred to forecasts obtained through proration of a forecast of the whole market.[1] In each instance, the entire market is a large selling unit partitioned into a set of smaller units called segments. This may occur in many ways, including states versus counties in that state, retailers versus wholesalers serving that region, product line versus product packages within that line, and yearly versus monthly sales in a region. The operational issue as stated in practice is whether to forecast bottom up or top down. The bottom-up approach is a forecast of the whole market obtained by summing forecasts of that market's segments. The top-down approach is a forecast of an individual segment obtained by proration. Most of the discussion of bottom-up and top-down approaches in this literature is oriented to minimizing forecasting errors of various types, errors that are magnified by one or the other of the approaches, depending on the forecasting methods and resources used at each level and some characteristics of the underlying universe. Few of these methods, however, deal with the problem(s) occasioned by policies generated at the top level that affect—and are affected by—actions and perceptions at the bottom levels:[2] in public sector top-down systems, we have seen, this is likely to be the norm, not the exception.

The Advantages of Bottom-Up Methodology

The idea of performing analysis from the level where the policy consequence is expected ultimately to impact has intuitive appeal. In an extreme example, to look at the regional impacts of national policy from a bottom-up perspective, one would simply refer to the area of interest, derive estimates of the localized effects, and integrate these across all the local- or regional-impact analyses. Analyses of this sort would be made with the belief that better information, more sensitive to regional needs and issues, can be gathered by performing assessments closer to where the impacts actually are. These more detailed studies would have the benefit of tending to

Some Bottom-Up Techniques 137

correct the errors created by using global-average statistics to calculate national impacts, for they would automatically introduce the correct weights and coefficients to specific areas and processes. Let us look at one possible set for structuring a bottom-up analysis, the objective of which is to yield a national impact of a particular policy. Features of this example can be used as a reference point for discussing the benefits and weaknesses of this approach.

1. Divide the nation into regions that will be the bases of individual partial analyses. This segmentation can be arrived at analytically, based on some clearly specified objective criteria, or to be arbitrary. Ultimately, regardless of the criteria used for partitioning, the only requirement is that the entire nation be covered.

2. A study design must be formulated beforehand and agreed to by investigators in all subareas. This sort of preplanning reduces the amount of intellectual entrepreneurship allowed to the investigators responsible for specific subareas and often meets with resistance on the basis that it stifles creativity.

3. Because the information gained at each individual area is to be used not only to analyze local issues but also as input to derivation of a national total, the necessary data bases have to be agreed upon and calibrated. Among the more obvious difficulties this presents is that of relative availability of specific bits of information. By denying the inclusion of information from an area rich in data, the homogenization of data reduces the richness of a local impact. Conversely, the difficulty of preparing an assessment of a specific area may be substantially increased if data sets are missing that are deemed necessary for national analyses.

4. To perform analyses of the subareas, several techniques will likely be used. In all cases, these tools will have to be the same for each area and calibrated with the same assumptions. These include not only the adjustments required for using such well-defined tools as analytic models but would extend to all techniques, inluding those that are comparatively subjective. It is clear that often these tasks will be extremely difficult to accomplish and will frequently require enormous investments of time and effort. Here, too, there will be resistance from investigators who see model and technique development as ways to exercise their creative abilities while at the same time effectively putting their own individual stamp on the results. Standardization of techniques might inhibit otherwise-creative approaches to national/subnational analysis.

5. With reference to the calibration procedures, of special importance is the need to ensure that all data are of the same vintage and that all assessments are done on and to the same years. Further, for the policies or issues analyzed to be agreed upon, there has to be a meeting of minds as to exactly what the study topic really implies, both in general and to the indi-

vidual subareas. Finally, all assumptions of the data bases, techniques, and analyses must be made consistent.

There will probably have to be a central group or a committee of all groups to guarantee that all these steps are taken. The design, staffing, and funding of such a group and the recognition of its authority to set standards and guidelines or to arbitrate disputes will have to be agreed on by all. These arrangements guarantee significant institutional and administrative headaches through the effort. One of the numerous responsibilities the central coordinating group should assume is to ensure that each subarea carries out its analysis so that all its individual components would be ready at the same time to permit integration. Among the delays involved are several checks with the large number of professionals and groups involved in the analyses and with the various government agencies that should be consulted before any analysis is released.

The subnational accuracy and structural validity potentially obtainable from a bottom-up approach needs to be compared—traded off, in real cost terms—against the organizational framework that would be required to link the various subarea analyses together. In addition, the coordinating group would have to assume analytic responsibility for accounting for the interregional transfers of such things as people, goods, pollution, resources, and the like, which lie outside the purview and technical capability of individual regional assessments, and these transfers would have to be fed back to the analysts in the various subareas for inclusion in their studies.

With all this apparent difficulty one might legitimately ask, why bother? In addition to the personal preferences and research biases of those who prefer bottom-up to top-down analytical techniques, there are several other benefits that might accrue to those who use this approach.

For one, the use of detailed analyses of specific areas does not necessarily mean use of the same data or even the same modeling techniques. On the one hand, even if the same general techniques are used, it might be possible to design the models to handle more-detailed data or enrich the information obtained from the models and weight it by inputs of local-area residents or situations. The data base, though consisting of the same general variables, may also be made more specific.

On the other hand, the use of subarea analyses may allow the shift of one set of model forms to another. For example, in the substantive areas of land use and transportation, it is possible to use several techniques for locational analysis to relate land uses, population, and economic characteristics to one another. It is not feasible, however, to use such spatial models to do national assessments. As a variant, it is possible to use one set of modeling techniques for general purposes and to extend the power of these forecasts, looking further into the data by carrying out subarea studies. For example,

Some Bottom-Up Techniques

it is possible to perform a detailed spatial analysis of a subarea for one or two variables of interest and to use other techniques to produce information that is more or less ancillary to the variables of greatest interest.

In summary, the preferred technique chosen to study national policy should depend on several factors. The paradigm presented here of how to organize a bottom-up analysis capable of being integrated at the national level is only one way the problem could be addressed. In this section we shall discuss several concrete examples of such analytic techniques currently in operation, ranging from the purely analytic to the purely organizational. Some we refer to as traditional, in that no two-way link is attempted; these reflect the regional-analysis standpoint. The illustrations cover almost all subnational levels, from large multistate regions to individual counties.

Jurisdictional Levels Suitable for Analytic Purposes

State Levels

Others have recommended that an important way to improve the accuracy, acceptability, and credibility of federal/subnational-model assessments is to increase substantially subnational involvement in the assessment processes.[3] Further, in many cases not only does the subnational unit want a part in the assessment process; it also wants some voice in what the scenario being assessed is in the first place. The top-down, federally inspired scenarios take into consideration international trade, national defense, and the like. The regional planners also want to ensure that their scenarios are included in national forecasts. Frequently, the exclusion of their input results in a refusal by regional planners to become involved in the federal exercise because the forecast does not take their scenarios into account. Furthermore, many agree that the state should be the basic subfederal unit or region for implementing these kinds of involvement. One of the reasons for selecting the state as the basic unit is the feeling that implementation of, say, federal energy and environmental policies is dependent on state concurrence and support. Specifically, those favoring state-level input argue that, regardless of the fact that the activity is most likely to be carried out in some lower level's jurisdiction:

1. The basic subfederal political boundary is the state.
2. Many decisions critical to energy futures are made at the state level (such as power-plant siting, state energy emergency plans, and intrastate natural-gas regulations).
3. The states are in a position to define and enact energy policies of their own.

4. The states are in a position to act as a focal point for the collection, dissemination, and analysis of local-energy, demographic, and environmental data.

Focusing on the two-way communication of analytical concerns, Ritschard notes that

> ... the design and operation of a modeling system should allow (as a minimum) for both the transmission of, and consideration of, goals and constraints between state and Federal levels. The resulting format can serve as a basis for interactive communication between Federal and state actors. Consistent with the concept of constraints is a hierarchical system of environmental impact assessment. . . .
>
> [The Federal level] would directly calculate (using SEAS or other appropriate models) only those impact best addressed at a national level. Resulting siting patterns and total activity levels would be used by regional laboratories and/or the individual states as drivers and control totals. . . .[4]

Regional Levels: Boards and Councils

There are many impacts that are best analyzed at a multistate level: long-range transport of sulfur-dioxide pollutant; major regional trends (such as the Sunbelt-Frostbelt phenomenon) related to multistate climatic differences (among other variables); multistate economic structural conditions such as a recession-ridden steel industry; multistate resource availability, such as Appalachian or western coal; and others.

Not unexpectedly, a number of organizational arrangements have been developed to deal with the incredible complex problems occasioned by the hierarchical tiering of governmental agencies and functions. Given the history of federalism and regionalism over the years, the creation of the Federal Executive Boards and Federal Regional Councils is a logical outcome. Their continued existence after almost two decades and one decade, respectively, should be no suprise either, because governmental organizations tend not to disappear. That they might provide a useful mechanism for relating and resolving federal and regional policy matters is less likely. A brief review can tell us where they stand today.

Federal Executive Boards. In November 1961, President John F. Kennedy, through an executive memorandum, created twelve Federal Executive Boards to serve as a coordinating mechanism for management improvement and cost reduction, intergovernmental and community relations, coordination of interrelated federal programs at local levels, and communication and joint-action programs of presidential interest. In creating the boards, the president reemphasized the continuous responsibility of the Bureau of the Budget (the predecessor to the current Office of Management and Budget) in the management area and stressed the importance of cooperation between the newly created boards and the organization and method-analysis functions of the bureau. Thus, the primary purpose of these boards has been to improve internal federal management practices and to provide a central focus for federal participation in civil affairs in major metropolitan centers of federal activity.

Federal Executive Boards (FEBs) are composed of heads of federal field offices in the metropolitan area. A chairperson is elected annually from among the membership to provide overall leadership to the board's operations. Committees and task forces carry out interagency projects consistent with the board's missions. The boards currently receive overall policy direction from the Office of Management and Budget (OMB).

The boards are scattered throughout major cities of the nation. Since their inception, they have represented a major departure in management approach. They are based conceptually on the premise of improvement of relationships between the federal departments and field agencies outside Washington. Though reporting to the OMB, they are very much oriented to the field and involved in field problems by their physical grass-roots location. Increasingly, the FEBs have become an important management mechanism serving local-area needs. However, most commentators have concluded that, by and large, the exclusively voluntary nature of cooperation has prevented the FEBs from realizing their full potential.

The effectiveness of the FEB concept as a management-coordinating device cannot be fully assessed at this time. The boards, on and off, have had to contend with pervasive uncertainty for years at a time. Their full potential may only now be beginning to be realized. If their progress is to be measured significantly, it must be measured in their potential as a future management tool, driving toward unity of purpose and a focus of the overall effort and better government. Can the FEBs serve as a foundation for future management improvement? Only time will tell. An examination of their *modus operandi* provides some preliminary insights.

The boards typically have no or little staff and all work is carried out by voluntary cooperative means. The voluntary nature of the board enables a functional harmony not normally found in legally instituted ventures. The cooperative spirit enables them to avoid bureaucratism, at least at the decision stage, which in itself is an accomplishment when one considers the bureaucratic nature of the federal government. With the work at hand, lack of power of enforcement does not seem to hinder FEB operations. Tasks to be accomplished appear to be expedited through mutual agreements.

The boards can best be described as ad hoc action-type high-level problem-solving groups. Because FEBs have few or no formally assigned tasks, their work does not become routine. A board's involvement is not with internal problems but with correlation of interagency problems. Furthermore, its major concern seems not to be in improving quality of performance or agency-management problem solving, but rather in allocating unsolved issues to agencies possessing the know-how for solving them. The boards increasingly claim to have certain in-house capabilities and to be able to absorb, in a somewhat beneficent parental fashion, various work-problem excesses on a functional basis. For example, a large department in the New York FEB area possessing facilities for data processing absorbs the work of departments lacking these facilities. Through FEBs, work is channeled to these larger departments.

Federal Regional Councils. The Federal Regional Councils (FRCs) were established by Executive Order 11647 of 10 February 1975.[5] A council was created for each of the ten standard federal regions. The councils were mandated to improve coordination of the categorical-grant system and to develop closer working relationships among themselves and with state and local governments.[6]

The Federal Regional Councils are composed of the principal regional officials of the Departments of Agriculture; Commerce; Energy; Health, Education and Welfare; Housing and Urban Development; Interior; Labor; Transportation; the Community Services Administration; and the Environmental Protection Agency. The president annually designates one member of each council to serve as chairperson.

In January 1979, linkage was established between the Federal Regional Councils and the Interagency Coordinating Council. The latter is comprised of agency officials directly responsible for managing domestic-assistance programs and is chaired by the assistant to the president for intergovernmental affairs. The Office of Management and Budget continues to provide policy direction to the councils and delegates to them the implementation of various OMB circulars and management initiatives.

Three board missions characterize the functions of the Federal Regional Councils: intergovernmental relations, interagency-program coordination, and delivery of services such as emergency aid during crises and disasters. Councils are the major interagency mechanism in the field to ensure that implementation of federal policies is consistent with overall administration policy and that federal policies are responsive to the concerns of state and local governments.

A recent criticism of the FRCs, after passing off a successful FRC coordination action as a "fluke," stated that, in general:

Some Bottom-Up Techniques 143

> The federal regional councils commonly provide little help to states and local governments; sometimes they actually represent a stumbling block to intergovernmental relations, which is why so many people are unhappy with them. . . .
>
> The federal regional councils suffer from high expectations. They were oversold and underpowered. . . .[7]

The continuing assessment has not been completed, but there has been increased thinking that the councils can and should be very helpful in the federal-regional-local decision-making process. A recent Department of Commerce Regional Round Table (25 July 1978) examined the possibility that the councils might, together with an extension of the regional-commission concept, provide nationwide federal/regional policymaking coordination, with the FRC chairman serving as the foremost regional advocate with a total federal perspective. So far, no decision has been made about this or other methods for strengthening the FRCs. Some question remains as to how seriously these councils are taken by state and local decision makers; to the extent that they are not taken seriously, buttressing from the federal level is apt to be successful. Again, as with most cooperative organizations, time, people, and experimentation are required elements for potential success.

We have already discussed a number of other multistate organizations: the Appalachian Regional Commission, the Title V Commissions, and the various multistate regional organizations used by the Corps of Engineers and other federal agencies. For the most part, we have seen that these organizations are performing subnational analyses almost exclusively.[8] This does not necessarily mean that these organizations could not be used in the future for the same two-way communication discussed above with regard to states.

Traditional Methods for National-Subnational Analysis

The national top-down modeling reviewed briefly above does not pretend to address regional variety but rather to average these differences across all national geographic diversity so that national—not regional—economic consequences can be analyzed. However, a number of techniques are available to assess regional economic-energy-employment impacts. These are traditional analytic methods in the sense that, by and large, no two-way communication between the top and bottom is utilized in these approaches.

As might be anticipated, significant variations exist in the procedures, assumptions, and quality of these techniques. The selection of a given technique may be dictated by constraints of time and/or cost. A relatively simple approach for estimating regional impacts involves the use of various types of economic multipliers. Two common types are: the economic-base multiplier, which measures the change in total economic activity due to a change in the base or export sectors; and the input-output multiplier, which measures the interdependence among economic sectors. In terms of existing techniques, the Regional Industrial Multiplier System (RIMS), developed by the Bureau of Economic Analysis, can be used to estimate required state- and substate-level impacts of changes in any category of final demand by any number of industries. Various application of economic ratios (such as sales to earnings, earnings to employment, and employment to output) also can be used to estimate regional impacts.

Alternatively, regional econometric models offer a more sophisticated approach to estimating economic impacts. In terms of design and structure, these models are similar to the national macroeconomic models. They include the Data Resources, Inc., and Chase econometrics regional models and the NRIES model. The DRI regional model provides a consistent forecasting system of the key dimensions of all fifty state economies, nine regional economies, and selected SMSA economies. This system provides a framework for both assessing a region's (or state's) economic performance and simulating the effects of alternative national-level economic occurences on the future economic prospects of a state or region.

A second alternative, the Chase Econometric State Forecasting Service, can provide forecasts of economic activities at the regional, state, and SMSA levels. Furthermore, this model can be adjusted to respond to cyclical business fluctuations, long-term national-growth trends, and local economic conditions. Other regional models that might be considered are the Economic Activity Analysis Model, developed by the Bureau of Land Management; the Multi-Regional Input-Output (MRIO) model of the Harvard Economics Research Project; and the Multi-Region, Multi-Industry (MRMI) model, developed at the University of Maryland.

The National-Regional Impact Evaluation System (NRIES) model, developed by the Bureau of Economic Analysis, is a medium-term (five to ten years) impact-analysis tool. It is composed of fifty-one state econometric models integrated into a model of the U.S. economy. NRIES offers what its developers claim to be a bottom-up approach to regional analysis, because the national-model component of NRIES is derived as the sum of the fifty-one independently constructed state models. This approach both accounts for individual regional-growth patterns and ensures that regional growth is consistent with national growth. This model, which can be used to analyze the regional effects of policy actions as well as the concurrent effects on national and regional variables, is described in more detail below.

Some Bottom-Up Techniques

Before describing the state of the art of these econometric models further, it is useful to describe briefly the concepts and procedures of the so-called OBERS (Office of Business Economics Research Services, U.S. Department of Commerce) projection system, for OBERS is possibly the granddaddy of them all. This venerable system, which for many years has provided estimation services for countless users, has many features of the traditional bottom-up model, plus others.

OBERS Projections

Philosophically, the OBERS programs are purported to be no more than extensions of present behavior. As a start, a comprehensive data base for the metropolitan-area and county levels has been assembled on present employment, population, and income. These data are used to forecast the same variables the year 2020, with forecasts for subareas controlled by an independently estimated national total. For these projections, the economy is assumed to be in equilibrium with reasonable full employment assumed nationwide. The full set of assumptions based on OBERS documentation, follows.

1. Growth of population will be conditioned by a fertility rate representing replacement-level fertility.
2. Nationally, reasonably full employment, represented by a 4-percent unemployment rate, will prevail at the points for which projections are made. As in the past, unemployment will be disproportionately distributed regionally, but the extent of disproportionality will diminish.
3. The projections are assumed to be free of the immediate and direct effects of wars.
4. Continued technological progress and capital accumulation will support a growth in private output per manhour of 2.9 percent annually.
5. The new products that appear will be accommodated within the existing industrial classification system; therefore, no new industrial classifications are necessary.
6. Growth in output can be achieved without ecological disaster or serious deterioration, although diversion of resources for pollution control will cause changes in the industrial mix of output.

The regional projections are based on the following additional assumptions:

1. Most factors that have influenced historical shifts in the location of regional-export industry will continue into the future with varying degrees of intensity.

2. Trends toward areal economic self-sufficiency in local-service industries will continue.
3. Workers will migrate to areas of economic opportunities and away from slow-growth or declining areas.
4. Regional earnings per workers and income per capita will continue to converge toward the national average.
5. Regional employment/population ratios will tend to move toward the national ratio.

The technique first forecasts the economic activity of the nation in industrial detail; this economic activity is then distributed regionally by means of expected growth in regional areas. Specifically, the GNP is forecasted using an economics supply approach, which proceeds through a series of four steps: population is forecasted based on assumptions concerning migration and age-specific birth and death rates; these population forecasts are then used to generate an employed labor force; private-level employment is estimated from the total, and assumptions are made about hours worked per year per person and private GNP per person per hour; finally, from these data, the constant-dollar GNP (private and government) is calculated.

The methodology also requires that industrial-level detail be calculated for economic activity. This is done by projecting the gross product and earnings by industry at the two-digit SIC level. The gross product by industry is then converted to industry-level share of GNP. Similar procedures are used for the agricultural sector (see figure 7-1).

The projection methodology used for BEA area forecasts is carried out using individual special-purpose models. The first handles basic industries, the second agriculture, the third residential industries, and the fourth, population from projected employment.

The basic-industry model is based on the so-called shift-share technique. In essence, it specifies a proportional-growth variable and a differential-growth variable between a specific region and the nation for each industry or income component:

$$E_{ij}^t = (E_{io}^i / E_{io}^x) E_{ij}^x + C_{ij}^{x-t}$$

where i, j = the ith industry and the jth region;

o = the summation of regions (the nation);

t, x = the projected time and base, respectively;

C_{ij}^{x-t} = the difference between the hypothetical level attained at the national growth rate of an industry in the period x to t and

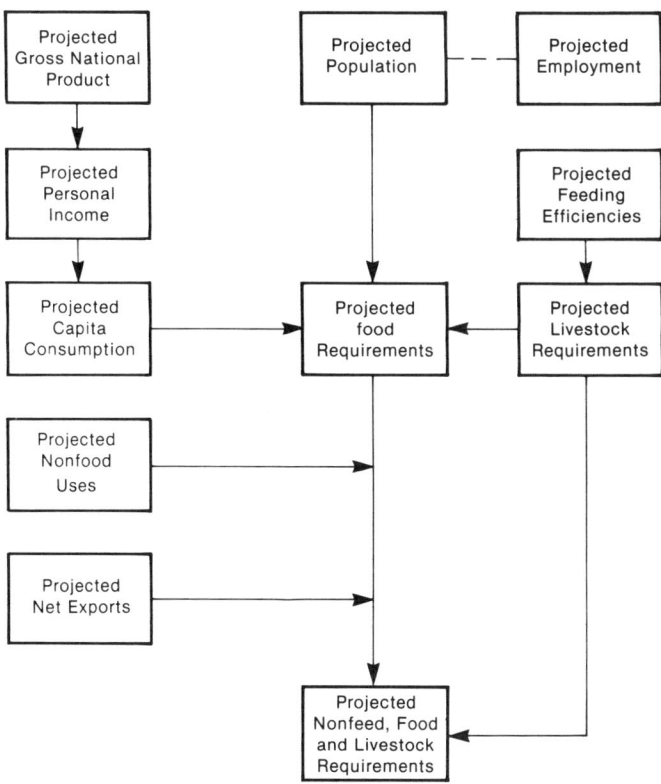

Figure 7-1. Projected National Framework of Production Requirements: Agricultural Sector

the actual regional level attained by the industry over the same period.

The term $(E_{io}^i/E_{io}^x)E_{ij}^x$ is used to calculate the proportional growth of the regions to the nation or the shift coefficient. The other term is the regional share (C_{ij}^{x-t}) whenever the amount produced in a region is proportionally greater than the national average. The region is said to be an example of the goods and services of that industry. The relative growth of a region depends on the comparative advantage of its export industries. The larger the composition advantage, the greater the expected growth of the region. Earnings and employment for each basic industry are each forecasted using this technique.

Earnings and employment are also projected for the agricultural sector.

Except for some assumptions that tend to smooth out differences in agricultural sectors, the technique consists in extrapolating earnings and employment area.

Residentiary industries (local-service sectors) are derived on the basis of relationships between the basic and service sectors. In general, the technique requires first calculating the ratio of regional industry's share of total area earnings. The same national ratios are projected for the industries. These two data sets are then related to the basic industries in the area. Regional totals of each service industry are calculated to give a proportion of the national total as a regional share. The shares are then summed for all service industry share. By projecting the basic component of this calculation (done earlier), all industry earnings are derived. The total is then disaggregated to industry/regional levels and forced to fit previously derived national totals.

Finally, population is forecasted as noted above (birth minus deaths plus migration by area). In the main, the local population is calculated by relating it to employment, and employment to the labor pool:

[1]   [2]   [3]   [4]

$$\frac{P_j^t}{E_j^t} = \frac{P_o^t}{E_o^t} + \left(\frac{P_j^{1970}}{E_j^{1970}} - \frac{P_o^{1970}}{E_o^{1970}} \right) \cdot \left(1 - .15 \frac{t - 1980}{10} \right)$$

where
P = population 15–64;
E = employment;
t = time (t = 1980, 1990, 2000, 2010, 2020);
j = region j;
o = U.S. total;
factor [1] = the regional ratio
factor [2] = the national ratio
factor [3] = the initial difference
factor [4] = the closure factor.

The methodology just described would be almost classically top down, with some regional sophistication of the data, were it not for the fact that the actual OBERS technique requires considerable checking and formalized inputs from regions across the country. Many of the discrepancies, real or apparent, are resolved on the basis of information provided by persons in the affected area who are in a position to have special, local-area knowl-

Some Bottom-Up Techniques

ledge.[9] It is this extensive checking and feedback from the local area that gives this technique its bottom-up flavor.

Regional Econometric Models

A survey of the literature indicates that several dozen models have been developed in the past decade for forecasting regional economic growth. Table 7-1 lists some of the principal ones that forecast economic activity for regions that cover the United States (all states, all counties, all BEAs, and so on). (For a listing of references, see appendix 7A, below.)

Analysis of these models suggests that they can be divided into three categories. First, there are models that rely entirely on behavioral equations based on time-series and cross-section data and are extensions of the early single-region models of L'Esperance, Crow, Glickman, and others (table 7-2). Next, there is the pioneering work of Polenske and her colleagues

Table 7-1
Partial List of Comprehensive Regional Models of the United States

Author (Reference)	Regional Delineation
Bureau of Economic Analysis	50 states + District of Columbia
Chase Econometrics	50 states + District of Columbia
Mathematica: Comprehensive Human Resources Data System (King, 1977)	50 states + District of Columbia
Data Resources, Inc.: State Area Forecasting Service (1977)	50 states + District of Columbia
Oak Ridge National Laboratory MULTIREGION (Olsen, 1977)	173 economic areas defined by the Bureau of Economic Analysis
Federal Energy Administration: Regional Energy Activity and Demographic Model—READ (Donnelly, 1977)	County level
Federal Energy Administration: Regional Earnings Impact System (REIS) (U.S. DOE, 1976)	50 states + District of Columbia
Polenske: The Multiregional Input-Output Model (1970)	50 states + District of Columbia
Golladay and Haveman: Regional Impact and Distribution Model (1976, 1977(a), 1977(b))	23 regions (aggregations of states)
Treyz, Friedlaender, and Stevens	States[a]

[a]The model so far has been estimated primarily for Massachusetts; Treyz, Friedlaender, and Stevens are planning to develop such models for all states.

Table 7-2
Partial List of Regional Modeling Efforts

Region Covered	Author (Reference)
State Models	
California	Burton and Dyckman (1965)
Hawaii	Licari, Deventer, and Studenmund (1973)
Massachusetts I	Bell (1967)
Massachusetts II	Friedlaender, Treyz, and Tresch (1975)
Michigan	Research Seminar, University of Michigan (1965)
Mississippi	Adams, Brooking, and Glickman (1975)
New York	Wharton Econometric Forecasting Associates
Ohio	L'Esperance (1975)
Pennsylvania	Klein and Glickman (1975)
Puerto Rico	Dutta and Su (1969)
Washington State	Bourque, Conway, and Howard (1977)
Multistate Models	
Northeast Corridor	Crow (1969)
New England	Wharton Econometric Forecasting Associates
Coastal Plain States	Richter (1970)
Other Regional Models	
Buffalo SMSA	Crow et al. (1974)
Cleveland SMSA	Loxley (1976)
Luzerne County	Schink (1974)
Philadelphia SMSA	Glickman (1971)

Note: See appendix 7A for references.

on multiregional input-output models. Finally, there are some models that attempt to bridge these two trends and incorporate a mix of input-output and time-series analysis.

Modeling of State Economies

Different modeling approaches to state economies have different strengths and weaknesses. The approach suggested below—currently at the forefront of such modeling—is one that draws upon the major developments in national and regional modeling to form a core model that can be used for making a baseline forecast and for carrying out alternative policy simulations. The model is designed specifically to facilitate its further development. Figure 7-2 shows how the model depends on previous work.

Some Bottom-Up Techniques

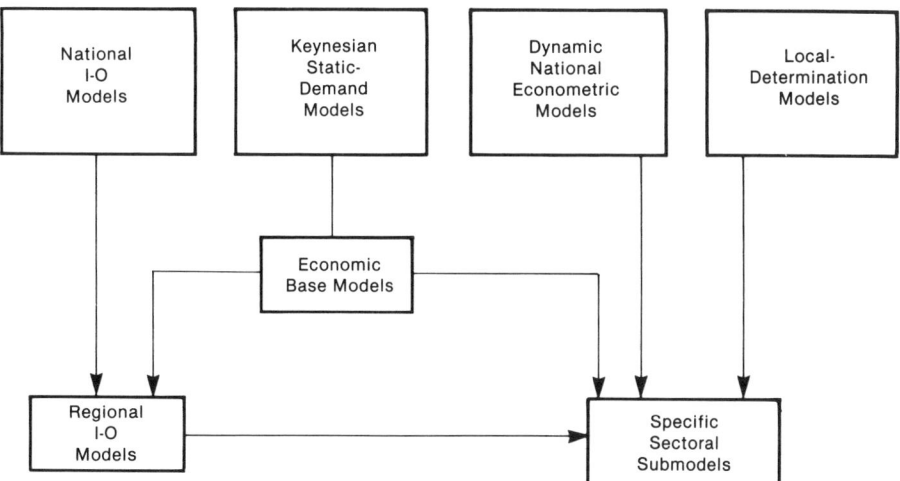

Figure 7-2. Modeling of State Economies: Generalized Framework

The model includes the input-output structure of the economy, Keynesian-type demand relationships, time-dated variable values, and changes in technology, wages, prices in line with changes in the national economy, and responses to changes in relative costs in the state that affect the comparative advantage of the state as a location for production.[10] It is also designed so that supply functions can be incorporated as the model is further developed.

The important endogenous features of the model can be seen in Figure 7-3. The following list explains the causal arrows linking the endogenous sectors.

1. Exports (sector 1) from the state depend on national and international demand, and on the relative advantage of the state as a location for production for the industry in question. In this model, changes in relative state costs of production play a key role in determining changes in business location. The second arrow pointing to sector 1 indicates that relative-factor intensity (such as capital-labor ratio) of production must also be known before export-dependent factor (input) demand can be derived from output demand. In this core model, factor ratios are held constant because a fixed input production function is used.

2. Intrastate-use-dependent factors (sector 2) also depend on factor intensity. In this sector, intermediate input demand for each industry is deter-

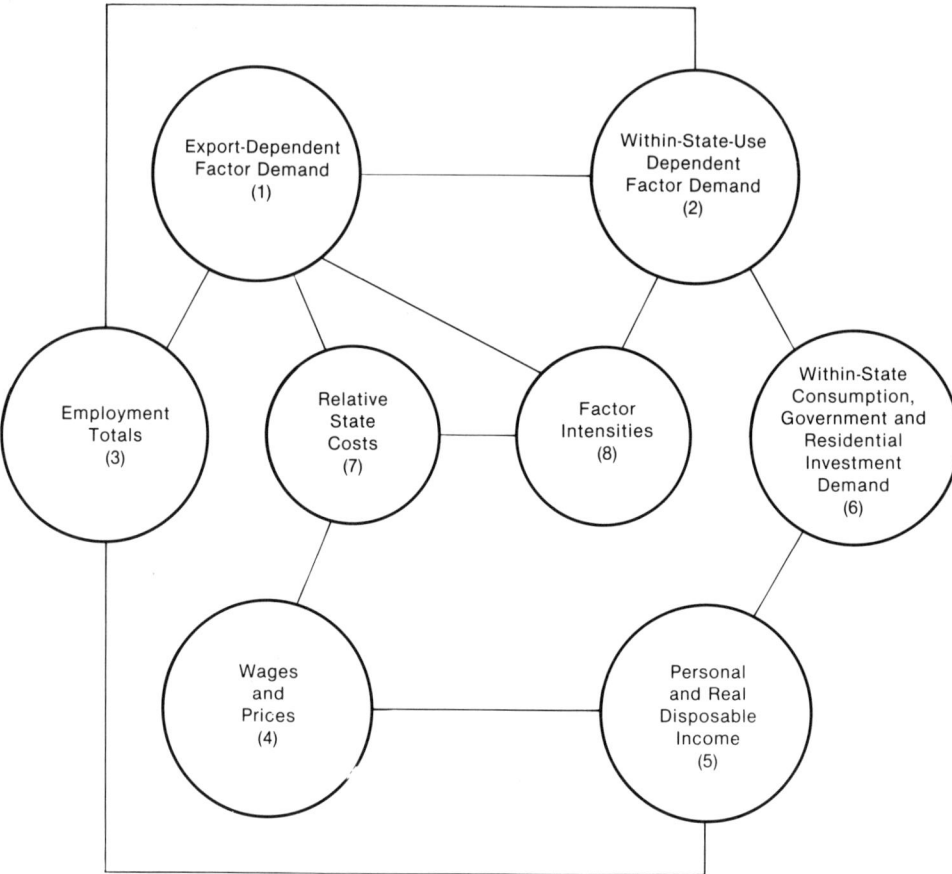

Figure 7-3. Endogenous Sectors

mined based on relative input costs and the state input-output relationships embedded in this sector. Intrastate final demand comes from the local-demand sector (6). Investment demand is derived from changes in capital-stock demand. Total employment (sector 3) is simply the sum of export and local-use-dependent employment.

3. Because this is basically a demand model, wage rates in sector 4 are largely determined exogenously. Consumer prices, however, will be affected by change in input costs in the state and by consumer taxes.

4. Personal income (sector 3) is made up of identities based on wage rates, employment, taxes, prices, property incomes, and transfers. Local-

consumer demand (sector 6) depends on real disposable income in the state, but could also allow for import substitution based on relative state costs, as well as price-induced substitution among products and income distribution. State and local government spending are based on real income and on trends in state and local government spending for the nation.

5. Relative state costs of production (sector 7) are determined by equations based on a specific production function and on tax, capital, fuel, intermediate inputs, and labor costs. The last sector (8) determines factor intensities of production based on a production function, relative-factor costs, and an assumed equality of marginal costs with marginal productions, for each factor of production, when new capital purchases are made. In the version of the model presented, fixed-input production function is used.

The production functions for both local and export activities allow for substitution among labor, capital, and energy. Thus, differential changes in state-factor input costs relative to the country will also change the relative intensity of use of these factors of production.

This highly structured approach to regional economic modeling makes substantial use of basic economic and regional economic theory and of existing data, while minimizing the use of regression equations. The use of such equations, in most state and regional forecasting models, involves the implicit assumption that the relationships between state-specific and national measures of economic activity will remain the same in the future as they have been in the past. Aside from the many possible questions about this underlying assumption, models based heavily on regression equations provide less flexibility for policy simulations. Economic relationships in regression models tend to be locked into the equations in such a way that it is difficult to simulate the effects of changes in state-policy instruments such as its tax, energy, and employment policies. Such changes can be simulated with the model described in figures 7-2 and 7-3.

At the same time, the transparent structure of the proposed model is intended to provide the analyst with the facility to change the structure, if desired, and to add other modules for specific purposes. It is not always possible to make structural changes in a model based only on regression equations, because the structure to be changed (such as interindustry flows or factor intensities) is buried in a regression coefficient. In the model presented here, however, such structural changes can be incorporated either directly or through the automatic mechanism in the model that transmits U.S. technological and other changes to the state economy. It may be difficult to add modules that feed back into regression-based models because the regression coefficients estimated on the basis of short time series may lead to unstable results when the model is expanded. In short, the core model described here has an explicit structural specification and uses regression techniques only when relationships cannot be specified by theory or other available data. This makes it possible for the analyst to use it as an instrument for forecasting and analysis rather than as a black box.

More Two-Way Communication between the Top and the Bottom

There are a number of exploratory methods beginning to address the development of analytic, two-way models.[11] And there is a substantial increase in methods used in the national-forecasting units of the federal government involving interdepartmental efforts at federal and subnational levels.[12] The purpose of such schemes is, minimally, to promote subnational review and, maximally, to obtain an interactive two-way process. To develop a standard set of state-population projections for allocation of federal funds and yet avoid the chamber-of-commerce effect, the Office of Management and Budget (OMB) has recommended a set of proposed procedures that would: establish a methodology for producing a single set of baseline population projections for the states; and establish requirements and procedures for the use of population projections by all federal agencies distributing funds to state and/or substate programs or projects on the basis of projected population.

According to the Office of Federal Statistical Policy and Standards:

> The projections produced with the proposed procedure will be baseline projections, i.e., projections which reflect the essence of historical growth trends. Such projections will not attempt to take into account changes in intervention strategies by any level of government or by the private sector. Such projections will in no sense be intended as a goal, an assigned share, or a constraint on a State's economic activity or demographic growth. They should carry no connotation as to desirability or undesirability. . . .
>
> The proposed procedure consists of three major steps. First, preliminary baseline projection of the economic base in each State will be produced by BEA. These will then be used by Census in the preparation of a set of preliminary baseline State population projections. Following review of the preliminary projections, a set of final projections will be issued.[13]

These methods represent a very good beginning; however, even given the two-way interactions, none of these methods is designed to take into account public interventions, introduced through either federal and/or lower-level policies and programs. Policy analysis with this objective requires a good deal more; at least one approach, described in the next section, attempts to achieve this objective.

Some Bottom-Up Techniques

The National-Regional Impact Evaluation System (NRIES)

Perhaps the most ambitious of the multiregional nationalmodels is the NRIES model of the Bureau of Economic Analysis. Originally utilizing an economic base and an input-output approach, the model is now a full-fledged fifty-one state multiregional system, combining time-series econometric estimations of state variables with explicit linkages in what its developers call a bottom-up national framework.[14] The purpose of this modeling system, which is still in its experimental stages, is to forecast conditionally measures of both the regional effects of policy or resource constraints and the impact caused by the resultant redistribution of economic activities among states.

General Description

In describing the evolution of the NRIES, the developers explain their rejection of earlier modeling concepts:

Single-region models, rejected because of their omission of impacts outside the region

Subnational multiregion models[15] (of states, Appalachia, the Northeast Corridor, and so on), rejected because of the openness of the economic systems remaining outside the region under consideration.

National and multiregional models,[16] rejected because of their predominantly top-down philosophy.[17]

Features of the NRIES modeling approach that seek to overcome these shortcomings of other systems are:

1. NRIES is applied in a closed economic environment: that is, most of the regional economic impacts occur inside the national modeling framework. In this way, NRIES offers a bottom-up approach to regional analysis. The national model is derived simply as the sum of the fifty-one independently constructed state models.
2. The NRIES model deals with interregional linkages by including specific interaction variables in the state-variable estimations. Interaction variables are derived for each state and represent distance-deflated economic activity in all other states. The use of these interaction

variables in the state estimations establishes explicit links in economic activity among all states.

3. Because NRIES is an econometric formulation, it can deal with nonlinear estimation of certain equations. Clearly, dynamic, structural changes can and do occur in subnational areas, making the nonlinear properties of some NRIES equations a major advantage for the system.

Several advantages are claimed for NRIES by its developers:

First, because one of its elements is an interregional model, NRIES can be used to analyze the regional or spatial distribution of policy impacts. . . .

Second, by integrating regional and national models, the NRIES structure insures that the sum of regional activity will always be consistent with forecasts of national activity. . . .

Finally, the system simultaneously determines the level of both national and regional activity.[18]

In the typical NRIES state model, the magnitude of economic activity in the state (such as industrial output or employment in an industry) is generally expressed as a function of three types of variables: economic activity in related sectors within the state, economic or demographic interaction among states, and certain nationally determined levels of economic activity. The ties among activities of related sectors within state economies form the internal linkages for each state submodel. The interaction variables are indexes of economic and demographic activity in all other states.[19] The state submodels also include two types of national variables: national totals, which are expressed as the sum of an activity in all states; and certain variables that typically show little spatial variation (such as interest rates and sector prices) and thus are modeled as a function of national activity. Both types of national variables when used in the state equations form an additional linkage between the individual-state submodels and the national economy. As a result, NRIES is a highly detailed model of regional economic and demographic interrelationships within the national economy.[20]

Several interregional-linkage variables are included in the typical state model. The first set of linkages, relative-cost variables, is often incorporated into multiregion models to reflect the factor input or price advantage of a particular state vis-à-vis the remainder of the states. NRIES, for example, employs manufacturing-sector wage rates in a particular state relative to national rates as a relative-cost variable in the durable-goods output equations. In other, similar models, regional-output shares are related to relative labor and energy prices, designed to reflect supply-function differences (such as comparative advantage) between regions.

A second set of linkages, adjacent-area-demand variables, is included in multiregion models to reflect the magnitude of markets in selected areas surrounding the region in question. NRIES employs market-area disposable-income and population variables to explain the demand for output in nondurable manufacturing, finance, and trade. Determination of the NRIES geographic bounds of the market areas for each state is based on the availability of interstate highway and other transportation links between large population areas in adjacent states. Market potential in other similar models also is defined in terms of effective distance (such as travel times) and variables reflecting effective demand.

The third major linkage mechanism incorporated in multiregion models focuses on the interaction between economic activity in the reference region and that in all remaining regions in the model. This level of activity is captured in NRIES through the linkage of each region to the remaining regions, based upon a gravity concept. A series of interaction indexes is calculated for each state to represent the level of economic activity in all other states, weighted by the distance from other states to the state in question. These indexes are calculated from such state variables as gross output, personal income, retail sales, and population. Their purpose is to provide estimates of distance-deflated demands by other states for a particular state's product. Interaction variables have been incorporated into NRIES output equations for durables and nondurables manufacturing, retail sales, and transportation, communication, and public utilities.

An NRIES Multiregional Application:
A National Coal Scenario

To illustrate the operation of NRIES in an energy application, the authors of the first NRIES monograph selected two subnational applications—a single-region and a multiregion case—and, finally, a national application.[21] Each application highlights different features of NRIES. We shall describe the multiregion application, which captures elements of both the single-region and national levels and illustrates the bottom-up feature as well.[22]

Here, NRIES has been applied in a national context with the direct impacts occurring in several (but not all) states. This scenario, involving a strategy of advanced coal development in fifteen of the major coal-producing states, is based on the Energy Information Administration, Department of Energy's *1977 Annual Report to Congress,* which presents six hypothetical scenarios of national coal development that might be achieved by 1985. The differences in the scenarios, which are listed for each of the twelve DOE multistate coal-producing regions, are caused by varying assumptions about the future supply, demand, and price of energy sources. NRIES, in turn, is employed to generate the economic and demographic impacts resulting from the differing coal-production and price levels.[23]

Certain direct regional impacts are modeled as exogenous inputs to NRIES. The top half of figure 7-4 shows the steps necessary to obtain these direct impacts. The DOE regional coal-output totals are distributed to the states based on surveys of coal-mine capacity. This increased output of coal presupposes certain construction inputs and inputs of manufacturing equipment from both coal-producing and non-coal-producing states. (For states with recently enacted severance tax laws, which would not be effectively modeled by NRIES, the direct additional taxes are calculated.)

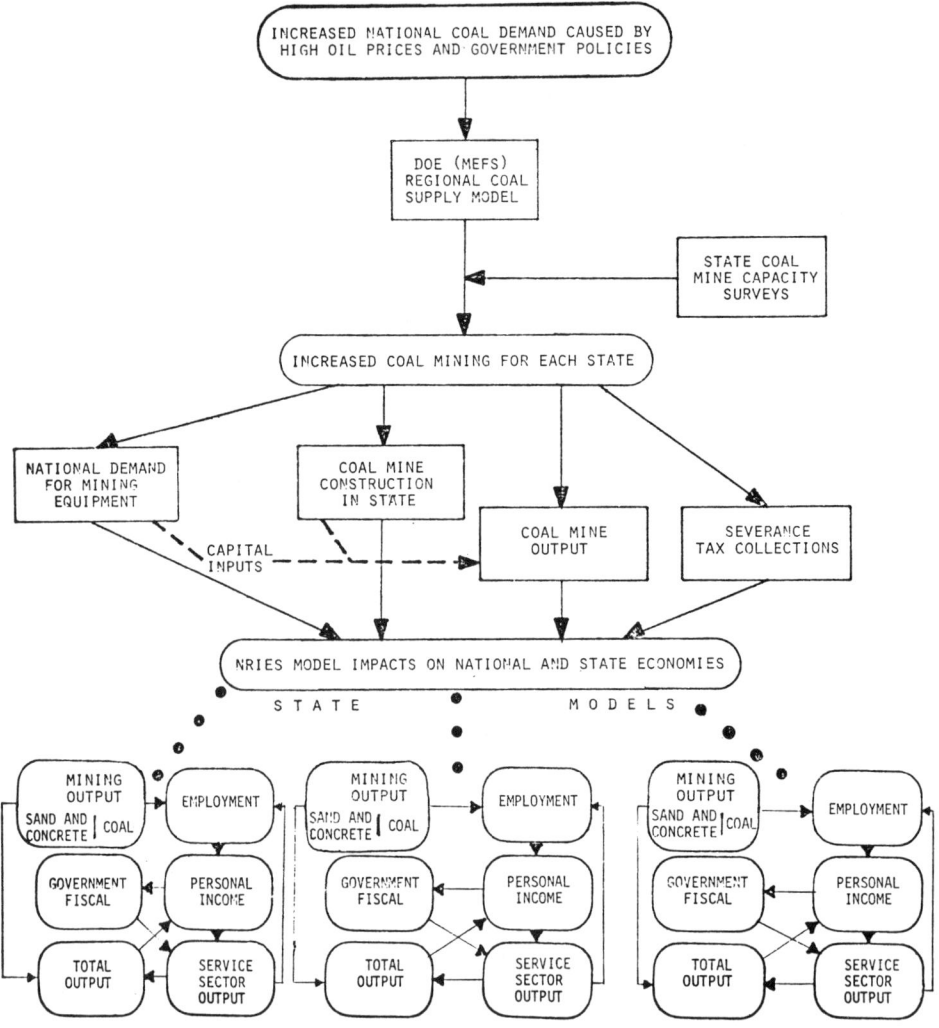

Figure 7-4. NRIES Flow Diagram for a National Coal Scenario

Some Bottom-Up Techniques

The lower half of figure 7-4 represents the structural linkage between the direct inputs for the alternative national coal-development scenario and the NRIES model.

Impacts on state (and BEA region) gross output that results from the national coal-development scenario are listed in table 7-3. The results indicate that the total-output impacts for the United States increase annually from $324 million in 1978 to $3.7 billion in 1985.[24]

Across the nation, non-coal-producing states such as California and Michigan generally show stronger output advances in the earlier years during the construction and capital-equipment-purchase period. Conversely, the coal-mining states show greater impacts in the later years.

Table 7-3
Regional Impacts on State Gross Product Originating in a National Coal-Development Scenario, Present and Projected
(millions of 1972 dollars)

	1978	1979	1980	1981	1982	1983	1984	1985
Regions								
New England	9.7	20.3	28.7	32.6	34.3	29.3	23.9	20.4
Northeast	55.1	125.9	218.2	297.4	363.6	399.2	427.2	470.2
Great Lakes	87.0	202.0	346.1	489.6	658.3	867.2	1020.4	
Plains	16.9	33.4	58.2	84.2	107.5	121.8	142.3	163.0
Southeast	57.7	113.2	352.0	534.8	683.1	820.5	953.3	1117.3
Southwest	25.1	50.7	105.8	157.2	215.6	262.8	310.7	350.8
Rocky Mountains	38.4	59.0	142.9	208.5	274.6	328.6	373.8	440.8
Midwest	34.0	71.5	104.7	124.5	139.8	133.8	127.1	127.9
States								
Alabama	1.4	3.1	6.6	10.8	16.2	22.3	29.7	38.5
Alaska	.1	.1	.1	.2	.3	.3	.3	.5
Arizona	2.3	5.8	10.1	14.3	17.8	20.8	22.6	25.4
Arkansas	1.0	2.5	5.5	8.6	12.0	15.6	19.3	23.7
California	26.6	55.6	80.1	92.6	99.5	88.5	75.8	68.7
Colorado	6.8	11.6	33.6	48.6	65.4	76.5	79.5	94.4
Connecticut	4.5	9.9	14.6	18.4	21.7	21.9	22.5	24.2
Delaware	.3	1.2	2.5	4.2	6.0	7.9	9.6	11.5
District of Columbia	.2	.3	2.3	4.6	6.4	8.0	9.9	12.5
Florida	5.8	14.3	25.3	35.4	45.9	54.3	62.7	73.4
Georgia	2.7	6.5	14.9	23.1	30.5	36.5	40.7	45.6
Hawaii	.1	.2	.4	.6	.9	1.1	1.3	1.6
Idaho	.7	1.4	2.3	3.1	4.0	4.5	5.2	6.1
Illinois	27.9	60.2	115.8	190.7	269.7	336.7	416.9	507.3
Indiana	16.7	38.4	64.0	87.9	125.4	144.9	168.4	195.3
Iowa	3.3	7.0	11.1	15.0	19.0	21.0	23.3	27.0
Kansas	2.2	4.7	7.4	9.3	11.3	12.3	13.5	15.6
Kentucky	10.4	20.1	55.8	91.9	134.1	189.2	245.3	310.2
Louisiana	1.3	2.7	5.0	7.2	9.3	11.5	14.3	18.9
Maine	.5	1.1	1.5	1.6	1.6	1.2	.8	.4
Maryland	2.7	6.1	15.0	23.6	30.6	36.9	44.1	53.1

Table 7-3 continued

	1978	1979	1980	1981	1982	1983	1984	1985
Massachusetts	3.1	6.2	8.2	8.1	6.8	3.7	−.1	−3.1
Michigan	22.8	57.4	92.2	121.3	155.4	164.6	178.4	208.5
Minnesota	2.1	4.6	9.6	13.8	17.5	20.9	22.9	26.2
Mississippi	2.2	4.9	7.8	10.1	12.4	13.3	14.5	16.4
Missouri	4.8	10.1	19.0	27.5	36.4	43.8	51.3	61.1
Montana	8.7	13.8	22.0	32.7	42.9	49.3	54.6	63.5
Nebraska	1.1	2.3	3.8	5.0	6.0	6.5	6.6	7.2
Nevada	.1	.2	1.4	3.0	4.7	6.4	7.8	9.3
New Hampshire	.2	.3	.5	.3	−.3	−1.1	−2.3	−3.7
New Jersey	8.8	21.0	30.4	39.6	42.2	43.5	38.9	39.4
New Mexico	4.0	7.7	15.3	22.2	34.9	45.9	54.2	67.5
New York	21.3	49.6	79.3	100.8	119.3	120.9	117.9	114.9
North Carolina	5.6	12.6	25.1	37.5	49.2	58.1	67.2	78.4
North Dakota	3.5	4.7	7.4	13.9	17.6	18.0	25.5	28.0
Ohio	13.4	30.6	49.4	55.6	65.0	58.4	47.6	43.8
Oklahoma	1.3	2.7	4.1	4.8	5.5	5.6	5.9	6.7
Oregon	4.1	9.3	14.0	18.1	22.1	23.7	25.8	29.1
Pennsylvania	21.7	47.8	88.8	124.5	159.1	182.0	206.8	238.8
Rhode Island	1.0	2.1	2.8	3.1	3.1	2.4	1.9	1.6
South Carolina	1.7	4.2	7.3	10.5	13.5	15.7	17.7	20.4
South Dakota	.0	−.0	−.0	−.2	−.4	−.6	−.9	−1.0
Tennessee	5.5	13.4	24.7	37.6	51.0	63.4	76.2	92.1
Texas	17.5	34.4	76.2	115.9	157.4	190.6	228.0	251.2
Utah	1.2	2.2	5.1	6.7	8.0	8.9	11.2	13.6
Vermont	.3	.7	1.0	1.3	1.4	1.3	1.1	1.0
Virginia	5.4	10.3	24.0	38.9	47.6	57.3	65.1	75.6
Washington	3.0	6.2	8.6	9.9	12.3	13.7	16.1	18.7
West Virginia	14.7	18.6	150.1	223.2	261.2	283.2	300.8	323.6
Wisconsin	6.2	15.5	24.3	34.0	42.8	49.6	55.9	65.6
Wyoming	21.0	30.0	79.9	117.3	154.6	189.3	223.3	263.2
Total	323.8	676.0	1356.4	1928.8	2476.8	2850.3	3225.6	3711.9

Future Directions of NRIES

Several directions are being worked on simultaneously in the BEA NRIES effort:

1. Correcting weaknesses; for example, remedying the paucity of regional data (such as commodity and sector prices and capital expenditures and stock), a long-term process; and further sectoral and spatial disaggregation
2. Integration of the NRIES with other systems, such as the Regional Industrial Multiplier System (RIMS) model,[25] employed in a recent DHUD-Commerce study of the effects of local public-works expenditures[26]

Some Bottom-Up Techniques   161

3. Work to bridge the NRIES model with DOE's Multiregional Energy Forecasting System (MEFS) to develop an energy-economic-model bridge[27]
4. Use of NRIES as a general-purpose model to a recursive submodel, such as to forecast major aggregates that in turn are used to drive specific industry and/or area submodels[28]

Concluding Remarks: NRIES

Apropos of these model linkages, the following statement provides a good perspective of the possibilities:

> Currently, hundreds of different general purpose regional models exist in the United States, each focusing on somewhat overlapping phenomena. Usually, these models cannot be integrated. . . . In many cases, a practical alternative to constructing a new model is the development of an external link, or "bridge," so that the models can interact with one another. Where feasible, this technique can produce large savings. . . .[29]

NRIES is in the early stages of development. Its progress should be watched closely by those involved in analysis assignments where the most advanced bottom-up/top-down modeling is required. Whether or not the sectoral detail and structure of the sectoral and areal submodels and their interaction are adequate for the policy-analysis tasks ahead, only time will tell. But NRIES, along with developments reported in the next chapter, appears to represent a substantial improvement on previous methods.

Concluding Remarks

In comparing modeling approaches that can most accurately be considered bottom up, we have seen a multitude of characteristics. Some of the models, particularly the traditional ones, could well suffer from the so-called chamber-of-commerce effect: with no top-down constrain, use of such models could lead to combined estimates that do not accurately reflect best-estimates national totals. These models may serve a narrow purpose, but they are inadequate for the vast majority of policy analyses generated at the federal level.

The more sophisticated bottom-up modeling approaches are beginning to find remedies to some—but not all—of the problems inherent in top-down models. For one, there is generally no inherent limitation on the intra-areal structural complexity each subnational area can represent and assume in some of the bottom-up models. We have seen in NRIES, for example, that each of the states—the basic subnational geographic unit of that system—can be represented in the substantial structural detail that a combined input-output, econometric formulation can represent. However, there are many aspects of subnational-area structure and detail that cannot be easily captured through such formulations. For example, when resources are underemployed, specific plans for increasing an area's output and productivity—particularly if there are a host of public and private economic-development tools available—require in-depth insight and knowledge of that area's institutional structure, leadership attitudes, and traditions. Similar agreements can be made regarding subnational environmental and energy plans, the implementation *modus operandi* that translate national policy into locally acceptable, satisfying, and even optimum actions. Given the plethora of policy tools, implementation choices, and subnational variation, even the most sophisticated and complex bottom-up formulation will frequently produce poor, invalid, and inaccurate representations of local economic, environmental, and energy activities.

As for interareal flows (the second key desideratum), all the multiregional national models and NRIES include representation of interarea trade flows—crudely, perhaps, in that transportation impedance (or distance) is taken as the key variable affecting the degree of interaction. Other flows—such as population commuting or migrating, industrial relocation, communication, money, capital, and many others—are generally omitted.

The third key criterion—the ability to handle scale economies and diseconomies—is not explicitly recognized in any of these modeling formulations, although NRIES does have the capability—essential for representing scale issues—to deal with nonlinear equations. Even with this feature, however, in its present formulation NRIES cannot readily deal with the changing regional boundaries (such as multistate regions, or boundary lines cutting through states as in the Appalachian Regional Commission's coverage), which proper treatment of scale economies requires.

In varying degrees, bottom-up formulations incorporate one or more of the ten additional positive features (see chapter 5) of desirable policy-analysis models. Probably most absent, as mentioned above, are the nuances, subtleties, and uncertainties that can come about only through dynamic two-way communication and interaction between the top and the bottom. In addition to inadequate representation of intra-areal complexity, interareal flows, and scale issues, the strictly bottom-up formulations necessarily omit problems and opportunities growing out of a two-way (top-bottom) communication over policies, implementation, and their combination. Some bottom-up formulations are beginning to utilize such two-way communications as checking and validation mechanisms. To the degree these communications are more than window dressing, they begin to bring bottom-up models into the realm of two-way systems.

Notes

1. E. Shlifer and R.W. Wolff, "Aggregation and Proration in Forecasting," *Management Science* 25 (1979):594-603. See also L.E. Oller, "A Method for Pooling Forecasts," *Journal of Operations Research Society* 29 (1978):55-63; M.P. Singh and R. Tessier, "Estimates for Domain Totals," *Journal of American Statistical Association* 71 (1976):322-325; S.D. Wood and B.M. Steece, "Forecasting the Product of Two Time Series with a Linear Asymmetric Error Cost Function," *Management Science* 24 (1978):690-701; Andrew Whinston, "Price Guides in Decentralized Organizations," in William W. Cooper, H.J. Leavitt, and M.W. Shelly II, editors. *New Perspectives in Organization Research* (New York: John Wiley & Sons, 1966); Kenneth Arrow, "Optimization, Decentralization, and Internal Pricing in Business Firms," in *Contribution to Scientific Research in Management* (Los Angeles: University of California, Western Data Processing Center, 1959); and H.J. Kruisinga, ed., *The Balance between Centralization and Decentralization in Managerial Control* (Leiden: H.E. Stenfert Kroese, 1954).

2. However, see M.A. Geisler and W.A. Steger, "How to Plan for Management and New Systems," *Harvard Business Review* 40, no. 5 (1962), pp. 103-110.

3. Ronald L. Ritschard, "Proceedings of the Workshop on National/Regional Energy-Environmental Modeling Concepts" (Reston, Va., 1979).

4. Ibid., pp. 28-29, 31.

5. This section is adapted from the *U.S. Government Manual, 1979-1980* (Washington, D.C.: Government Printing Office, 1980), appendix D, pp. 858-859.

6. Executive Order 11731 of 12 July 1973 broadened the Federal Regional Council mandate, including coordination of direct federal program assistance to state and local governments. Executive Order 11892 of 31 December 1975 increased the membership of the Federal Regional Council system, further expanding interagency cooperation and improving coordination of services to state and local governments.

7. "Federal Regional Councils—Can Carter Make Them Work?" *National Journal*, 18 June 1977, p. 949.

8. The Corps of Engineers is attempting to design and develop methods to permit the division of impacts into subnational versus national effects: no methodology, however, has yet been found completely acceptable. But see the Water Resources Council, "Procedures for Evaluation of National Economic Development (NED) Benefits and Costs in Water Resources Planning (Level C)," 18CFR, part 713, *Federal Register* 44 (5 December 1979):72892-990.

9. This is based on discussions with Bureau of Economic Analyses OBERS research staff.

10. For a review of recent work in regional modeling, see Norman J. Glickman, *Econometric Analysis of Regional Systems: Explorations in Model Building and Policy Analysis* (New York: Academic Press, 1977); and John J. Knapp, T.W. Fields, and R.T. Jerome, Jr., *A Survey of State and Regional Econometric Models* (Charlottesville, Va.: Tayloe Murphy Institute, 1978).

11. Sidney Saltzman and Hua-Shan Chi, "An Exploratory Monthly Integrated Regional/National Econometric Model," *Regional Science and Urban Economics* 7 (1977):49-81; Steven Caldwell, William Greene, Timothy Mount, Sidney Saltzman, and Richard Broyd, "Forecasting Regional Energy Demand with Linked Macro/Micro Models" (Ithaca, N.Y.: Working Papers in Planning, Cornell University, 1979).

12. U.S. Department of Commerce, *State Quarterly Economic Developments* (EDA, OMB, and BEA, various dates); Office of Federal Statistical Policy and Standards, U.S. Department of Commerce, "Population Projections for Use in Federal Fund Allocation," *Federal Register* 44 (5 December 1979):700076.

13. Ibid., p. 70078.

14. K.P. Ballard and R.M. Wendling, "The National-Regional Impact Evaluation System: A Spatial Model of U.S. Economic and Demographic Activity" (Paper presented at the National Meeting of the Regional Science Association, Chicago, November 1978).

15. K.P. Ballard and N.J. Glickman, "A Multiregional Econometric Forecasting System: A Model for the Delaware Valley," *Journal of Regional Science* 17 (August 1977):161-177; R.T. Crow, "A Nationally Linked Regional Econometric Model," *Journal of Regional Science* 13 (August 1973):187-204; S.H. Putman, *An Empirical Model of Regional Growth,* Monograph Series 6 (Philadelphia: Regional Science Research Institute, 1975); and George Treyz, A.F. Friedlaender, E.N. McNertney, Benjamin Stevens, and R.E. Williams, "The Massachusetts Economic Policy Analysis Model," mimeographed (Amherst, Mass.: University of Massachusetts, Department of Economics, 1977).

16. S.P. Dresch and R.D. Goldberg, "IDIOM: An Inter-industry, National/Regional Policy Evaluation Model," *Annals of Economic and Social Measurement* 2 (July 1973):323-356; C.C. Harris, Jr., *The Urban Economies 1985: A Multiregional Multi-Industry Forecasting Model* (Lexington, Mass.: Lexington Books, D.C. Heath and Company, 1973); W.J. Milne, N.J. Glickman, and F.G. Adams, "A Framework for Analyzing Regional Decline: A Multiregional Econometric Model of the United States" (Philadelphia, University of Pennsylvania, Department of Economics Discussion Paper 398, 1978); R.J. Olsen, Richard John, et al., *MULTIREGION: A Simulation-Forecasting Model of BEA Economic Area Population and Employment* (Oak Ridge, Tenn.: Oak Ridge National

Laboratory, 1977); and K.R. Polenske, "The Implementation of a Multiregional Input-Output Model for the United States," in *Input-Output Techniques,* ed. Andrew Brody and Anne P. Carter (Amsterdam: North-Holland Publishing Co., 1972), pp. 171-189.

17. "Multiregional models are restricted, however, since they place little emphasis on individual regional-growth patterns, but rather allocate shares of national growth to each region. In the top-down approach, multiregional growth is constrained to a predetermined national solution. There is little or no feedback from the regions to the Nation. In addition, the top-down approach often precludes the effective modeling of interactions between regions"; Ballard and Wendling, "National-Regional Impact Evaluation System," p. 2. *Journal of Regional Science,* 20, 2 (May 1980):143-158; K.P. Ballard, R.D. Gustely, and R.M. Wendling, *NRIES: Structure, Performance and Application of a Bottom-Up Inter-Regional Econometric Model* (Washington, D.C.: Department of Commerce 1980).

18. Ibid., pp. 3-4.

19. These indexes are defined as the activity of certain sectors, deflated by the physical distance to the particular state in question, and summed over all states in the nation. When incorporated into the state equations, these indexes form explicit interregional linkages among the states.

20. Each state model consists of 264 equations, of which 68 are behavioral. There are, in addition, 98 total and 20 behavioral equations in the national model. Thus, the full model system has approximately 3,500 behavioral and 14,000 total equations.

21. K.P. Ballard, J.V. Cartright, R.D. Gustely, and John Kort, *National-Regional Impact Evaluation System* (Washington, D.C.: Bureau of Economic Analysis, U.S. Department of Commerce, 1980). See also R.M. Wendling and K.P. Ballard, "Projecting the Regional Impacts of Energy Development," *Growth and Change* 11 (1980):7-17; Urban Systems Research and Engineering, (1980); "Inputs to NRIES for Montana Coal Development Scenarios" (Report to the Energy Information Administration, U.S. Department of Energy, 1979) (mimeographed, Cambridge, Mass., 1979).

22. Partially excerpted from Wendling and Ballard, "Projecting Regional, Multiregional, and National Economic Impacts."

23. An NRIES *control solution* is first estimated, which in this case is matched as closely as possible to one of the coal scenarios. Any of the other scenarios may then be defined as the *alternate solution.*

24. Except for two years, Illinois registers the highest impacts during the period. This is not surprising, for two reasons: first, it is one of the states where high-level advanced coal development is assumed; second, it has a very high manufacturing-durables base and is a source for not only mining equipment but also construction-related equipment.

25. RIMS is an input-output model used to estimate impacts for areas as small as counties and for any combination of the 478 industries in the national input-output table. It is capable of providing a substantial degree of both industrial and spatial detail, but has only limited interregional feedback capability and no explicit time dimension.

26. See Ballard et al., *National—Regional Impact Evaluation System*.

27. Ibid.

28. For a similar application, see R.W. Thomas and H.J. Stekler, "A Model of Construction Activity in Subnational Areas," (IDA Paper P-1446, Institute for Defense Analyses, Arlington, Va., 1979).

29. Ballard and Wendling, "The National-Regional Impact Evaluation System," p. 180.

Appendix 7A: References to State Economic Models

Adams, F.G., Brooking, C.G., and Glickman, N.J. "On the Specification and Simulation of a Regional Econometric Model: A Model of the Mississippi." *Review of Economics and Statistics* 57 (August 1975): 286-298.

Ballard, Kenneth, and Glickman, N.J. "A Multiregional Econometric Forecasting System: A Model for the Delaware Valley." *Journal of Regional Science* 17 (1977):161-179.

Bell, F.W. "An Econometric Forecasting Model for a Region." *Journal of Regional Science* 7 (1967):109-127.

Bourque, P.J., Conway, R.S., and Howard, C.T. *The Washington Projection and Simulation Model.* Seattle, Wash.: University of Washington, 1977.

Burton, R.P., and J.W. Dyckman *A Quarterly Economic Forecasting Model for the State of California.* Berkeley: Center for Planning and Development, Research Institute of Urban and Regional Development, University of California, 1965.

Crow, R.T. *An Econometric Model of the Northeast Corridor of the United States.* Washington, D.C.: U.S. Department of Transportation, 1969.

Crow, R.T. "An Econometric Model of the Buffalo SMSA: A Progress Report." Mimeographed. State University of New York at Buffalo, School of Management, 1974.

Danzinger, Sheldon, and Haveman, Robert "Tax and Welfare Simplification: An Analysis of Distributional and Regional Impacts." *National Tax Journal* 30 (September 1977):269-284.

Data Resources, Inc. "State and Area Forecasting Service: Technical Documentation." Lexington, Mass., 1977.

Donnelly, William A.; Havenner, A.M.; and Hopkins, F.E. "Estimating a Comprehensive County-Level Forecasting Model of the United States: A Presentation of the READ Model." Mimeographed. Federal Energy Administration, Washington, D.C., 1977.

Dutta, M., and Su, V. "An Econometric Model of Puerto Rico." *Review of Economic Studies* (1969):319-334.

Freidlaender, A.F.; Treyz, George; and Tresch, Richard. "A Quarterly Econometric Model of Massachusetts and Its Fiscal Structure." Report to the U.S. Senate Ways and Means Committee, 30 June 1975.

Glickman, N.J. "An Econometric Forecasting Model for the Philadelphia Region." *Journal of Regional Science* 11 (April 1971):15-32.

Golladay, Frederick, and Haveman, Robert "Regional and Distributional Effects of a Negative Income Tax." *American Economic Review* 66 (September 1976):629-641.

──────. *The Economic Impacts of Tax Transfer Policy.* New York: Academic Press, 1977.

Harris, C.A. "Evaluation of the Regional Economic and Environmental Effects of Alternative Highway Systems." Report prepared for the U.S. Department of Transportation, 1975.

Kendrick, J.W., and Jaycox, M.C. "The Concept and Estimation of Gross State Product." *Southern Economic Journal* 32:(1965):153-169.

King, Jill A. "The Distributional Impact of Energy Policies: Development and Application of the Phase I Comprehensive Human Resources Data System." Report prepared by Mathematica Policy Research, Inc., for the Federal Energy Administration, 1977.

Klein, Lawrence, and Glickman, N.J. "An Econometric Model of Pennsylvania." Philadelphia: Economics Research Unit, University of Pennsylvania, 1975.

L'Esperance, W.L.; King, A.E.; and Sines, R.H. "Conjoining an Ohio Input-Output Model with an Econometric Model of Ohio." Paper presented at the Twenty-second Annual Meeting of the Regional Science Association, 1975.

Licari, J.; Deventer, D.; and Studenmund, A.H. "An Impact Analysis of the Hawaiian Economy." Mimeographed. (Los Angeles, Calif.: Occidental College, Dept. of Economics, 1973).

Loxley, Colin John. "A Quarterly Economic Model of the Cleveland Metropolitan Area." Ph.D. dissertation, Case Western Reserve University, 1976.

Olsen, R.J. "MULTIREGION—A Simulation-Forecasting Model of BEA Economic Area Population and Employment." Oak Ridge, Tenn.: Energy Research and Development Administration, Oak Ridge National Laboratory, 1977.

Polenske, Karen "A Multiregional Input-Output Model for the United States." Cambridge, Mass.: Harvard Economics Research Project, 1970.

Research Seminar in Quantitative Economics. *Econometric Model of Michigan.* Ann Arbor: University of Michigan Press, 1965.

Richter, C. "An Econometric Model of the Coastal Plains States." Mimeographed. Chapel Hill: University of North Carolina, Department of Economics, 1970.

Schinck, George "An Econometric Model of Luzerne County." Report prepared by Wharton EFA Inc., for the U.S. Department of Commerce, 1974.

Treyz, G.I.; Friedlaender, A.F.; and Stevens, B.H. "The Employment Sector of a Regional Policy Simulation Model." Philadelphia: Regional Science Research Institute, 1978.

U.S. Department of Energy. "Regional Earnings Impact System (REIS)." Mimeographed. Washington, D.C., 1976.

U.S. Water Resources Council. *1972 OBERS Projections: Regional Economic Activity in U.S., Series E. Population.* Washington, D.C., 1974.

**Part III
Discovering Some
Two-Way Methods**

8 Some Two-Way Applications for Modeling National-Regional Analysis

We have come full circle, from maintaining that forecasting the future is a very risky business (chapter 1) to supporting the development and use of methods to perform both national forecasting that incorporates regional needs and characteristics (chapters 5, 6, and 7), and regional modeling that thoroughly captures whatever national forces make themselves felt at that regional level. The federal government has to make the most responsible effort it can to perform such conditional forecasts, both for planning and for budgetary purposes. The complexity of making these forecasts is exacerbated by several factors, among them changing national and subnational trends and the uniqueness of regional impacts to each locality and subarea. The central issue of using forecasts at any level is whether they really add anything useful to a policy debate or planning decision. Clearly, their purpose is forecasting, or at least conditionally projecting; their actual *utility*, however, has to be carefully monitored. Overzealous claims for their results in terms of prognosis or specific attention to analytic precision is likely out of order. Here, we are focusing on bringing forward the best techniques and information available to enrich the decision-making process—not to replace that process.

We have also devoted a good deal of attention to explicating the terms *top-down* and *bottom-up* so that they take on more meaning to the systems analyst as different conceptual approaches to model development. The beliefs and strategies of proponents of these approaches often make for interesting reading and have provided stimulating controversy—and entertainment—at several professional meetings. They represent different types of information capabilities that are needed in formulating national policy.

To recapitulate briefly, top-down analyses suggest methodologies that attempt to produce, as outputs, global perspectives of the relationship between the variable in question and other variables that might impact it or that it impacts. Normally, these analyses are relatively holistic and attempt to investigate strategic questions of national policy. Data are collected at a relatively gross level of detail (state or federal region as opposed to city block, for example), and relationships between the variables (given certain actions) are average coefficients representing groups of people, processes, or actions rather than specific activities of individuals or units. Such models are used both for research and analysis, to test the first-order consequences of various strategy alternatives, and for prediction, to look for unanticipated macro effects resulting from proposed courses of action.

Bottom-up analyses, on the other hand, normally entail integration of the results of a series of detailed analyses to produce a complete national or global picture. These individual analyses are comparatively detailed and represent more clearly the specific subnational areas, or spatial portions of a problem. They are often used in assessments of national strategies whenever time and resources allow a more detailed survey. Often issues of a less analytical nature are introduced into these analyses to permit a weighting of empirical results. The detailed data and relationships modeled in these studies might, for example, contain spatial analyses to locate impacts of various policies in a more precise and areal fashion.

Debating the relative merits of these approaches becomes a meaningless exercise when real-life policy issues are involved. It then becomes clear that there is no simple response to which approach is the better. The answer depends on a whole series of factors, including the specific policy, time and resources available, and where and for what purpose the decision is being made. Ideally, an agency would have both types of models available and that the results of a top-down analysis could be directly utilized by the family of bottom-up models, and vice versa. Such a capability would allow an agency to utilize the analysis produced by the more macro approach as a bounding condition and allocative capacity to permit more-detailed analysis by a collection of micro models. To some extent, this would solve the problem of having results obtained by the top-down models that are too general and insensitive to, say, local differences, but it would also impose a tyranny of total-value limits on the bottom-up segments. The essence of the bottom-up approach is that the totals are discovered by summing the values obtained in the several detailed studies.

A true bottom-up approach is likely to be less than totally useful to federal policymakers if their use is meant to be repetitive or frequent on a relatively short time demand. The organizational and administrative problems of continually exercising such a network would be nearly impossible or would require impressive managerial skill. Further, there is an inherent weakness in producing unbounded partial analyses of policies: each study area makes up its own mind as to the share of the total policy or impact it will have or cause. The chamber-of-commerce effect, often noted in geographic analyses when inordinate localism creeps into the results, produces unrealistically integrated impacts.

Of particular interest are answers to questions of the following sort:

> Can there conceptually be a successful integration of the top-down and bottom-up approaches? If yes, what would each of these systems contain? How would they link?

Two-Way Applications

Institutionally, how would an integrated system of models and analyses be organized and maintained? Should it be housed inside or outside the government, or both? How would all or part of this system be run for analysis? How can it be decided what parts to run for what analysis?

Administratively, what should such a system cost to build, to run, and to maintain? Should it belong to only one agency?

Scientifically, how can validation of the results obtained from the system be demonstrated? How should the system be improved?

These questions, though not exhaustive, provide a starting point for investigation. Creating and implementing such a system would be difficult, but if it can be done and can be demonstrated to give superior answers to our increasingly complex policy issues, there is little doubt it will be used.

Before we describe and evaluate several approaches to combining top-down and bottom-up methods, two observations are necessary.

First, it is difficult to draw the line, as we have done here, between approaches that are a bit of both and those that are predominantly one or the other. For example, some of the models discussed in chapter 7 could have been labeled "incipient combined approaches," such as the OBERS two-way-communication model (see pages 145-149). In fact, it is more likely that the predominantly bottom-up approaches can be adapted to the combination than that the purely top-down ones can. Selecting the former for inclusion in this chapter rather than in chapter 7 is, admittedly, partially arbitrary, based as much on the *intentions* of the designers of these methods as on the methods themselves. Nevertheless, we believe that the approaches described in this chapter are more oriented to a combined approach than any of those already discussed.

Second, because none of the methods has been employed long enough for any pattern of validity or usefulness to emerge, we have no fully developed set of criteria to perform assessments of the models. Instead, we will apply some of the criteria developed and discussed in previous chapters (particularly chapter 5). These are primarily assessments of characteristics rather than of *ex post* effectiveness. Nevertheless, they may enable readers to develop and refine their own ideas and concepts for both improved two-way analytic methods and ways to assess the effectiveness and costs of these methods. Although we have not yet focused on the costs of each class of methods, we need to be aware of the resources and completion times associated with each. Obviously, methods that are equally effective and require fewer resources are the most desirable. Rarely, however, is the choice that simple; as we have seen, no two methods produce equivalently relative to each of the criteria discussed in chapter 5. In the end, users will have to measure the advantages of each additional resource and/or time increment against what they are willing to spend.

In this chapter we describe the following methods, illustrating each with appropriate application(s):

Regional Environmental Assessments—DOE Style

Regional Characterization: The Use of Factor- and Cluster Analysis

Urban- and Community-Impact Statements

Subnational Programming in the Federal System

Regional Environmental Assessments—DOE Style

Perhaps because it is a latecomer to the cabinet; perhaps because it originated as an overriding national and presidential priority; perhaps because the regional laboratories are such an extensive resource; or perhaps because it is regionally so differentiated: whatever the key reasons, DOE—particularly that part dealing with energy, environmental, and economic tradeoffs—insisted from the very first on regional assessments. The rationale was that without a thorough understanding of differences in states and regional acceptability, subtle, often crucial, conflicting state and regional objectives and issues are often missed in formulations of national energy policies and programs. Failure to identify and address regional issues is believed to restrict significantly the success and the benefits of national energy programs.

As a result, regional-impact assessments have become vehicles for analyzing state and regional environmental issues related to the national energy-policymaking framework. More-sensitive and more-responsible planning is intended to result. To support the development of such regional-impact assessments, the regional-assessment effort was developed at the Department of Energy, Office of the Assistant Secretary for the Environment (DOE/EV).

Historically, regional analyses have concentrated on the interrelationships of different activities in the same region, with only cursory consideration of the three major reasons for concern about subnational consequences and trends: the presence of important interareal relationships; detailed and crucial intra-areal structural variations; and scale economies resulting from multiareal policies and programs.

Based on the information contained in subnationally developed baseline data and scenarios of energy futures, the Office of Environment constructs regional-energy characterizations, performs analyses of impacts of energy development, and determines environmental conflicts associated with such development (see figure 8-1). Impacts are quantified, classified,

Two-Way Applications 177

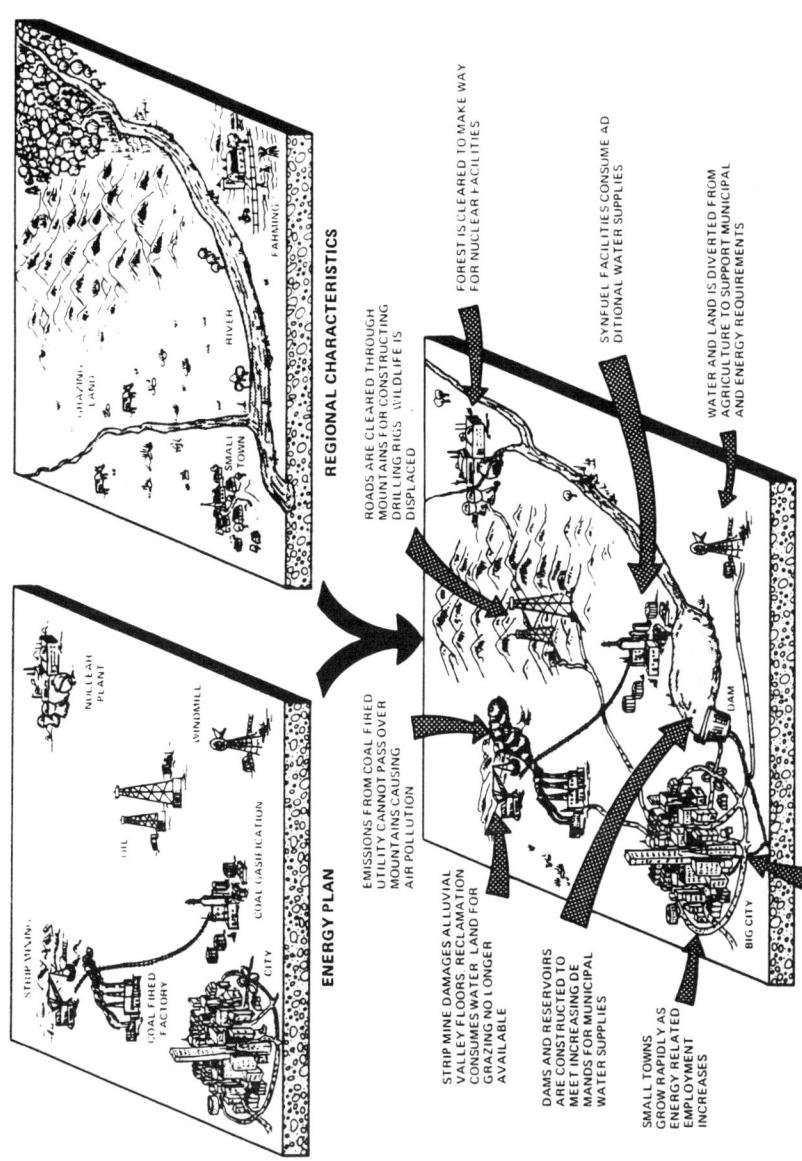

Figure 8-1. Conceptualization of the RIIA Process

and evaluated on a state-by-state basis and presented in annual summary reports for each federal region (see figure 8-2).

National energy policies and plans, intended to address future needs, are used to develop alternative future policy scenarios for use in these analyses. Although the DOE/EV effort does not develop scenarios per se, it does identify and assess the environmental impact of selected scenarios at the regional level. Figure 8-1 is an example of what a federal-level laboratory-coordinated Regional Issue Identification and Assessment (RIIA) effort deals with in studying the prospective impacts occurring in a region where a concerted energy-development effort is being implemented. The hypothetical multistate region of figure 8-1 is shown with a representation of the disaggregated national energy plan for that subnational area. The subnational environmental issues resulting from the interaction of the energy plan with this environment are characterized in the lower frame of the figure.

Currently, the DOE/EV effort is determining environmental, health, and safety, social, economic, and institutional impacts from demands for technologies as depicted in the Energy Information Administration (EIA) medium-energy-supply/demand (mid-mid) scenario for 1985 and 1990.[1] In subsequent years, this DOE office will routinely examine the effects of alternative DOE scenarios that will include business-as-usual (that is, status quo) cases and assumptions regarding future legislative and executive actions, including the National Energy Act. Let us look briefly at these methods.

Regional Assessment Methods and Results

The primary purpose of the regional-assessment effort is to support national policymakers in delineating the subnational impacts of national energy demand-and-supply projections, whether or not these consequences cross state boundaries. The process and products are objective and made consistent from region to region by disaggregating national control totals to the subnational areas.

The methodology designed to produce the DOE RIIA report takes the results of the energy, economic, and environmental assessments produced by the department to the federal regional level(s) and further aggregates them to the county level on the supply side. These forecasts are provided to six of the national laboratories engaged in research for the department.[2] Each laboratory is responsible for providing the regional-impact assessments for one or more federal regions and the composite states.

Procedurally, each laboratory is responsible both for producing a segment of the regional analyses, the specific segments being a function of their individual expertise, and for serving as the general expert on this area, cri-

Two-Way Applications 179

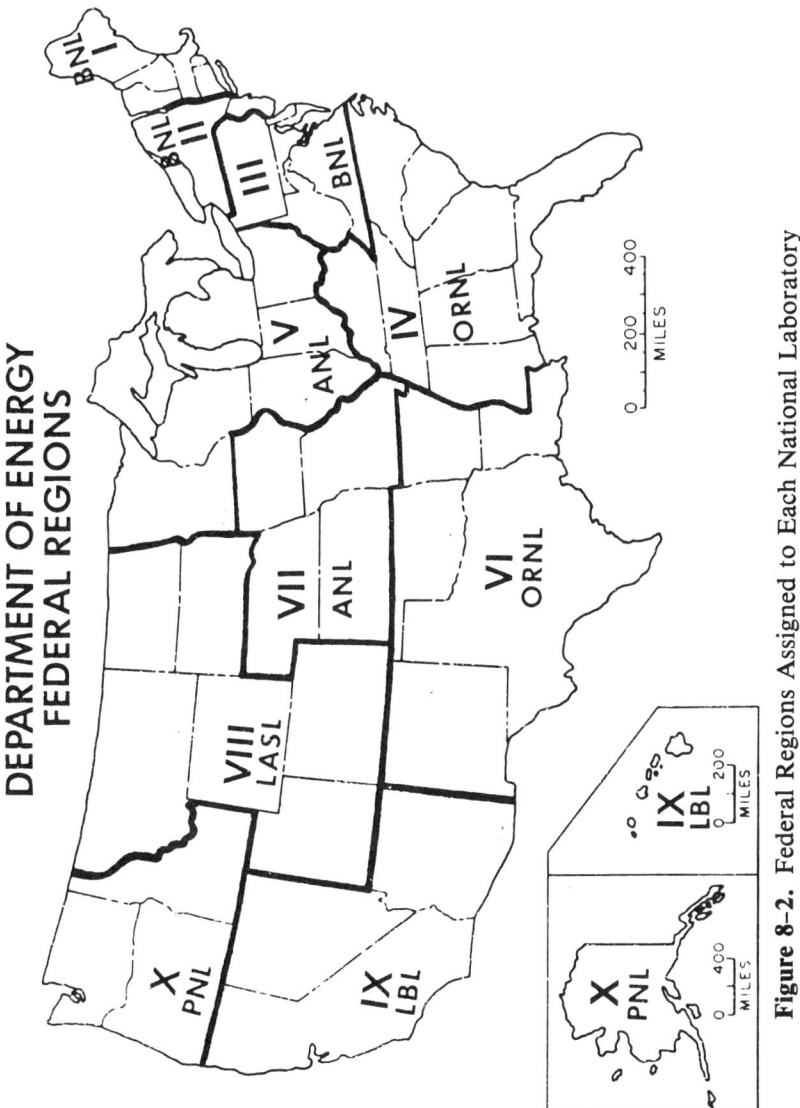

Figure 8-2. Federal Regions Assigned to Each National Laboratory

tiquing national assumptions and other laboratories' forecasts and enriching the segment information. The segments include these specialties: utility and industrial siting, air quality and long-range transport, water quality and quantity, solid waste, public and occupational health and safety, ecology/ land use, visibility, and socioeconomic impacts. Individual laboratories are expected to produce a forecast of the regional impacts of the national scenario provided, and the other laboratories provide feedback on the validity of the estimates and add information not available through the particular analytical techniques used. For several impact areas, the process has to procede more or less intuitively; siting determinations, for example, have to be completed before the air-pollution models are run. Let us look at the process in detail.

In the first step of the RIIA process, a basic DOE mid-term (through 1990) national projection (scenario) of future energy development is chosen. This is the mid-mid scenario discussed earlier (in chapter 6). The next step specifies the fuel mix of coal, nuclear, oil, gas, oil shale, geothermal, hydroelectric, and solar power predicted by the scenario and locates these for the years 1985 and 1990. Power plants, major fuel-burning industries, and mines are sited in counties and regions across the United States for these years based on the projected federal regional fuel mix.

After locating of the projected energy facilities, each participating laboratory performs two distinct tasks. First, it determines the impact of future energy development on one or more environmental-impact areas (such as air quality and/or water quality) for the nation. This exercise is referred to as the *lead-laboratory impact analysis.*

Laboratories responsible for lead impacts identify the environmental consequences suggested by these siting projections. The lead-analysis concept attempts to capitalize on unique capabilities of specific laboratories to evaluate certain environmental-issue areas and to facilitate uniform analytical methods across regions.

The laboratories conduct impact analyses in ten categories (see figure 8-3). The air-quality analysis is subdivided into two sections: local and interregional. The laboratory having the lead responsibility for the local air-quality analysis applies appropriate air-quality simulation models to estimate the changes in the annual and short-term concentration levels in the ambient air for several air pollutants such as sulfur dioxide, total suspended particulate matter, carbon monoxide, and nitrogen dioxide. For the interregional air-quality impact analysis, the lead laboratory employs regional atmospheric transport models to quantify the pollutants (mostly sulfates) affecting distant areas because of long-range atmospheric transport processes.

The lead laboratory conducting the water-quality analysis produces estimates of the cumulative basin loadings of water-pollutant effluents and

Figure 8-3. RIIA Development Program

estimates future water quality. It also performs a water-availability study producing estimates of total consumptive and nonconsumptive demands for energy facilities and activities, plus nonenergy demand where water scarcity is apparent.

A projection of energy solid-waste materials (such as overburden, tailings, and ash) is also produced. Land-use impact analyses produce estimates of the total area requirements for energy activities.

The lead laboratory responsible for the ecology analysis develops a protocol for conducting ecological assessments based on environmental-quality calculations, identification of endangered species, and energy-facility siting conflicts. Each laboratory uses this protocol in conducting its own regional ecological analyses.

The assessment of economic impact includes quantification of employment, capital-investment, pollution-damage, and mitigation costs associated with regional energy development. The social-impacts assessment might include analyses of aesthetics, archaeology, psychological impacts of changing life-style, demography, and the like.

Finally, effects on the scenario of state and local institutions are also identified. Institutional constraints to energy development are addressed and include intent, enforcement, and effects of related development laws and statutes, political and economic mechanisms used in making local public policy, and operational effectiveness of organizations having authority over energy development.

Upon completion of air-quality, water-quality, and solid-waste-management studies, pertinent data are furnished to the lead laboratory responsible for estimating risk on public and occupational health and safety. This information is used to calculate probable numbers of persons affected, degrees of impact, and economic evaluations of these impacts.

Each laboratory utilizes these lead analyses to support its own additional regional assessment, the sacred distinct task. These assessments bring to the fore the specific problems unique to a particular region(s) for which the laboratory is responsible and, based on a consistent set of high-, medium-, and low-impact ratings, rank the issues in terms of environmental severity. Further details of this analytic process are described in the next section.

Disaggregation of National Scenarios to Subnational Levels

Two integrated models (Oak Ridge National Laboratory's MULTIREGION and the Regional Balance System [REBS]) were used to disaggregate the national mid-mid scenario to workable subregional levels. Brief descriptions of the two models follow.[3]

ORNL's MULTIREGION model, which utilizes the Bureau of Economic Analysis (BEA) area as the functional regional unit, provides the regional economic and demographic base for subnational energy-consumption projections. MULTIREGION is a formal econometric/simulation model for projecting regional activity. It incorporates a top-down approach in which national projections of population, labor supply, and employment are allocated to the BEA level. The model views a region's economy as a labor market in which labor supply is a function of mortality, fertility, migration, and labor-force participation; and labor demand is related to a region's ability to grow in such sectors as natural resources, manufacturing, and services as a function of employment trends.

MULTIREGION generates BEA-area projections for sixteen age

groups by sex. Employment is forecasted for thirty-seven sectors categorized by basic industrial structure. MULTIREGION is not designed around a single algorithm as are many of the models discussed earlier, but instead matches the economic sector and its general characteristics with a forecast technique most apt to capture the essence of the growth and development of that sector. Consequently, resource-oriented industries are projected within a shift-share framework, manufacturing industries by a regional-advantage approach, while service-oriented industries are projected by a regional-base model.

MULTIREGION recognizes interregional linkages through an economic-potential approach such that the projections for a given BEA area are determined by the level of activity in nearby areas measured by distance, as well as in endogenously generated growth. Similarly, each industry is linked spatially and structurally to other industries that are purchasers or suppliers of inputs to its product. Adjustments for interregional migration and for labor-force-participation rates are incorporated in the model and related to underlying changes in potential regional employment.[4]

REBS was originally designed to bridge the gap between national energy models and the specific regional detail needed for energy-related economic-impact assessments. As a step in bridging this gap, the REBS system was designed to use the MULTIREGION forecasts of population and employment. However, for the REBS system to be able to provide energy projections for a variety of regions, it was necessary to increase still further the regional detail available from the MULTIREGION-BEA forecasts. Consequently, ORNL developed a simple computer algorithm that allocates the BEA-area projections provided by MULTIREGION to the constituent counties of each BEA area. The model retains the detailed age/sex-cohort structure and employment categories used in MULTIREGION. County projections of population are made using 1970 census estimates of county populations by age/sex cohort (as a base for the first forecast period) and then aging the population—similar to the procedure used in MULTIREGION. Any differences in the projected BEA-area total, as computed from the summation of county forecasts and the MULTIREGION forecasts, are allocated proportionate to each county share. These county projections are then used as the base for the next forecast period.

Similarly, employment projections are initialized by 1970 county/sector employment data with any growth by sector allocated proportionally to past employment patterns by sector. If a new industry appears in the BEA forecast, this is allocated based on total county employment. The procedure is straightforward but allows for differential county growth depending on which industry is growing in the BEA. At this level of detail, the REBS system can be used to forecast energy information.

The REBS system incorporates three component modules to provide a comprehensive view of regional historical and projected energy conditions: an energy-consumption submodel, a primary-energy-production submodel, and an energy-transformation submodel.

Energy consumed by final end use in the residential, commercial, industrial, and transportation sectors is estimated using historical energy-consumption patterns and regional economic activity by sector. As with many models, the forecast and apportionment algorithms are straightforward, but the data to make them operate are either not available or not in a consistent form. For example, because substate consumption data are not consistently available for all fuels considered in the REBS system, an estimating scheme had to be used to develop historical-data series. In the case of the historical energy-consumption series, state-level consumption data developed by the Bureau of Mines are regionalized to the BEA area using employment data from *County Business Patterns*. The energy-consumption estimates are generated separately for each fuel considered, each of the employment sectors projected by the MULTIREGION model, and a residential sector represented by total population. The regional unit utilized may be the county or any aggregate of counties. Because of the large number of fuels usually considered in any given analysis, multicounty regions were utilized in RIIA for the unit of analysis in order to facilitate the data processing.[5]

Facility-Siting Methodologies. Because the magnitude and significance of environmental and socioeconomic impacts depend on the geographic and demographic settings to which energy development is introduced, effective assessment of these impacts requires that their potential sources be located as specifically as possible. As a result, the second major step in the RIIA process is the establishment of plausible county-level siting patterns for the major energy user and product facilities, such as electric utilities, major industrial facilities, and fuel-extraction and -processing plants: these siting patterns in effect form the basis for all subsequent environmental and socioeconomic residual calculations and assessments.

Utility Siting. Electric-utility siting patterns are an extension of the energy supply-and-demand forecasts at the regional level. As previously mentioned, the national scenario was disaggregated to multicounty forecasts of electric-energy demand as well as possible technology mixes (the proportion of coal, nuclear, oil, gas, and so on) that may be used to meet the demand in 1985 and 1990. In developing utility-siting patterns, ORNL attempted to match the proportionate mixes specified by the national scenario as closely as possible.[6] ORNL developed a computerized site-selection procedure capable of multiple-resource analyses, using different constraints and scenarios. However, because some decisions cannot be completely simulated by the computer, the design also accommodates manual operation whenever human judgment is required. This computerized site-selection procedure is known as Oak Ridge Spatial Analysis Model (ORSAM). ORSAM involves a collection of models. The components of the system are illustrated in figure 8-4.

Present and future energy-facility siting patterns, up to 1985, are based on historical expectations of existing and proposed generating-capacity data unless otherwise modified by the scenario. A fundamental reference for information on existing and proposed electricity-generating facilities is available from the Federal Energy Regulatory Commission (FERC).[7] ORNL updates and modifies the FERC data substantially through communications with utility companies, use of published data on plant cancellations, and assistance from other laboratories participating in the RIIA program. Using this data base, a detailed picture of the supply infrastructure was developed for any given year up to about 1990. Included in the data file is a description of the capacity, plant type, fuel type, cooling type, and location of generating units over ten megawatts. The file also indicates the year a facility came on line or is scheduled to come on line, and the scheduled date of retirement for some generating units.

A portion of the 1985 siting patterns is readily determined by the announced expansion plans of the utilities. Most of the existing and proposed facilities will be operating in 1990. However, to the extent that the national scenario calls for growth in electricity-generating needs beyond that currently anticipated by the utility industry, the location of the required plants is less certain. As a first step, these deficits must be located as specifically as possible. To do this, local energy demand is expressed in terms of required capacity so that existing and proposed capacity can be subtracted to show net deficits or surpluses of power production by subregion. Before a siting analysis is begun, surplus power is normally redistributed to the nearest deficit region. After these calculations are complete, a more forward siting analysis can proceed.

The disaggregation of the national scenario to the federal regions is intended to provide basic information on the level of demand for which capacity must be sited and also provides the relative amounts of generating or processing capacity in each technology and fuel type that must be sited in a given federal region. The technology mixes serve as guidelines and control totals in the allocation of capacity within a given region, but do not necessarily determine the final mix sited in any given county or BEA area. The fuel mixes in the regional disaggregations specified in the national scenario were often substantially different from those planned by the utility companies in the regions. Once again, the disparity in data sets required a more-or-less arbitrary decision by the analysts. For the sake of consistency, the analysis discussed here stayed with the national forecast.

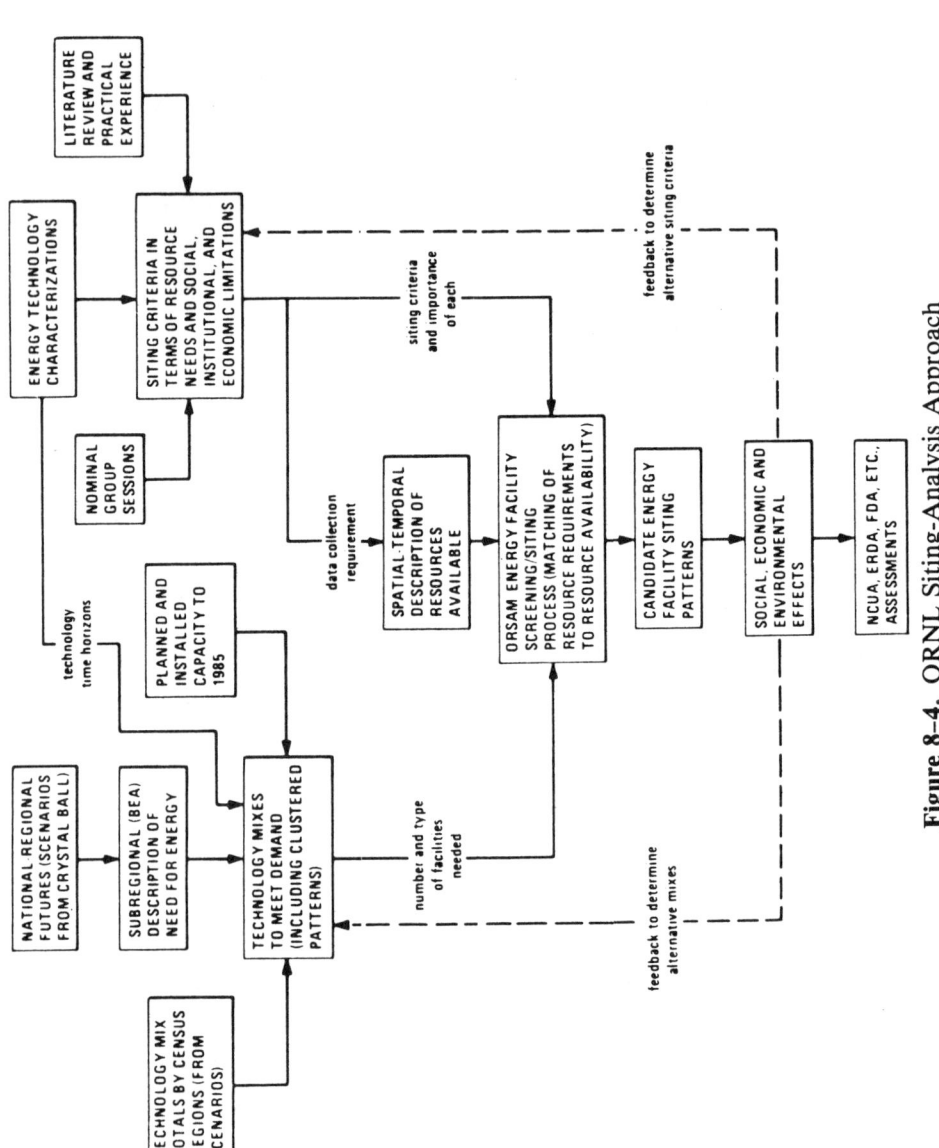

Figure 8-4. ORNL Siting-Analysis Approach

One of the first steps in developing the siting methodology for RIIA was to identify the factors that are normally considered by utilities and state agencies in locating acceptable energy-facility sites. To accomplish this, two nominal-group sessions were conducted to obtain expert opinion from power-plant-siting specialists.

The nominal-group technique is a highly structured, interactive approach that has been widely accepted in health and social services, education, industry, and government.[8] The process consists of four basic steps: (1) nominal (silent and independent) generation of ideas in writing by a panel of participants; (2) round-robin listing of ideas generated by participants in a serial discussion; (3) group discussion of each recorded idea for clarification and evaluation; and (4) independent voting, with the group decision resulting in a mathematical ranking. The strengths of the technique lie in enhanced participation by group members, step-by-step movement toward a goal, and cross-education of participants. To some extent, the technique is a variant on the Delphi process, developed by Dalkey at the RAND corporation years ago.[9] Delphi was developed in recognition of the fact that there were numerous situations that for one reason or another, were not amenable to computer modeling and therefore had to be dealt with by some form of human opinion. Lack of rigor and concern with individual pressure from dominant or individual situational factors made obtaining such opinion difficult. Delphi was designed to overcome these. As with the nominal-group technique, it is a form of structured expert opinion and can enhance formal analytic techniques if used carefully.

These sessions resulted in lists of weighted factors that became the basis for the factor models used in the siting method. The regional siting factors, identified by a member of the nominal-group panel, are listed in table 8-1.

The minimum criteria, based on subfactors, to be considered in the county-level siting analysis for coal-fired electricity-generating facilities were specified by a DOE siting worksession held in 1975 at Argonne National Laboratory. These criteria are:

1. Proximity to load centers. The factor to be considered is the distance to the load center or centers as an indication of the cost of transmission from each political site.
2. Water availability. Water availability is considered in terms of the flow available 95 percent of the time and the seven-day/ten-year low flow. The percentage of this flow actually available for energy use may vary from region to region; precise estimates cannot be obtained for most areas.
3. Coal availability. The relative availability of coal, as indicated by magnitude of reserves and by transport distance, has been established at a subregional level using methods provided by the siting work group.

Table 8-1
Definition of Criteria for Rating of Impacts

Impact Category	High Impact	Medium Impact	Low Impact
Air quality	Major facilities in proposed siting scenario could be constrained by one or all of the following issues: Persistent and continued violations of primary national ambient air-quality standards Inability to attain acceptable PSD increment limitations Limited probability that improved emission-control efficiencies or offsets would result in NAAQS attainment	Some major facilities in proposed siting scenario could be constrained by high-impact issues. Violations occur but are amenable to extensive control technology, fuel (coal and oil) purchasing policy, and/or offset.	Air quality and emission level are within acceptable standards; no major adjustments to siting of plants because of air-quality issues.
Visibility	There is a significant decrease in calculated visual range in class I areas.	There is a moderate decrease in visual range but the reduction is amenable to mitigation measures.	No decrease in visual range or new siting impacts amenable to mitigation measures; no major adjustment in siting.
Water quality	Significant economic burden to meet WPCA requirements.	Treated effluents meet effluent standards but occasional localized stream standard violations will occur in receiving water body.	Receiving body capable of handling all projected effluent additions; few or no violations of stream standards anticipated.
Water availability	No water available without major shifts in current water uses, e.g., either energy development of agriculture, even with low-flow augmentation, or water available through major structural and nonstructural alternatives, e.g., structural-construction of dams and reservoirs. Groundwater mining with no recharge potential	Water available at moderate economic cost to the region. Groundwater mining with recharge potential available or possible.	No conflicts except for recreational use. Groundwater withdrawal where annual recharging occurs.

Solid waste	Severe potential contamination problems are likely to require complete containment of wastes	Minimal environmental impacts with proper control technology, indication that many areas may experience problems and in some of these areas suitable options may not be available.	Minimal environmental impacts with proper control technologies; some potential problems but generally amenable to current technology options at additional cost.
Ecology	Critical natural habitats will be disturbed.	Critical natural habitat or large acreages of cropland may be disturbed.	Localized impacts that may be readily mitigated by structural or siting alternatives.
Land use	Conflict with high-value land use, such as loss of habitat, parkland, seismic risks, scenic resources, indian lands, and agricultural land.	Similar conflicts, with alternative sites or mitigation measures costly but available.	Few conflicts, or a range of alternatives available.
Public health	Significant increases in morbidity and mortality rate due to exposure to energy-related pollutants.	Moderate increases in morbidity and mortality rate due to exposure to energy-related pollutants.	No significant impact; all impacts subject to mitigation.
Occupational health and safety	Significant increases in occupationally related deaths, injuries, and disease due to increased energy development.	Potential significant increases in respiratory and other diseases but improvements in OSHA, NRC, and EPA regulations and workplace conditions expected to alleviate much of the problem.	No significant increases in occupationally related deaths, injuries, and disease due to increased energy development.
Local sociological factors	Implementation delayed or possibly blocked due to potentially severe changes in community's quality of life; heavy demands placed on physical infrastructure including services, facilities, housing; conflict in values and lifestyle between immigrants and long-time residents; immigrants represent a statistically significant	Potential delays due to community and local government resistance to facility; potential increased costs to local government; some community fears for changes in the quality of life accompanying influx of population; mitigation strategies available, but usually costly; moderate capacity of affected	Minor changes in local government's infrastructure; few immigrants or few cultural and lifestyle clashes expected; mitigation costs easily absorbed by affected communities.

Table 8-1 continued

Impact Category	High Impact	Medium Impact	Low Impact
	portion of the baseline population; extended negotiations likely between developer and affected communities; affected communities will have great difficulty absorbing high social and economic costs of project without outside assistance.	communities to absorb these impacts.	
Local economies	Implementation is blocked due to unacceptable economic demands on local infrastructure.	Potential delays due to lack of skilled personnel; financial impacts on local government.	Infrastructure impacts minor; adaptability of community government high.
Regional economies	Causes adverse capital or employment impacts on region, decreases competitive position compared to other regions.	Potential employment, capital, or competitive impacts but mitigation strategy possible.	No significant impacts.
Institutional and legislative	Prohibition of implementation based on available strong legal constraints, anticipated legislative prohibition, absence of effective organizational responsibilities, statutes, etc.	Delays possible due to legal or political constraints; low to moderate public or private interest in enforcement.	No significant opposition, legal constraints, or organizational problems.

This information, relating to delivered price, was considered in selecting the location of the plant relative to the producing mine.
4. Air-quality constraints. Air-Quality Maintenance Areas (AQMAs) defined by the Environmental Protection Agency as being nonattainment have been considered exclusionary areas for coal-fired plants except when other overriding constraints make use of these areas mandatory. Regulations for the prevention of significant deterioration (PSD) have not been used in the initial baseline siting patterns.
5. Seismic risk. Areas of high seismic risk (zone 3 as designated by U.S. Geological Survey seismic-risk maps) are excluded as sites for nuclear facilities.
6. Population distribution. Population constraints exclude areas containing 500 or more people per square mile for siting of nuclear facilities. AQMA constraints often exclude coal-fired facilities as well.
7. Public lands. No facilities have been sited on state or federally owned lands.

Limitations of Siting Analysis. The ORNL siting methodology is based on the recent behavior of the electric-utility industry. This has been an expanding industry, not a contracting one. Because these facilities are in the nature of so-called natural monopolies, they are highly regulated in many aspects of their operation, but not all. Expansion has been in fairly small increments, with little control or coordination of siting by public decision makers. The siting methodology attempts to simulate these trends, although for analytic purposes it makes the simplifying assumption that the nation as a whole or multistate regions are served by a single utility company rather than the hundreds that now operate.

The methodology as designed is inadequate for disaggregating short-term forecasts such as those for 1985 and 1990. Short-term forecasts frequently show sharp reductions from existing generating capacity, as well as reductions from future plans. Consequently, ORNL had to resort to ad hoc procedures to retire or postpone (that is, unsite) excess generating capacity. These procedures vary among scenarios and among regions within a scenario, depending on the severity of the projected reduction. As with all subjective assessments, these opinions are difficult to verify and are open to argument by users and other technicians.

In addition, the current methodology is inadequate for disaggregating projections that show increased hydroelectric, peaking, or solar technologies. Suitability scores, one of the variables in site selection, were developed only for new coal-fired and nuclear steam-electric plants and for coal-conversion facilities. ORNL assumed that any projections for new oil- and gas-fired steam plants could be handled using the coal-suitability scores. The emphasis on coal-fired and nuclear-steam plants seemed appropriate because these technologies will probably account for most of the increase in the nation's base-load generating capacity during the middle term. Moreover, the most severe environmental and social impacts have been associated with these technologies.

Other problems, gaps, and/or methodological issues exist in the current siting-methodology procedure, but most are relatively minor given the level of detail of the analyses. As with all such techniques, the analyst has the responsibility of recognizing the large number of simplifying or limiting assumptions that have to be made to come up with a forecast, and to take these into consideration when communicating the level of confidence with which he credits the forecast.

Additional Analyses: Institutional Aspects

In implementing energy policies, specific laws, regulations, and interpretations of these must be complied with, certain organizations must be relied on, and certain political processes may become engaged. For example, a number of legal, organizational, and political constraints may stand in the way of achieving the desired outcome of an energy policy. These constraints can appear at the national level (such as new source performance standards), at the state level (such as state implementation plans) or at the local level (such as local zoning ordinances). In addition, legal, organizational, and political impacts (such as lawsuits) may result from decisions and actions taken at each stage of policy implementation. Concomitantly, achieving the desired outcome of a specific energy policy may require designing new institutional relationships if existing arrangements tend to constrain the implementation of a new policy. Furthermore, institutional constraints, impacts, and design choices may require readjusting calculations about technical performance, environmental impacts, economic performance, and socioeconomic impacts.

No consistent methodology has yet been adopted by the laboratories for assessing the institutional implications of alternative-energy programs at regional levels. Rather, each laboratory has been encouraged to develop its own methodology based upon general guidelines. The purpose of these guidelines has been to provide the laboratories with rough boundaries within which to conduct their analyses.

Essentially, each laboratory identifies federal, state, and local regulations that could constrain the energy-development goals incorporated in a given scenario. The laboratories also identify types of institutional behavior and activities that tend to interact most commonly with energy development. In identifying these interactions, the laboratories seek answers to some basic institutional questions—legal, organizational, and political—

Two-Way Applications

and their relation to the energy/environmental issues raised in the region for which each lab is responsible:

1. Legal
   a. What are the relevant federal, state, and local statutes, regulations, and adjudicatory decisions?
   b. What are the relevant legal principles?
   c. What standards must be met?
   d. What licensing procedures must be followed?
   e. What legal conflicts and uncertainties may arise?
   f. What processes may be used to resolve conflicts and uncertainties?
2. Organizational
   a. What are the relevant public and private organizations; that is, what organizations must take action?
   b. What are each organization's goals and missions, standard operating procedures, resources, and approaches to recruitment and training of members?
3. Political
   a. What are the relevant political interests, both within and outside government?
   b. Who participates? Whose interests are affected?
   c. What is the likely position of each participant with respect to relevant issues?
   d. What determines each participant's preferences and interests?
   e. How are preferences combined; that is, what are the action channels?
   f. What are the sources of influence?
   g. Whose preferences count; that is, which participants are influential and which participants not influential in the process?
   h. How stable is the distribution of relative influence among participants?

Answers to these and similar questions are obtained by the laboratories through literature searches and through interviews with state and local officials and representatives from regional commissions, public utility commissions, and interest groups. The literature consulted includes local newspapers, various newsletters, reports, and position papers provided by the states. The federal regional offices of DOE and EPA are also consulted. Laboratories also convene workshops to identify, from various perspectives, the important energy-related environmental issues relevant to their regions.[10] The participants represent diverse views, including state energy offices and regulatory agencies, public-utilities commissions, utility companies, local government, several public-interest groups, DOE, and EPA.

A Perspective on Regional Issues beyond State Boundaries

The discussion by each laboratory focuses on region-specific issues. However, it is important that the material developed at the state and federal regional level is also viewed in terms of impacts that transcend regional boundaries. The following comments provide some insights into this larger, multistate regional perspective.

Among the air-related issues, of particular importance from the perspective of interregional impacts is the long-range transport of pollutants. This problem clearly illustrates the interrelationship of energy-development activities in several states or regions. For example, emission of sulfur oxides and sulfates in one part of the country can expose other regions to potential environmental impacts such as acid rain and health risks.

In the East, problems of water availability are most often tied to periodic droughts resulting in low stream and river flow. In general, these instances are rare. Water-usage and flow rates are important in eastern rivers because these rivers receive significant quantities of municipal and industrial waste. When their flows are subjected to consumptive water uses (such as evaporation from cooling towers) or when drought occurs, concentrations of pollutants above acceptable levels may result.

In contrast, the West experiences a continuous high demand for water and has relatively meager resources for all potential users. This physical reality is made worse by institutional practices that can cause site-specific water shortages. Low-flow problems and pollution are a continuing multiregion issue in the West.

Let us now turn to some specific regional issues from region 5, which includes some of the key north-central states.[11]

Regional Overview—Federal Region 5. Each regional description begins by defining the physical, economic, social, institutional, and energy setting on which the EIA scenario and the lead-laboratory analyses are set.

The energy supply-and-demand scenario for Federal Region 5 is summarized in figure 8-5. These projections were utilized as the basis for the county-level utility, industrial, and mine-siting patterns (tables 8-2 and 8-3), which in turn provide the basis for the impact assessments that follow.

In 1977, the states in region 5 had a population of 45 million and an average density of about 148 people per square mile. The average annual increase in net population has slowed significantly in the last several years. In the 1950–1960 period it was 1.6 percent, in 1960–1970 1.1 percent, and in 1970–1976 it declined to 0.3 percent, with a relatively low emigration rate, a slowdown of new households, and an older median age (27.4).

The median income in the region is $10,376, average per-capita income $6,594 (1976). The primary industries are farming and manufacturing, the latter employing 107 persons per thousand population (1975).

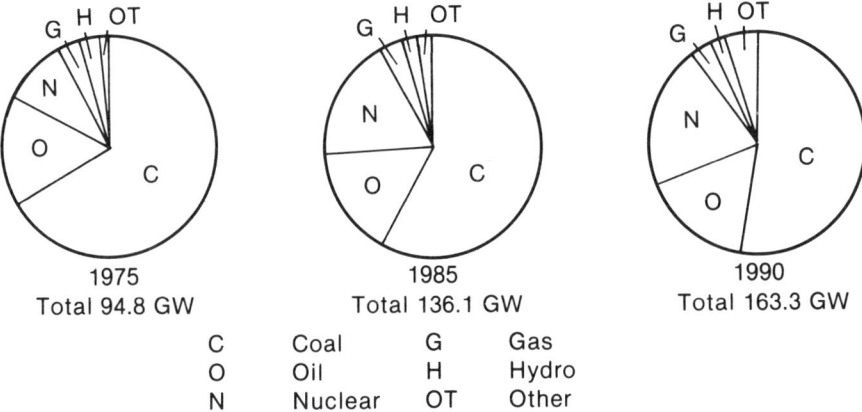

Figure 8-5. Projected Electrical-Generating Capacity, by Technology: Region 5

Air. Coal use is a central energy issue in federal region 5. Large reserves of high-sulfur coal exist in Indiana, Illinois, and Ohio, and historically these have been the preferred sources of fuel for much of the industry in the region. However, the 1970 Clean Air Act required the installation of desulfurization devices, principally scrubbers, and is expected to improve the air quality in many areas of region 5. In 1975, areas around Minneapolis-St. Paul, Gary, Peoria, Indianapolis, Lansing, and most of the industrial urban centers in Ohio were in nonattainment for sulfur dioxide (SO_2). This potentially affects not only human health but also vegetation. Damage induced by SO_2 exposure can result in decreased productivity and yield: soybeans, wheat, small grains, vegetables, and fruits and berries are major crops of all or part of the region and these are particularly sensitive to high SO_2 levels. The coniferous forests of the northern part of the region are also sensitive to SO_2. Levels of sulfur dioxide are projected to decrease below damage thresholds throughout the region in 1985, but in some urban industrialized areas they are projected to increase again in 1990, primarily due to industrial use of coal. Increases in atmospheric levels of SO_2 in the last twenty years have also contributed to the formation of acid rain (precipitation in much of region 5 is below pH 5). Acid rain is suspected to have significant agricultural ecological implications because, among other effects, it increases the mobility of nutrients and metals in soil. State and local impacts include these:

> In Region 5, Michigan, Wisconsin and Ohio are the states most likely to experience regulatory impediments as a result of the scenario-projected energy development. Michigan's primary air quality problems are expected to be in the eastern portion of the state where utility coal growth is projected to occur in nonattainment areas. Wisconsin has similar problems in the southeastern and central portions of the state. Additional emissions offsets and improved control efficiencies will not significantly mitigate air

Table 8-2
Electrical-Generating Capacity, Coal Extraction, and Industrial Fuel Use: Region 5

	1975	1985	1990
Electrical—Generating Capacity (10^3 Mw)			
Coal	63.9	79.5	86.9
Oil	15.5	22.0	26.2
Gas	2.4	4.7	4.1
Nuclear	9.7	24.3	34.5
Combined cycle	0.2	0.2	5.6
Hydro	3.1	3.1	3.2
Solar	0	0.1	0.6
Geothermal	0	0	0
Other	0	2.2	2.2
Total	94.8	136.1	163.3
Coal Production (10^6 tons)			
Deep mines	476.6	629.8	669.9
Surface mines	839.1	851.7	795.3
Total	1315.7	1481.5	1465.2
Industrial Fuel Use (10^{12} Btu)			
Coal	16.3	1056.7	1109.4
Oil	296.3	459.3	531.8
Gas	0.4	0.3	0.3
Total	313.0	1516.3	1641.5

Table 8-3
Disaggregation of National Impacts to the Regional Level: Region 5

Energy Resource	Air Quality		National Socioeconomics	Water Resources[b]
	Visibility	Long-Range Transport[a]		
Coal				
Electric	L	L	L	L
Oil	L	L	L	—
Gas	L	L	L	—
Nuclear	L	L	L	L
Solar	L	L	L	—

Note: L = Low; conflicts are unlikely to occur.
— = not applicable.

[a]Long-range transport of pollutants may become an issue in local areas where ambient levels for criteria pollutants are near standards. Although the average contribution from long-range transport may be small, it may nevertheless be sufficient to ambient levels over national standards.

[b]Water-allocation issues may arise for proposed utility or industrial facilities located along the Great Lakes.

quality problems in these areas. Nearly 30 percent of the projected utility coal growth in Ohio could be restricted because air quality regulations primarily NAAQS.

Projected growth of utility oil capacity in nonattainment areas appears to be greatest in the industrial states of Illinois, Indiana, and Ohio. Mitigation of impacts through fuel purchasing practices could greatly reduce the air quality impact from these facilities. Specific areas, such as the four county nonattainment areas surrounding Chicago, might require special attention.

Industrial growth projected by the scenario could be restricted by nonattainment air quality regulations in industrialized areas like Chicago, St. Louis, Detroit, and Cleveland. Specific restrictions will depend upon fuel selection and available emissions offsets in each locality.[12]

Water. Water quantity and quality issues are raised because the region has extensive agricultural areas. Further, the Ohio River basin has severe air- and water-pollution problems. Water quality from point sources is obviously important but not a major issue. However, pollution from agricultural runoff is significant.

Region 5 lies primarily in the Ohio, Great Lakes, and Upper Mississippi drainage basins. The major water-quality problems in this area result from municipal and industrial loadings that often exceed the assimilative capacity of particular streams and sections of streams. The Ohio River and its tributaries have experienced particularly severe industrial pollution, including thermal pollution from power plants. In addition, streams in Ohio, Illinois, and Indiana are often excessively polluted by acid mine drainage from abandoned coal-mining operations.

> The utility activities analyzed for water-related impacts were coal, gas, oil, combined cycle (assuming coal type) and nuclear. Of these categories, 8.8 percent of the projected incremental increase in utility activity up to 1990 was identified as having a potential water related impact (assuming that effluent treatment beyond statutory point source requirements is implemented and/or that the 7 day-10 year low flow is maintained). This fraction represents 2.1 percent of the total utility activity projected by 1990 for Region 5.[13]

The upper Mississippi River basin is predominantly agricultural, and runoff from agricultural land contributes large amounts of sediments as well as nutrients and pesticides to receiving streams. Reducing the discharge of nutrients, particularly phosphorus, into the lakes is a major goal of Great Lakes planning agencies. Specifically, the mesotrophic status of some deep-water parts of Lake Michigan and the advanced eutrophic state of some shorelines and bays are the major water-quality problems. On the other hand, the water in many parts of central and northern Minnesota and Wisconsin is considered to be of good or superior quality and is a valuable resource to the entire region.

Historically, water availability has not been a major problem in region 5: the Great Lakes and the Mississippi, Ohio, Illinois, and Wabash Rivers have provided plentiful supplies for utilities and industry. Large withdrawals in the Chicago area, however, have led to a U.S. Supreme Court ruling limiting withdrawals by Illinois. Allocations could be extended to other states if activities requiring large amounts of water continue to expand. Activities that may affect water quality and water supply in the Great Lakes are also subject to international agreements. These considerations, as well as state shoreline-development policies and coastal-zone plans, may affect the siting of large energy or industrial facilities along the Great Lakes.

Solid Waste. Disposal of all kinds of solid waste has become an important issue nationally. Historically, solid-waste disposal has not been a constraint on new development; however, inexpensive dumping at nearby locations is a thing of the past. The filling of nearby sites, growth in industrial wastes, and the rapid increase in scrubber waste portends increasingly serious problems over time. Although all regions face the challenge of disposing of ash, sludge, and other wastes in an environmentally acceptable manner, region 5 will likely have more problems because of the large amount of waste involved.

The quantity of residuals generated from industrial coal use is the highest in the nation (3.7 million tons in 1975). Industrial coal usage is projected to increase 38 percent by 1990; however, land requirements for solid-waste disposal are expected to grow by nearly 400 percent because the application of gas desulfurization (GDS) systems will increase the amount of solids generation. Large quantities of waste are also produced by the utilities in this region. Coal-fired utility capacity is estimated to increase by nearly 40 percent for the period 1975—1990, to 88,000 megawatts.

Industrial disposal requires a large number of small sites. Some industries have their own disposal sites; others have municipal facilities. In crowded urban and industrialized areas, finding available land can be a problem; however, the institutional constraints associated with siting a new disposal facility can pose even greater problems. In most areas, technically feasible and environmentally acceptable sites can be found, but local opposition may block the construction of new landfills in those areas.

Because of the historically agricultural nature of the region, the large acreages disturbed by surface-mining activities present the greatest potential for adverse ecological and land-use impacts. Mining in the region is projected to occur in central and southern Illinois, southwestern Indiana, and eastern Ohio, areas where the present land use is a mix of forested tracts and row-crop agriculture. State and federal (Office of Surface Mining) regulations require that mined lands be returned to their original productivity and land use. Reclamation costs in region 5 will be high because mining in most of the region is most likely to disturb row crops or forested land.

Socioeconomic. The socioeconomic impacts discussed are principally those related to the boom-town phenomenon. Somewhat surprisingly, several areas of the region could be expected to experience several boom-town impacts.

Facilities totalling more than 70,000 megawatts (Mw) of new generating capacity are sited for region 5. The scenario indicates that the majority of these new facilities—depending on the proposed timing of the developments, size of the facilities, and the types of technologies to be sited—will create adverse socioeconomic impacts (resulting from a population increase greater than 10 percent in only one year) in many of these counties. Other sited energy developments throughout the region will incur adverse impacts, but their negative effects will be overshadowed by increased employment, growth in local income and tax bases, and other socioeconomic benefits. In these counties, because of their economic and demographic characteristics, the projected population growth due to the employment and capital requirements of the site development(s) will not exceed 10 percent of the baseline population.

Seven counties in region 5 would experience rapid population increases, extensive economic growth, sociocultural impacts, and institutional problems. These counties are expected to incur more of the negative adverse consequences of resource development because their existing workforce and infrastructure are insufficient to satisfy the manpower demands during the construction phase(s) and therefore require the inmigration of a transient labor force. in Indiana, Illinois, and Wisconsin the negative effects of development are primarily attributable to construction of coal and nuclear facilities.

Health and Safety. Finally, potential health and safety impacts on the regions' energy growth will increase significantly, particularly in relation to occupational health. Emissions-related deaths from sulfates are expected to decrease because of better pollution-control equipment.

Large amounts of energy-related activities, ranging from extraction to electricity generation, occur in region 5. Coal extraction presents the highest risk to occupational health (see figure 8-6). Occupational impacts of deep mining—injuries, disease, and deaths—are historically more severe than those from strip mining because of differences in dust exposure and risk of accident (figure 8-7). Illinois, Indiana, and Ohio contain the major coal reserves found in region 5. Death, injuries, and disease from coal extraction in region 5 account for approximately three-quarters of all energy-related impacts on occupational health. Regional impacts of oil and gas extraction

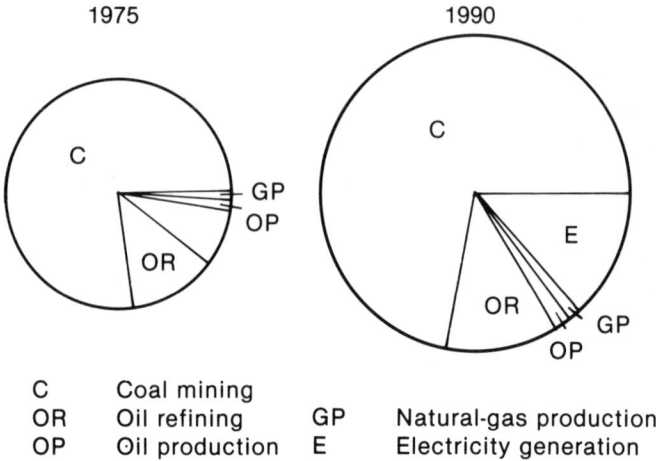

C	Coal mining		
OR	Oil refining	GP	Natural-gas production
OP	Oil production	E	Electricity generation

Figure 8-6. Relative Contribution of Energy Activities to Energy-Related Occupational Deaths under the Mid-Mid Scenario: Region 5

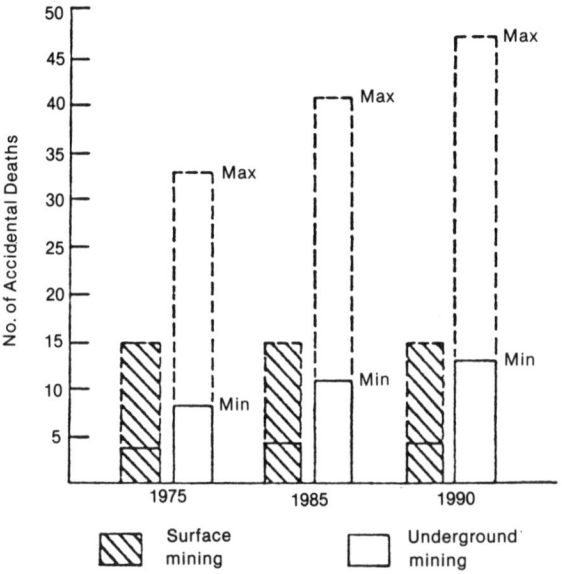

Figure 8-7. Range of Potential Accidental Deaths in Coal Mines under the Mid-Mid Scenario: Region 5

and refining and electricity generation are minimal, although these activities exert significant effects in Michigan, Wisconsin, and Minnesota, where coal extraction does not occur.

The scenario projects an overall 11-percent increase in tons of coal extracted in region 5, and an increase in the proportion mined underground (from 36 percent in 1975 to 45 percent in 1990). This could cause a 20-to-40-percent increase by 1990 in the number of accidental deaths and injuries due to coal mining. Cases of chronic respiratory disease (CRD) and deaths due to CRD could increase 35 to 40 percent (figure 8-8).

Utility and industrial use of fossil fuels is the primary source of energy-related effluents that affect public health in region 5. Most fossil-fuel use occurs near densely populated areas. When fossil fuels are burned near highly populated areas, adverse health impacts increase. Although combustion of fossil fuels produces many effluents, the adverse impacts of sulfur oxides and particulates are best documented (see figure 8-9). Inhalation of these pollutants can adversely expose populations—most severely the high-risk groups such as asthmatics and young children, cardiovascular patients, and the elderly. Fifty to sixty percent of all deaths in region 5 are attributable to cardiovascular and respiratory diseases, both of which are aggravated by emissions from fossil-fuel use. Over time, such deaths are projected to decrease despite an increase in electricity generation of 40 percent and an increase in industrial fuel use of 240 percent by 1990. The decrease is primarily due to sulfur-emission controls instituted during the assessment period as dictated by the Clean Air Act. Public-health impacts, measured in terms of individual risk and potential number of deaths, will drop by 48 percent and 35 percent, respectively.

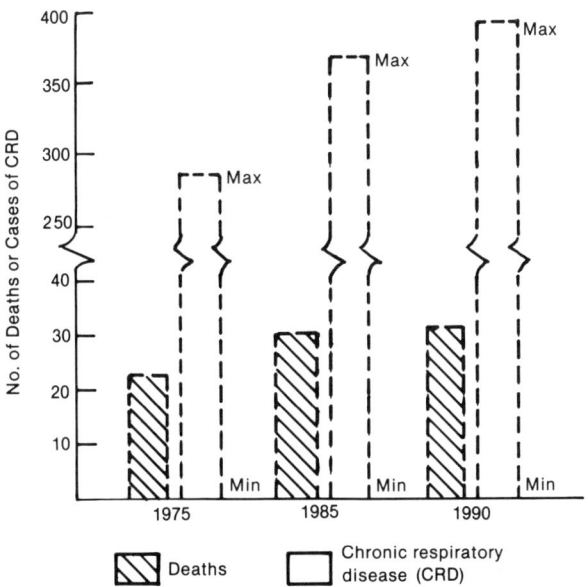

Figure 8-8. Range of Potential Deaths and Cases of Chronic Respiratory Disease Due to Coal-Mining Occupational Exposure under the Mid-Mid Scenario: Region 5

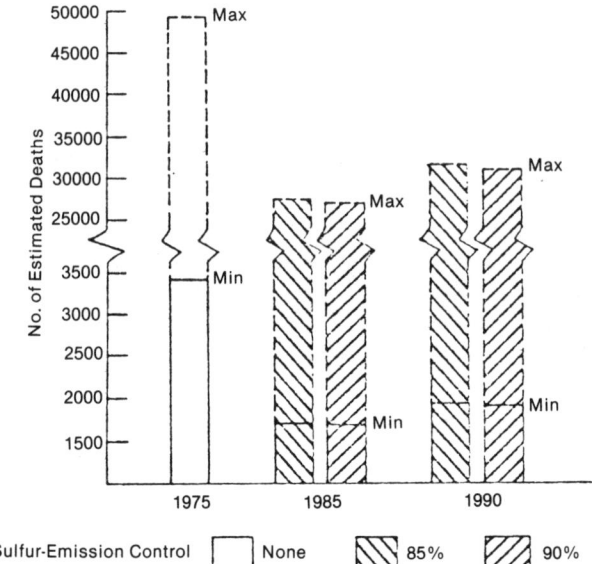

Figure 8-9. Range of Potential Deaths from Sulfate Exposure Due to Utility and Industrial Use of Fossil Fuels under the Mid-Mid Scenario: Region 5

The RIIA analysis then discusses detailed impacts on a single state, Illinois, as an example of a more complete, state-by-state assessment. Each major issue is looked at generally, some background given, and state-specific implications presented. The following section based directly on the RIIA report, presents only the air and water impacts, as examples of the type and depth of information presented.

Illinois. The scenario (see table 8-4) projects an additional 14,571 Mw of electrical-generating capacity in Illinois by 1985 and 21,622 Mw by 1990. Coal production is projected to increase from a 1975 value of 59.7 million tons per year to 68.5 million tons per year in 1985 and 70.2 million tons per year in 1990. More than half of the coal is mined underground.

Seventy percent of the fuel used in Illinois was imported from out of state in 1975, including 25 percent of the coal, 99 percent of the natural gas, 77 percent of the liquid fuels, and all the uranium. Illinois, which ranks fourth in the nation in coal production, exports 40 percent of its own coal. The sulfur content of Illinois coal is high (3-5 percent).

Table 8-5 summarizes the impacts discussed in the following section.

Air: Description and Background Issues. Despite its vast coal reserves, Illinois consumes more than twice as much fossil fuel as it produces. Illinois

Table 8-4
Projected Increases in Electrical-Generating Capacity under the Mid-Mid Scenario: Illinois

Period[a]	(Mw) Coal	Oil	Gas	Nuclear	Hydro[b]	Other[c]	Total
1975-1985	2,665	2,794	1,231	7,840	0	35	14,571
1975-1990	5,558	4,067	1,111	8,796	0	2,095	21,622

[a]Base year: 1975
[b]Includes conventional hydro and pumped storage.
[c]Includes solar, combined cycle, and other.

produces over $61,500 \times 10^3$ tons of coal annually (the second-largest producer in the region). The majority of Illinois coal is burned locally or shipped to adjacent states. Because of its large and rapidly expanding energy requirements, Illinois must import increasing amounts of other fuels for purposes not fulfilled by coal. The state currently imports over 740 billion cubic feet of natural gas annually. Faced with an increasing demand for fuel and dwindling supplies of available fuels, pressure to meet fuel demands with local coal production may increase. Illinois coal has an average sulfur content of 3.2 percent. Use of fuel with such a high sulfur content places greater pollution-control requirements on new facilities.

Illinois air-quality problems are most pronounced in the northeastern, central, and southwestern portions of the state. In the metropolitan Chicago interstate AQCR, which includes several major industrial centers, nonattainment sites have been designated for total-suspended-particulates (TSP) standards. With the increasing economic activity, additional pressure will be placed on air quality. The air quality in the metropolitan St. Louis interstate AQCR is characterized by TSP-standard violations, and the air quality of Granite City has been ranked the worst of ten sites within the state. A decrease in violations in the area has not been noticeable even with more restrictive air-pollution standards. The metropolitan Dubuque interstate AQCR has shown improvement in total particulate emissions, with fewer violations of primary particulate standards.

Impacts on Air Quality/Visibility. Air quality should improve throughout Illinois between 1975 and 1990 assuming attainment by existing sources due to improved control technologies and the enforcement of state implementation plans; however, continued TSP and SO_2 primary national ambient air quality standards (NAAQS) violations are projected for several areas in region 5 AQCRs (see figure 8-10). Forty-three percent of the projected 1990

Table 8-5
Environmental Impacts of the EIA Trendlong Mid-Mid Scenario at the State Level: Illinois

	Air	Water		Land			Health and Safety		Local Socioeconomic[a]	
Energy Source	Quality	Quality	Availability[b]	Ecology	Land Use	Solid Waste	Occupational Safety	Public Health	Economics	Sociological Factors
Utility										
Coal	L	L					L	L	M	
Oil	M[c]						L	L	M	
Gas	L						L			
Nuclear	L						L	L	M	
Combined cycle	L									
Solar	L								M	
Hydro										
General										
Utility	M	L	H	L	L	L	L	L	M	M
Industry	H			M	M	L	M	L	L	L
Mining	L									

Note: H = High; there is a high degree of certainty that conflict will arise at several facilities, with little or no opportunities for cost-effective mitigation.
M = Medium; specified concern could occur at a few facilities, but potentially cost-effective mitigation strategies will be available.
L = Low; conflicts are unlikely to occur.
Blank entries indicate either no impact or impact not addressed.

[a]The socioeconomic entries reflect growth only in counties with a projected immigration (for energy-facility developments) in excess of 10 percent of the baseline population in any one period. Because actual impacts are extremely localized and thus vary significantly by county, the utility of the aggregated state-impact index presented in the matrix is limited.
[b]Includes ground water.
[c]Fuel switching to premium-quality fuel may be required.

Two-Way Applications

utility oil increases and 33 percent of the combined-cycle increases sited by the scenario in these areas are subject to review. Because over 65 percent of projected growth of industrial capacity may occur in nonattainment areas, proper emissions offsets may be required in these areas.

Scenario-Induced Changes. Illinois does not have coal-utility siting projected in nonattainment areas. Although new-source performance standards, control efficiencies, and local regulations must be satisfied, no significant air-quality issues exist for utility coal expansions.

Over 43 percent of the proposed utility oil growth is expected to occur in nonattainment areas. The northeastern corner of the state will be most affected by utility oil development. Selective fuel-purchasing policies will mitigate air-quality problems cause by emissions, but unavailability of offsets and nonattainment provisions could constrain development.

One-third of the proposed combined-cycle capacity could be constrained because of the inability of local areas to attain NAAQS air-quality standards. Fuel selection for these plants will depend on availability of appropriate offsets. Approximately two-thirds of the proposed industrial growth in Illinois will occur in nonattainment area. Fuel use, emission limitations, and offset requirements may also be necessary for these plants to meet new-source review requirements.

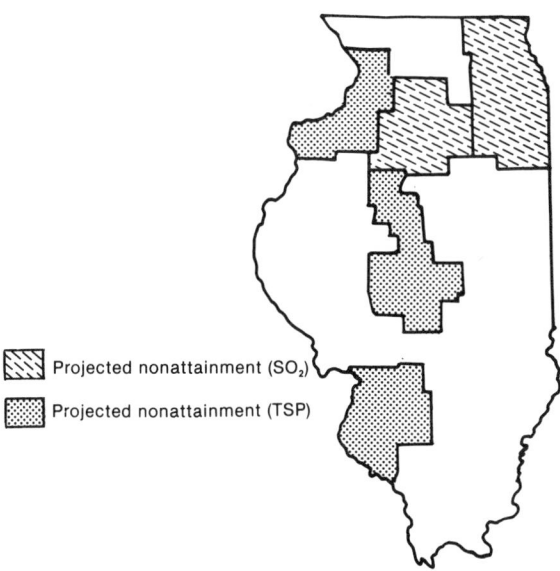

Figure 8-10. Potential Air-Quality Impact Areas: Illinois

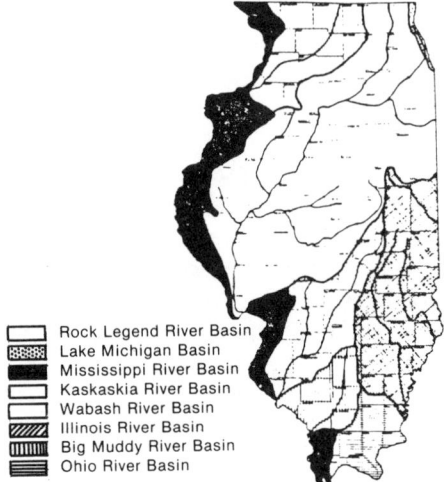

Figure 8-11. River Basins: Illinois

Water Description: and Background Issues. Major increases in utility siting are projected in the upper Illinois River basin and nearby tributaries that drain northern and northeastern Illinois (see figure 8-11). Because of artificial flow reversal of the Chicago and Calumet Rivers, the Illinois basin also receives metropolitan Chicago waste water that would flow to Lake Michigan under natural conditions.

The southern portion of the basin has a large assimilative capacity, diminishing the effect of waste loads from the northern part of the state. However, parts of the southern Illinois River basin experience mercury, phenol, and biological-oxygen-demand (BOD) violations below industrialized areas and large municipal treatment facilities.

Water quality and availability are most threatened in Illionois northeastern river basins. The Fox and Sangamon Rivers are frequently unable to assimilate industrial and municipal waste loads because of seasonal low flows. Further, water removal from Lake Michigan is subject to allocation under federal mandate. Water from the lake is used for drinking water, process water, and for sewage dilution by many municipalities in northeastern Illinois.

Impacts on Water Quality/Availability. More-stringent waste-load allocations and/or river-basin management will be required to alleviate projected total dissolved solids, copper, chromium, and sulfate violations in the Fox, upper Illinois, and Sangamon Rivers (Illinois River basin).

Water availability may restrict projected utility siting in the northern counties because of seasonal low flows of the Rock and Fox Rivers and in central Illinois on the Sangamon River. Water-allocation issues may restrict siting in the Lake Michigan basin.

Scenario-Induced Changes. Three rivers are impacted by the scenario: the Fox, the Illinois, and the Sangamon.

Increases in total dissolved solids (TDS) and copper concentrations are projected in the Fox River, primarily from an increase in utilities. River-basin management and implementation of discharge standards would be expected to reduce the incidence of the copper violations. The assimilative capacity of the Illinois River, on the other hand, diminishes the severity of violations that occur upstream. Although efforts are being made to improve the quality of the upper reaches, TDS levels are expected to increase (figure 8-12). Finally, the upper reaches of the Sangamon River would experience significant water depletions from increased activity by utilities, causing TDS, sulfate, copper, and chromium violations without flow augmentation and/or discharge management. High residual concentrations would diminish downstream.

Concluding Comments: Lead Labs and the RIIA Process

The lead-lab concept and the notion of national-regional linkages to perform Regional Issue and Identification Analyses (RIIAs) are evolving

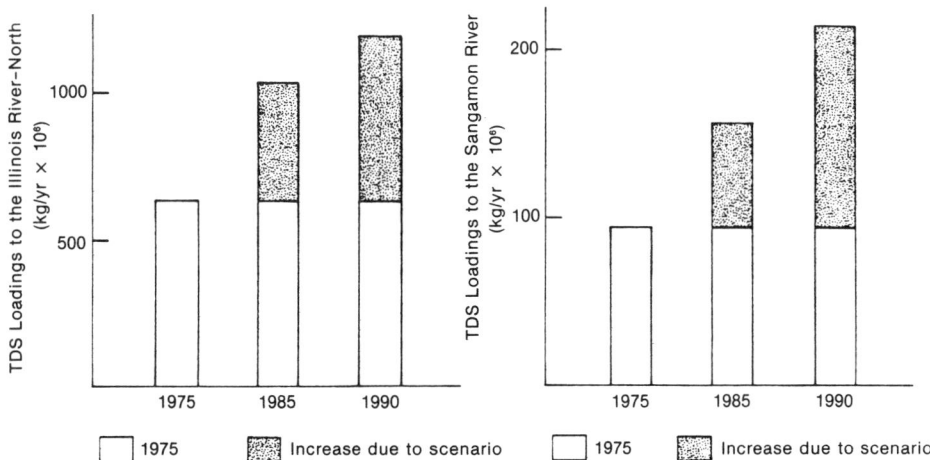

Figure 8-12. Projected Increases in TDS Loadings to the Northern Illinois and Sangamon Rivers, 1975-1990

rapidly. The lead lab concept is relatively new. During the first iteration (1977-1978), each participating national laboratory was responsible for assessing the environmental and socioeconomic impacts of a given national scenario for all impact categories for its region. Although the resulting analysis represented a comprehensive assessment of the regional implications of a national-policy scenario, no attempts have yet been made to aggregate or compare the results among regions: there were numerous differences and possible inconsistencies incorporated in the laboratories' basic assumptions and analytical procedures. To begin to remedy this situation, in the second iteration of RIIA (1978-1980), each laboratory computed the impacts of the scenario for one or more impact categories of the nation, utilizing a consistent set of assumptions and consistent methodologies across regions. The assignment of a particular laboratory to a specific impact category was based upon that laboratory's expertise.

The lead-lab process is extremely complex, requiring constant monitoring, expediting, feedback, and interaction, as illustrated in figure 8-13. The advantage, however, is a finer level of detail and subnational realism, made possible by continued analysis of a national model to provide boundary conditions, and by models that provide more-specific impacts and then a mix of qualitative assessments of these impacts for the states within the laboratory's region of responsibility. From this first attempt several lessons were learned, to be applied in the next round.

For one, the laboratories were reluctant to perform more impact analyses and repeatedly questioned the results of the economic and energy scenarios provided them. Possibly the biggest single problem, however, was managerial. Six laboratories and an average of five or six people per lab is a lot of integration. These people had not worked together as a team before, and their wide geographic dispersion made communication somewhat difficult. Numerous meetings were necessary to break down these barriers and to help ensure that each component of the analysis was produced on time and in a form that all could use.

Numerous meetings were also necessary to establish and agree upon definitions, protocols, and criteria that all the laboratories could use in their individual area assessments, to ensure the highest degree of interregional comparison possible.

The lead-lab concept had both positive and negative features. On the one hand, it allowed individual laboratories to specialize in areas where they had the greatest expertise. On the other hand, this practice did little more, at least at this stage, than perpetuate a top-down analysis approach. The only real difference from the earlier, single-model approach was that segments of the model at DOE were run by laboratories using their own models. In the second round, one lab still sited utilities and industrial boilers, but the other laboratories demanded considerably more input to improve the estimates of these projected locations. The rest of the impact models (except for long-range transport) became more of the responsibility of the individual labs, with help from the former lead lab. This procedure enriched the output by making the analyses more sensitive to local conditions. However, care had to be exercised that the methods used were constant in all areas other than those required to deal solely with local peculiarities.

In the main, this lead-lab approach has proved highly successful in terms of the expectations of its developers and the needs of the Department of Energy. It has provided invaluable, in-depth information to DOE about regional sensitivities of the environmental impacts of the department's policies. The process is built upon a substantial analytic capability already existing at the six national laboratories participating in the program. The transferability of this technique will be discussed later.

Regional Characterization: The Use of Factor- and Cluster-Analysis Techniques

Regional Characterization

To identify and evaluate regional resources and constraints affecting utilization of potential national-energy strategies in more detail, another technique was used that assessed the characteristics of the various regions of the nation. The purpose of this regional characterization effort was to:

> Compile data for selected (representative) regions, including information on ambient environmental quality, energy consumption and production, geography, topography, climate, demography, industrial activity, and political, social, and financial institutions

> Apply statistical clustering techniques whereby similar Bureau of Economic Analysis (BEA) areas or other recognized standard regional designations are grouped according to a given set of variables, including demography, physical environment, ambient environmental quality, government and related infrastructure, industrial activity, energy consumption, and variables unique to each energy technology

> Select representative areas for case studies for evaluation in terms of potential strategies for mitigation of environmental impacts

A major task of the regional characterization effort is to apply a clustering technique that groups commercial and industrial areas (BEAs) in the ten federal regions according to similar characteristics. The categories eventually chosen include the following:

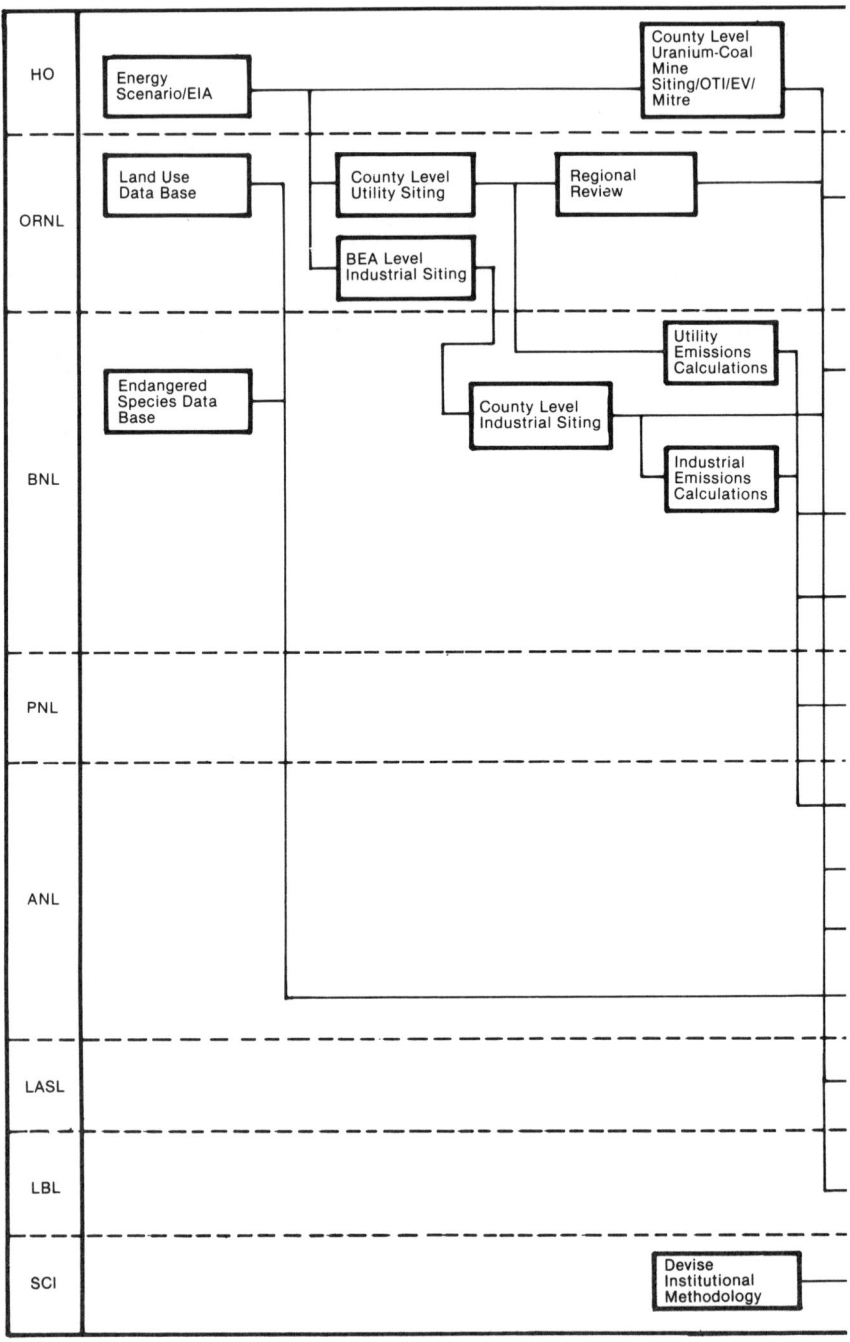

Figure 8-13. Regional-Issue Identification and Assessment: Lead-Lab Process

Two-Way Applications

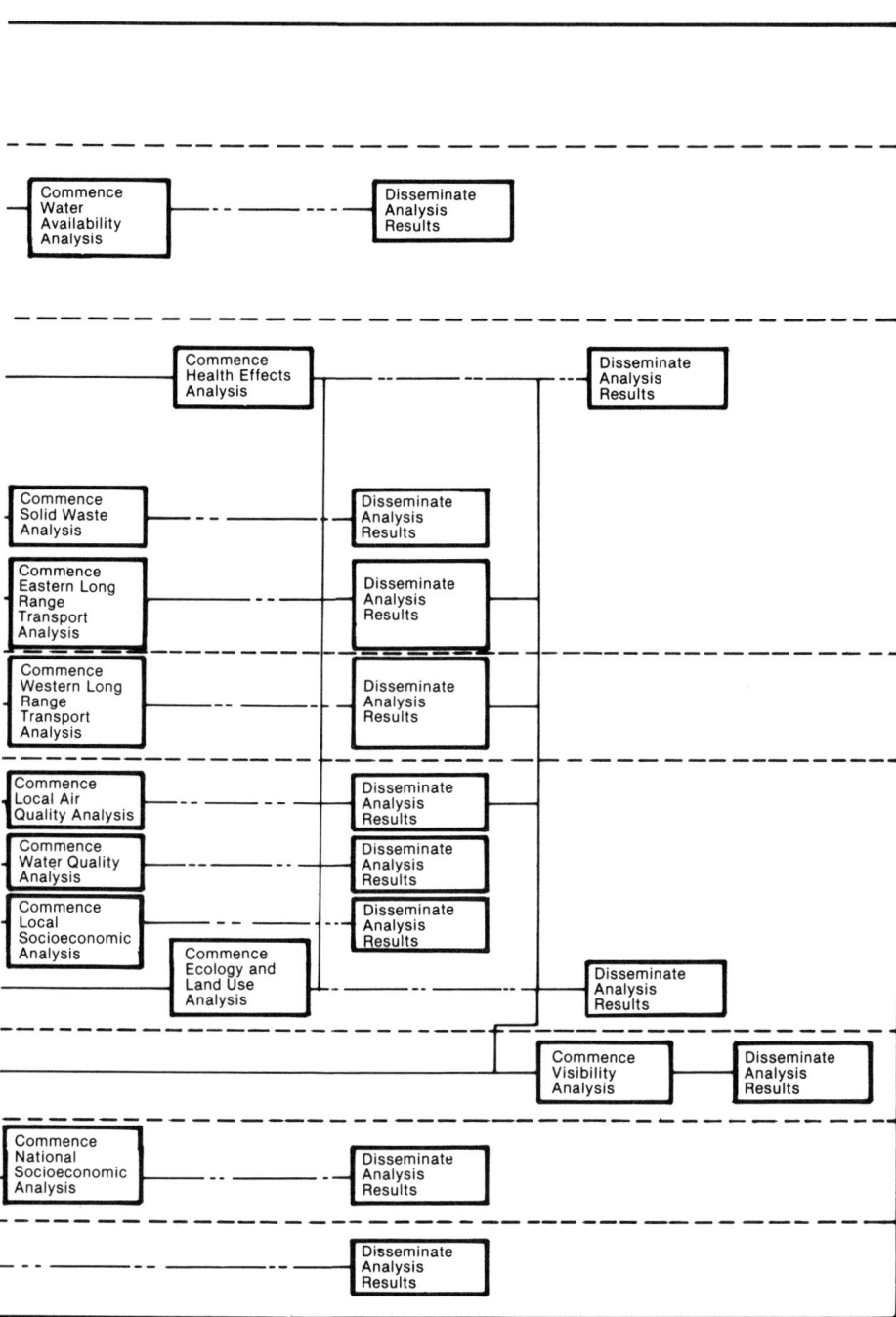

Demography: characteristics of the population, housing quality and living conditions, economic welfare, population and income changes, and transportation usage patterns

Public sector: government expenditures and community concern and involvement

Industrial activity: Indicating the importance of manufacturing, the industrial mix, wholesale and retail trade, services, and patterns of energy consumption

Physical environment: distribution of activities within the BEA area, its density and urbanized portions, its assimilative attributes, and information on climate and geography

Ambient environmental quality: existing air quality, water quality, and waste management

Residuals: types and quantities of pollutant residuals being discharged

These groupings serve as a basis from which it is possible, for example, to select potential sites for conducting case studies of environmental, social, economic, and institutional constraints associated with development and deployment of energy technologies. The BEA areas are clustered for each technology, within each region, and within the nation, reflecting parameters unique to the technology being addressed. For example, the parameters for selecting a site to conduct a case study concerned with institutional constraints on decentralized solar-energy development are considerably different from the parameters for selecting a site to conduct a case study concerned with the institutional constraints on coal development. Clustering techniques are intended to reflect these differences and to allow reasonable extrapolation of results from the case-study to other, comparable areas.

A clustering technique that embodies these characteristics and was used in the regional characterization process is the principal-components approach to factor analysis. Variables of the parameter that correlate highest with each other are grouped together under a specific factor, and from this factor a site is selected. For example, if the results of the oil-shale technology analysis show six BEA areas grouped together, two things are indicated: first, the BEA areas are similar, and second, there is a high probability that selecting a BEA area from this group would provide a representative candidate for ensuring the validity and generalizability of the case studies. This factor-analysis methodology is described in more detail in the next section.

Two-Way Applications

Regional Impacts

Once a set of regions has been selected, the groupings are used to study the postulated impacts of selected policies on modal areas. For example, recently DOE and the Environmental Protection Agency engaged in extensive discussions about the impact of various interpretations of the New Source Performance Standards (NSPS) of the 1977 Clean Air Act amendments for electric-utility boilers. One useful piece of information absent from this analysis was the relative probabilities that various impacts flowing from this regulation would occur. Assuming that all other sections of the act were also implemented locally (and in the states) and that the ten modal areas were truly representative of the other areas in their respective groupings, then it was believed that performing ten case studies would provide a good notion of the differential impact of NSPS on various types of localities across the nation. We will test this hypothesis later in an example of urban- and community-impact assessments.

Factor Analysis: The Techniques

Statistically, the concept of factor analysis is relatively well known. Though originally conceived to carry out analysis in the field of psychology, it was soon seen to have applications in several other areas. As early as 1943, for example, Margaret Hogood was using the technique to apply to regionalization and agriculture in the United States.[14] Although much controversy remains as to whether the technique can be usefully applied to regional issues, proponents maintain that, properly used, it is a very useful tool.

In general, factor analysis, when used as a data-reduction technique, defines the parameters describing a major portion of the total variance and eliminates items that do not explain a significant amount of variance, under the assumption that the most significant factors are also the most important ones for the policymaker. This, however, may not be the case, particularly when some areas of interest have much more information available than others, or certain factors are more critical to some areas than to others.

Factor analysis is really little more than an expansion of the basic idea of statistical-correlation analysis. Its specific uses are many, but all can be reduced to two general uses: as a way to recognize patterns in a data set, and as a way to transform data, normally into fewer numbers of variables. In either case, the technique has to be used with care because the process requires considerable subjective input. On the one hand, the pattern-recognition use can result in undue attention to spurious relationships as correlations between data items are noted and attempts to theorize connections unduly forced. In the same way, using factor analysis to reduce the number of variables in a data set to a number sufficiently small to facilitate study may result in the choice of inappropriate surrogates. Clearly, the technique works best when used by someone who both understands its strengths and limits and is also familiar with the subject area, so that the chance of introducing nonessential information is reduced to a minimum. Several variants of factor analysis have been constructed, and it is up to the researcher to choose the one most appropriate to his needs. Rummel suggests ten factors to consider when making this choice.[15]

1. Grouping requirements. Some techniques require input variables to be grouped together according to the research hypothesis.
2. Number of factors. Some techniques are constrained to a given number of factors (normally one or two), whereas others deal with the generalized case of multiple factors.
3. Variable complexity. The major option here is between identifying all relevant factors and limiting the solution to a small number of dominant factors for each variable.
4. Factor complexity. The degree of complexity—the number of variables having at least moderate loadings on a given factor—reflects the choice of general factors, which load on all variables; grouping factors, which load on more than one but not all variables; and specific factors, each of which is unique to a particular variable.
5. Factor variance contribution. The researcher must decide whether the factors should all contribute equally to explaining variance, or whether the first should explain the most variance, with others explaining a decreasing proportion, and so on.
6. Sensitivity to error. Not all methods give specific consideration to measurement and stochastic error, and those that do estimate the error use differing approximations.
7. Determinateness. This criterion, the uniqueness of the solution, implies a tradeoff, for certain assumptions are required in order to reach a unique solution.
8. Resources. Some methods are not feasible without the aid of high-speed computers.
9. Hypotheses. The method must be consistent with any hypotheses. Normally, this is a question of factor and variable complexity.
10. Theory. This is a special case where factor analysis is applied to geometry.

These ten criteria are applied in the research-design process to choose, first an approach and then a specific solution technique from a large number of alternatives. Discussion here will center on the inherent assumptions of three alternative approaches. Alternative-solution techniques are applied within the three approaches but will not be enumerated here. Rummel provides a concise discussion of these methods.[16]

The technique of factor analysis leaves ample opportunity for abuse in specific instances. Not only does it require that some simplifying assumptions be made about the data set, but also the subjectivity of data selection and interpretation opens the way for considerable misunderstanding. Possibly the principal way to reduce the potential for misinterpretation, deliberate or otherwise, would be to specify clearly the assumptions made and technique used throughout the particular application so that any other analyst could arrive at similar conclusions by replicating the steps taken. By this means, the area of disagreement about the results can be made explicit and the opportunity increased for making the issue more explicitly one of interpretation of data than of the technique itself.

Factor Analysis: DOE Application

In 1979 and 1980 the Department of Energy joined the EPA, Department of Transportation, and DHEW in attempting to use factor analysis to improve regional assessments.[17] As with many other groups in the federal government, most regional analysis was carried out by means of case studies designed to focus attention on areas where the particular policy issue was thought to be most pervasive. This practice had many worthwhile features, including making the most-detailed information available to the policy level concerning specific sites and impacts; however, the practice also has many obvious deficiencies. In the first place, the utility of the case study to the policy issue at hand is a function of the care with which the study area is chosen. If the choice is not made by someone adequately skilled or is made for other than purely analytic reasons, then the case study results are correspondingly less useful. Further, the typical case study requires considerable time to perform the functions of information collection and analysis. It is not always possible to make the results in time for those who might use the information for decision analysis. Finally, although this technique allows collection of a great deal of specific information about the potential impact of a policy on a particular area, it does not usually provide a means for generalizing these findings to the whole nation.

To overcome such deficiencies, a technique was sought that would allow consistent and timely analysis of the regional/land impacts of federal policy, a method that combined the rigor and speed of computer-based, top-down analysis with the detail and specificity of bottom-up case studies. For RIIA, this has been achieved through incremental (multiphased) analysis, looking at federal policy impacts in ever-increasing detail and keeping the analysis in the perspective set by the original macro- analysis. Primarily, the technique is areal in form and is designed to present policy impacts in a comparative fashion on different places in the nation.

One alternative to a locational analysis is a modified, case-study factor analysis approach designed to provide a different perspective. To accomplish this, several steps were taken. First, a substantial data base was assembled on local areas and used for segregating areas into like categories. The data were then used to perform factor analyses, both to group the locales into like categories and to make these categories as few as possible. Typical locales could be chosen in each of these categories and case studies. The results could be taken as typical of what could be expected to be found in other locales belonging to the same category. Finally, an institutional method had to be devised to gather the original case-study data on the typical locales, to keep it updated, and to perform the requisite analysis.

The extensive data base, collected on over 300 variables (see figure 8-14),[18] provided the foundation for the factor analysis. The variables included measures of energy supply and demand, transportation, socioeconomic measures, physical features, land use, and environmental quality. The reference year used was 1975.

Crude Oil Production in 10^{12} joules/year
Natural Gas Production in 10^{12} joules/year
Total Coal Production in 10^{12} joules/year
Coal Production, Auger Method, 1000 short tons/year
Coal Production, Strip-Auger Method, 1000 short tons/year
Coal Production, Strip Method, 1000 short tons/year
Coal Production, Underground Mining, 1000 short tons/year
Coal Reserves, Strippable, Lignite, 10^4 short tons/year
Coal Reserves, Strippable, Anthracite, 10^4 short tons/year
Coal Reserves, Strippable, Bituminous, 10^4 short tons/year
Coal Reserves, Deep, Anthracite, 10^4 short tons/year
Coal Reserves, Deep, Bituminous, 10^4 short tons/year
Oil & Gas Exploration, Total Exploratory Well Feet Drilled in '75, Scaled Number
Number of Wells Drilled in '75
Electric Production w/o Transformation, Hydroelectric, in 10^{12} joules/year
Electric Production w/o Transformation, Nuclear, in 10^{12} joules/year
Electric Production w/o Transformation, Geothermal and Solar, in 10^{12} joules/year
Number of Underground Bituminous and Lignite Coal Mines
Number of Bituminous and Lignite Strip Mines

Ambient Water Quality

Water Temperature, °C
Streamflow, cu. ft./second
Turbidity, jtu

Figure 8-14. Factor-Analysis Data Base

Dissolved Oxygen, mg/liter
Acidity, pH
Alkalinity, mg/liter of $CACO_3$
Total Nitrogen (Organic and Inorganic), mg/liter
Total Phosphorous, mg/liter
Total Organic Carbon, mg/liter
Hardness, mg/liter of $CACO_3$
Total Arsenic, μ/liter
Total Chromium, μ/liter
Total Copper, μ/liter
Total Lead, μ/liter
Total Zinc, μ/liter
Radioactivity Level, pc/liter of
Fecal Coliform, coli/100 ml
Dissolved Solids, mg/liter
Suspended Solids, mg/liter

Water Use

Total Fresh Surface Water Withdrawn, millions of gallons/day
Fresh Water Consumed, millions of gallons/day
Ground Water—Total Withdrawn, millions of gallons/day
Public—Industrial and Commercial Use, millions of gallons/day
Public—Domestic Use and Losses, millions of gallons/day
Public—Total Consumed, millions of gallons/day
Agriculture—Total Withdrawn, millions of gallons/day
Agriculture—Consumptive Use, millions of gallons/day
Agriculture—Conveyance Loss, millions of gallons/day
Electric Utility—Total Fresh Water Withdrawn, millions of gallons/day
Manufacturing—Total Fresh Water Withdrawn, millions of gallons/day
Manufacturing—Total Fresh Water Consumed, millions of gallons/day
All industries—Total Fresh Water Consumed, millions of gallons/day
Rural Water, Domestic (Withdrawn and Consumed), millions of gallons/day
Rural Water, Livestock (Withdrawn and Consumed), millions of gallon/day

Acres of Urban Land Use
Acres of Agricultural Land Use (Crop and Pasture)
Acres of Rangeland
Acres of Forest
Acres of Water
Acres of Total Land Use
Acres of Unusable Land
Acres of Federally Owned Land
Acres of Existing and Potential Wilderness Areas
National and Scenic River in or Bordering County (0/1 Indicator)
National and Scenic River Under Study (0/1 Indicator)
National Scenic Trail, Existing and/or Under Study (0/1 Indicator)
National Wildlife Refuge (0/1 Indicator)
National Park (0/1 Indicator)
Existing Wilderness System and/or Study Area (0/1 Indicator)
Wilderness Area Proposed for Study (0/1 Indicator)
Existing Class I Areas (0/1 Indicator)
Average Daily Solar Radiation (Langleys/Day)
Mean Annual Mixing Heights—Morning (1000's Feet)
Mean Annual Mixing Heights—Afternoon (1000's Feet)

Figure 8-14 continued

\# Days High Meteorological Potential for Air Pollution
Annual Heating Degree-Days
Annual Cooling Degree-Days
Annual Air Conditioner Compressor Operating Hours
Average Relative Humidity for July
Near Great Lakes or Ocean (0/1 Indicator)
Mean Annual Wind Power (w/m²)
Indicator—Inland Waterway

Number of In-Service Coal Plants
Number of In-Service Oil and Distillate Plants
Number of In-Service Gas Plants
Number of In-Service Nuclear Plants
Number of In-Service Hydroelectric Plants
Number of In-Service Geothermal Plants
Number of In-Service Solar Plants
Number of In-Service Wind Plants
Number of In-Service Wood, Refuse and Organic Plants
Number of In-Service "Other" Plants
Nameplate Rating of Coal Plants
Nameplate Rating of Oil and Distillate Plants
Nameplate Rating of Gas Plants
Nameplate Rating of Nuclear Plants
Nameplate Rating of Hydroelectric Plants
Nameplate Rating of Geothermal Plants
Nameplate Rating of Solar Plants
Nameplate Rating of Wind Plants
Nameplate Rating of Wood, Refuse and Organic Plants
Nameplate Rating of "Other" Plants
Number of Refineries
Crude Oil Distillation Capacity in Operating Mode, Scaled Number

Natural Gas Processing Plants—Output of Other Hydrocarbons, 10^{15} joules/year
Natural Gas Processing Plants—Input of Natural Gas, 10^{12} joules/year
Electric Generation, 10^{15} joules/year
Oil Refining, Crude Oil Input, 10^{15} joules/year
Oil Refining, Natural Gas Input, 10^{12} joules/year
Oil Refining, Distillate Oil Output, 10^{12} joules/year
Oil Refining, Residual Oil Output, 10^{12} joules/year
Oil Refining, Gasoline Output, 10^{15} joules/year
Oil Refining, Other Organics Output, 10^{15} joules/year
Electric Generation, Distillate Oil Inputs, 10^{12} joules/year
Electric Generation, Residual Oil Inputs, 10^{12} joules/year
Electric Generation, Natural Gas Inputs, 10^{12} joules/year
Synthetic Natural Gas Production—1975 Production, in 10^8 cubic feet
Synthetic Natural Gas Production—# of Existing Facilities
Electric Generation, Coal Input, 10^{15} joules/year

Air Pollutant Emissions—Particulates, tons/year
Air Pollutant Emissions—SO_x, tons/year
Air Pollutant Emissions—NO_x, tons/year
Air Pollutant Emissions—HC, tons/year
Air Pollutant Emissions—CO, tons/year
Indicator—Heavy Metal Emissions, 0/1 Indicator
Radioactive Waste Volume in Storage, 1000 m³

Figure 8-14 continued

Water Pollutant Discharges—BOD, tons/year
Water Pollutant Discharges—Suspended Solids, tons/year
Water Pollutant Discharges—Dissolved Solids, tons/year
Water Pollutant Discharges—Nitrates, tons/year
Water Pollutant Discharges—Phosphates, tons/year
Water Pollutant Discharges—Nitrogen, tons/year
Water Pollutant Discharges—Phosphorous, tons/year
Water Pollutant Discharges—Oil and Grease, tons/year

Copper, $10^4 \times$ mg/m^3
Lead, $10^3 \times$ mg/m^3
Nickel, $10^4 \times$ mg/m^3
Vanadium, $10^4 \times$ mg/m^3
Sulfate, Scaled Number
Acid Rainfall, Scaled Number
Indicator—Arsenic, 0/I Indicator
Chromium, $10^4 \times$ mg/m^3
Co, 9 ppm for 8 hours
O_3, 0.12 ppm for 1 hour
NO_2, 0.25 ppm for 1 hour
SO_2, 0.139 ppm for 24 hours
TSP, 269 g/m^3 for 24 hours
Median Visibility, Scaled Number
Water Temperature, °C
Streamflow, cu. ft./sec.
Turbidity, jtu
Dissolved Oxygen, mg/liter
Acidity, pH
Alkalinity, mg/liter of $CACO_3$
Total Nitrogen (Organic and Inorganic), mg/liter
Total Phosphorous, mg/liter
Total Organic Carbon, mg/liter
Hardness, mg/liter of $CACO_3$
Total Arsenic, µg/liter
Total Chromium, µg/liter
Total Copper, µg/liter
Total Lead, µg/liter
Total Zinc, µg/liter
Radioactivity Level, pc/liter of
Fecal Coliform, col/100 ml
Dissolved Solids, mg/liter
Dissolved Solids, mg/liter
Suspended Solids, mg/liter
pH
Hardness, Total
Calcium, Dissolved
Magnesium, Dissolved
Potassium, Dissolved
Chloride
Sulfate, Total
Fluoride, Dissolved
Iron, Dissolved
Manganese, Dissolved

Natural Gas Demand, 10^{12} joules/year
Coal Miscellaneous Demand, 10^{12} joules/year

Figure 8-14 continued

Electricity Miscellaneous Demand, 10^{12} joules/year
Total Miscellaneous Energy Demand, 10^{12} joules/year
Distillate Oil, Miscellaneous Demand, 10^{12} joules/year
Residual Oil, Miscellaneous Demand, 10^{12} joules/year
Other Hydrocarbons, Miscellaneous Demand, 10^{12} joules/year
Distillate Oil, Residential and Commercial Demand, 10^{15} joules/year
Distillate Oil, Industrial Demand, 10^{15} joules/year
Distillate Oil, Transportation Demand, 10^{15} joules/year
Residual Oil, Residential and Commercial Demand, 10^{15} joules/year
Residual Oil, Industrial Demand, 10^{15} joules/year
Residual Oil, Transportation Demand, 10^{15} joules/year
Gasoline, Industrial Demand, 10^{15} joules/year
Gasoline, Transportation Demand, 10^{15} joules/year
Other Hydrocarbons, Residential and Commercial Demand, 10^{15} joules/year
Other Hydrocarbons, Industrial Demand, 10^{15} joules/year
Other Hydrocarbons, Transportation Demand, 10^{15} joules/year
Natural Gas, Residential and Commercial Demand, 10^{15} joules/year
Natural Gas, Industrial Demand, 10^{15} joules/year
Natural Gas, Transportational Demand, 10^{12} joules/year
Coal, Residential and Commercial Demand, 10^{12} joules/year
Coal, Industrial Demand, 10^{15} joules/year
Coal, Transportation Demand, 10^{12} joules/year
Electricity, Industrial Demand, 10^{15} joules/year
Electricity, Transportation Demand, 10^{12} joules/year
Total Residential and Commercial Demand, 10^{15} joules/year
Total Industrial Demand, 10^{15} joules/year
Total Transportation Demand, 10^{15} joules/year
Net Export ($-$) or Import ($+$) of Energy to Region, 10^{12} joules/year

Total Employment
Total Unemployment
Civilian Labor Force
Federal-Civilian Employment
Federal-Military Employment
Total Employment
Agricultural Services, Forestry and Fisheries Employment
Mining Employment
Construction Employment
Manufacturing (Total) Employment
Food Employment
Tobacco Manufacturing Employment
Textile Mill Products Employment
Apparel and Other Textile Products Employment
Lumber and Wood Products Employment
Furniture and Fixtures Employment
Paper and Allied Products Employment
Printing and Publishing Employment
Chemicals and Allied Products Employment
Petroleum and Coal Products Employment
Rubber and Miscellaneous Plastics Employment
Leather Employment
Stone, Clay and Glass Employment
Primary Metal Industries Employment
Fabricated Metal Products Employment
Machinery Except Electrical Employment

Figure 8-14 continued

Electric and Electronic Equipment Employment
Transportation Equipment Employment
Instruments Employment
Miscellaneous Manufacturing Industries Employment
Transportation and Other Public Utilities Employment
Trucking and Warehousing Employment
Wholesale Trade Employment
Retail Trade Employment
Finance, Insurance and Real Estate Employment
Services Employment
Unclassified Establishments Employment

Total Employment
Miles of Interstate Highway
Total Rural Vehicle Miles Traveled, by Area
Total Urban Vehicle Miles Traveled, by Area
Aircraft Landing/Take-Off Cycles—Military
Aircraft Landing/Take-Off Cycles—Civilian
Aircraft Landing/Take-Off Cycles—Commercial
Transportation Employment
Cross-County Commute Patterns, Inside County
Cross-County Commute Patterns, Outside County
Means of Transportation to Work, Via Automobile
Means of Transportation to Work, Via Mass Transit
Means of Transportation to Work, All Modes
Passenger Car Registrations
Fixed Route Mass Transit System, 0/1 Indicator
Surface Water, Indicator—Includes Inland Waterway
Surface Water, Indicator—Border Ocean or Great Lake

Effective Tax Rate—Property Taxes, Thousands of Dollars
Effective Tax Rate—Total Tax Revenue, Thousands of Dollars
Total Sewerage Expenditures, Dollars
Expenditure on Other Sanitation, Dollars
Expenditure on Water Supply, Dollars
Median Household Income, Dollars
Per Capita Outstanding Debt, Dollars
Total Retail Sales, Thousands of Dollars
Total Wholesale Sales, Thousands of Dollars
Central City Population, Central City Area
Central City Population, Outlying Areas

Urbanized Area, Central City Area, Square Miles $\times\ 10^{-1}$
Urbanized Area, Outlying Areas, Square Miles $\times\ 10^{-1}$
Family Income Distribution, Percentage Below Poverty
Family Income Distribution, Percentage over $15,000
Population Change, 1970–1975, Percentage
Annual Average Percentage Change in Per Capita Income, 1969–1974
Male, 0–19 years, 1975
Male, 20–39 years, 1975
Male, 40–64 years, 1975
Male, 65+ years, 1975
Female, 0–19 years, 1975
Female, 20–39 years, 1975
Female, 40–64 years, 1975

Figure 8-14 continued

Female, 65+ years, 1975
Federal-Civilian Employment
Federal-Military Employment
State/Local Government Employment
Total Dwelling Units
Single Family Dwellings, Percentage
Local Government—General Expenditures, Millions of Dollars
Full-Time Employment by Federal Government
Total Value of Production by Mining Sector, Millions of Dollars
Value Added by All Manufacturing, Millions of Dollars

State Administers Its Own NPDES Permit System, 0/1 Indicator
State Can Control Development of Wetlands, 0/1 Indicator
State Can Site Power Plants and Energy Facilities, 0/1 Indicator
State Has Legislation Authorizing the Regulation of Flood Plains, 0/1 Indicator
State Has Limited or Full NEPA Statute Requiring State EISs, 0/1 Indicator
Indicator, State Policy on Land Spreading of Sludge

Males, 0-19 years, 1975
Males, 29-39 years, 1975
Males, 40-64 years, 1975
Males, 65+ years, 1975
Females, 0-19 years, 1975
Females, 20-39 years, 1975
Females, 40-64 years, 1975
Females, 65+ years, 1975
Cancer, Buccal Cavity, Pharynx—Mortality Rate/100,000 White Male Population
Cancer, Alimentary System—Mortality Rate/100,000 White Male Population
Cancer, Respiratory System—Mortality Rate/100,000 White Male Population
Cancer, Breast—Mortality Rate/100,000 White Female Population
Cancer, Cervix, Uterus, Other Female—Mortality Rate/100,000 White Female
    Population
Cancer, Kidney—Mortality Rate/100,000 White Male Population
Cancer, Central Nervous System—Mortality Rate/100,000 White Male Population
Cancer, Residual—Mortality Rate/100,000 White Male Population
Cancer, Ill-Defined and Secondary—Mortality Rate/100,000 White Male Population
Cancer, Lumphomas and Leukemia—Mortality Rate/100,000 White Male Population
Neoplasms, Benign and Unspecified—Mortality Rate/100,000 White Male Population
Influenza and Pneumonia—Mortality Rate/100,000 White Male Population
Chronic Respiratory Disease—Mortality Rate/100,000 White Male Population
Cancer, Bone—Mortality Rate/100,000 White Male Population
Cancer, Thyroid—Mortality Rate/100,000 White Male Population
Cancer, All Sites and Forms—Mortality Rate/100,000 White Male Population
Heart Disease—Mortality Rate/100,000 White Male Population
Accidents—Mortality Rate/100,000 White Male Population
Homicide—Mortality Rate/100,000 White Male Population
Suicide—Mortality Rate/100,000 White Male Population
All Causes—Mortality Rate/100,000 White Male Population

Figure 8-14 continued

Two-Way Applications

Bureau of Economic Analysis Units

The data base was collected on the basis of BEA areas (see figure 8-15). These areas are nationwide whole aggregates of counties defined by BEA area, using central-place theory to include the labor market and supply regions for a hub city. Thus, BEA areas are named for the urban area around which they are centered. This approach simplifies the analysis considerably, since certain types of data are readily available on a county basis. However, no single regional designation can perfectly serve all purposes or possible applications. For example, environmental-quality measures are typically defined on the basis of an airshed or watershed, which is not coincident with BEA-area boundaries, for the latter are defined by economic and political characteristics. A second problem is that the BEA areas cross state boundaries, so that state estimates cannot be made directly. This problem can be minimized by collecting as much data as possible at the county level and also by using the State Economic Areas (portions of BEA areas), which can be aggregated to state totals. Subject to these limitations, the BEA areas, based on economic characteristics and county boundaries, are the most practical choice.

Clustering BEA Areas

A two-stage approach to factor analysis was utilized: small analyses were first classified on parameters hypothesized to be closely related, and the results were used in a more general, second-stage analysis. Application of factor-analysis methods involves considerable skill. The two-stage approach permitted significant hypothesis testing and interpretation and also controlled for inconsistencies in the quantity of available data in various subject areas.

The factor-analysis technique provides a grouping of the BEA areas according to variables selected to describe groups of BEA areas sorted according to a particular question, such as air quality, socioeconomic impact, water quality, or land use. Because the purpose of using factor analysis was to reduce the data set to a number of like areas, the following strategy was chosen:

1. The data were used to reduce the approximately 300 variables to groupings of BEA areas that were sorted and grouped according to selected factors such as air quality or water quality.

224   Modern Federalism

Figure 8-15. BEA Economic Areas

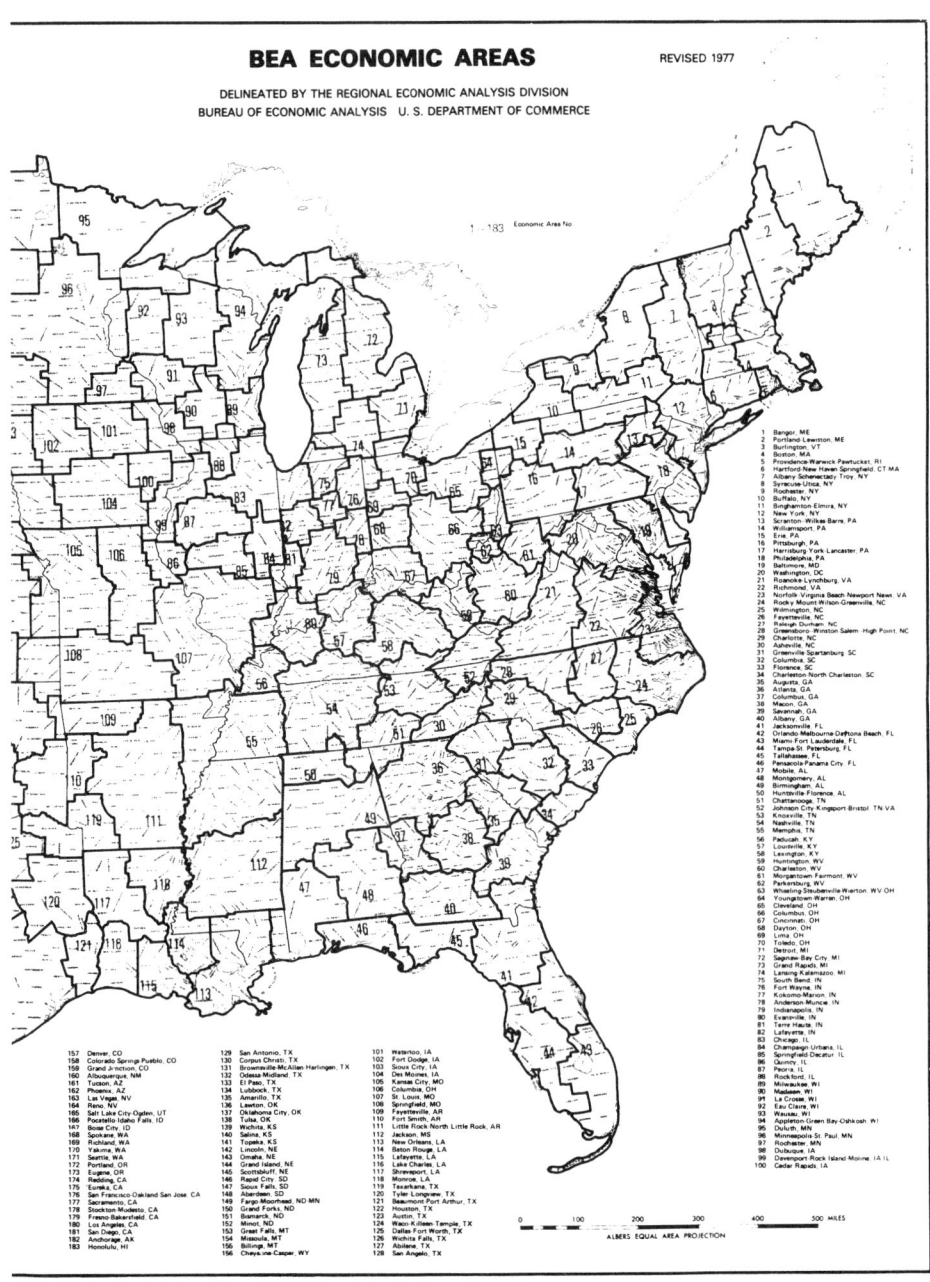

2. These groupings were analyzed for a representative BEA area that fell into each category in a specific discrete fashion which maximized that area's characteristics from those of other representative areas. The groupings were constrained to be as near to a half-dozen as possible. Thus, within each grouping (say, six), a representative or model BEA area was chosen as being exemplary of all others in the same group. One of the criteria for these representative BEA areas was that the six also fell in the other grouping in a unique fashion; that is, no grouping contained two or more from a previous sort.
3. A data base was constructed for each of the six BEA areas that served as the basis for selected case studies of federal energy policies.
4. These case areas were fairly well dispersed geographically and were used as the basis for describing the impact of a selected federal energy policy on these selected areas.
5. The specific case studies that resulted were used to extrapolate the potential impacts on similar BEA areas across the nation.

In short, the most probable impacts of a particular federal policy could be inferred on the basis of six case studies of areas selected as being representative of the remainder of the 1973 BEA areas.[19]

Some Applications—and Limitations

Factor analysis has come to be used a great deal in investigations by federal agencies where regional and local conditions need to understood better in terms of depth, realism, and analytic power. DOE's Office of Environmental Assessment has commissioned several applications of factor analyses to a variety of policy and regulatory analyses.[20] One of these examined the interactions of certain forms of energy supply and air quality on a regional basis. Another was concerned with the local effects of large-scale energy facilities, including impacts on air quality, water availability, water quality, and socioeconomic factors. Both studies used factor-analysis approaches to classify geographic areas into groups based on quantitative measures for the variables of interest. The first included the whole of the continental United States, using data for BEA areas; the second looked at selected coal-rich counties. Both analyses depended on the comprehensive data base—including information on energy resources, extraction and reserves, water resources, land use, geography, energy production, residuals, ambient environmental quality, transportation, energy demand, industry structure, demographic characteristics, regulations, and damage effects—briefly described above.

The results of the energy-supply/air-quality application indicated that:

Gulf Coast and southern Great Plains areas appear to offer more air-pollution-carrying capacity to accommodate coal-fired power plants than other regions, because of the low incidence of air pollution and the lowest probability of Prevention of Significant Deterioration (PSD) siting conflicts.

Of the seven BEA areas identified by EPA as areas in which the majority of new energy facilities would be located, none are in the Gulf Coast or southern Great Plains.

The results of the large-scale-energy-facility impact analysis concluded that:

Patterned variation among counties of impacts caused by large-scale energy facilities may be described by key factors such as land-use, environmental-quality, economic, and institutional considerations. Counties in the West appear to possess unique characteristics—relating to location and land-use variables such as population density, distance to the nearest SMSA, and proportion of acreage in rangelands and federal lands—that distinguish them from county clusters in the East.

National air-quality attainment goals (such as prevention of significant deterioration [PSD] may serve as a constraint to facility siting in the West, whereas other air-quality regulations (nonattainment) may serve as a constraint to siting in the East.

The two eastern clusters differ mainly in their carrying capacity in terms of population density and air quality. Boom-town scenarios will not result from the siting of major energy facilities such as synthetic-fuel plants, but air quality will be an important consideration in choosing sites.

Those who conducted this study, and its clients, believed that the methodology was powerful, valid, and very useful. However, the authors of the report put forth this statement about the method's limitations:

> ... no single regional designation can perfectly serve all purposes or possible applications. For example, environmental quality measures are typically defined on the basis of an airshed or watershed. These natural territories do not coincide with county or BEA area boundaries that are defined by economic and political characteristics. A second problem is that BEA areas cross state boundaries, so that state estimates cannot be made directly. This problem has been minimized by collecting as much data as possible at the county level. While states and other regions can also be used, they are defined must less consistently; much of the analytic effort must be directed at removing from the results the effect of these various geographic boundary lines. ...

Most of the study data are readily available from secondary sources and are of reasonably high quality. This is true of economic data on industrial activity, personal income, and population, as well as the data on energy supply activities, climate, natural conditions, and environmental quality.... However, in other areas such as energy demand, land use, mineral reserves, and waste production, data have been more difficult to collect, and may be less accurate. Clearly, the validity of the analytic results depends on the quality of the data used.[21]

Others have used factor analysis beyond the relatively descriptive mode depicted above. In one case, a more normative application was used to attempt to classify and analyze regional-welfare elements, that is, the elements of quality of life that make some regions better off—or at least appear so—than others. An author of one of these investigations, though finding the technique useful, states these caveats:

Factor analysis has been a very popular instrument for deriving welfare scores for different regions. In my opinion it is not clear at all why the specific maximisation assumptions underlying a factor-analytical method would be attractive for deriving *ex-post* welfare weights. A better alternative procedure might be a revealed preference approach.... It will appear that revealed preference approaches also imply arbitrariness on the analyst's behalf, as several restrictive assumptions have to be made to reach conclusions in an empirical context. The assumptions frequently show a lack of intuitive appeal and this restricts the usefulness of the derived welfare weights. Consequently, an *a priori* specification of welfare weights is to be preferred.... This specification is a matter for policy makers, who could also use attitudinal surveys. The modest aim of this study is only to make a useful contribution on the welfare elements concerning the welfare evaluation functions. For complete regional welfare evaluation the policymaker himself will have to specify the trade-offs, implicitly or explicitly.[22]

Put into proper use, factor analysis appears to have excellent potential for making top-down/bottom-up analyses more efficient and effective, but is not likely to offer much help to the policymaker looking for evaluative weighting schemes.

Urban- and Community-Impact Statements

The concept of impact analyses appears to have sprung from the environmental movement of the late 1960s and early 1970s. The first of these, the environmental impact statement (EIS), was based on the ecological principle that everything is relative to everything else. Clearly, the people who conceived this idea believed that an explicit requirement that environmental concerns be taken into consideration as part of the formal decision-making process would ensure that more of the issues they believed were significant would actually be taken into account. Although it is hard to tell just how significant these statements have been generally, it is certain that in many specific cases they had discernible effect. If imitation is still considered the sincerest form of flattery, then EIS inventors should be very flattered indeed, for the number of imitators has become large. Today there are inflationary-impact statements, regulatory-impact statements, and, recently, urban- and community-impact analyses (UCIA). The last type is the focus of this section.

On 27 March 1978, President Carter announced his urban policy, which included some nine policy options. Among these were efforts to improve local planning-and-management capacity, greater involvement of states and neighborhoods in urban issues, provision of fiscal and employment growth from both the private and public sectors, and improvement of the social, health, and physical-cultural environment, particularly for the disadvantaged. To ensure that these and other goals would be accomplished by the administration's policies, the president created the concept of the "urban- and community-impact statement." On 16 August 1978, the President signed Executive Order 12174, which stated (in part):

> By the authority vested in me as President by the Constitution of the United States of America, and in order to establish an internal management procedure for identifying aspects of proposed Federal policies that may adversely impact cities, counties, and other communities, it is hereby ordered as follows:
>
> The Director of the Office of Management and Budget shall: (a) develop criteria for identifying major policy proposals to be analyzed; (b) formulate standards regarding the content and format of impact analyses; and (c) establish procedures for the submission and review of such analyses.

The basic idea behind these analyses was quite straightforward. Many urban-policy experts felt strongly that the plethora of federal programs, policies, and regulations often worked at cross-purposes with one another, often canceling one another's intended efforts.[23] This clearly unintended and often undesirable effect was to be mitigated, at least to some extent, by requiring that prospective effects, both direct and indirect, of agency policies be taken into account before those effects would occur. To carry out this mandate, the Office of Management and Budget (OMB) issued *Circular No. A-116,* which addressed the preparation of these statements.[24]

Proposals to Be Assessed

Urban- and community-impact analyses are to be prepared on proposed major policy and program initiatives identified by each agency. All types of initiatives were to be considered candidates for this type of analysis, including new programs, expansions in budget outlays, program changes leading to shifts of resources among recipients, program changes in affected state and local governments, changes in tax provisions, new regulations, new regulatory authority, and other changes in policy or program direction. The circular was not intended to require urban- and community-impact analyses of individual projects.

Of the types of initiatives identified above, agencies are to subject only their *major* initiatives to urban and community analysis. It is recognized, however, there is no simple, uniform rule that can be applied to all agencies to identify the initiatives that are major. The following general criteria are therefore intended to furnish some guidance to agencies in making these selections:

1. In the case of regulations, major initiatives were those that were the subject of economic analyses under Executive Order 12044.[25]
2. In the case of all other initiatives, major initiatives are those that are clearly the most important agency proposals in terms of any of the following:
    a. direct budget cost, either immediately or over time;
    b. costs for entities other than the federal government;
    c. centrality to the agency's or administration's mission or purposes;
    d. public visibility;
    e. likely impact on cities or other types of communities, either in absolute terms of giving advantages to one type of city or community over other types; or such other factors as the agency considers necessary or appropriate to identify its major initiatives.

As specified more fully in the procedures section below, agencies are to indicate in advance which initiatives they consider major and therefore subject to the requirements of the circular. The OMB, in consultation with the domestic-policy staff, is to review these agency designations and make any necessary modifications.

Impacts to Be Analyzed

In order to guarantee uniformity and focus in agency efforts, sections 1, 2, and 3 below outline the general guidelines agencies should follow in conducting urban- and community-impact analyses. Not every category or locus of impact is expected to be appropriate in each agency's analyses, however, and some agencies may anticipate urban or community impacts not identified in the guidelines. Therefore, agencies may, with OMB's concurrence, add to or amend the guidelines in order to report the urban and community impacts that are most relevant and useful to their mission.

1. Types of impact. To the extent analytically feasible, analyses should identify the impact a proposed major initiative is anticipated to have with respect to:
   a. employment, especially minority employment;
   b. population size and composition, including the degree of racial concentration or deconcentration;
   c. income, especially that of low-income households;
   d. the fiscal condition of state and local governments;
   e. such other factors as the agency may consider appropriate and feasible to analyze, such as neighborhood stability, housing availability, availability and quality of public services, degree of urban sprawl, environmental quality, or cost of living.
2. Locus of impacts. For each of the foregoing types of impact, the analysis should seek to identify:
   a. absolute impacts, including direct or indirect benefits of costs, on the following types of places:
      i. central cities
      ii. suburban communities
      iii. nonmetropolitan communities
      iv. communities with higher-than-average rates of unemployment
      v. communities with per-capita income lower than the U.S. average, taking account, when possible, of differences in tax rates and cost of living
      vi. such other categories of places as the agency considers appropriate and necessary;
   b. relative impacts, that is any differential effects that an initiative is likely to have on one type of place as compared to other types, with special attention to the types of places noted in 2a above.
3. Time period. Analyses should clearly identify the time period over which the indicated impacts are anticipated. When appropriate, impacts that are short term (under three years) should be differentiated from those that are long term (three years or more).

Types of Analysis and Procedures

Projected urban and community impacts should be quantified to the greatest extent possible. However, when reliable quantification is not possible, qualitative assessments are acceptable. Urban- and community-impact analyses are to be brief (about fifteen to twenty pages) and should contain a two-to-three-page summary of impacts, accompanied by explanatory material indicating the basis for the judgments in the summary.

The procedures to be used for different types of major initiatives, under Executive Order 12044, which immediately preceeded the Reagan Administration's regulatory relief Executive Order 12291, were as follows:

1. Regulations. The procedures outlined in Executive Order 12044 are to apply. Urban- and community-impact analyses should be incorporated into the economic analyses of significant regulations required in Executive Order 12044.
2. Legislative and budgetary proposals.
    a. By August 31 of each year, each executive department or agency, unless specifically exempted by the director of OMB, shall submit to the director of OMB, with a copy to the assistant to the president for domestic affairs and policy, brief summaries of all initiatives it tentatively expects to include in its legislative program or budget submission, and nominate those it will subject to urban- and community-impact analysis. OMB, in consultation with the domestic-policy staff, is to review these agency nominations and request additions or deletions as appropriate. When proposals are advanced at other times of the year, a similar procedure is to apply to determine which should be subjected to urban- and community-impact analysis, and this procedure should be activated as far in advance of the final executive-office decisions as possible.
    b. For the initiatives so identified, agencies are to submit urban- and community-impact analyses as part of their regular legislative and budget submissions, according to the procedures outlined in OMB Circular A-19 for legislation and OMB Circular A-11 for budget proposals. OMB, in consultation with the domestic-policy staff, is to review the resulting analyses to determine their compliance with the requirements of this circular (EO 12044) and may request revisions by either the submitting agency or any other agency with expertise in the area.
3. Other major initiatives. For other proposed major policy or program changes, agencies should submit urban- and community-impact analyses to OMB and the domestic-policy staff as far in advance of decisions as possible. Such analyses will form part of the material required for final action.

Later in 1978, to facilitate agency preparation of these documents, the OMB issued a handbook.[26] For our purposes here, the most interesting parts of the handbook are those devoted to explaining the methodology to be used in implementing the UCIA. Unfortunately, the handbook is notable for its vagueness in this significant area, as one example shows:

> Developing Appropriate Methodology
>
> An agency should use the methodology appropriate to the nature of the Federal action being analyzed: its complexity, its specificity, it amenability to quantitative analysis, and its relative importance. An agency's choice of

Two-Way Applications

methodology will be influenced by its staff capability, its experience with similar policies and programs, and the availability of data. No single methodological approach will be appropriate for all analyses; it may be necessary to use more than one approach in a single analysis. Where it is possible, an agency should use quantitative methods and present its data in a systematic format. But when it is not possible to do so, an agency should use qualitative methods, including the use of case studies, reviews of the literature, judgment, and common sense.[27]

And in another:

In most cases, analysts should proceed by familiarizing themselves with the results of past program performance, be exploring analogies with existing programs, by learning from studies of how urban and political, economic and social systems operate, and by seeking advice and guidance from experienced administrators and staff and outside experts. When staff capacity is readily available and resources as well as time permit, analyst may want to use modified versions of such analytic techniques as cost-benefit analysis, input-output analysis, simulation models, and various conversion formulas (which link the volume of expenditures to such factors as jobs generated or taxes produced) to help in their impact analyses.[28]

In short, although it is deemed desirable to perform urban- and community-impact analyses, little guidance is actually given as to how to go about doing them. Despite this lack of guidance, the Department of Energy, in attempting to carry out these analyses of its programs, has made use of innovative techniques for systematically grouping urban areas to facilitate the preparation of its impact analyses.

A DOE Illustration

Within DOE, the assistant secretary for environment was given responsibility for conducting urban- and community-impact analysis. The case-study selection process was developed by DOE's Office of Environmental Assessments (OEA), which has primary responsibility for energy-related environmental issues and problems. OEA used cluster analysis for selection of modal sites. Fiscal, economic, and social impacts were calculated on a site-specific basis using modal BEA areas or counties. The results of these studies were then generalized to other counties with similar attributes. Variables for county screening were chosen from a larger county/BEA data base of environmental, energy, demographic, social, and economic characteristics. Cluster analysis was selected as a technique because it allowed analysts to evaluate the data and select modal BEAs that could be expanded to typify impacts to the nation as a whole. (Such a technique, we have already seen, had already been utilized by HUD and EPA in calculating distribution effects of specific projects.) Typically, a five-stage approach was used for conducting UCIAs: first, program selection; second, application of factor-analysis methods; third, use of clustering techniques to screen modal BEA areas for case-study analysis; fourth conducting case studies; and fifth, generalization of the case-study results to other communities nationwide exhibiting similar characteristics.

Program-Selection Approach. So noted, the lead for the performance of the urban- and community-impact analyses within DOE rests with the Assistant Secretary for Environment. This office was given responsibility for reviewing UCIAs submitted by various program offices and for preparing interprogram analysis when initiatives cut across program lines. Examples of UCIA interprogram analysis might include conservation, energy-supply initiatives, government regulation, oil-shale demonstration, and industry-conservation cost-sharing with the private sector.

Within DOE, economic, employment, demographic, and financial criteria were established for the selection of an initial UCIA energy initiative. These criteria include:

1. Economic.
   a. If the program or policy initiative resulted in aggregated costs to the economy of $100 million or more in any one year, or of $150 million or more for any two-year period, then the proposed program or policy was determined to be major and could receive substantive urban- and community-impact analysis.
   b. If the result of any DOE-proposed program or initiative imposed costs in excess of $50 million in any one year on an industrial or regional sector of the economy, or costs in excess of $75 million dollars in any two-year period, the initiative could be determined to be significant and could be reviewed by the department under UCIA.
2. Employment. If the proposed program or policy initiative resulted in a 0.2-percent or greater change in the rate of employment (approximately 200,000 people) in any one year in the aggregate, then the initiative was determined to be significant.
3. Demographic. If the result of the proposed program or policy initiative was a change in population in any community or region of 10 percent or more, the initiative was determined to be significant.
4. Fiscal. If the program or policy initiative resulted in a change in local or state revenues or expenditures of plus or minus 5 percent, the initiative was determined to be significant.
5. Administrative.

a. If the cost of implementing the proposed program or policy initiative was $50 million or more in any one year, the initiative was determined to be significant.
b. If the proposed program or policy initiative resulted in a change in energy supply or demand greater than 1 percent in any one year, the program or policy initiative was determined to be significant.
c. Any program or policy initiative that was highly visible at local, state, or federal levels as determined by the program office or EV was determined to be a significant initiative.
d. Any program or policy initiative that was deemed important by the president, the secretary of DOE, or his designee was significant.

DOE has attempted to present systematically econòmicy, demographic, and environmental criteria that could allow program selection on a national basis for UCIAs, given a commonly agreed-upon set of criteria. From a demographic, economic, social, and administrative perspective, the synthetic-fuels program was selected for analysis as the first large-scale test case.

Synthetic-Fuel Analyses. The first step was to delimit and define what aspects of the synfuels program were most suited to urban- and community-impact analysis. Rather than address the entire program, the analyses covered only the impacts of several types of specific but characteristic synfuel plants in specific but characteristic communities. Example plants and communities were used because actual plants and their locations were not known. This limited coverage was best suited to a prototype effort because it was analytically manageable and responsive to UCIA guidance, which exempted individual projects from analysis.

Only four synfuel technologies were considered commercially feasible and available for integration into this analysis of synfuels: coal liquefaction, coal gasification, biomass conversion, and oil-shale retorting. Information for these technologies was also the most available for this type of analysis. Because oil-shale development is economically limited to the reserve location (that is, mining and processing activities occur at the same site), decisions on alternative plant locations are greatly reduced and are less responsive to the results of a UCIA analysis; therefore, oil-shale development was not included in the study. The plant sitings of the remaining three technologies are less constrained by resource location and are therefore more appropriate for UCIA. A brief description follows of the three technologies covered.

Biomass Conversion. The biomass-energy resource includes terrestrial and aquatic plants and agricultural, forestry, industrial, and municipal wastes.

Biomass resources can be collected and burned directly or converted by a number of methods into liquid, gaseous, or solid fuels, chemicals, or energy-intensive products.

The biomass application with the greatest potential for expanded commercial use (and the example used in this UCIA) is the fermentation of grains and agricultural-process wastes into ethanol, which can be blended with gasoline as an automotive fuel. U.S. production levels are increasing rapidly in response to recently established incentives to produce ethanol for gasoline/ethanol blends (gasohol). Production capacity to sixty million gallons per year was available at the end of 1979. The Energy Security Act's target is an annual production rate of twenty-two million barrels by the end of 1982.

Coal Gasification. Although coal gasification in the United States is currently limited to few small installations, literally hundreds of coal gasifiers are in use commercially around the world.

More energy is available in the U.S. deposits of coal than in petroleum, natural gas, oil shale, and tar sands combined. Known U.S. reserves are about one-half of the known world reserves. Over 400 billion tons are considered minable under current economic and technological conditions. The reserves are distributed through the country, with about 20 percent in the Appalachian region, 30 percent in the central region, and 50 percent in the West. Although most U.S. coal is currently obtained from the East, production is increasing more rapidly in the West.

The primary chemical process used to generate a fuel gas is to react steam (water) with crushed and dired coal (carbon) or oxygen at elevated temperatures and pressures to produce a mixture of carbon monoxide, hydrogen, and other gases. This reaction produces a medium-Btu gas (MBG), which, after further processing, produces a high-Btu or synthetic natural gas.

Coal Liquefaction. There are two substantially different methods of producing liquids from coal: indirect and direct liquefaction.

The indirect liquefaction processes are so named because coal is first converted to a gas, and the gas is then catalytically converted to liquid products. In the direct processes, hydrogen is reacted with finely crushed coal, producing liquids directly. Generally speaking, the indirect processes have the advantage of being in or near commercial use today. The direct processes are still in the pilot or demonstration stage, but promise improved efficiency and costs, and possibly other advantages, over the indirect processes.

The alternate route to indirect liquefaction is to produce methanol from a synthetic gas (hydrogen and carbon monoxide) obtained through first gasifying the coal. Methanol can, in turn, be burned directly in combustion gas turbines, blended with gasoline in much the same way that ethanol is used today to make gasohol, or used directly in modified automotive engines.

The first commercial liquids-from-coal plants in the United States will probably produce synthetic fuels using indirect methods that are available and that entail minimum technical risk. Direct liquefaction has been under intensive development by DOE and by industry.

Three Analytic Approaches

Little precedent existed to guide UCIA analyses, but *Circular A-116* encourages agencies to develop impact-analysis methods appropriate to their missions, allowing flexibility as long as they address the key impact categories. DOE devised three separate approaches that varied as to data sources, modeling techniques, level and units of analysis, costs, complexity, time to complete, staff analytical requirements, and other factors. The three approaches, representing different levels of analytic effort and sophistication, were designed for the ultimate purpose of comparative analysis, both of the approaches and their results, to determine their relative utility in the decision-making process and their degree of responsiveness to UCIA. After such comparison, an optimum approach could be developed for future efforts. These approaches are hereafter identified as type A (detailed analysis), type B (alternative analysis), and type C (simplified analysis).

To make their results comparable, all three approaches had to proceed from similar assumptions and analyze the same geographic areas. Type A used the statistical clustering technique described above to aid in case-study selection, based on degrees of similarity of a wide range of data. Six distinct clusters of BEA areas were developed, and one was chosen from each cluster as most representative (table 8-6). These six areas (Portland, Oregon; Springfield, Illinois; Waterloo, Iowa; Albuquerque, New Mexico; Nashville, Tennessee; and Grand Forks, North Dakota) then became the geographic-base cases used by the type A and B analyses. These areas are significant not only because they are used as illustrative communities, but because they may typify other BEA areas within the same cluster that show similar responses to synfuel-plant development. Use of the same six clusters and their base case areas represented the common point of departure for all three approaches, from which took a widely disparate direction (table 8-7).

Type A Analysis. Type A methodology characterized in depth the extreme breadth in industrial size, technology, time frame, location, and impact dimensions. A process was devised to select case-study areas and facilities that represented meaningful ranges of locational and technological variety.

Table 8-6
Cluster-Analysis Results

Case-Study Regions	Other Representative BEA Areas

Cluster 1: Grand Forks, North Dakota (29 BEA areas)

Low population and population density
Small central city
Above-average labor-force participation
Low unemployment
Decreasing population
Oil and gas production
Some strippable coal reserves

Abilene, Texas
Eau Claire, Wisconsin
Lubbock, Texas
Wausau, Wisconsin

Cluster 2: Waterloo, Iowa (26 BEA areas)

Below-average population
Larger, central cities
Above-average population density
Stable, high-quality farming areas
Above-average income
Decreasing population
Above-average labor-force participation
No energy production or reserves

Fort Wayne, Indiana
Peoria, Illinois
Rockford, Illinois

Cluster 3: Springfield, Illinois (16 BEA areas)

Above-average population and
 population density
Larger central cities; government and
 commercial centers; high-quality
 farming areas
Decreasing population
Above-average income
Considerable coal reserves

Columbus, Ohio
Harrisburg, Pennsylvania
Louisville, Kentucky

Cluster 4: Nashville, Tennesee (46 BEA areas)

Slightly above-average population and
 population density
Generally southeastern, developing central
 cities with lighter industries
Low-income, high nonwhite populations
Increasing population
Above-average debt

Greenville, South Carolina
Mobile, Alabama
Roanoke, Virginia

Cluster 5: Portland, Oregon (38 BEA areas)

Above-average population and
 population density
Older industrial cities; transportation and
 commercial centers
High income, high per-capita debt
Slightly decreasing population
Little energy production or reserves

Cincinnati, Ohio
Indianapolis, Indiana
Toledo, Ohio

Cluster 6: Albuquerque, New Mexico (6 BEA areas)

Low population and population density

Colorado Springs, Colorado

Table 8-2 continued

Case-Study Regions	Other Representative BEA Areas
Rapidly increasing population High minority Substantial energy production Greater-than-average income Low per-capita debt Few central cities, large outlying areas	

Fifteen candidate facilities within the three generic technologies—coal gasification, coal liquefaction, and biomass—were characterized in detail.

Choosing and characterizing the geographic impact area was a complex and significant part of the entire analysis. Although the BEA area is designed to encompass contiguous areas whose economic activity is somewhat homogeneous, it generally represents regions whose economics are rather large and widely dispersed. Consequently, the population and employment impacts on local areas of deploying any of the candidate synfuels technologies, even as single plants, could be readily lost at the BEA-area level of analysis. Therefore, the county was chosen as the appropriate geographic unit of analysis for the following reasons: it is a common political unit of appropriate size where data are systematically gathered; growth and impact management issues are most important at the county/community levels; and DOE has built at this level detailed impact-modeling capability that estimates key demographic and employment effects.

Case-study selection began with construction of an extensive data base of over 300 variables for 1975, chosen for their ability to reflect a wide range of impacts from energy development. This data base was compiled from numerous secondary sources and includes information on energy supply and demand, transportation, socioeconomic and demographic attributes, land use, pollutant emissions, and environmental quality. Aggregated at levels defined by regional economic and demographic factors, BEA areas were characterized by 40 distinct variables according to the types of impacts most nearly matching the requirements of OMB *Circular A-116*. This process yielded six clusters of BEA areas; from each of these were selected four modal-base case counties.

Cluster 1: Grand Forks, North Dakota. By completing a case study on Grand Forks, analysts could generalize impacts to a set of BEAs in counties located mainly in the Great Plains and eastern Rocky Mountain regions. Counties and BEAs with the highest density functions were located in West

Table 8-7
Characteristics of Analyses of Varying Complexity

	Type A (Detailed Analysis)	Type B (Alternate Analysis)	Type C (Simplified Analysis)
Design Methodology	Relatively complex	Relatively simple	Simple
Geographical unit of analysis	Modal counties	The 6 modal BEA areas	Generic, nonspecific communities
Impact causal factor	15 district types of synfuels-conversion facilities from within the 3 technologies: coal gas, coal liquids, and biomass	The 3 generic synfuels-conversion technologies	Facilities described as large or small based on new employment
Population impacts	Used multipliers that vary by county	Used a single-stage multiplier that was constant for all case-study areas.	Compared new primary employment to range of existing county populations in the U.S.
Employment impacts	Estimates separate employment trajectories for each of the 15 technologies	Used separate employment trajectories for each of the 3 generic facilities	General evaluation of required skill levels
Use of models	Employed a dynamic model to estimate jobs, primary and secondary population growth, and public-cost impacts	No models used	No models used
Incremental impacts calculated	Yes	No. Calculated single-year peak-growth impacts only	Impacts inferred from past experience
Baseline population growth	Projected by a model	Used updated 1970 population data	None used
Time required to complete	Several months	Several weeks	Few days
Costs (approximate magnitudes)	$5,000	$5,000	$500
Format	Standard report format	Approximate UCIA format	White paper
Use of contractors	Heavy	Moderate	None
Percentage done by in-house professionals	10–20	50–75	100

Texas, Oklahoma, and Kansas. They were areas of low population and low population density. In many cases, they had small central cities with little or no suburban population. During the early 1970s, the population of these regions was decreasing. In many cases, labor-force-participation rates were somewhat above average, and unemployment rates were very low. Income and per-capita debt were not distinguishing characteristics. The BEAs in this cluster tended to be oil and gas producers, many with strippable coal reserves.

Cluster 2: Waterloo, Iowa. By an analysis of this modal BEA, analysts could generalize results to other BEAs in the rural areas of the Pacific Northwest and the Midwest. The modal BEAs in cluster 2 were located primarily in Indiana, Ohio, and Illinois. They were relatively small in area, so that even though they were somewhat below average in population, their population density was high. The central cities were small, and their population was also decreasing. They had low unemployment rates and a high rate of labor-force participation. Personal income in many instances was well above average. In terms of energy resources, the BEAs did not have oil and gas production or coal reserves.

Cluster 3: Springfield, Ill. By analysis of the modal BEA of Springfield, analysts could generalize results to other modal BEAs in the Midwest. In many instances they were above average in population and population density, and their population in the last decade had decreased slightly. Like the first two clusters, their central cities were small. Their labor-force-participation rates and unemployment rates were slightly below average, but their income was above average. The per-capita debt tended to be high. They were characterized by having large reserves of strippable and underground coal. They were also producers of oil and gas.

Cluster 4: Nashville, Tennessee. By an analysis of Nashville, analysts could make certain generalizations to BEAs in the rural South. The modal BEAs had somewhat above-average populations and population densities. This cluster was the only one characterized by a large nonwhite population and an increasing population. Labor-force-participation rates were slightly above average. However, they were in many cases poor areas with an above-average per-capita debt. Some of the BEAs in this cluster had oil and gas production and coal reserves.

Cluster 5: Albuquerque, New Mexico. By an analysis of Albuquerque, analysts could make some assessment of impacts on BEAs located predominantly in the intermountain West. This cluster was the only one characterized by low labor-force-participation rates, low population densities, and significant oil, gas, and coal reserves.

Cluster 6: Portland, Oregon. Finally, analysis of modal BEAs in cluster 6 allowed analysts to make generalizations about middle-sized and larger cities. In many instances the population and population densities were higher; however, central cities were relatively small compared to outlying areas. Most of the modal BEAs in this cluster had high labor-force-participation rates and low unemployment and were losing population. Per-capita income was the highest of any cluster; so was per-capita debt. Most BEAs in this cluster were not energy producers.

Each of the fifteen facilities was then assumed to be built in each of the twenty-four counties. A matrix was developed addressing impacts on employment, population growth, low-income groups, opportunities for minorities, local public expenditures, and other social and economic conditions.

The most dramatic socioeconomic impacts of synfuels plants resulted from the associated population increase in the areas around the plants. The community growth induced by synfuel or other kinds of basic industrial development is diagrammed in figure 8-16.

This technique in its most basic application is little more than an algorithm formalizing the economic-base theory of Homer Hoyt, developed during the 1950s. The application of such models in low-population areas automatically results in so-called boom-town effects, in which community support services are outstripped by a surge in local demand. When this demand disappears, it leaves an overbuilt, underfinanced infrastructure.

Specifically, the model postulates that the construction and operation of the plant will result in new jobs in the region. The plant will generate increased business for supplying and supporting industries (such as construction materials and transportation facilities), and this activity will also generate increased employment. The magnitude of the population influx will depend on the degree to which the increased employment opportunities are filled by local residents or by newcomers. If most of the primary and secondary jobs are filled by local residents, inmigration will be minimal. If, on the other hand, most jobs are filled by inmigrants, the effects of the population change could be quite severe, especially in sparsely populated areas. The increased income generated by the plant and increased population will result in heightened demand for publicly and privately provided goods and services such as schools, shopping, housing, water, and sewage treatment. Provision of these goods and services will again result in employment opportunities, some of which will be filled by current residents and some by inmigrants. The industry depicted in figure 8-16 consisted of fifteen processes within the three broad types of technologies. Table 8-8 lists these plants and their significant variables.

The Social and Economic Assessment Model (SEAM) used in this analysis identified a county's assimilative capacity, that is, its ability to tolerate

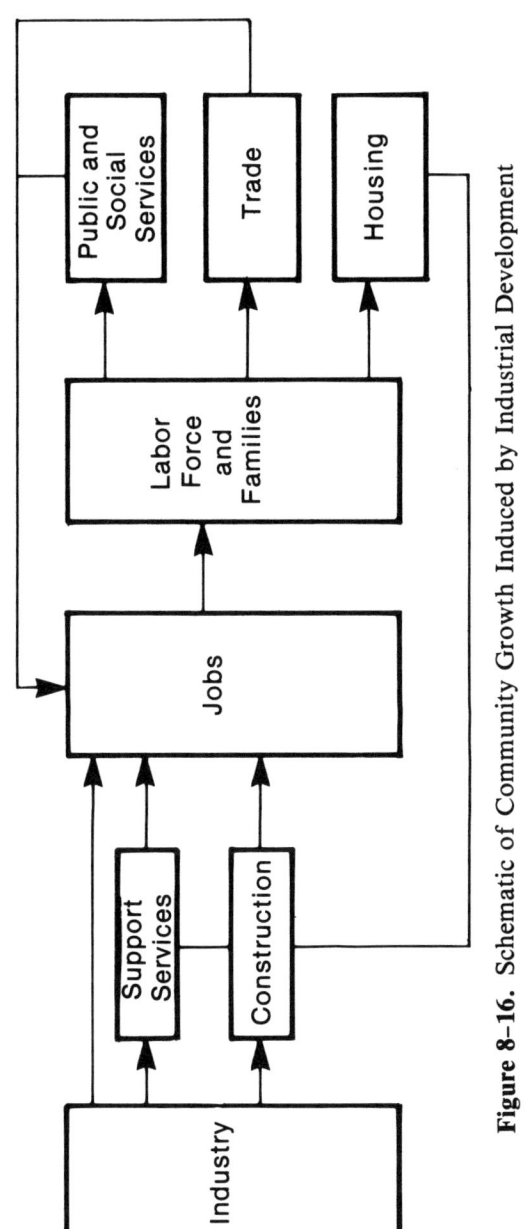

Figure 8-16. Schematic of Community Growth Induced by Industrial Development

Table 8-8
Synthetic-Fuel Technologies Incorporated in Analysis

Type	Process	Size	Labor Force Peak Construction	Operation
Coal liquefaction	Fischer-Tropsch (SASOL)	44,950 OEB/D	10,000	925
	Mobil M-Gas	45,550 OEB/D	7.400	750
	H-Coal	50,000 OEB/D	6,000	2,385
	Exxon donor solvent	60,000 OEB/D	6,000	725
	SRC III	100,000 OEB/D	5,425	500
	Lurgi/ICI (methanol)[a]	50,000 OEB/D	4,150	1,230
	Indirect (PEIS)		2,100	638
	Lurgi/ICI (methanol)[b]	50,000 OEB/D	2,080	615
Coal gasification	HYGAS (hi-Btu)	250 × 10⁶ Scf/D	2,953	660
	UGAS/MGLW (med-Btu)	250 × 10⁶ Scf/D	686	270
	UGAS/IGT (med-Btu)	300 × 10⁶ Scf/D	651	118
	UGAS/IGT (low-Btu)	600 × 10⁵ Scf/D	553	104
Biomass conversion	Ethanol production[c]	50mm Gal/yr.	89	62
		5 mm Gal/yr.	56	24
		1 mm Gas/yr.	15	15

Note: DOE/EV, "Energy/Environmental Data Study."
[a]Three-year construction period.
[b]Five-year construction period.
[c]A generic product was assumed because detailed information on specific technologies is currently being evaluated for development assistance within different governmental agencies and is therefore still proprietary.

the often-rapid growth associated with a major energy-conversion facility. To capture the dominant range of assimilative capacities in each of the selected BEA areas representing the six clusters, all counties were characterized and distributions of the assimilative capacities recorded by BEA area and cluster. This permitted the special character of each cluster to be preserved as the level of analysis was disaggregated from the BEA area to the county level. A county was then defined on an interval scale as possessing high, medium, low, or extra-low assimilative capacity. Four counties, representing the full range of assimilative capacities present in that particular BEA area, were then chosen in each of the six BEA areas for detailed impact analysis. The impact calculations at the county level were then performed by the SEAM model, which was devised to examine detailed county-by-county population and employment impacts resulting from energy development.

Twenty-four case-study counties were examined for their response to the construction and operation of fifteen different types of synfuels facilities. Some 360 simulation runs were performed detailing the dynamic impacts on these counties, which were growing at different rates as a function of varying degrees of urbanization and labor intensiveness of a given technology. Figure 8-17 shows an example of one of these runs. Some commuting from surrounding areas is assumed, but no mitigation strategies such as federal, state, or private financial aid were included. The results estimate what the maximum expected effects would be without growth-management efforts.

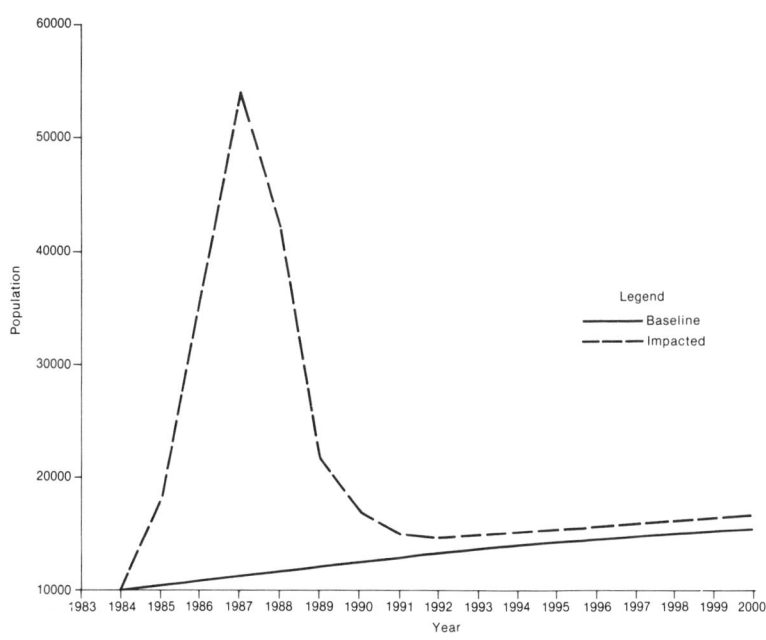

Figure 8-17. Projected X Low Annual Population Impact of Fischer-Tropsch Synthetic-Fuels Development: Torrance, New Mexico

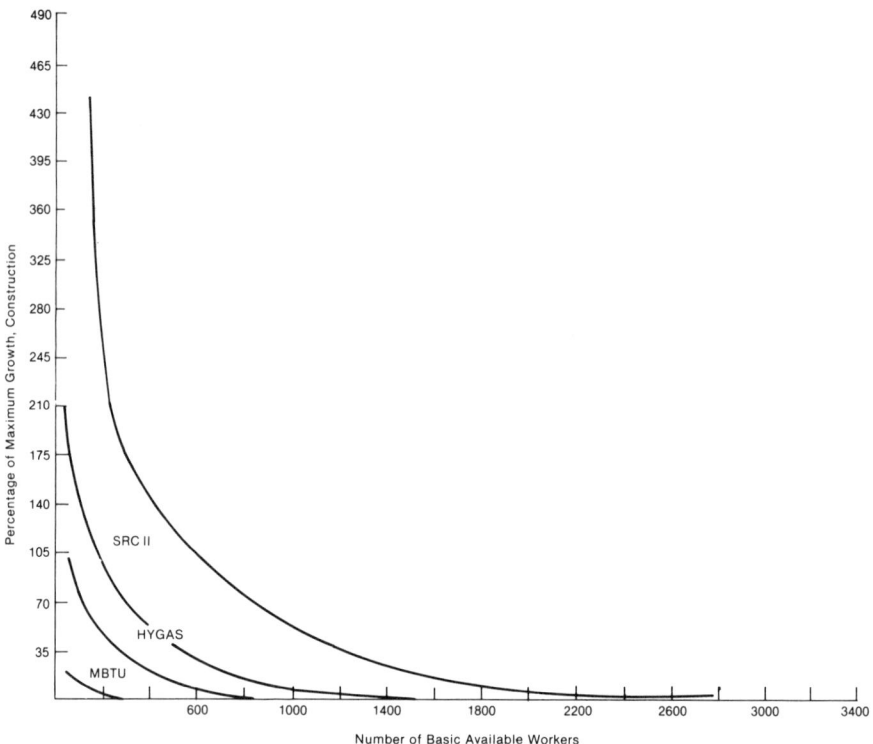

Figure 8-18. Illustration of a Time Impact: Maximum-Growth Effect of Commuting Distance on Available Construction Workforce

Figure 8-18 is an example of the time impact reflecting the effect of varying levels of available workforce within commuting distance of a particular county when maximum growth occurs. Maximum population growth is expressed on the vertical axis; this is the peak value estimated during the construction phase for four synfuels-conversion technologies.

Figure 8-19 is a sample summary of the maximum growth during the construction phase (for the counties in which they occurred), rank ordered by descending impact.

Type B Analysis. The absolute and relative impacts of synfuels plants obviously depend on the nature of the plants, the nature of the impacted communities, and their interaction (that is, the same logic flow as shown in the type A schematic). Therefore, the framework and methodology for type B consisted of characterizing the three illustrative synfuels plants, characterizing six illustrative communities, and deriving impacts by interfacing the characterizations. The analysis attempted to be responsive to OMB *Circular A-116* in both form and substance; thus, all characterizations and analyses were oriented to UCIA variables.

For representative plants, the most recent information was used to characterize each of the three basic synfuel technologies by selected variables. Because commercial-size plants do not yet exist for each technology, some plants were scaled-up estimates of demonstration plants, but when possible, empirical observations of actual plants were used. Those variables and the figures for an example technology are listed in table 8-9. Since type A and B efforts were independent, the latter figures differ from those in type A analysis; however, we believe that they capture the proper sense of proportions, taken both independently and relative to one another.

To extrapolate the facility labor requirements into actual total induced employment and population, standard assumptions and multipliers were used. These results are shown in table 8-10.

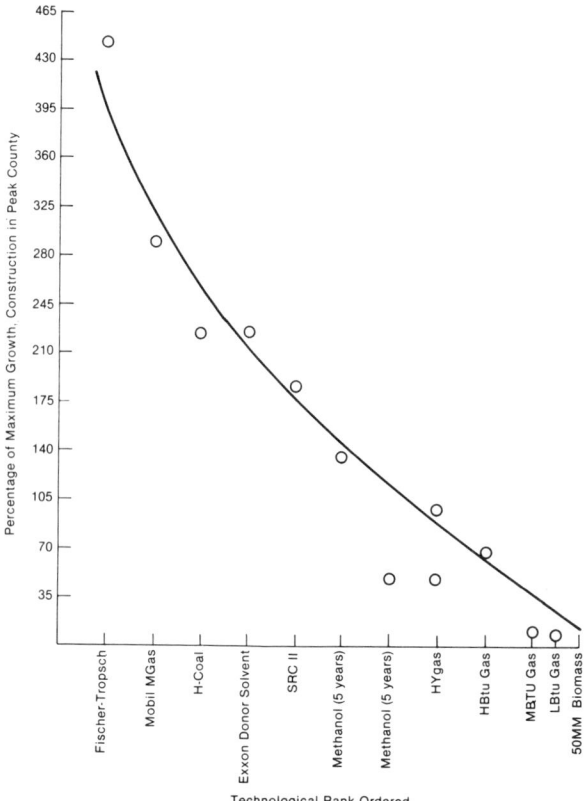

Figure 8-19. Summary of Maximum-Growth Construction Potential, by Technology

Table 8-9
Variables Used to Characterize a High-Btu Coal-Gasification Plant

Size (daily or annual production rate)	250 million SCF/d	
Capacity (feedstock delivery rate)	20,000 TPD coal	
Plant cost (capital requirement for construction)	$4,600 million	
Construction time (length of time [design to initial operation] to construct a green-grass facility)	4 years	
Construction (labor requirements to build the facility)	*Average*	*Peak*[a]
Skilled	1,632	2,956
Unskilled	200	375
Total	1,832	3,166
Operation (labor requirements to operate the facility)		
Professionals	59	
Skilled	464	
Unskilled	66	
Total	589	

[a]Peaks for skilled and unskilled do not occur simultaneously.

The six BEA areas were characterized from standard statistical sources. Available social, demographic, and economic data were used to show relevant variables within the four UCIA impact categories: population, income, employment, and fiscal condition. This allowed comparisons and distinctions to be made, and for each BEA area these were shown both as absolute numbers and as comparative rankings relative to the other five BEA areas, to indicate relative assimilative capacity and potential to respond to UCIA target variables. Table 8-11 is an example of such a characterization for two impact categories.

The impact analyses were derived by interfacing the characterized communities with the characterized plants; that is, impact magnitudes of all three illustrative plants were assumed for all six illustrative communities. Like numbers were then matched (minority unemployment with induced employment, available skill levels with plant labor profiles, and so on) arithmetically to show absolute and relative impacts in narrative and tabular form. Emphasis was placed on how the siting of each plant would allocate absolute benefits and costs for various demographic groups within each BEA area, as well as the relative benefits and costs among BEA areas. Many of the results are qualitative and subjective because of the limited scope of the effort and of available data. Certain relative impacts became apparent for UCIA variables, as shown in table 8-12.

Table 8-10
Workforce Requirements for Characteristic Synfuel Plants

Type of Plant	Primary Employment[a]	Induced Secondary Employment[b]	Total Employment[c]	Total Induced Employment[d]
Biomass				
Construction phase (2 years)				
Skilled	48	84	140	350
Unskilled	8			
Total	56			
Operation phase				
Professional	23			
Skilled	80			
Unskilled	54			
Total	154	235	392	970
Coal Gasification				
Construction phase (4 years)				
Skilled	2,956			
Unskilled	375			
Total	3,166	4,749	7,915	19,787
Operational phase				
Professional	59			
Skilled	464			
Unskilled	66			
Total	589	883	1,472	3,680

	SASOL	SRC	SASOL	SRC	SASOL	SRC	SASOL	SRC
Coal Liquefaction Construction phase	(5.5 years)	(4.0 years)						
Skilled	—	6,447						
Unskilled	—	579						
Total	15,000	7,026	22,500	10,539	37,500	17,565	93,750	43,913
Operational phase								
Professional	—	85						
Skilled	—	453						
Unskilled	—	22						
Total	560	560	840	840	1,400	1,400	3,560	3,560

[a]Weak period, secondary.
[b]Multiplier = 1.5.
[c]Equals primary and secondary employed.
[d]Equals total employment × 2.5.

Type C Analysis. The type C analysis, representing the opposite extreme from type A in terms of analytic level of effort and sophistication, is shown in the impact quadrants depicted in figure 8-20. It is intended to represent an analyst's intuitive response to sets of either known or rapidly obtained information factors. These factors include an approximation of the generic

**Table 8-11
Characterization of Illustrative BEA Areas by Two Major UCIA Impact Categories: Springfield, Illinois**

Major UCIA Impact Category	Variable		Relative Rank Among 6 BEA Areas (1 = highest, 6 = lowest)
Fiscal condition	Total fiscal revenues	$183,100,000	5
	Percent from federal government[a]	4	5 (tie)
	Total fiscal expenditures[a]	$175,700,000	5
	Total government debt[a]	$158,400,000	4
	Per-capita debt[b]	$334	4
Business activity	Manufacturing[c]		
	Employees	316,000	2
	Payroll	$304,300,000	3
	Value added	$736,700,000	3
	Wholesale sales[c]	$1,386,900,000	4
	Retail sales[c]	$1,109,710,000	4
	Agricultural sales[d]	$594,400,000	3
	Selected services (receipts)[c]	$186,816,000	4

Source: U.S. Department of Commerce (Washington, D.C.: Government Printing Office, 1978).
[a]*County and City Data Book, 1977,* (Washington, D.C.: Government Printing Office, 1978). Data for fiscal year 1971-1972.
[b]Lawrence Berkeley Laboratories, Berkeley, Calif.
[c]*County and City Data Book, 1977;* 1972 data.
[d]Only farms with sales of $2,500 are included.

communities in which a plant is presumed and of the labor demands and other characteristics of the facilities. Such information is readily available from DOE and other documents, studies, or staff members.

Quadrant I represents areas having few people and synfuels plants that are not labor intensive would have little impact of interest to the UCIA. The higher densities in quadrants III and IV suggest an ability to absorb influxes of reasonable numbers of workers associated with a synfuels plant and so would also tend to have little noticeable impact on the interest area of the UCIA. The second quadrant, with low population densities and high labor requirements, poses greater difficulty, requiring further UCIA investigation.

Given this highly aggregated and generalized information, the analyst proceeds through the same analytic process as for the other two methods; that is, data of certain plants with specific impact-causal factors are varied

Table 8–12
Employment Impacts for UCIA Variables

Impact		Biomass						Coal Gasification						Coal Liquefaction					
		A	B	C	D	E	F	A	B	C	D	E	F	A	B	C	D	E	F
Assistance for areas with high unemployment rates	High	X						X						X	X				
	Medium		X						X	X						X			
	Low			X															X
Assistance for areas with low unemployment rates	High					X													
	Medium				X		X				X	X	X				X	X	X
	Low						X												
Increased job opportunities local skilled unemployed	High	X						X						X					
	Medium		X						X	X	X	X	X		X	X	X	X	X
	Low		X	X	X	X	X												
Increased job opportunities local unskilled unemployed	High											X	X					X	X
	Medium									X	X						X		
	Low	X	X	X	X	X	X	X	X					X	X				
Increased job opportunities local unemployed minorities	High	X						X	X	X	X	X	X	X	X	X	X	X	X
	Medium		X	X	X	X	X												
	Low																		
Incentive for business and industries to remain, expand, or locate within the BEA	High	X						X	X					X	X	X	X	X	X
	Medium			X	X	X	X			X	X	X	X						
	Low		X																
Impact on efforts to maintain or increase economic diversity	High	X						X	X					X	X	X	X	X	X
	Medium			X	X	X	X			X	X	X	X						
	Low	X	X																

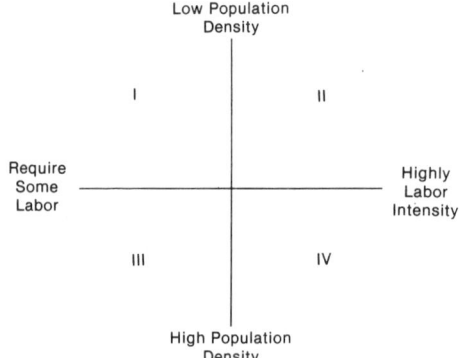

Figure 8-20. Type C Analysis Impact Quadrants

with respect to the derivative of certain characteristic communities. The difference between type C and the other levels is that this analysis permits impact estimates and responses to be drawn largely from professional judgment, self-evident assumptions, theories, and the like, which are interpreted and presented as generalized and qualitative conclusions.

Results and Conclusions of the Three Analytic Approaches. *Type A Analysis.* The type A methodology produced numerous detailed charts, graphs, and figures showing the relative impacts of various technologies on various counties. The report, produced the following significant overall conclusions.

1. Depending on the labor demands of a particular synfuels technology and the particular siting patterns, facilities have a very wide range of effects. Of the fifteen technologies examined in twenty-four counties across the United States, biomass facilities were most likely to be environmentally benign; the Fischer-Tropsch coal-conversion process was judged most likely to have the greatest amount of impact.

2. When locally available supplies are small, then very large construction projects require a great deal of inmigration: Fischer-Tropsch facilities exacerbate these effects. Except for highly industrialized and urbanized areas, the Fischer-Tropsch process may cause local population-growth rates from 200 to over 400 percent at the county level.

3. Inmigration effects associated with the Fischer-Tropsch process are multiplied at the local level; for areas with low assimilative capacity, liquefaction processes from coal generally induced much greater growth rates than with gasification or biomass conversion; boom towns may be unavoidable. For similar output sizes, the very large construction-labor-force requirements of all the liquefaction processes (5,000-10,000 workers on site at the peak) induce unavoidable problems at the local level if a county has a low capacity to assimilate development: rapidly increasing demand for pub-

lic services that cannot be met; increased sprawl and neighborhood instability; inadequate housing; rapid localized inflation; increases in crime, divorce, social stress; and substantial reductions in worker productivity.

4. Local benefits from increased construction-job opportunities, especially in rural areas, may be limited for all but the highly skilled or quickly retrainable worker. Skill-level requirements, especially in the construction phase, do not encourage much localized labor-force participation if that area has seen little industrial development in the past. The secondary needs for further services, retail and wholesale jobs, are much more attractive alternatives for locals, especially for minorities and low income populations. For most areas, low-income and minority groups are already a very small proportion of the population. Inmigration is unlikely because such groups are generally poorer and are far less mobile than skilled workers.

5. The impacts of synfuels initiatives will most likely be felt in rural and outlying areas; public investment and risks are high at both the national and local levels. Synfuels facilities will be very large and expensive, and most likely sited near primary resources required for conversion to liquids, gases, or solid fuels; virtually all coal and oil-shale resources are in remote or rural areas. Transportation links may permit intermediate siting between the resource base and the demand centers for fuels. Large public-subsidy and incentives programs may be required.

6. Impacts estimated for all technologies varied largely by assimilative capacity, which is highest for urbanized areas and lowest for remote rural regions. There was less variation across regions characterized by alternative demographic and economic indicators. Effects were consistent for each of the technologies examined among several BEA areas, representing a wide range of attributes. County characteristics most strongly affecting the ability to assimilate growth are: proximity to metropolitan areas and their larger skilled labor force; willingness at the local level to incur large, new debt; political management of change; very active local, state, and federal government cost sharing; and cooperation with industry.

7. The systems effects of several interacting impacts make mitigation strategies and planning crucial to the success of building a large industry based on innovative technologies: many economic benefits at the local level can be readily eliminated by large social costs, especially for liquefaction facilities. Large, rapid, complex construction projects in rural areas often are accompanied by dramatically lowered worker productivity and sharp reductions in the local quality of life. Fischer-Tropsch and other first-generation technologies may be more costly in terms of site-specific external costs. Their tendency to use more coal per Btu output further exacerbates problems surrounding a very large construction peak. Conscious economic-development strategies may need to be formulated to ensure that in the middle term, liquid fuels from first-generation technologies can be made worth the public cost.

Type B Analysis. A wide range of absolute and differential impacts became evident throughout the type B analysis. Impacts were discussed quantitatively and qualitatively in narrative form, and relative impacts (between BEA areas and between technologies) were shown in matrix form. Impacts were characterized by twenty-three impact descriptors within the four UCIA impact categories. Conclusions regarding the results included the following.

> Regardless of which synfuel technology is used and where it is sited, there will be certain changes in the existing infrastructure of each BEA area. For the biomass plant, since the plant is extremely small and requires a minimum amount of labor, each BEA area studied should have no problem assimilating the plant into its current structure. The impacts of the gasification plant will be larger and a certain amount of growth will be required in most of the BEA areas to house the plant. The liquefaction plant—SASOL—will most probably cause total disruption *wherever* it is sited. This plant will potentially create boom towns in the four smaller BEA example regions (Albuquerque, Springfield, Waterloo, and Grand Forks). Nashville and Portland are large enough that the boom-town scenario would not totally develop; however, these two BEA areas could suffer economically if the right actions and procedures were not taken.

> Larger urban BEA areas are better able to assimilate any plant than smaller or more-rural areas.

> The infrastructures of a Nashville-type or a Portland-type BEA area are best able to handle any synfuel plant; however, these two BEA areas least need the resulting increase in growth and business activity.

> Nashville has the greatest number of unemployed minorities. If the siting goal is to assist minorities, the Nashville BEA area would be a leading candidate.

> The Waterloo and Grand Forks BEA areas have very few minorities, employed or unemployed. These areas would appear to satisfy least that target objective of the urban policy.

> The systems effects of several interacting impacts make mitigation strategies and planning crucial to the success of building a large industry based on innovative technologies; any economic benefits at the local level can be readily eliminated by large social costs, especially for liquefaction facilities.

> Large construction projects such as the gasification plant and the liquefaction plant (especially the SASOL process) require large inmigration to fill the created jobs.

Two-Way Applications

Many construction companies will bring in their own skilled and professional workers regardless of the size of the locally unemployed labor pool.

BEA areas that host large construction plants may have problems coming up with the large amount of front-end financing required.

The coal-gasification and the coal-liquefaction processes will increase the income of the BEA area.

Both the Waterloo and Springfield BEA areas have low growth rates and may therefore have problems housing a large synfuel plant.

Inmigration of minorities to plant-induced jobs may be limited because minorities are generally poor and far less mobile than skilled workers. This would imply a lower capability for the facilities realistically to provide employment opportunities for minorities and low-income populations, and a corresponding increase in inmigrants for facility-induced jobs.

The report also listed several significant conclusions and evaluations regarding process and methodology. Some of the more significant conclusions, which suggest objective limitations to the use of the approach, follow.

1. Characterization and analyses required data generalization and aggregation at topical and geographic levels. In keeping with the mission of this office and the intent of the UCIA process, the results are considered generic and regional in nature, with little site-specific application.

2. Previous clustering methodology and results do not carry a high degree of confidence. Because the variation within a cluster of BEA areas is great, results of the base cases analyzed may not be reliably extrapolated to other BEA areas in the same cluster.

3. Results of analyses using BEA areas are misleading because their large sizes tend to mask local impacts, indicating that assimilative capabilities are sufficient for many technologies. In reality, if technology impacts are telescoped from the BEA-area level down to the county or local level where they actually occur and where assimilative capacities are much less, such impacts and responses (both positive and negative) would be much more pronounced.

4. Plant-induced impacts and resulting socioeconomic responses are highly variable and are largely determined by very local and specific conditions. Although BEA area-specific data (including assimilative capacity) can be theoretically used to match certain broad siting criteria and objectives with certain BEA areas, a wide range of actual effects is possible depending entirely on where within the BEA area the facility was sited.

5. The types and magnitude of actual impacts could be further influ-

enced by the degree to which effective growth-management policies and strategies are developed by the industries and communities involved. Industry strategies could range from policies to develop self-contained housing and to hire locally (thus minimizing impacts) to, conversely, policies to use local facilities and to import labor (thus maximizing impacts). Impacted communities could develop response mechanisms through fiscal strategies, local land-use plans, policies, controls, and political pressures that could selectively modify (increase or decrease) the actual impacts.

6. UCIA guidances call for analyses and discussion of many vague issues that could not be addressed except in extremely broad and qualitative generalities. Many cannot be addressed with any level of confidence and were not discussed.

7. Use of any UCIA results for siting purposes would first require the decision maker to establish and prioritize siting goals and objectives, because some objectives could be mutually exclusive: satisfying one could be adverse to another. For example, a siting goal to reduce minority unemployment could suggest a BEA area that might also have the greatest problem in generating revenues to accommodate or manage growth. Quantitatively assessing such tradeoffs to reach an optimum solution was not possible within this particular UCIA's level of effort and available time.

8. Given that a BEA-area level of analysis is not entirely appropriate, certain modeling capabilities exist to analyze UCIA-relevant parameters at the county level. Dynamics of employment, demographics, and public cost for siting major industrial facilities (including synfuel plants) are available at the county level through SEAM, developed for DOE at the Argonne National Laboratory, and this model was used extensively for the expanded UCIA effort previously mentioned. Though not used for this UCIA, which analyzed at the BEA-area level, SEAM may have considerable utility for limited-effort UCIAs in the future whenever analysis at the county level is felt appropriate.

9. The specific base cases are mostly large urban areas well removed from coal resources and not entirely representative of candidate coal-conversion sites; such facilities generally need to be located close to the coal deposits, which are generally in rural areas. Base cases may be considered representative of eventual candidate sites only to the extent that they characterize BEA areas in or near coal deposits.

Type C Analysis. Results and conclusions from this minimal-level analytic effort include the following:

> Rapid growth—defined by experience as growth in excess of 10 percent per year—is generally problematic in a community.

The smaller facilities will have no significant impacts, regardless of location.

The large plants can cause significant rapid growth impacts in most communities under 100,000 population. Some combination of federal, state, local, and private assistance can ease these impacts.

Because most plants will locate in rural areas near sources of raw material, impacts are expected.

Synfuel plants require mostly highly trained workers for construction and operation. Therefore, without special training and relocation programs, new jobs would not be available for disadvantaged, unemployed minorities.

Comparative Analysis and Evaluation of the Three Analytic Methods

The synfuels-technology analysis project was a sample initiative: the overall effort was considered a prototype intended to provide DOE with UCIA experience, rather than to provide a functional UCIA. The three disparate analyses of this initiative were intended to permit comparison and help determine the optimum approach to future UCIAs. Unfortunately, there are few criteria to evaluate the analyses against the perceived goals of UCIA and their real-world technical, administrative, and policy use within the budget cycle. The intent was to respond to UCIA guidance documents to the extent that they existed; lack of additional guidance motivated the three alternative approaches.

It was not considered axiomatic that the degree of responsiveness to UCIA was measured by—or was a direct function of—such factors as cost, time to complete, or level of detail or sophistication (although these may affect the degree of confidence in the results). Tradeoffs are required to determine which particular or conceptual level of analysis or detail best supports the intent of UCIAs.

SEAM, used in the type A analysis, calculates numerous localized effects as a function of time and can display the results graphically. The type B analysis, in contrast, selects the peak growth year from the primary-workforce trajectory and compares it to the 1970 (updated) population for the BEA area, thereby permitting only a single-point comparison. SEAM, however, calculates a baseline population throughout the years when development may occur, then varying this baseline, utilizing the primary and secondary-workforce trajectories for fifteen different technologies rather than three generic types. The result is a time-series estimate of overall population growth in the county in which the plant is sited; this estimate also accounts for the effects of commuters and neighboring economic centers that act as proximate areas for the support of the impacted area. Finally, SEAM estimates the incremental public costs for both services and infrastructure and annualizes them to examine dynamic fiscal effects on county governments.

SEAM relies on sets of population multipliers that vary by county but are difficult to validate. The type B effort depends on a single-stage multiplier that is constant for all case-study areas.

The type B analysis, which lacks the dynamics and detail of the growth process and which uses the BEA as the unit of geographic analysis, encountered limitations in estimating the magnitude and direction of growth effects. It shows, for instance, that a Fischer-Tropsch liquefaction facility sited in the Springfield, Illinois BEA area induces a maximum single-year growth rate of 16 percent. The type A dynamic analysis at the county level, however, shows that for the four counties analyzed within the BEA area, dramatically larger growth increases are evidenced. A county with an extra-low assimilative capacity shows a maximum single-year incremental population increase compared to the baseline of 444 percent. Single-point growth estimates of an excessively large geographic area underestimate many effects of rates and magnitudes and provide a weak means of comparing the relative impacts of construction and operation. Furthermore, they yield few hints about the duration of the impacts and changes—either acceleration or deceleration—in the rates.

Critical features of growth occur at the level managed by local and state governments. Although knowledge of an approximate-requirement profile for a particular plant (type B) is helpful, comparison with a baseline population growth without development (type A) is more instructive. Expected increases and decreases in public services and infrastructure expenditures are also important in helping growth managers to estimate rapid-growth costs and to search for the resources and institutional arrangements necessary to cope with those costs.

Type C emerges as a viable approach for this initiative, largely because DOE had the information readily at hand to apply to the necessary characterizations, and the staff expertise to perform the analyses quickly. Type C methods might apply best to initiatives on which extensive analyses have already been done, especially those involving hardware deployment. However, the nature, complexity, and lack of background information on many grants programs might not be amenable to a type C approach.

Ultimately, the conclusions of types A and B show considerable consistency and agreement. Type C states or infers similar conclusions, but at a more generalized level of detail. Because it is not certain that details of the growth process or impact results at the county level are necessary for UCIAs that address policy at the national level, this comparative evaluation does not conclude that highly sophisticated approaches or detailed levels of analysis are always necessary or optimal. It does concede the obvious, however: that because type B and especially type C required massive samplings and aggregations of data bases and units of analyses and the use of standard and nondifferential assumptions (that is, constant rather than variable multipliers), type A is theoretically a more credible approach.

There are, however, some advantages to not using county impact models and to avoiding such levels of detail. Type B and especially type C analyses are much simpler to design, the results are easier to interpret, they are less costly and are available sooner. These efforts could be conducted by DOE staff with minimal lead time and contractual assistance and with a flexibility and a turnaround time that accommodates the budget cycle.

In conclusion, a sophisticated and expensive type A analysis could evolve into a long-term, expensive research project. Although its results might be more supportable, quantified, and validated, they might also be late, unnecessarily complex, and carried to irrelevant detail. The type B and C results could be less costly, more timely, and easily understandable, but they might also be less supportable, less quantified, and more subjective. The paramount criteria for evaluating the three approaches must be the perceived responsiveness to *Circular A-116* and the actual use made of the UCIA during the decision-making process. Unfortunately, such criteria are not now explicit and must be assumed or inferred. Even so, the three approaches must not be evaluated against the standards of a general study, for such criteria would consistently favor type A merely because it is more exhaustive. Other strengths, limitations, qualifications, and caveats related to each approach are contained in the reports themselves.

Subnational Programming of Public-Works Investment within the Federal System

The UCIA, a recent phenomenon oriented to urban-area decision making, has just begun to enter the bottom-up/top-down analytic scene. A much older and, in a sense, more pervasive set of issues is concerned with how every public-works investment (PWI)—roads, hospitals, prisons, airports, waterways, and myriad others—is selected, planned for, programmed, and implemented. Clearly, when federal funds are involved, a host of top-down considerations enter the scene; for one, is there a national purpose, a national net benefit from the federal provision of a local (subnational) PWI? This section is concerned with the bottom-up, top-down nature of the PWI decision process.

PWI Information Requirements

Table 8-13 summarizes, for a dozen federal programs that provide funding for public-works investment (PWI) to subnational levels, the following information, in addition to the types of PWI created through each of these programs:

Legislative needs satisfied

Program objective

Factors used in determining need

Key factors in needs assessment

Our intent here is to show how the larger national purpose of each of these programs, basically in the third and fourth columns of the table, is implemented in each of the nation's regions, states, and localities. These statements of national purpose, culled from the enabling legislation for each program, are interpreted—in the last two columns—based on the legislation and then through the implementing regulations.

What is most noticeable is the use of a number of subnational indicators, statistical indexes of current and future projected, estimated need for each program. Current levels and changes in population, data relating to low-income ("poverty") level populations, school-district membership, financial capacity, facilities, consumption, utilization and occupancy, and current captial stock are used, typically in some weighting scheme broadly (and politically) interpreted from the legislative intent, to provide the subnational PWI obligational authority and levels of funding each year, and for future (budgeted) years.

In most of these programs, the national purpose is to achieve at least a minimum level for each PWI-type standard everywhere in the nation. To the extent that this is the purpose, matters of interpersonal equity and income redistribution are the primary focus—not economic efficiency or national-growth objectives per se. However, many of these programs do have a national-level objective. For example:

Travelers and shippers use airports, highways, and railroads everywhere. The ubiquity of transporation provides the national glue linking all otherwise spatially separated activities.

The economic development of an otherwise underdeveloped (or undeveloped) area may raise the economic levels of other areas as well, even given subsidization by these other areas to the underdeveloped area.

Pupils educated in one place may migrate to other areas and, in any case, contribute to both the subnational and national good wherever they are productive (in a net sense).

Reduced use of imported oil through increased use of mass transportation is a national as well as subnational benefit.

For each program, there are likely to be both actual and alleged benefits, both to the nation and to the recipient subnational area. Whether these are net benefits or not, however, depends (as we have seen in previous sections, especially chapter 5) on a number of key intra- and interregional factors:

Whether the economic effectiveness of that recipient subnational area has increased (more than the losses to the "giving" areas are decreased) through the detailed workings of the economic system following use of the resources

Whether there are scale economies present, such that the receiver gains more than the givers lose

Whether interregional-trade activities are so substantially enhanced that these gains offset the losses to the givers

Assessment of the PWI Decision-Making Process

Unfortunately, the factors used in PWI decision making provide no information about the three potential rationales for national betterment; all are subnational measures of localized need and thus provide insights primarily into equity rationales for federal intervention at subnational levels. In this sense, most PWI programming offers bottom-up analytic insights, with few or no top-down factors taken into account. This tends to produce pork-barrel solutions to the distribution of federal public-capital funds. Some top-down features exist whenever there are requirements for tying in changes in subnational transportation networks to national grids (as, partially, in the highway, rail, and aviation-facility programs). The factors used could in fact lend themselves to improved national-level analyses, although other variables would also be required, including cost functions for producing the specific service, interareal activity flows, and projected demand functions (for both local and other area users). The PWI policy area represents an excellent place in which to make substantial progress in bottom-up, top-down analysis.[29]

Table 8-13
PWI Programs: Factors in Top-Down/Bottom-Up Needs Assessment

Program Title	Type of Public Investment	Legislative Needs Satisfied
Construction, reconstruction and renovation of higher-education academic facilities Office of Education, DHEW	Higher-education academic facilities Undergraduate academic facilities Graduate academic facilities Community colleges and technical schools	Equity considerations Improve quality of life
Hill-Burton Program Health Resource Administration, DHEW	Hospitals and other health-related facilities	Protection of citizenry: public health Improve quality of life Equity considerations
Federal Prison Construction Bureau of Prison, Department of Justice	Federal prison	Protection of civil rights Protection of citizenry:defense Improve quality of life
Law-Enforcement Assistance to State and Localities Law Enforcement Assistance Administration, Department of Justice		Protection of civil rights Protection of citizenry: defense Improve quality of life

Two-Way Applications

Program Objective	Factors Used in Determining Need	Key Factors in Needs Assessment
To carry out a program of grants and loans to institutions of higher education for the construction, reconstruction, and renovation of academic facilities	Number of high-school graduates in state and state-allotment ratio Number of students enrolled in institutions of higher education	Not specified in public laws Planned enrollment growth Capacity enrollment Serious deficiencies in quality of programs Age and conditions of existing facilities Functionally inadequate facilities 10-percent increase in current capacity instructional and library space
To assist in survey of state needs and to develop state plans for construction of public and other voluntary nonprofit hospitals and other health facilities To assist in building such facilities	Population and square of the states allotment percentage Population, per-capita income, and relative need for modernization Financial need Eliminate or prevent safety hazards Avoid noncompliance with state licensure	Population Utilization Occupancy Current capital stock: age, condition
To provide suitable quarters and provide for the safekeeping, care and subsistence of all persons charged with or convicted of offences against the United States, or held as witness or otherwise	Existing and estimated prison population Actual available bedspace by region Projects prioritized for new facilities Deficiencies within security levels Age and condition of capital stock Ability to acquire existing surplus military or government facilities	Long-range forecast of in-state population by custody (security) level Capacity of existing facilities to be retained Optimum capacity of new facilities to be constructed Number of federal inmates that could be housed in nonfederal facilities
To encourage states and localities to carry out programs and projects to improve and strengthen law enforcement and criminal justice	State population Year-to-year changes to accomplish certain agency initiatives Alternatives to incarceration	Not specified except that advanced techniques in design/construction must be used. These are defined by the National Clearinghouse on Criminal Justice

Table 8-13 continued

Program Title	Type of Public Investment	Legislative Needs Satisfied
Rural Community Facilities Program Farmers Home Administration, USDA	Public buildings Fire protection	Protection of civil rights and property Encourage economic development Improve quality of life
Economic Development Grants and Loans for Public Works and Development Facilities Economic Development Administration, U.S. Department of Commerce	Water and sewer systems	Encourage economic development Countercyclical measures
Community Development Block Grants, Entitlement Grants Community Planning and Development, Department Housing and Urban Development	Neighborhood facilities Basic water supply and distribution sewer lines	Encourage economic development Improve quality of life
Construction of school facilities in federally affected areas Office of Education, DHEW	Elementary and secondary education	Equity considerations Improve quality of life

Two-Way Applications

Program Objective	Factors Used in Determining Need	Key Factors in Needs Assessment
To encourage states and localities to develop and implement programs and projects for the construction, acquisition and renovation of correctional institutions and facilities and for the improvement of correctional programs and facilities	Physical condition of facility Need based on inmate population Deficiencies in jail-inspection reports Use of advanced techniques	Planning and architecture. There must also be an emphasis on development and operation of community-based correctional facilities (halfway houses, release programs, etc.).
To construct, enlarge, extend, or improve community facilities providing essential services to rural residents	Survey of community facilities in rural areas Inventory of present facilities Need on a state-by-state basis	Financially needy of the rural community, as shown to county and state officials by way of evidence that the applicant's bonds were offered on the open market and did not sell
To improve the opportunities for successful establishment or expansion of industrial or commercial plants or facilities To assist in the creation of additional long-term employment opportunities To benefit long-term unemployed or members of low-income families To assist communities in providing decent housing and a suitable living environment,	Population loss Median family income Per-capita employment Duration and severity of economic distress Average annual unemployment over the last four years Special factors Long-term benefits Labor intensity Sponsorship by a local government unit	Reason for population loss (e.g., caused by sudden and severe changes in economic conditions or imports) Median family income Per-capita employment Average annual unemployment Long-term economic deterioration
To expand economic opportunities, principally for persons of low and moderate income. To create viable urban communities where decisions are made by local residents and performance of local government is improved	Population, poverty figures (counted twice) and extent of housing overcrowding. While in transition to a full entitlement program, guarantees no major drop in funding for cities that participated in categorical urban-aid programs in past	Population Overcrowded housing Poverty
To provide assistance for construction of urgently needed minimum school facilities in school districts that have had substantive increases in school membership as a result of new or increased federal activities	School districts must absorb an increase of 6 percent or 1500 pupils (whichever is less) in average daily membership Four-year increase period involved	Increased average daily membership over 4-year period Percentage of federally connected children to total number at end of 4-year period Percentage of federal land to

Table 8-13 continued

Program Objective	Factors Used in Determining Need	Key Factors in Needs Assessment
Airport Development Aid Program Office of Airports, FAA, DOT	Airports Protection of citizenry	Promotion of commerce
Federal Aid Highway Program Federal Highway Administration, Department of Transportation	Highway, bridges, streets	Promotion of commerce Protection of citizenry: defense

Two-Way Applications

Program Objective	Factors Used in Determining Need	Key Factors in Needs Assessment
	Inadequate housing	total land in a school district
	Ability to finance minimum school facilities, local agency's tax efforts	Percentage of children inadequately housed to total children in district
		School district's ability to finance needed school facilities
		School district's effort to obtain financing through taxes and/or other sources
		Normal capacity of school district's facilities
To bring about, in conformity with the National Airport System Plan (NASP), the establishment of a nationwide system of public air ports adequate to meet the present and future needs of civil aeronautics	Relative population and relative land area	Relationship of each airport to local transportation system
	Number of passengers planed	Forecasts in technological developments in aeronautics
	Safety, capacity, and security	Forecasts in demand for air transportation
	Efficiency of operation, security	Other modes of intercity transportation
	National Airport Plan, and timing of need	Factors affecting quality of environment
		Airport system plans
		Airport master plans
		Current airport facilities and relationships to FAA's standards
To assist state highway agencies in in constructing and rehabilitating the interstate highway system	Population	Program of proposed projects balanced with other modes to satisfy national, regional, and local requirements
	Area mileage	
	Road mileage	
To build or improve primary, secondary, and urban-system roads and streets, and to provide aid for their repair following disasters		Provide economic movement on highways
		Provide highway access to and within federal lands
		Promote economic growth development
To foster safe highway design and replace unsafe bridges		National defense
		Enhance environmental values
		Traffic forecast, highway classification design standards, and service adequacy

Table 8-13 continued

Program Title	Type of Public Investment	Legislative Needs Satisfied
Urban Mass Transportation Capital Improvement Grants and Loans Urban Mass Transit Administration, Department of Transportation	Mass transit	Improve quality of life Promotion of commerce Equity considerations
Water and Waste Disposal System for Rural Communities Farmers Home Administration, Department of Agriculture	Water supply and distribution Sewer lines and treatment plants	Protection of citizenry: public health Encourage economic development Improve quality of life
Construction Grants for Wastewater Treatment Works/Environmental Protection Agency	Construction of Treatment plants	Improve quality of life Protection of citizenry: health

Two-Way Applications

Program Objective	Factors Used in Determining Need	Key Factors in Needs Assessment
To provide railroads with financial assistance for the rehabilitation and improvement of equipment and facilities or such other purposes approved by the secretary of transportation	Public-benefit standards based upon national goals Ability of applicant carrier to provide essential service Preferability to alternative service	Safety Travel time Capacity (volume/capacity ratio) Productivity (vehicle miles of travel) Energy consumption Displacement (highway acres, jobs lost) Environmental (air quality, trucks vs. rail)
To assist in financing the acquisition, construction, reconstruction, and improvement of facilities and equipment for use by operation, lease, or otherwise in mass transportation in urban areas and a coordinating service with highway and other transportation in such areas	Size of system: prevention of cessation of services; demonstrate noncapital intensive means to reduce traffic congestion Impact of potential bus ridership; changes to service level; condition of present vehicles Traffic congestion; transit ridership Improve quality of urban development and environment Effect on efficiency of current facilities; Consistent with major development and redevelopment projects Improvements in efficiency	Prevention of cessation of service Reduction of traffic congestion Demonstration of noncapital-intensive alternatives Conservation of natural resources and environment Mimimize disruption of desirable community development and growth
To provide basic human amenities, alleviate health hazards, and promote orderly growth of nation's rural ares by meeting need for new and improved rural water and waste-disposal systems	Formula that considers each state's proportion of the total U.S. population in the open country and towns of less than 20,000 outside urban areas Each state's rural per-capita income	Financial need of a rural community as shown to county and state officials by way of evidence that the applicant's bonds were offered on the open market and did not sell
To enhance the quality and value of the nation's water resources and establish a national policy for prevention, control, and abate-	Cost factors Nature and extent of pollution problem Natural conditions	Reasonable nature, and cost of facilities reported in the survey for the population and industries to be served

Table 8-13 continued

Program Title	Type of Public Investment	Legislative Needs Satisfied
Watershed Protection and Flood Prevention/Soil Conservation Service, Department of Agriculture	Civil works: dams and flood control	Protection of property Encourage economic development Improve quality of life
Flood Control Works, Navigation Project/Office of the Chief of Engineers, Department of the Army	Harbor facilities: ports Civil works: dams and flood control	Promotion of commerce Protection of property Improve quality of life

Source: CONSAD Research Corporation, *Federal Agency Methods for Determining Public Works Investment Need,* vol. 3 (Pittsburgh, 1980).

Two-Way Applications

Program Objective	Factors Used in Determining Need	Key Factors in Needs Assessment
ment of water control. Grants are awarded to any state, municipality, or intermunicipal or interstate agency for construction of necessary treatment facilities to prevent discharge of untreated or inadequately treated sewage or other waste into any waters	Construction costs Nature and size of facilities	Costs for treatment facilities justified by data such as population (Bureau of the Census "E" Series) to be served (1990) Wastewater pollutants and flows expected, and reference to legally required effluent standards Costs for collection facilities supported by such data as pipe sizes and lengths and special problems with construction and design
To provide technical and financial assistance in planning and carrying out works of improvement to protect, develop, and utilize land and water resources in small watersheds	Contribution to conservation Development and utilization of water resources Benefit to a large number of people Economic justification Cost of flood protection	Erosion, floodwater, and sediment damages Loss of life Damages to property Preservation and protection of land and water resources Local citizen's perception of need Assistance to rural community development
To plan, construct, and operate water resources projects authorized by Congress for navigation, flood control, and such related purposes as irrigation and hydroelectric power development.	Physical needs Income redistribution equity Regional allocations Establishment of basin budgets Establishing regional project priorities Project selection	Control of water damage Meeting water supply/demand Meeting navigation needs Providing recreational opportunities Providing hydroelectric power to minimize use of fossil fuel

Whether or not the new federalism will lead to more top-down, national perspectives for PWI decision making is not yet clear; however, that new PWI decision-making arrangements are being considered *is* clear. On 15 April 1981 the Reagan administration announced the creation of a presidential task force to examine federalist issues in terms of the philosophy of more limited roles for government. The implication for decision making at each hierarchical level—and their interactions—will surely be a major issue for discussion. Public-investment decision making would be an excellent place to begin.

Notes

1. The first stage in this process was detailed above. See also Energy Information Administration, *Annual Report to Congress, 1977,* DOE/EIA-0036/2, (Washington, D.C., 1978).

2. The laboratories are Brookhaven (New York), Oak Ridge (Tennessee), Argonne (Illinois), Los Alamos (New Mexico), Berkeley (California), and Pacific Northwest (Washington). See figure 8-2.

3. This section is adapted from U.S. Department of Energy, *Regional Issue Identification and Assessment: Study Methodology, First Annual Report* (Washington, D.C.: Government Printing Office, 1980), pp. 9–12.

4. For more-detailed information regarding MULTIREGION see Richard Olsen, *MULTIREGION: A Simulation Forecasting Model of BEA Economic Area Population and Employment* (Oak Ridge, Tenn.: Oak Ridge National Laboratory, 1977.) Available from National Technical Information Service as report number ORNL/RUS-25.

5. Multicounty units are defined as the largest grouping of counties that will allow simple aggregation to the different grids required in a study.

6. See R.B. Honea, E.L. Hillsman, and R.F. Mader, *Oak Ridge Siting Analysis: A Baseline Assessment Focusing on the National Energy Plan* (Oak Ridge, Tenn.: Oak Ridge National Laboratory, 1979.)

7. Federal Energy Regulatory Commission, Office of Public Information, *Generating Unit Reference File* (Washington, D.C., 1978.) Updated by Oak Ridge National Laboratory.

8. A.L. Delbecq, A.H. Van de Ven, and D.H. Gustafson, *Group Technique for Program Planning: A Guide to Nominal Group and Delphi Processes* (Glenview, Ill.: Scott Foresman, 1975).

9. N.C. Dalkey, *The Delphi Method: An Experimental Study of Group Opinion* (Santa Monica, Calif.: RAND Corporation, 1969).

10. For more information on the LBL workshop see R.L. Ritschard and K.F. Haven, *Regional Energy Issues: Summary of a Workshop Held at Lawrence Berkeley Laboratory* (Berkeley, California: Lawrence Berkeley Laboratory, 1979).

11. Taken largely from the recent report by DOE/Office of the Environment *Regional Issue Identification and Assessment,* U.S. Department of Energy, Washington, D.C., 1980.

12. DOE/Office of the Environment, *Regional Issue Identification and Assessment.*

13. Ibid.

14. Margaret J. Hogood, "Statistical Methods for Delineation of Regions Implicit to Data on Agriculture and Population," *Social Forces* 21 (March 1943):287-297.

15. R.J. Rummel, *Applied Factor Analysis* (Evanston, Ill.: Northwestern University Press, 1970), pp. 333-347.

16. Ibid., pp. 333-347, 101-313.

17. U.S. Environmental Protection Agency, *Classification of American Cities for Case Study Analyses* (Washington, D.C., August 1976).

18. Taken from Urban Systems Research and Engineering, Inc., "Energy/Environmental Data Study" (Report prepared for the Office of Technology Impacts, U.S. Department of Energy, 1979). See also Joan Hock, "Urban Community Impact Analysis" (Washington, D.C.: U.S. Department of Energy, 1980).

19. There were 173 in 1972; recently the number has been increased to 183.

20. For example, Urban Systems Research and Engineering, Inc., "Energy/Environment Data Study."

21. Ibid., pp. 15, 18.

22. C.P.A. Bartels, *Economic Aspects of Regional Welfare* (Leiden: Martinus Nijhoff, 1977), p. 5.

23. Lester Salamon and John Helmer, "Urban and Community Impact Analyses: From Process to Implementation," (Office of Management and Budget, Washington, D.C., 1977); and Stephen Barro and Roger Vaughan, *The Urban Impacts of Federal Policies,* vol. 1, *Overview* (Santa Monica, Calif.: RAND Corporation, 1977).

24. Since preparation of this section, President Reagan's Executive Order 12291 has superseded Executive Order 12174; the role to be played by urban-impact analysis in the Reagan administration remains unclear at this time. Plans to reduce its influence and use are under consideration.

25. Requiring "regulatory analyses" of "major, substantial" regulations. This order was superseded in February 1981 by Presidential Executive Order 12291.

26. Office of Management and Budget, *Urban and Community Impact Analysis: Handbook and Prototypes* (Washington, D.C., 1978).

27. Ibid., pp. 23-24.

28. Ibid.

29. CONSAD Research Corporation, *A Study of Public Works Investment in the United States* (Washington, D.C.: U.S. Department of Com-

merce, 1980); also Pat Choate and Susan Walter, *American in Ruins: Beyond the Pork Barrel* (Council of State Planning Agencies, Washington, D.C., 1981).

9 Summary and Conclusions

The expressed purpose of this book has been to examine whether regional or other subnational interests can be seriously, routinely, and systematically considered in national decision making—and, if so, how; how the impacts of these proposed policies can be expected to affect various regions of the nation; and how these forecasted impacts can be factored into the evaluation of a proposed national policy.

Whether the new federalism is more or less extreme in terms of state and local decentralization, there will continue to be some degree of federal policymaking. National security, regulatory reform, coping with inflation and unemployment, and a host of other public responsibilities will continue to be national-level concerns. Public policy will, in these areas, be a combination of top-down and bottom-up influences.

The focus throughout the book has been on three matters: assessing the difficulties of federal policymaking in the light of unanticipated and unintended subnational consequences; describing a variety of analytic methods to assist federal policy analysts seeking insights into such consequences before they actually occur, so that anticipatory and ameliorating action can be taken; and performing a preliminary evaluation of a number of analytic techniques, characterized as top down, bottom up, and combined.

To reinforce the notion that federal decision makers cannot—by virtue of their lofty position as well as the complexity and vastness of the national economy and each of its subareas—be omniscient, we have discussed the potential effect of several possible trends on the future of our urban and regional environments. These descriptions were not meant to be prophetic or even argumentative vis-a-vis current national-level forecasts of regional and local growth and development. They do, however, suggest plausible futures for some subnational areas and, as such, should be seriously considered in national-level decision making, so as to assist in some national purpose and/or to prevent or mitigate unwanted consequences of implementing a specific policy. In fact, if such futures were introduced into current projections for national-level energy demand and supply, estimates of the potential impacts of some present-day national policies could very well be significantly altered, which in turn might lead to reconsideration of the policies in question.

These and other examples have been proffered to illustrate the fact that subnational impacts are indeed important and must be considered in national policymaking to ensure that the ultimate effects of policies are not counterproductive or, equally important, do not frustrate the espoused goals of other important national policies. Indeed, some people might suggest that there is, in reality, no such thing as national policy and that public policy ought to be reoriented to a regional set of analyses that explicitly account for the very different needs of specific regions of the country. We do not concur in this view in its extreme forms, but to the extent that subnational considerations do not enter into national-level policymaking, the potential for emergence of this view significantly increases. Furthermore, while emerging trends in federalism make state and local considerations even more important, these trends also heighten the importance of—and the focus on—whatever federal policymaking *will* continue to exist.

Following this critique of policy analysis at the federal level, we looked at the current information base from the perspective of several disciplines. This attempt to set definitions and define analytic structures allowed us to begin to inquire more deeply into what is known about two very different approaches to considering regional impacts of public policies, which we broadly characterized as top down and bottom up. Users of the top-down approach attempt to construct methods that measure the impacts of national policy broadly across the nation and, where they believe useful and/or necessary, to disaggregate these impacts to subnational areas. There are numerous examples of this philosophy at the federal level; it is in fact the more common method of policy analysis in use today. The school of macroeconomics, for example, has been designed, and is built around, the forecasts of policy-sensitive national-level GNP estimates, which are largely insensitive to subnational structural variations. Policy analysis is performed in terms of changes in the level or growth of this measure or its sectoral components. In chapter 6, the Bureau of Labor Statistics (BLS) model was presented as illustrative of this methodology. We made similar observations about DOE's PIES model (presently called the Mid-range Energy Forecasting Model) and the EPA-DOE Strategic Environmental Assessment System (SEAS), which views energy and environmental impacts of economic patterns primarily from a top-down perspective, notwithstanding that subnational computations are made to disaggregate these national-level projections after the national forecast is done.

Chapter 7 investigated some bottom-up techniques that have as their conceptual basis the projection of policy impacts by regional area and the integration of these impacts across the whole nation. From a strictly analytic perspective, fewer of these methods appear to be available, although there have been several institutional administrative efforts made to factor regional perspectives into federal decision making. An example of this is the development of the Federal Regional Councils, which coordinate federal

Summary and Conclusions 277

policies in each of the ten federal regions. There is some question whether these groups currently do much more than coordinate and implement federal policy, and a feeling that they have little significant input into the actual development of national policy. They appear to be bottom up only in an implementation—not a policy or decision-making—sense.

Two analytic techniques were discussed that illustrate the bottom-up approach: the National-Regional Impact Evaluation System (NRIES), which is being developed at the Bureau of Economic Analysis, U.S. Department of Commerce; and the OBERS system for projecting local employment and economic activity, developed jointly in the early 1970s by the Departments of Commerce and Agriculture.

Having examined these two rival analytic approaches in some detail, we arrived at a rather obvious conclusion: what is needed is a technique that uses the strengths of both. In essence, this combination would entail using the top-down method to generate boundary conditions for the analysis of policy options and a subnational analysis capability both to provide a validation check on the national forecasts and to allocate the impacts in subnational areas in a more meaningful fashion. The two examples chosen from the Department of Energy illustrate how such a process could be used to carry out high-quality national-subnational policy analyses.

The first method, called Regional Issue Identification and Assessment (RIIA), further extends the national-level forecast of models such as the MEFS and SEAS to smaller subunits, while adding the dimension of rigorously performed, integrated analyses by regional research teams. The responsibility of these teams is to perform assessments of these national policies or programs using methods common to such teams but also sensitive to the physical, institutional, and political features of their subregion that make it different from the others.

The second technique is the use of a statistical methodology known as factor analysis. This technique permits the grouping of geographic subunits into categories that can be considered more or less homogeneous in terms of anticipated policy impacts. This homogeneity permits the choice of the typical or modal subunit, whose characteristics are representative of all the units in the group. The choice of a relatively small number of subunits to represent the entire universe of subunits (say, counties or BEA areas) means that impact analysis can be performed on these units and the results extrapolated from each representative unit to all others in their category. Performing analysis by this method makes it possible to carry out fairly detailed impact analyses of national policies in each type of subject subunit and to use these regionally developed results to infer national impacts. In chapter 8 we discussed the use of this technique in performing the urban- and community-impact analysis (UCIA) required of all federal agencies since 1978 by the U.S. Office of Management and Budget.

Both techniques demonstrate that it is technically feasible to perform regional-impact analyses of national policies or programs. On the other hand, the experience also makes it clear that such undertakings are generally foreign to the way national policy analysis is currently done. Consequently, a move in this direction requires, and would continue to require, enormous investments in institutional and organizational resources. Before such experiments can be judged successful, considerably more experience will have to be accumulated and evaluated.

These methods, we believe, are only first steps toward providing the kind of analytical techniques and support bases that will be required if subnational perspectives are truly to be taken into consideration in national policymaking. Before attempting to devise a strategy for institutionalizing such a process, let us summarize some of the requirements, problems, and realities of implementing this need, discussed in the previous chapters.

1. Every attempt, even a conditional one, to forecast the impacts of a policy initiative faces criticisms regarding its adequacy, veracity, and the appropriateness of the technique(s) used. Such questions do, and should, recur often: the successful use of a technique in one application does not protect it from scrutiny in another. To the extent that the questions and potential difficulties are associated with models and other such analytic techniques, some standards and procedures exist to help assure the user of the quality of the tool. Further, there are relatively well-known procedures and guidelines for building, improving, updating, and otherwise exercising these techniques, however imperfect. The addition of expert opinion and informed insights (often from peers) provides a dimension to the analysis that may be incompatible with insights formed only from more rigorous, less judgmental scientific sources. Such inputs are familiar to the policy analyst, however. The quality of expert opinion is a function of the veracity of the information and the skill of the analyst. Both veracity and skill are notoriously difficult to quantify and replicate but are nonetheless useful.

2. Constructing an organizational arrangement that combines a mixture of the various forms of top-down and bottom-up modeling is a technically complex, time-consuming, unexciting, and expensive task. Once such a system is in place, the task assigned to it can be repeated at regular intervals. Models must be completely documented and feedbacks and linkages clearly understood. Moreover, using specific models for particular regions means more complexity, further exacerbated if these subnational models are to be maintained in their respective regions. Finally, if it is useful to have subnational perspectives enriched by adding qualitative inputs to the process, then the task of ensuring consistency and quality becomes even more important—and more difficult.

3. Time and again, problems associated with institutionally housing the models and analytic capability become preeminent. Knowing where to begin the calibration process to ensure data consistency, deciding what poli-

Summary and Conclusions 279

cies to evaluate, and resolving similar questions requires, minimally, a central coordination group that may also have other, more-technical functions. This same group might also be responsible for administering and funding the model systems and for many dozens of operational details. Evaluating the policy of a single agency requires one kind of arrangement. Evaluating a multiagency policy analysis requires deciding where to locate the coordinating or planning group used to perform the national forecasts. Similar questions arise when attempts are made to institutionalize such a system at the regional level. Where to put it, who pays for it, how those responsible are to be held accountable, and other, similar issues must be addressed. Furthermore, no matter how these issues have been resolved in the past, they will have to be reviewed and reassessed in terms of the new federalism.

4. Although there may be some room for real disagreement, the most promising combination of techniques seems to be that of using a top-down national model to set limits and boundary conditions and concomitantly to use subnational sectoral and spatial models to provide allocation and feedback guidance and in-depth areal and structural detail. Whenever possible, analysts performing this regional assessment should be extremely knowledgeable, in all respects, about the area under question.

Clearly, all formal methods have both benefits and problems associated with them. Not only are there those who argue for the technical superiority of one method over another, but also there are strong political and personal biases for one or the other technique that tend to complicate the issue further. In earlier chapters, we discussed each of these strategies as they are currently practiced in order to understand the advantages and disadvantages of each approach. In so doing, we described a variety of specific methods, past and present, for systematically evaluating subnational perspectives in federal decision making. Our discussions were largely methodologically oriented, with a focus on techniques that have progressed beyond the conceptual stage and are being, or have been, used in a decision-making mode.

We have demonstrated how these methods are beginning to be used to perform sophisticated assessments of both national and subnational policies, and their relationship to decision making. The ultimate objective of such analysis is to improve federal decision making by including in the federal consciousness major consequences and broad trends on the one hand and such specifics as affected parties, places, and elements—including land use, socioeconomic class, transportation and communication, housing costs, energy and other natural resources, and environmental quality—on the other.

In a sense, we have come full circle, from suggesting that the business of forecasting the future is very risky, to supporting national forecasting that incorporates subnational interests, trends, and characteristics. To be responsible—whether it espouses the new federalism or not—the federal government has to make its best effort to perform such forecasts for both planning and budgetary purposes. These forecasts are difficult to make, and their complexity is compounded by several factors, among them changing national trends and the uniqueness and complexity of subnational impacts. Such difficulties, however, are no excuse for not trying, experimenting, evaluating, and improving.

Given this brief review, let us now combine the threads of discussion and look at the feasibility of formally introducing regional perspectives into national policymaking.

There are several institutional dimensions to be considered in constructing an implementation strategy for integrating subnational impacts and concerns into national policymaking. These include politics and budget, two dimensions which subsume matters for analytic capability, timing, sensitivity, adversarial skills, and other realities of the policymaking process; all affect the present and future institutionalization and location of policymaking activities at national and subnational levels. Let us turn each of these factors in turn and consider the variety of issues that might emerge in connection with them.

Politics

Although considerable rhetoric is put forth about the need for, and desirability of, having each subnational interest involved in a fundamental way with federal decision making, the very fact that they are *not* more involved—at least not now—suggests either that the majority policy-sensitive political opinion and power wants it that way or that no workable method for achieving that involvement has been yet devised. Whereas it is clear that legislators in the Congress are beholden to local constituencies for survival, it is equally clear that their political futures (for a variety of reasons) are also tied to their role as statesmen, as movers and shakers in the arena of important national issues, rather than in more-narrowly-parochial matters. It is possible that the legislator who spends his time serving only the interests of his constituency and ignores the limelight (and public coverage) of national events may fare less well, in the long run, than one who reorders priorities more toward highly visible national needs. Thus, congressional policymakers share a mixed, unpredictable set of attitudes and approaches as to when parochialism can and should dominate, and when (or even whether) the larger, national public interest should prevail.

Further, the executive and judicial branches are not consciously subnationally structured, and even though there are meetings with such formal and informal, legislated or unlegislated groups as the National Governors'

Summary and Conclusions 281

Conference, the National Conference of Mayors, the Appalachian Regional and Title V Commissions, and dozens of other such groups, the input received at the federal level is seldom sufficiently timely or well-enough organized to be of sustained, focused, and effective use in the policy arena. Generally, at best, a particularly powerful local interest may marginally change an ongoing policy direction.

Finally, decision makers at the federal level see themselves only as decision makers, not as implementers, of policies initiated by their peers at the local or state level. If politics is a profession of power-brokering, then those who practice it tend to see themselves as powerful. In metaphorical terms, each would more likely see himself as captain of the ship of state, as opposed to a mere navigator.

None of this should be surprising to the observer of U.S. politics and of political science generally. The greater American public has never been comfortable with increasing centralization of public responsibilities and authority. Students of the evolution of the Constitution are quick to point out how the intensely pragmatic U.S. citizen has favored moves toward centralization only as a military necessity and, unless there are strong technological imperatives to the contrary (that is, immense economies of scale and the need for centralized authority and control), seeks a return to subnational (federalist, decentralized) power and its perceived freedoms as quickly as prudence allows.[1] Clearly, the complex relationships among democracy, the state and local levels, and capital market structures are only now beginning to be understood:[2] none of the theoretical rationales for a so-called national public interest appears to outweigh, in either intellectual or attitudinal force, the sheer economic self-interest and needs for power of individuals living in each of the nation's subareas. Ultimately, economic more than philosophical imperatives appear to favor subnational levels for policymaking.[3] Furthermore, technological advances favoring decentralization, the so-called appropriate technology, and an increased ability to function (comparatively) independently are increasing the trend toward local, subnational me-too-ism, though admittedly more within a global than a nation-state setting.[4]

One does not have to be in complete agreement with the trend of the 1980s toward localism/federalism/inwardness to sense its meaning for our major thesis: If national-level policymakers are to achieve their national objectives better, they will have to convince better each of the subnational interests what, where, and how a national policy can help that interest more than any other, purely subnational, policy. The executive branch and congressional policymakers who occasionally think in national terms will need, more and more, to turn to those who can best help them make the point that some policies are best that have both favorable national and subnational outcomes (or, at least, for which subnational losers can be compensated).

Here, the policy analyst whose tools permit this type of top-down/bottom-up conditional forecasting can be of help and may well be sought after. Whether the policymaker will merely use the analyst as a resource if and only if he (the policymaker) can gain support for a preconceived opinion, is a serious matter for the responsible, professional analyst. Nevertheless, we believe the current political trends should not and do not put the analyst in a necessarily weaker position relative to the policymaker. If anything, such political trends favor increased use, independence, and responsibility for the analyst who can bring the bottom-up perspective effectively and efficiently into national-level policy analysis. We believed this before the November 1980 election presaged a more rapid trend toward a new federalism and increased decentralization. We believe it even more strongly today.

Budget

To set up systematically a formal, analytically based policy-response mechanism that integrates regional perspectives into national policymaking in a timely fashion, the cost will be large. Rather than try to estimate the exact actual cost, we shall concentrate instead on some of the components that would be needed.

> First, there would have to be a location agreed upon to perform the analysis at both the national and subnational levels. These locations would have to be staffed and housed regardless of how often they were used.
>
> Communication and transportation capabilities would have to be provided both to solicit, access, receive, and refine subnational inputs generated within each area and to communicate these data bases and analyses to other subnational levels and to the national level.
>
> Analytic tools would have to be provided in terms of analysts, software and hardware, and budgets would need to be devised and implemented to purchase and maintain them. The continual gathering, updating, and validating of data is very expensive, indeed. It is even more expensive when the data set is required to be so extensive that it covers all the variables considered useful by all the participants for all policy issues.

In general, the cost in resources to set up a formal network is certain to be substantial—at least in terms of what such functions ordinarily tend to cost. Decentralized, public-sector, data-base pilot projects of years past provide some indication of that cost. The DHUD Urban Systems Advisory Committee's multicity Integrated Municipal Information System project

Summary and Conclusions

attempted (in the late 1960s and early 1970s) to set up a comprehensive computer-based information system, using a few pilot cities' functional-area demonstrations (such as human resources, physical resources, economic development, and criminal justice). On a cost-shared basis, the demonstrations—for four cities—cost tens of millions of dollars (some federal, some local, some private-sector). The care and feeding of large macroeconomic or other energy or economic systems data bases and analytic methods tend to run to millions a year. An integrated effort to pull these all together would without doubt require a very substantial figure. A truly ambitious, formal program could well run into hundreds of millions of dollars.[5]

Although this is a very large figure, it is dwarfed by the realization that it would be used to help make rational, meaningful decisions on budgets that are measured in hundreds or thousands of millions of dollars and would thus affect subnational public- and private-sector lives, decisions, income and wealth of equal or even greater magnitudes: were it as much as $100 million, this would represents .02 percent of the federal budget and less than .005 percent of the GNP. Nonetheless, large funding of unproven, politically volatile programs is hard to come by, particularly as federal budgets are pared in real dollar terms.

Of course, it might be asked: Couldn't we better consolidate the various data bases, analysis tools, and methods by integrating them across federal agencies so that resource savings would result with little or no adverse affect on the ability of independent users to pursue further analysis and/or varied interpretations? House and Williams, in their study of forecasts of federal statistics and projections and forecasting agencies, did not recommend a single, consolidated entity for the purpose of achieving resource savings or generating fewer forecasts; however, readers of *Planning and Conservation* can only judge that better evaluation and monitoring of these activities can produce the same or better quality and diversity—if this is desired—at a lower total cost to the federal taxpayer. And it is even more likely that subnational data and analysis system users will find considerably less expensive ways, in this decade and the next, for reaching more effectively and more efficiently into the enormous masses of federal statistics and analysis techniques.[6]

The bottom line of this discussion is that, in the medium-to-longer run—if and only if the concept of political usefulness takes hold—budgets can and will be made available. Furthermore, the software/hardware learning curves are such that a considerable decrease—perhaps in order of magnitude, in real terms—could very well be the fruits of labor of hardware, software, and system developments of the 1980s. Until serious use at subnational system levels is achieved, the pressure for such comprehensive, large-scale budgets will not be there; nor will the consolidated budgets for this purpose. Given this pressure, the budgetary constraint will probably lessen or disappear, as is the general case of most current national statistics programs.

Institutional-Organizational Issues

Possibly the most difficult issues that will have to be resolved in institutionalizing an effective, formal system are administrative and public-management ones. They fall into a number of categories.

1. At the federal level, there has been considerable effort expended in attempting to combine the various forecasting and policy-analysis capabilities of the federal agencies into a single unit. But questions surface everywhere; how could one coordinate the various models and methods currently used when there is no agreement on such fundamental issues as data accuracy, model validity (or even methodology), and forecast utility? In addition to real technical issues, there is a territorial resistance to any interagency discussion of this issue. Where does the coordination begin: with units of a single executive agency, among agencies, between the legislative and executive branches, and/or between the public and private sectors? A continuing, permanent, centralized analysis system for federal policymaking is clearly a powerful tool (or weapon); its characteristics are not likely to be casually agreed upon, or easily altered once they are.

2. Issues of who decides what is valid, what policies will be addressed, and how and what the role of the other federal units will be are certain to be subjects of continuous conflict. For example, one method of integrating and using the joint capabilities of the various federal agencies would be to leave the analytic units where they are and orchestrate the analysis from a single place, say the Office of Management and Budget. There are several difficulties with this model but one will serve here. Using this design, one agency has to begin the analysis and the rest are then performing sequential impact analyses of the original forecast. Clearly, it is important who starts such a process; how are feedbacks taken into account?

The House and Williams study[7] summarized the conclusions of those who have wrestled with the problem, after reviewing several needs for a central planning unit and the difficulties of establishing one. Such a unit was visualized as incorporating four functions: data coordination and calibration; analysis of the resource budget; comprehensive and impact-analysis capability; and a methods-coordination and analytic unit. The study investigated these aspects of such a centralized information and planning center: desirability, content, implementation, location, and feasibility.

In the section on alternative locations, House and Williams discussed the relative benefits and associated problems with locating such a function in: the executive branch (OMB and an independent agency); the legislative

Summary and Conclusions

branch (Joint Economic Committee, Office of Technology Assessment, or Congressional Budget Office); a separate commission; a fourth branch of government; and/or the private sector. They also discussed regional involvement:

> It is difficult to envision how a group of centers would actually be designed to handle regional interest. In the first place, there would have to be as many of these regional centers as there are regions. Consequently, a first task would be the definition of a region; for a first approximation the ten Federal regions might suffice. At the same time, it would have to be decided whether or not to create a central coordinating group at the Federal level to collect the regional inputs or whether to allow the center for formulate and report findings on its own. In addition to the question of which operating mode is chosen, the trade-off between the potential for cooperation by coordination and confusion by segmentation is a complex one.
>
> The specific charters of these centers might vary considerably. For example, they might carry out such functions as: (1) identify regional resources, opportunities, and problems; (2) assist the regions in forming necessary public and private development organizations; (3) provide knowledge to the regions so that each regional organization—public and private—would have the information necessary to the fullest development of its region; (4) provide viable regional plans coordinated with national plans.
>
> Regional development centers would be responsible to both national planning and goals and to the regions that they serve. They likely should be formed and guided by the regions and not imposed by the Federal level. While Federal funding would be used to assist in their early development, they should eventually be funded by and be answerable to their respective regions.
>
> The question of development would be the responsibility of regional and local public and private organizations, community groups, and individuals. The regional development centers would provide key knowledge and organizational assistance.[8]

When many regions have problems in common, a single center might serve all the regions. The nation now has a number of such problem-oriented centers, which could be coordinated by a central office and could given responsibilities to aid problem-solving in all regions. In other instances, centers could be created to serve multistate regions. The resources represented by each of these centers would then serve many interrelated needs of its region in a coordinated manner.

3. These organizational issues do not resolve the complexities introduced by the need to organize and integrate inputs from several regions. Furthermore, in each of the individual regions, one can anticipate similar difficulties to those discussed at the national level. For example, where does it go? what department has precedence? what models should be used? and many others.

Further, because regions are interdependent, there is the additional question of how one keeps track of interregional flows of goods, services, and people. How does one get two or more regions to agree about estimated anticipated impacts? Who adjudicates if there is disagreement? It is clear, at all levels of government, that decisions are not likely to be made or forecast merely on the basis of information from a computer model. At the local level, where citizen participation is more of an everyday occurrence than at the federal, the importance of understanding the dynamics of personal and institutional forces becomes more obvious. Consequently, it is at the local level that attempts are surely to be made to factor more qualitative information into policy analysis and public decisions. As a result, two additional facets of developing regional input to national policy need to be carefully thought out. First, subjective and qualitative policy inputs are difficult to make sufficiently explicit so that others can feel comfortable about using them, particularly since they did not generate them firsthand. Second, in a related vein, is it necessary to routinize these inputs so that they can be formally integrated across all regions, or is it necessary to be concerned that the inputs from all the regions are not commensurable?

Clearly, we are not the first analysts to have discovered these important national/regional policymaking/policy-analysis issues. Regional commissions, particularly the Appalachian, have begun to evaluate how effective their planning process and development strategies—achieved through combinations of quantitative analysis and qualitative insights—have been, relative to where they might have been without these (and with or without the funds that have, as a result, flowed into the ARC states).[9] Federal departments seek to build the planning and analysis capabilities at regional, state, and local levels through technical assistance (such as specialists sent to the locality) and/or methods for developing and enhancing the so-called residual capabilities of the subnational jurisdictions.[10] The Departments of Energy, Commerce, and Housing and Urban Development, among others, have made serious, sincere, and prolonged commitments to this institutional objective, with varying degrees of success. And evaluations by the General Accounting Office have focused on regional perspectives, assessing if—and how—the federal government's responsibilities required more inputs to, about, and from the concerned subnational levels. For example, with reference to the Northeast region's energy and transportation problems:

> There are many ways the Federal government could address regional concerns, including: making Federal spending requirements flexible enough that States within regions can use them for their highest priorities; considering cost, usage, and productivity factors in awarding Federal funds; providing special or additional assistance for particular regions, based on spe-

Summary and Conclusions

cial needs; and assessing the impact of proposed/present programs on the varying regions. . . .

Merely considering a proposed program's long- and short-term impact on regions—perhaps through a "regional impact statement"—may raise issues that otherwise might not have surfaced. This would not necessarily mean the proposed program's components would change, as there may be sufficient benefits in some regions to justify adverse effects in others. However, the Federal government would have the opportunity to alter programs or take other actions to counteract the negative impact in regions where they occur. This concept was put forth by the White House Conference on Balanced Growth and is reflected in President Carter's executive order that agencies prepare urban impact statements for government policies.[11]

What we have attempted to do here is to bring the entire matter—across its entire scope and breadth—to the attention of readers interested in broad issues of better policymaking by government in a world made, simultaneously, both more complex and more understandable by decision-making policy-analysis techniques. We do not believe this world is rationally manageable *without* such analytic tools and hope our review of such approaches encourages decision makers to develop and utilize them to the fullest extent possible.

Methodology

We have said, in this and previous sections, as much as needs to be said about the current state of the art in top-down/bottom-up modeling, data bases, and general analytic approaches. Although we might have left the general reader with a sense of complacency about the current capability to perform top-down/bottom-up analysis, however, we wish also to prepare those interested for some dramatic, perhaps even revolutionary, contributions that may be made, in the mid to late 1980s, in the modeling of top-down/bottom-up phenomena:

1. Adaptation to the public sector of modern strategic corporate planning methods for dealing with hierarchical problems[12]
2. Operationalizing and adapting "hierarchy theory" as applied in regional-science theory[13]
3. Development of methods for operationalizing the Pareto concepts of real national income and welfare economics to subnational levels[14]
4. The application and adaptation of cognitive psychology concepts concerning the brain's ability to perform top-down/bottom-up thinking and planning and improved meshing of the computer with mental (thinking) processes[15]

5. Breakthroughs and adaptations of methodological advances in measuring the contributions of subnational areas to larger (national) areas, and vice versa[16]

These and other, similar technical advances may, separately or together, dramatically find a home in improving methods of top-down/bottom-up policy analysis: if anything, this would serve only to enhance the current state of the art and would therefore strengthen a major conclusion of this study. Methodology is not the major stumbling block in the advance toward the application of better, more scientific policy analysis methods.

There are several points which need to be briefly revisited here as we bring this book to a close. Although the start-up cost to tie regional assessments formally into national policymaking may have a high price tag relative to the total budget level for such endeavors—or, more important, relating the overhead and maintenance (O&M) costs to the annual budget estimate—the dollar cost is relatively small. In the long run, it is not money that is likely to be the real difficulty behind trying to take regional perspectives into account in Federal policymaking. The real obstacles are likely to be found elsewhere—in the political scene. Considerable rhetoric calls for— and constitutional doctrine dictates—the separation of powers, and the pyramiding shift of power that might possibly occur might shift the relationship between these units. Although such a shift (currently, to a decentralized new federalism) may or may not be in the best long-term interests of the nation as a whole, the losers in the shift of power and influence would be less than pleased with the prospects. As such, there is apt to be considerable foot-dragging and procrastinating over how, when, and in what specific ways the shift will occur. One way for input about subnational, regional impacts to occur without a power shift would be in those instances where such information is used only to enhance the quality of federal decision making. Although such a goal may seem harmless enough on the surface, it is hard to believe that the regions favored by a particular policy would not immediately begin to lobby to ensure that such a policy would be implemented. Those that do not benefit by the proposed policy but might by an alternative—or, worse, are injured by the policy—will begin to push to cancel or reverse the policy option.

One useful way of understanding how subnational, analytic inputs might come to form a part of national decisions is to view the decision-making process as being made up of, say two components: analytic and political. It is clear that decisions have to be made and that those who are in power will make decisions based on whatever resources and information they have. In the absence of analytic input, political factors will prevail.

The almost purely political side of decision making (which includes all the qualitative, hard-to-measure factors that go into making a decision) is

Summary and Conclusions 289

the most common way decisions are currently made and have been made in the past. This is not to say that no analytic inputs have been available, but merely that such inputs have been somewhat sparse, and have been used even more sparsely. Rigorous, consistent analytic inputs from regional units on the impacts of national policy have been all but nonexistent. Among all the constraints we have mentioned, the most striking is the need to overcome organizational, political, and institutional barriers. It is to these difficulties we now turn.

1. It is probably quixotic to attempt to resolve the issue of whether or where a central coordinating body should be in the Federal government while trying to address questions about the regional impacts of national policymaking. Instead, although several problems will occur later, it is adequate to begin by allowing (or requiring) that each federal department set up its own capability for integrating subnational impacts into its proposed policies and plans.

2. It is probably not necessary to formally reorganize the entire public sector to accomplish the analytic link between federal and subfederal units. The most straightforward way to develop an organizational network is to house it in each of the federal regions. Each of these regions currently has one or more representatives for political or administrative purposes. These capabilities would also have to be extended to encompass analytic capabilities.

Though relatively straightforward from a conceptual perspective, the details of providing sufficient personnel and budget to the regional offices to carry out this additional function would require commitment at all levels of government. More important, care would have to be taken that the professionals chosen were of sufficiently high caliber to ensure both that the product is credible and that it would be accepted by peers in other regions and in Washington.

3. In each federal department, depending upon the structure of the department itself, arrangements would have to be made to care for and integrate these regional inputs. On the one hand, this could be done in an office of intergovernmental affairs, which exists in one form or another in every department and also as a White House office function. Its functions at present are a mixture of liaison, public relations, politics, and administration. To the extent that such an office is asked to take on the additional role of analytic coordination, it will either have to obtain the assistance of other groups within its agency to perform technical support and quality control, or it will have to build such a capability on its own. Alternatively, the function could be assigned to a policy shop and a section of such a shop could be concerned with the analytic input from the regions just as it is with inputs from any other part of the agency. This possibility would be somewhat less troublesome from a technical perspective but would likely result in some

administrative difficulties, because arrangements would have to be made to coordinate inputs from all the regions through channels not yet in place.

4. The technical process would also have to be one of compromise. Several of the models mentioned earlier in this book made use of a mixture of top-down and bottom-up analyses. Probably the best that can be hoped for, given the limits on resources and time, is a technique that uses the top down (or macro) results as boundary conditions for the analysis performed at the regional levels. In time, as the analysts work together, a new balance would tend to evolve featuring the strengths of each group's expertise.

Ultimately, the balance along the continuum from political to analytical inputs into political decision-making process will shift. It is our contention that decisions that involve the lives and futures of individuals should not be made solely through a political process that does not take advantage of state-of-the-art analytic methods and data bases developed to provide public-sector decision-making impacts. On the other hand, public policy should not be made and implemented solely through the analytic route. The conceit of the technocracy, which manifests itself in a belief that all policies can be handled in a rational, formal, empirical fashion, is equally naive and unrealistic. The balance lies somewhere in between. The capabilities exist to move the balance more toward harder information, but some real difficulties stand in the way.

National policy is presently being made about some very knotty issues: energy, environment, economics, agriculture, transportation, and the like, at a time when those decisions are increasingly interdependent, critical, and harder to make. Each of these decisions impacts one or more regions of the nation in a fundamental fashion. And all of this is occurring at a time when the regions, for a variety of reasons, are beginning to shift to new economic bases and to larger or smaller population masses. It is also a time for increasing debate about federalism—but no one can doubt that increased decentralization of decision making will emergy the victor. The mere existence of all these forces, combined with the fact that the capability exists to carry out the mission, suggests that the change will come to pass. Whether or not the change will be a rebalanced federalism is still to be determined. We hope that the ideas presented here will assist in this crucial transition.

Notes

1. Gary Wills, *Inventing America* (Garden City, N.Y.: Doubleday, 1978).

2. Gordon L. Clark, "Democracy and the Capitalist State: Towards a Critique of the Tiebout Hypothesis" (Harvard University, Department of City and Regional Planning, Discussion Paper D79-P, 1979); also Samuel

Bowles and Herbert Gintis, "The Invisible Fist: Have Capitalism and Democracy Reached a Parting of the Ways?" *American Economic Review* 68 (1979):358-363; R.A. Dahl, *Preface to Democratic Theory* (Chicago: Chicago University Press, 1966); Anthony Downs, *An Economic Theory of Democracy* (New York: Harper & Row, 1957).

3. Richard Corrigan and R.L. Stanfield, "Rising Energy Prices—What's Good for Some States Is Bad for Others," *National Journal,* 22 March 1980, pp. 468-474.

4. Alvin Toffler, *The Third Wave* (New York: William Morrow & Co., 1980); E.F. Schumacher, *Small Is Beautiful: Economics As If People Mattered* (New York: Harper & Row, 1973); Rene Dubos, *Man Adapting* (New Haven, Conn.: Yale University Press, 1965); Amory Lovins, *Soft Energy Paths: Toward a Durable Peace* (Cambridge, Mass.: Ballinger Press, 1977); Paul Halmos, *The Personal Service Society* (New York: Schocken Books, 1970).

5. Peter House and E.R. Williams, *Planning and Conservation: The Emergence of the Frugal Society* (New York: Praeger, 1977).

6. Ed Zimmerman, *The Domestic Information Display System* (Washington, D.C.: Department of Commerce, 1979); James Morten, *The Wired Society* (Englewood Cliffs, N.J.: Prentice-Hall, 1978); J.M. Nilles, F.R. Carlson, Jr., Paul Gray, and G.J. Hanneman, *The Telecommunications-Transportation Tradeoffs: Options for Tomorrow* (New York: John Wiley & Sons, 1976).

7. House and Williams, *Planning and Conservation.*

8. Ibid., pp. 214-215.

9. "ARC Puts the Pieces Together," *Appalachia Review,* September-October, 1979.

10. See D. Harrison, Jr., and M.H. Shapiro, "The Local Government Role in Energy Policy" (Cambridge, Mass.: Harvard University, Department of City and Regional Planning, 1979).

11. General Accounting Office, *Northeastern Energy and Transportation Problems* (Washington, D.C., 1979), pp. 52-53.

12. Working Group, European Industrial Research Management Association, "Top-Down and Bottom-Up Approaches to Project Selection," *Research Management* 21 (March 1978):22-27.

13. Vedia F. Dokmeci, "Analytical Planning of Multi-Level Facility Systems"; Stephen J. Gould, "The Hierarchical Structure of Evolutionary Theory"; and Howard H. Pattee, "The Principle of Complementarity: An Epistemological Basis for Viewing the World as Hierarchical Levels" (Papers presented at International Regional Science meetings, 1980).

14. S.S. Chipman and J.C. Moore, "Real National Income with Homothetic Preferences and a Fixed Distribution of Income," *Econometrica* 48 (March 1980):401-422; William Baumol, "Theory of Equity in Pric-

ing for Resource Conservation," *Journal of Environmental Economics and Management* 7 (1980):308-320.

15. Howard Gardiner, "Thinking: Composing Symphonies and Dinner Parties," *Psychology Today,* April 1980, pp. 18-22; Martin Gross, *The Psychological Society* (New York: Random House, 1978); Joseph Weizenbaum, *Computer Power and Human Reason: From Judgment to Calculation* (San Francisco, Calif.: W.H. Freeman, 1976).

16. The Water Resources Council and the Army Corps of Engineers are continuing their long-term studies of subnational-national economic linkages: see Water Resources Council, "Procedures for Evaluation of National Economic Development (NED) Benefits and Costs in Water Resources Planning (Level C)," *Federal Register,* 14 December 1979, pp. 72892-72990; also Mark Abrahamson and Michael DuBick, "National Dominance and Urban Exploitation," *Urban Affairs Quarterly* 15 (December 1979):146-163.

Index

ABATE model, 102-103
Acid rain, 194, 195
Advisory Commission on Intergovernmental Relations, 3
Aggregated Statistical Areas (ASAs), 108
Agriculture, 23, 83, 147-148
Airlines, 10, 48
Air pollution, 76-78, 103; abatement costs, 101, 102-103; analysis, 180, 182; forecasts, 115-116, 120, 126-127, 195-197; long-range, 28, 180, 194; and urban areas, 195-197; and utility siting, 191. *See also* Air quality
Airport-construction programs, 20, 24, 260
Air quality, 6-7, 76-78, 80. *See also* Air pollution
Air-quality-control regions (AQCRs), 103, 106, 108, 111, 203-205
Air-Quality Maintenance Areas (AQMAs), 91
Alaska, 115; oil production, 95, 114
Albuquerque, 8, 241, 254
Alexander, Governor (Tennessee), 3
Alperwitz, Gar, 33
American Petroleum Institute, 95
Annual Environmental Analysis Report, 108
Appalachia, 115, 140, 236
Appalachian Regional Commission, 19, 23, 26, 46, 143, 283; effectiveness, 288; scale economies, 56, 162
Argonne National Laboratory, 187-191, 256
Atlanta, 7, 8
Automobile, 7, 10, 76-78
Avoidance costs, 67

Babbitt, Governor (Arizona), 3
Balance of trade, 79

Basic-industry model, 146-148
BEAs. *See* Bureau of Economic Analysis, areas
Berkeley (California) laboratories, 274
Best Available Technology (BAT) standards, 120
Best Practicable Control Technology (BPCT) standards, 120
BIA, 20
Biochemical-oxygen demand (BOD), 115, 120, 129, 206
Biomass conversion, 235-236, 239, 252, 254
Boom-town phenomenon, 199, 227, 242, 252, 254
Boston, 34
Bottom-up analysis, 135-166, 174-175, 261, 275, 276-278
Boudeville, J.R., 31
Brennon, Geof, 40-41
Breton-Scott report, 40-41
Bridge matrices, 81
Brookhaven laboratories, 274
Bureau of the Budget, 141
Bureau of Economic Analysis, 84-85, 111, 144, 277; areas (BEAs), 182-183, 184, 185, 209-212, 223-228, 233-234, 239-242, 244-259, 277
Bureau of Indian Affairs, 19
Bureau of Labor Statistics Economic Growth Model, 80, 81-87, 90, 111, 131, 133-134, 276
Bureau of Land Management, 144
Bureau of Mines, 93, 184
Business-assistance programs, 20

California, 76-78, 159
Calumet River, 206
Capital: accumulation, 145; flows, 65; and modeling, 82, 101, 145
Carbon monoxide, 115, 127, 180

293

Carter administration, 19-20, 25, 229, 287
Case-study techniques, 215-216, 226, 237-242, 245
Census data, 27, 107
Chamber-of-commerce effects, 66, 131, 154, 161
Chase Econometric model, 80, 144
Chase Econometric State Forecasting Service, 144
Chemical pollution, 121
Chicago, 17, 197, 198, 203, 206
Chicago River, 206
Chiniz, Benjamin, 32, 50-51
Chronic respiratory disease (CRD), 201
Cincinnati, 17
Circular A-116, 229, 237, 239, 247
Citizen participation, 5
Clean Air Act, 20, 76-78, 122; and desulfurization, 195, 201; and electric utilities, 213
Cleveland, 197
Climatic regions, 140
Cluster analysis, 209-212, 223-226, 233-234, 239-242
Coal, 7-8, 93-95, 108, 124-125; demand, 5; gasification, 122, 235, 236, 239; and health and safety, 199, 202; liquefaction, 235, 236, 239, 252-253, 254; and NRIES projections, 157-159; and pollution, 115-116, 120; regional forecasts, 114-115, 140; and solid waste, 198; and utility siting, 187-192
Cognitive psychology, 287
Communications, 9-10, 27-28, 279
Community-action grants, 19
Community-facilities program, 19
Community-impact analysis, 41-46. See also Urban- and community-impact analysis
Community Services Administration, 20, 142
Compensation, 12, 281
Comprehensive Employment and Training Program, 20

Computer models, 78, 283
Congressional Budget Office, 29, 285
Consistency of models, 66
Constant-share file, 133
Construction, impact of, 254-255
Copper pollution, 207
Corps of Engineers, 19, 20, 143, 163
Cost-benefit analyses, 12-16, 39-40
Costs: distribution of, 51; and impact analysis, 235; of regional organizations, 48; relative, 156; and state economies, 153
Counties, 131, 133, 277; and energy siting, 184; and impact analysis, 239-259; population, 183
Crow, R.T., 149

Dalkey, N.C., 187
Dams, 19, 65
Data, 6-7, 197, 137-138, 160, 280-281; and energy models, 185; and factor analysis, 215-223, 226; and housing of models, 280-281, 284; and states, 140
Data Resources, Inc. (DRI), 80, 89, 144
Decentralization, 281-282
Decision theory, 34-35
Deflators, 83, 86
Delphi process, 187
Demand, 83-84, 101-103; adjacent areas, 156-157; and energy models, 88-93, 109-110, 115, 124, 184, 216; and state economy models, 151-152
Demography, 4, 65, 209, 234, 241
Derthick, Martha, 52-53
Detroit, 17, 197
Dubuque, 203
Dynamic regionalization process, 133
Dynamics and analysis, 67, 88

Earnings, 144, 146, 147-148. *See also* Income; Wages
Eckstein, A.J., 86-87
Economic Activity Analysis Model, 144
Economic-base multiplier, 144

Index   295

Economic Development Administration (EDA), 19, 20, 26
Economic development programs, 4–5
Economic-impact analysis, 39, 41–46, 54 88, 144. *See also* Models; Urban- and Community impact analysis
Economic Information System file, 133
Efficiency. *See* Scale, economies of
Electricity, 114–115
Electric utilities, 95–98, 103, 108, 213; and demand, 114; and pollution, 116–119, 120–121, 129, 191; siting, 180, 184–192, 199, 206; water consumption, 122, 206–207
Employment, 32, 79, 152; and counties, 183; and energy policies, 181–182; estimates, 81–82, 85, 87, 145, 147–148, 183; government, 82; and impact analysis, 231, 234, 241–242, 248, 254–255; and minorities, 253, 254, 255, 257; and population, 148; regional, 109, 110, 145, 146; and synfuel plants, 242, 247, 250, 252–253, 256, 257
Energy: conservation, 8, 124, 125, 209; consumption, 184; costs, 79; demand, 88–93, 109–110, 115, 124, 216; and employment, 181–182; and environment, 100–101, 103–104, 226–227; institutional aspects of policy, 192–193; and private sector, 4; and states, 54, 139; and Sunbelt, 7–9; and supply, 88–89, 93–98, 107–110, 216
Energy-impact analysis, 76, 87–100, 103–104, 176–209
Energy Information Administration, 112–122, 131, 134, 157, 178
Energy programs, 4–5, 20, 48
Energy Security Act, 236
Environment, 4–5, 75–76; and energy, 100–101, 103–132, 226–227. *See also* Air pollution; Water pollution
Environmental-impact analyses (EISs), 41, 76, 93, 176–209, 228–229
Environmental Protection Agency, 7,

19, 20, 142, 213; and factor analysis, 215; and models, 193, 276
Errors, 64
Ethanol, 236
Executive Order 11647, 142
Executive Order 11731, 163
Executive Order 11892, 163
Executive Order 12044, 230, 231–232
Executive Order 12174, 273
Executive Order 12291, 231–232, 273
Export industries, 145, 151
Externalities, 32, 48, 87

Factor analysis, 212, 213–228, 277
Farmers Home Administration, 20
Federal administrative regions, 31, 285, 289
Federal Energy Administration, 87
Federal Energy Regulatory Commossion, 185
Federal Executive Boards, 140–142
Federal Highway Administration, 24
Federal Home Loan Mortgage Corporation, 19
Federal Natural Mortgage Association, 19
Federal Regional Councils, 142–143, 276–278
Federal Region 5, 194–207
Feedback loops, 63, 65, 149, 278
Fischer-Tropsch coal-conversion process, 252, 253, 258
Fixed-share file, 133
Firecasting, 4, 106–108
Forestry programs, 20
FOSSIL 2 model, 134
Four Corners area, 17, 132
Fox River, 206–207
Frostbelt, 5–6, 9–10, 21, 25
Fuel substitution, 87, 88, 184

Game theory, 34–35
Gary, Indiana, 195
Gas desulfurization (GDS), 198
Gasohol, 236
Geisler, M.S., 64
General Accounting Office, 286–287

Geothermal power, 132
Glickman, N.J., 149
Government National Mortgage Association, 19
Governors, 3, 280-281
Grand Forks, N.D., 237, 239-241, 254
Granite City, 203
Great Lakes region, 120, 122, 127, 134, 197-198
Great Plains, 115, 227, 239
Great Society programs, 54
Gross national product, 81-83, 101, 106, 146
Growth rates, 108, 110-111; and synfuel plants, 255, 256-257, 258
Gulf area, 115, 227

Halperin, Martin, 55
Harvard Economics Research Project, 144
Health and Safety analysis, 180, 199-202
Health services, 40
Hien, D.M., 86-87
Hierarchy theory, 287
Highway systems, 10, 20, 24, 56, 260
Hogood, Margaret J., 213
Holism, 76
Hoover, Edgar, 32
House, Peter, 283, 284-285
Housing, 212; costs, 21, 279; programs, 19, 48, 256; in West, 8-9
Hoyt, Homer, 242
Hydrocarbons, 115, 127
Hydropower, 132, 191

Illinois, 165, 195-197, 198, 199, 241; air quality, 202-205; coal reserves, 202-203; water quality, 206-207
Illinois River, 198, 206-207
Impact statements, 76, 229-230, 277-279
Income: disposable, 100, 153, 157; distribution, 32; family, 83; in Federal Region 5, 194; and impact analysis, 231, 241-242, 248; and modeling, 83, 86, 101, 146, 152-153, 212; and synfuel plant siting, 242, 255
Indiana, 195-197, 199, 241
Indianapolis, 195
Industry: classification, 145; fuel consumption, 103, 110, 115; impacts on, 78-79; modeling of, 81, 84-85, 106-107, 146-148; and pollution, 121; regional characterization, 212; water consumption, 122
Inflation, 79
Inflationary-impact statements, 76, 229
INFORUM Input-Output model, 80, 102-103, 106, 107-108, 109-110
Infrastructure, 23, 34, 209, 258; costs, 21
Inland waterways, 10, 19
Input-output analysis, 84-85, 86-87, 101-102; models, 80, 102-103, 106, 107-108, 109-110; multipliers, 144
INSIDE subsection, 107-108, 109
Integrated Municipal Information System, 282-283
Interagency Coordinating Council, 142
Interarea flows, 64-65, 90, 131, 162, 286
Interareal development, 23
Interest groups, 76, 193
Investment, 82, 83, 101, 152, 182
Iron ore mining, 133

Job opportunities programs, 20

Kansas, 241
Kennedy, John F., 140-141
Krier, James E., 76-78

Labor input, 81-83, 133, 182
Lake Michigan, 197, 206
Lamm, Governor (Colorado), 3
Land, 8, 9; management programs, 20, 21, 198-199
Land use, 106, 180, 279; and economic planning, 49; and energy, 180, 181, 227; factor analysis, 216

Index

Lansing, Michigan, 195
Lead-laboratory impact analysis, 180–182, 193, 207–209
Legal constraints, 192–193
L'Esperance, W.L., 149
Licensing, 193
Lindblom, Charles Edgar, 51
Load centers, 187
Lobbying, 76
Local governments, 4, 53
Local-service industries, 146, 148–149
Long, Norton, 33
Los Alamos laboratory, 274
Los Angeles, 7, 17, 78

Macroeconomics, 32–33, 34, 278; and modeling, 78–83, 101
Management science, 52–54, 55
Manual-share file, 108
Markets, 40, 79, 157
Mass transit, 8
Mercury pollution, 206
Methanol, 236–237
Metropolitan areas, 31–32, 34, 195–197, 203, 254. *See also* Standard Metropolitan Statistical Areas; Urban- and community impact analysis
Michigan, 159, 195–197
Microeconomic analysis, 78–79, 86
Middle Atlantic region, 120, 122, 127, 134
Midrange Energy Forecasting System (MEFS), 80, 87–100, 108, 111–112, 114–115, 278
Midrange Energy Market Model (MEMM), 134
Midwest, 241
Migration, 8, 65, 146; and synfuels, 242, 250, 254–255
Mining, 5, 198–199
Minnesota, 197
Minorities, 253, 254, 255, 257
Mississippi River Basin, 197–198
Mobile sources emissions, 77–78
Models, 41–46, 278–280; bottom-up, 135–166, 174–175, 276–277;

budgeting, 282–284; housing of, 278–279, 284, 291; linkages, 155–157, 159, 161; properties of, 64–73; top-down, 32, 72, 75–134, 136, 139, 154, 173–174, 261, 275, 279, 290; two-way, 154, 173–274, 275, 289–290
Modularity of models, 66, 108, 131, 133, 183–184
Multiple jurisdiction organizations, 40–41, 46, 140–143
MULTIREGION model, 182–183, 184
Multi-Region, Multi-Industry (MRMI) model, 144

Nashville, 237, 241, 254
National Commission on Air Quality, 78
National Conference of Mayors, 283
National Energy Act, 20, 178
National Energy Plan, 112, 122–129
National Governors Conference, 280–281
National Journal, 11
National Petroleum Council, 90. 95
National Regional Impact Evaluation System (NRIES), 41, 144, 155–162, 277
National Resource Committee, 25
Natural gas, 28, 95, 98, 112, 120; costs, 114; electricity generation, 122; synthetic, 201
Net national product (NNP), 32
New England, 115, 120, 134. *See also* Northeast
New sectionalism, 11–12
New Source Performance Standards (NSPS), 110, 211
Nitrogen oxide, 115, 116, 127, 180
Nominal-group technique, 187
North-Central states. *See* Federal Region 5
Northeast, 288–287. *See also* New England
Northeast Corridor Project, 10, 19, 46
Northwest, 115, 241
NRIES. *See* National Regional Impact

Evaluation System
Nuclear power, 5, 98, 116, 122, 124–125; siting constraints, 191–192; water consumption, 127
Nuclear wastes, 5

Oak Ridge National Laboratory (ORNL), 182–183, 184–192
Oak Ridge Spatial Model (ORSAM), 185–191
OBERS, 107–108, 109, 110–111, 175, 279; projections, 145–149
Occupational health, 199–200
Office of Environmental Assessment, 226, 233
Office of Federal Statistical Policy and Standards, 154
Office of Management and Budget (OMB), 141, 154, 229, 232, 277–278
Office of Minority Business Enterprise, 20
Office of Technology Impacts, 29
Ohio, 195–197
Ohio River basin, 120, 132, 197–198, 241
Oil, 95, 98, 112–114, 205; electricity generation, 122; price, 124, 125
Oil-shale retorting, 129, 132, 212, 235
Oklahoma, 241
Old West Regional Commission, 19
Ozarks Regional Commission, 19

Pacific Northwest laboratory, 274
Pareto optimality, 12–16, 287
Particulates, 115, 120, 127, 180
Permanent-share file, 108
Personal Consumption Expenditures (PCE), 86
Petroleum Administration for Defense Districts (PADDs), 98
Phenol pollution, 206
Phillips curve, 86
Phosphorus, 197
Pittsburgh, 34
Planning, 39, 48–52, 55; "balanced," 50–52; efficiency of, 40, 286–287; synoptic, 51
Planning-assistance programs, 20
Planning and Conservation (House and Williams), 283
Polenske, Karen, 149
Political factors, 40, 253, 280–282, 283, 288–289
Political scientists, 52–54
Politics and Markets (Lindblom), 51
Pollution. *See* Air pollution; Water, pollution
Population, 183, 212, 231; in Federal Region 5, 194, 199; and growth, 145, 146, 148; and impact analysis, 234, 241–242, 246, 248; and nuclear power siting, 191; and synthetic fuel plants, 242, 246, 247
Portland, Oregon, 237, 242
Postal system, 28
Price, 79, 83; determination, 86, 152; elasticities, 90–93; and models, 151; sensitivity, 87
Private sector, 4, 136, 287
Product forecasts, 84, 145
Productivity projections, 85, 87, 109
Project Independence Evaluation Systems (PIES), 80–81, 87–100, 276
Projection Series C scenario, 112–114
Proxy variables, 109
Public administrators, 52–54
Public sector, growth of, 27–28
Public works, 20, 160, 259–274
Pulp mills, 111

Quality-of-life issues, 10, 228

Railways, 5, 10
RAND Corporation, 77, 187
Ratios, 144
Rauner, Robert, 33, 34, 39–40, 50
Reagan administration, 3, 231, 272
Redistribution effects, 18
Refineries, 98
Regional Balance System (REBS), 182, 183–184
Regional Identification and

Index

Assessment (RIA) effort, 178-182, 187-209, 215-216, 277
Regional Industrial Multiplier System (RIMS), 144, 160, 166
Regionalism, 11-12, 52-53; and energy models, 88, 93-98, 99-111, 114-115; forecasting, 106-107
Regions: characterization, 209-228; delineation, 46-48; and environmental assessment, 176-209; impact of federal programs, 4-5, 11-12; linkages, 155-157, 159, 161, 183
Regulatory-impact analysis, 229
RESGEN, 103
Residentiary industries. *See* Local-service industries
Resource constraints, 87, 89-90
Ritschard, Ronald L., 140
River basins, 46, 48
Rockies, 115, 239
Rockefeller, Jay, 3
Rock River, 206-207
Rummel, R.J., 214
Rural areas, 23

Sagebrush rebellion, 27
St. Louis, 197, 203
St. Paul-Minneapolis, 34, 195
San Diego, 77
San Francisco, 7, 8
Sangamon River, 206-207
SASOL plant, 254
Scale, economies of, 39-41, 47, 48; and analytic procedures, 65-66, 131, 132, 162; and public works, 261
Schlesinger, James, 55
School busing, 28
Scrubbers, 122, 195, 198
Second National Energy Plan, 124
Sectoral decision making, 23-24
Self-sufficiency of regions, 146
Settlement patterns, 21, 49
Severance taxes, 158
Sewer programs, 19
Shift-share technique, 146-148
Siting, 180, 184-192, 199, 206, 256

Sludge, 115, 122, 129
Small Business Administration, 20
Smith, Adam, 47
Smog, 76-78
Social and Economic Assessment Model (SEAM), 242-259
Socioeconomic impacts, 21, 33-34, 199; and analytic models, 72, 180, 182, 216; and synthetic fuels, 242-259
Solar power, 191
Solid waste, 122, 129, 180, 181, 198-199; and water pollution, 206-207
South, 6
South Central region, 120, 122
Southeast, 122, 127. *See also* Sunbelt
Spatial disequilibrium, 32
Spillover effects, 28, 33-34, 39-40, 48
Springfield, Illinois, 237, 241, 254, 258
Standard Industrial Classification (SIC) level, 107, 146
Standard Metropolitan Statistical Areas (SMSAs), 106, 111, 144
State Economic Areas, 223
States: and bottom-up analysis, 139-140; and data collection, 140; energy policies, 54, 139, 192-193; and environment, 5; growth rates, 111-111; interaction variables, 155-156, 157; resistance to federal policies, 4; spending, 153
Statistical correlation analysis, 213-215
Statistical properties of models, 67
Steger, W.A., 64
Strategic Environmental Assessment System (SEAS), 80-81, 100-112, 115, 131, 134, 276, 277
Strip mining, 5, 198-199
Structural unemployment, 32
Subfederal impact of programs, 4-5, 11-16, 21-24; and analytic models, 67-68
Suboptimization, 47
Sulfur-oxide emissions, 115-116, 120, 127, 140; and acid rain, 194, 195;

analysis, 180; and coal, 202-205; health effects, 201
Sunbelt, 5-6, 25; air quality, 6-7, 76-78; energy, 7-9; immigration, 10, 21; water quality, 7
Sundquist, James, 53-54
Supply, 81-83; and energy models, 88-89, 93-98, 107-110, 216
Synthetic fuels, 8, 110, 235-237, 239-259
Synthetic Fuels Corporation, 8

Task Force on Regional Factors in National Planning and Development, 25
Team theory, 34-35
Technology, 87, 281
Tennessee Valley Authority, 23
Texas, 241
Time-series models, 149, 155, 246
Title V Commissions, 19, 23, 26, 31, 46, 143, 283; budgets, 40, 50; scale economies, 39-40
Top-down analysis, 32, 72, 75-134, 136, 139, 154, 173-174, 261, 275, 279, 290
Total dissolved solids (TDS), 120-122, 129
Transportation, 21, 27-28, 84, 88, 162, 279; assistance programs, 20, 260, 261; and energy modeling, 88, 95, 98; in Frostbelt, 9-10; scale economies, 65; and synfuel siting, 253
Two-way models, 143, 154, 173-274, 275, 289-290

Uncertainties and modeling, 67
Underemployment, 32, 34, 132
U.S. Congress, 27, 28-29; Joint Economic Committee, 29, 285
U.S. Department of Agriculture, 19, 20, 102, 142, 277
U.S. Department of Commerce, 19-20, 40, 41, 102, 107; models, 277; and planning, 286; and regional councils, 142; Regional Round Table, 143
U.S. Department of Energy, 20, 78-79, 142, 213; factor analysis, 215-228; impact analysis, 237-259; models, 80, 87-101, 112-122, 134, 157-161, 208-209, 228; planning, 286; regional environmental assessment, 176-209; and urban- and community-impact analysis, 233-237
U.S. Department of Housing and Urban Development, 6, 20, 142, 282, 286
U.S. Department of Interior, 19, 20, 102, 142
U.S. Department of Labor, 142
U.S. Department of Transportation, 19, 20, 142, 215
University of Maryland, 144
Urban- and community-impact analyses (ACIAs), 41-46, 76, 228-259, 277
Urban development, 23, 25
Urban Systems Advisory Committee, 282-283
Ursin, Edward, 76-78

Validation of models, 67, 111, 131, 175, 284
Valuation problems, 66-67
Veterans Administration, 19
Vocational education, 40, 48, 56
Von Neumann-Morgenstern utility, 34-35

Wabash River, 198
Wages, 83, 87, 151, 152, 156
Washington, D.C., 8
Water, 19, 180-181; consumption, 7, 115, 116-119, 122, 127; and electricity generation, 116-119, 187; and Federal Region 5, 197-198; pollution, 7, 103, 115, 120-122, 127-129, 194; shortages, 194; and siting, 187; and Sunbelt, 7
Waterloo, Iowa, 237, 241, 254
Water Resources Council, 111
Welfare economics, 289

West, 227; air pollution, 120; and coal, 7-8, 114, 236; environmental issues, 6-7; and water, 119, 194
Western Governors Policy Office (WESTPO), 8
Wharton Energy Model, 86
Wharton model, 80, 86
White House Conference on Balanced Growth and Economic Development, 25-26, 289
Williams, E.R., 283, 284-285
Wisconsin, 195-197, 199

Zero-sum game, regional development as, 34-35

About the Authors

Peter W. House is director of the Office of Environmental Assessment within the Office of Environment, U.S. Department of Energy. Before joining the Department of Energy, Dr. House served with the Environmental Protection Agency as director of the Environmental Studies Division. Authorized by an Intergovernmental Personnel Act Agreement, he was assigned to the Institute of Transportation Studies at the University of California as a visiting scholar from August 1975 to September 1977.

From April 1969 to October 1971, Dr. House was involved in management operations as president of his own company, Environmetrics, Inc. He has served as research associate and director of Urban Systems Simulation of The Washington Center for Metropolitan Studies. Dr. House has also served with the U.S. Department of Agriculture as Fiscal and Financial Economist in the Office of Economic Research Service.

Wilbur A. Steger is president and chairman of the board of CONSAD Research Corporation, a national private-sector think tank that he founded in 1963. He has been a consultant and advisor to several federal, state, regional, and local executive agencies. He has also served as an economic and systems analyst consultant to a number of corporations. He is currently an advisor to the Vice-Presidential Task Force on Regulatory Relief.

From 1955 through 1962, Dr. Steger was a member of the Logistics Department of the RAND Corporation, becoming chief economist of the RAND Logistics Simulation Laboratory in 1958. He participated in several inventory- and transportation-systems performances and cost analyses. In the course of designing, implementing, and analyzing results of several systems-simulation exercises, Dr. Steger assisted in developing methods for integrating large-scale information-retrieval systems and systems-simulation models for decision-making purposes.

Dr. Steger received the B.S. in economics from Yale University and the M.S. and Ph.D. in economics from Harvard University. He was a teaching Fellow at Harvard from 1952 through 1955 and adjunct professor at the University of Pittsburgh from 1963 through 1973.